IF THE GODS

HAD MEANT

US TO VOTE

THEY WOULD

HAVE GIVEN US

CANDIDATES

IF THE GODS HAD MEANT US TO VOTE THEY WOULD HAVE GIVEN US CANDIDATES

Revised Edition

JIM HIGHTOWER

Perennial

An Imprint of HarperCollinsPublishers

Grateful acknowledgment is made to the copyright holder for permission to reprint excerpts from the following:

"I Ain't Got No Home." Words and music by Woody Guthrie. TRO—© copyright 1961 (renewed), 1964 (renewed) by Ludlow Music, Inc., New York, NY. Used by permission.

"This Land Is Your Land."* Words and music by Woody Guthrie. TRO—© copyright 1956 (renewed), 1958 (renewed), 1970 (renewed) by Ludlow Music, Inc., New York, NY. Used by permission. (*The excerpt used in this book was taken from Woody Guthrie's original manuscript and is different from the published words.)

Designed by Lindgren/Fuller Design

This book was manufactured in the U.S. on totally chlorine-free paper made by Lyons Falls Pulp and Paper, and printed with soy-based ink.

Library of Congress Cataloging-in-Publication data is available.

ISBN 0-06-093209-0

01 02 03 04 05 ❖/RRD 10 9 8 7 6 5 4 3 2 1

To Susan DeMarco

*No man should ever be president
who doesn't understand hogs.*
—HARRY S TRUMAN

CONTENTS

ACKNOWLEDGMENTS

I owe a very special thanks to the research division of my office—our "Department of Betsy," as we call it—which produces so much work that it seems like a whole department of people, but actually consists of a one-woman wonder by the name of Betsy Moon. She is a jewel, capable of unearthing great volumes of information, nimbly sifting through it to find the important nuggets, and producing what's needed when it's needed. She does all of this with great humor, which makes her not only invaluable, but also a delight.

Much of her digging is done in the wealth of materials produced by America's unique and undervalued public-interest groups. Located throughout the country, these small research and advocacy groups are saddle-burrs that have bucked many a pompous corporate executive or government official off of his or her high horse. Since the media have largely abandoned investigative journalism, these underfunded but dedicated truth-seekers are the best source that We the People have for finding out who's doing what to whom and why. In all of my work, including this book, I make use of their information and insights, and I thank them for the enormous public service that they perform.

I owe a great big thank-you, also, to my co-workers Cheri Nightingale and Sylvie Salade, who have done the heavy lifting of production, proofing, and scheduling that has moved this book from my hand scribbles to computer disk (yes, in this exciting electronic era, I remain a proud pad and pen Luddite) and that has moved me around the country for assorted author appearances. Theirs is a difficult assignment, requiring more direct dealings with me than a sane human should have to bear, and I'm grateful not only for the excellent job they do, but also for their great spirit, which allows them to laugh at the impossible, rather than cry.

I'm grateful, too, for the work provided by Chris Johnson, Joe Sexauer, and Barbara Strickland, three interns who blessed our office and were assigned to our Salt Mine Division, tracking down sources, checking facts, and doing other essential grub work.

Mentioning such bright young lights as Chris, Joe, and Barbara brings to mind how optimistic I feel about young people these days. Despite the media image of teens and twentysomethings being hopelessly self-centered, consumer-obsessed, alienated, and apolitical, my experience has been that most of them are attentive to the big issues of injustice, alert to the possibilities for progressive change, and willing to agitate to get it. I would call them our "most valuable natural resource," but as Utah Philips once said to a group of students, "Have you ever seen what they do to valuable natural resources? Don't ever let them call you a valuable natural resource. They're gonna strip-mine your soul, clearcut your best thoughts for the sake of profit unless you learn to resist. . . . Make a break for it, kids! Flee to the wilderness!" Instead, I'll simply note that I place great hope in this generation, and I thank them for the good spirit, smarts, and sass that they are bringing to the rebellion against the mind-numbing, soul-numbing forces of Corporate World. In addition to the many young people I've been lucky to encounter and work with, I'm especially proud of the ones in my own family, so to put a personal face to this promising generation, I salute my nieces and nephews—Brent, Eric, Jenny, Jerry, Kelly, Kyle, Lisa, and Tommie. Keep agitating.

And I give a big *abrazo* to Adrian Zackheim, my editor and friend ("editor friend" being a concept that would strike most writers as oxymoronic, but it works for me when describing

Adrian). In addition to being a whiz with a red editing pencil, he has also been my savvy guide within the world of conglomerate publishing, moving my hardcore populist work into print and onto the shelves despite its defiantly anticonglomerate viewpoint. It took some *cojones* for him to do this—and I greatly respect and thank him for it.

PART ONE

ELECTION 2000:
A Space Odyssey

OH, GOD!

It's a little known fact that neck cricks are a common occupational hazard among your politicking class—right up there with wrist sprains, smile cramps, and cologne burn. Politicians suffer neck cricks because, as incongruous as it seems, American politics is damn near eaten up with prayer, so their heads are always bobbing down and up, down and up.

Even Congress begins its daily sessions with a pious bowing of every corrupt head in the chamber—this is not something you'll find normal prostitutes doing. On the campaign trail, too, every public event, whether Democratic or Republican, is kicked off by hauling some minister, rabbi, priest, or whatever to the podium, from whence the cleric beseeches the Almighty to side with the assembled partisans in their righteous cause and smite the infidels of the other party. As one who often speaks at political events—and, I confess, as one who once was a practicing politician myself (you didn't get a virgin here)—I've heard hundreds of these prayerful entreaties. Most are predictable, but every now and then you get a prayer that makes a statement.

My favorite came at a bipartisan meet-the-candidates breakfast in 1990. The head table was stocked with twenty or so buffed-and-grinning aspirants for state legislator, county constable, hide inspector, and whatnot. The collective IQ of the whole bunch wouldn't have outgunned a passel of possums, and none of the candidates had sparked even a flicker of interest, much

less enthusiasm, among the yawning public. Nonetheless, about
a hundred of their political diehards and kin were in attendance,
enjoying the grits and gravy, if not the lackluster campaign.

At 7:30 on the dot, the preacher was called forth. He was a
big and imposing man who possessed particularly powerful
pipes. He gripped the lectern as the crowd instinctively hushed
and bowed. Before uttering a word, the preacher looked deliberately down the line of candidates to his right, then turned
and gazed upon those to his left, after which he closed his eyes
unusually tight, not so much in prayer, but as though he hoped
to block out the sight he'd just taken in. Lifting his face to the
heavens, he thrust his arms wide and cried in a booming voice
that clearly was seeking deliverance: "Oh, God!" As his plea
rumbled across the room, he softly said, "Amen"—and sat
down.

As we cast our eyes on today's political process, most
Americans would say to the preacher, "My sentiments
exactly." Ask people anywhere in the country what they think
about the Democratic-Republican choice they were offered in
the presidential election and they'll roll their eyes and say,
"Oh, God." What about the system itself, with both parties
butt deep in the muck and mire of corrupt campaign funds:
"Oh, God," they moan, shaking their head. How about your
own Congress critter—does he or she represent you? "Oh,
God no!" Would you want your kid getting involved in politics? "OH, GOD!!"

What a shame that our nation's two-party leadership is so
corrupted and such an embarrassment these days, for America
really could have used an honest pulse-taking before plunging
blindly into the relentlessly ballyhooed millennial election. All
hoopla aside, the turning of a century, much less a millennium, is a significant marker, an attention-focusing opportunity to have a thorough public conversation—maybe even a
bit of national contemplation—about our people's progress
and our national direction. I realize I'm teetering on the brink

of squishy idealism here, but golly Pollyanna, if our political system was not totally fucked, this 2000 election could have been a time when the parties, the candidates, and the media all came out to us plebeians, actually listening to the reality of regular people's situations, debating a plethora of unconventional (i.e., noncorporate) ideas, and generally conducting a kind of coast-to-coast political Chautauqua—not quite a plebiscite, but at least a "whaddaya think" consultation on charting America's twenty-first-century course.

There's plenty to discuss. For starters, enough already with the official pretension that ours is one big fat-and-happy populace whose only real problem in today's "great economy" is deciding whether to stick with the Ford Explorer or move up to the newer and bigger Excursion. Reality check: Sticker price on that Excursion tops $50,000—more than the yearly income of eight out of ten American families. This real-world majority is fortunate if they can afford a used Escort, for the same 80 percent of the people have seen their incomes go flat or go down during the past decade, even as they have been ceaselessly bombarded with assertions that America is wallowing in luxury. For these families, middle-class opportunities are being shut off, and their political voice has been cut off—in both cases by an ascendant corporate/investor elite that now rules supreme, essentially owning the economy, the government, the media . . . and, sadly, the 2000 elections.

So, we did not get the kitchen-table consultation America needs and deserves, nor did the Powers That Be so much as get their feathers ruffled with any bothersome talk by either of the Big Two parties about returning to the gut-level values that working people hold dear: economic fairness, social justice, and equal opportunity for all. Instead, 2000 was like '98, '96, '94, and '92—another money-soaked, corporate-driven, issue-avoiding, made-for-television snoozer, completely unconnected to real life.

THIS IS CHOICE?

OK, presidential elections have not been about big ideas, contrasting philosophies, or even about people for several cycles now (going back at least to LBJ *v.* Goldwater thirty-six years ago), but this one was a particularly surreal space odyssey. In the Democratic primary, you had the unbridled excitement of a Bill Bradley–Al Gore matchup—two policy-wonkish, big-money corporatists who couldn't fire up grassroots America if we let them use flamethrowers. Listening to them was like having two competing insurance salesmen in your living room at once, both yammering nonstop about the term-life annuity clauses of their respective policies.

But at least Gore and Bradley are slightly sane. Check out the sideshow in the GOP primary. Among the featured acts were Stevie Forbes (a billionaire whose chief idea was to eliminate taxes on billionaires), Gary Bauer (a religious rightist caught up in the conundrum of whether mothers of homosexuals should have aborted), and Orrin Hatch (a Utah senator consumed by the ineffable joy of being himself, running on the exhilarating proposition that if everyone else failed, he was ready to be the nominee)—plus Goofy, Pluto, and Dan Quayle. Yes, Danbo! Or at least we had him as a contender for a while, before he dropped out of the race in September of '99, having finished a rather sad eighth in a highly contested Rebulican straw poll in Iowa, running just behind the blue-ribbon heifer at the Iowa State Fair. Still, it's a measure of how far we've tumbled down Mount Rushmore that Danbo will be recorded in history as having had enough money backers that he actually was a contestant in the millennial presidential run.

Perhaps some readers are too young to have known The Dan when he was elected veep with Bush the Elder back in 1988, so as a public service I offer a quick refresher course in Quayle Quotes:

- "It's time for the human race to enter the solar system."
- "What a waste it is to lose one's mind. Or not to have a mind is being very wasteful. How true that is."
- "It isn't pollution that's harming the environment. It's the impurities in our air and water that are doing it."
- "I have made good judgments in the past. I have made good judgments in the future."
- "For NASA, space is still a high priority."
- "I was recently on a tour of Latin America, and the only regret I have is that I didn't study Latin harder in school so I could converse with those people."
- "Welcome to President Bush, Mrs. Bush, and my fellow astronauts."
- "If we don't succeed, we run the risk of failure."
- "Verbosity leads to unclear, inarticulate things."
- "I believe we are on an irreversible trend toward more free-dom and democracy—but that could change."
- "Public speaking is very easy."

One notch up on the Republican's seriousness level was Bush the Younger, the golden boy of the party elders and Washington lobbyists. Carefully scripted, tightly managed, professionally posed, and stuffed with money, Bush quickly moved to the head of the pack—yet, fundamentally, this is a guy sporting a 10-gallon hat on a half-pint head. Despite the best efforts of his handlers to keep Bush's tongue from flapping out of control, that little sucker kept slipping out, revealing again and again that, like Quayle, deep down Bush is shallow. Here's a sampler of Bushisms from the late, great campaign:

- "Rarely is the question asked: Is our children learning?"
- "The most important job is not to be governor, or first lady in my case."
- "Actually, I—this may sound a little West Texan to you, but I like it. When I'm talking about—when I'm talking about

myself, and when he's talking about myself, all of us are talking about me."

- "This is still a dangerous world. It's a world of madmen and uncertainty and potential mential losses."
- "The important question is, How many hands have I shaked?"
- "I understand small business growth. I was one."
- "It's clearly a budget. It's got a lot of numbers in it."
- "I was raised in the West. The west of Texas. It's pretty close to California. In more ways than Washington, D.C., is close to California."
- "I know how hard it is to put food on your family."
- "The senator has got to understand if he's going to have— he can't have it both ways. He can't take the high horse and then claim the low road."
- "We ought to make the pie higher."
- "What I'm against is quotas. I am against hard quotas, quotas they basically delineate based on whatever. However they delineate, quotas, I think vulcanize society."
- "I have learned from mistakes I may or may not have made."
- "If you're sick and tired of the politics of cynicism and polls and principles, come and join this campaign."

But the lighter-than-helium essence of Dan, George W., and some of the other aspirants was not what made Election 2000 so surreal. Rather it was that none of the contenders, Democrat or Republican, came near the terra firma where we hoi polloi reside. Oh, there was plenty of jabbing and jabbering by the candidates, lots of dissecting and drawing of fine distinctions, but it amounted to a blinding blizzard of minutiae obscuring the solid corporatist core of each of these Jabberwockies. Instead of substance and solutions, they offered gobbledygook and the same lame nostrums that pols of both parties have been pushing for years. At times, they sounded

like a jumble of junior executives trying to impress senior executives by blurting out the buzzwords of the day almost at random: export enhancement . . . *game plan* . . . *smart growth* . . .
win-win . . . *synergy* . . . *enterprise zones* . . . *bandwidth* . . . *fast
track* . . . *bottom line* . . . *workfare* . . . *proactive* . . . *new economy*
. . . *hardball* . . . *global connectedness* . . . *result driven* . . . and
the always popular, *think outside the box.* The campaign also
got heavily into diversionary "issues"—Republicans vied for
who could be the Biggest Bubba on the question of keeping the
Confederate flag atop South Carolina's statehouse, and the
Democrats got into a serious pissing match over which one was
the most pro choice the earliest. It was the stuff of Jerry
Springer, though not as deep.

Meanwhile, those working class values of fairness, justice,
and equal opportunity got lost in the wash of candidates clam-
oring to claim credit for Wall Street's "Boom," and none of
them bothered discussing the kitchen table issues that are key
to the life, liberty, and happiness of America's get-up-and-go-to-
work majority.

Since the candidates were ignoring the needs and aspirations of these people, the people largely ignored the campaigns (only about 23 percent of eligible voters turned out for
the fun and games through the Super Tuesday primaries in
March, when both Bush and Gore effectively locked up their
nominations). And why would people flock to the polls? For
all of their manufactured, media-hyped differences, GoreBush-
BradleyMcCainAlexanderDoleetal were the same ol' same
ol'—candidates who have spent their entire careers in service
to Wall Street and the Fortunate 500, each of whom were
financed by the same corporate and investor interests, and all
comfortably committed to the full agenda of Rambo globalization that would enthrone those very campaign contributors as
sovereigns over workers, farmers, the environment . . . and
government itself.

This is choice? Which of the Y2K contenders could you

count on to be on your side when your interests collide (as they always do) with the interests of big money? Would Al Gore stand up for your family against the whims of global speculators and genetic manipulators, would George Bush take on the air polluters and tax loopholers on your behalf, would Bill Bradley go to the wall for you against finance industry finaglers and pharmaceutical ripoff artists, would John McCain be there for you to buck the downsizers and low-wage profiteers? You might as well expect a bird to fly backward. Of the contestants who had a prayer of being their party's nominee, all were tightly tethered to the same economic elite that has ruled both parties for decades, an elite that maintains control by employing a well-drilled corps of $500-an-hour, Gucci-clad lobbyists and deploying enough campaign cash to build an impenetrable wall around Washington.

BRADLEY'S AIR BALL. Even the supposed "outsiders" of 2000 were trusted insiders. Start with the Democratic primary challenger, Bill Bradley. The son of a midwestern Republican banker, Bradley grew to six-foot-five, rose to New York Knicks basketball fame, and ascended to the U.S. Senate—but he never rose above his corporate sponsors, who backed him generously throughout his career. Just as he was paid to play for the Knicks in Madison Square Garden, Bradley was a pay-to-play guy for corporations in Washington. For example, in his excellent book, *The Buying of the President,* Charles Lewis of the Center for Public Integrity writes that in Bradley's last Senate campaign he took more money from drug companies than any other candidate in the country. These pharmaceutical giants were not giving to Bill because they were old Knicks fans, but because they were avid fans of a loophole in the tax code called Section 936, and Senator Bradley, who sat on the tax-writing finance committee, was their chief defender to keep the loophole in play. Section 936 had been passed years ago as an economic development boost for the commonwealth of Puerto

Rico, allowing companies that created jobs there to avoid paying taxes on profits they made from their Puerto Rican operations. Fine, but in the 1980s, legal beagles for the drug makers twisted this good intention into a billion-dollar-a-year boondoggle for themselves.

Here's the trick. Profits from drug making mostly come from the marketing, development, and research stages, with the actual manufacturing of a pill being an almost inconsequential part of the process. The corporations, however, saw Section 936 as a bird's nest on the ground, for it allows them to shift good-paying medicine-manufacturing jobs from workers here in the States to low-wage Puerto Rican workers—not only pocketing a cheap-labor windfall, but also claiming that every dime of the profits they make on the drugs are tax free, since they are "Made in Puerto Rico." The bottom line on this Section 936 bookkeeping maneuver is that we taxpayers dole out a tax subsidy of some $70,000 a year to these giants for each and every pill-making job that they move to the island, even though the workers themselves are paid around $12,000 a year. When Senate reformers tried in the 1986 tax bill to stop this rip-off, Bradley defended the loophole with more frenetic energy and sprightly moves than he used in guarding John Havlicek in their basketball matchups, and he saved Section 936 for his drug-company contributors.

Asked by the Center for Public Integrity about the connection of such campaign contributions to legislative results, Bradley responded: "The assumption that the only reason anyone donates to a political campaign is to 'buy access to power' is insulting to those who participate in politics." Perhaps he's simply polite to a fault, but the New Jersey senator certainly never came close to "insulting" corporate executives by rejecting their checks, instead showing tail-wagging enthusiasm for them to participate in politics through him. He performed so consistently in their interests that *Investment Dealers' Digest* ranked him among "Wall Street's strongest advocates," and the official voice of corporate power, the *Wall Street Journal*, gushed in 1995 that Bradley was "the most admirable senator of this era."

Even in his proposals to help the poor and middle class he took care to structure them in a way that did not offend his sponsors. Like his fellow "New Democrat," Bill Clinton, he proposed running most of his programs through corporations—an approach that John Kenneth Galbraith once likened to feeding the sparrows by first passing the grain through a horse. An example was Bradley's widely touted campaign plan for health care. First, give him his due—he deserves high praise for trying to put the issue of universal health coverage back on the political table. But the praise stops there, because his idea amounted to a massive, money-sucking subsidy from taxpayers to insurance companies and HMOs. Rather than boldly advocating a single-payer plan that would eliminate the bureaucratic, wasteful, and fraud-ridden insurance middleman, Bradley wanted to hook up every American to these very insurance corporations, letting them control our medical decisions and continue their profiteering at our expense.

As always when assessing a politico, to know Bradley, follow the money. "I am raising money from ordinary citizens, not from special interest PACs," he proclaimed, and indeed he (and Gore) rejected PAC funds. But before you swallow that "ordinary citizens" line, note that 82 percent of his presidential funds came not from the twenty-five-dollar crowd, but from the big contributors. Also, he took more Wall Street money in the primaries than any other candidate in the race. Technically, corporations can't give money to presidential contenders, but they get around this legal inconvenience by bundling "individual" contributions from their top executives. The following six bundlers were Bradley's biggest sugar daddies:

Goldman Sachs	**$239,700**
Lehman Brothers	**$156,950**

Merrill Lynch	$121,940
Citigroup	$74,150
Morgan Stanley Dean Witter	$55,750
J. P. Morgan	$51,600

As a political adviser to institutional investors observed, "Wall Street likes Bill Bradley. He is a Wall Street kind of Democrat ... the kind of guy corporate executives feel comfortable around."

This was the people's champion? Yes Bill Bradley is smart, yes he's serious-minded, yes he's a decent and caring human being, yes he can hit the jump shot from the post—but, no, he would not take on the economic elites who are trampling America's workaday majority.

Even though he was well financed, Bradley's lack of populist punch (coupled with such a numbing dullness that he actually made Al "Too Dull" Gore seem to sparkle in contrast) left him with no particular popular appeal. Gore, with superior organizational support, slam-dunked the lead-footed Bradley in the first two contests, Iowa and New Hampshire, and the game was pretty much over for him after that.

THE McCAIN PHENOMENON. The real buzz of the primary elections came from, of all places, the Republican side, embodied in the unlikely, quasi-populist candidacy of Senator John McCain. This Arizonian suddenly came chugging over the hill in New Hampshire in his "Straight Talk Express" bus, campaigning as an "outsider." Well, not really an outsider-outsider, since he had been in Congress for seventeen years and was the sitting chairman of the powerful Commerce committee, which has long been a safe harbor for corporate interests. But McCain explained that "I've always been an outsider in the Senate." So, he was sort of an outsider-insider, or an inside-outer, or whatever. Nonetheless, he came into the "Live Free or Die" state thumping hard on the issue of corrupt money in politics, approaching startled voters with compelling candor, saying to them, in essence: "The system is corrupt . . . I know it's corrupt because I'm part of it . . . *I'm* corrupt." Score one for integrity, even if it's based on the lack of integrity.

The McCain candidacy very quickly became the McCain *phenomenon*, as even some card-carrying liberals rallied to his banner. Don't be fooled into thinking, however, that the senator himself contemplated any bleeding heart ideas about storming the barricades of the corporate powers, for he has a lifetime of loyalty to their causes. Lift the McCain log and you'll find all sorts of ugly squirmies under there, including a 100 percent voting record with the U.S. Chamber of Commerce; consistent support for NAFTA, WTO, and the whole alphabet soup of corporate trade scams; opposition to increasing the minimum wage, even in today's boom economy; use of his chairmanship to run errands for the telecommunications giants that contribute to his campaigns; repeated attempts to kill funding for public broadcasting; a nasty temperament toward antipollution initiatives; and a full embrace of every item in Newt Gingrich's infamous "Contract With America," which was a grab-basket of goodies and special favors that big business had long lusted after.

Any doubts about whether McCain might have been a sockless Jerry Simpson in pinstripes is put to rest when you look at the half-dozen members of the kitchen cabinet he assembled to shape policies for his presidential run: Herb Allison, former president of the Merrill Lynch financial empire, was top adviser on economics as well as the senator's guide into Wall Street's inner sanctums; Ken Duberstein, former chief of staff for Ronald Reagan's White House, who now lobbies for the likes of Time Warner, United Airlines, and General Motors; Kevin Hassett, a former Federal Reserve economist and a think-tanker at the corporate-funded American Enterprise Institute; and Vin Weber, McCain's chief adviser on domestic policies, was a GOP congressman from Minnesota before moving on to lobby for such clients as AT&T, Microsoft, and the association of electric utilities.

While that is the reality of the McCain candidacy, none of it mattered to the McCain phenomenon. The national media, of course, rushed to probe at and pontificate about McCain the person, which missed the point, for the phenomenon was not in him—it was in the voters. Just as a rambunctious, maverick electorate has reached out in recent years to Jesse Jackson, Ross Perot, Jerry Brown, and Pat Buchanan, using them as handy sledgehammers to wield against the politics-as-usual gang, New Hampshirites and other voters saw in John McCain the chance to whap that gang one more time. Who gave a damn who he was—people were looking for a sledgehammer, and here was a guy that wasn't totally scripted, who had a little quirky edge, who seemed genuinely to relish his bad-boy role, and who was putting front-and-center the only solidly progressive proposal of the whole dismal primary season, namely: Let's get a little bit of the corruption out of the system.

Poor George W. He never saw it coming. He felt he owned New Hampshire. He had deep, blue-blooded family roots in the neighboring states of Maine and Connecticut. He had his poll-tested slogan of "Compassionate Conservative" to appeal to independent New Hampshirites, and he had his multibillion-dollar tax-whack to satiate the red-meat Republicans of the state; he had a tsunami of campaign cash to saturate every TV set with his focus-grouped ads; he had the popular and properly preppie New Hampshire governor tight by his side; he had busloads of Washington lobbyists showing their affection by coming into the snows of January to go door-to-door for their boy; and he had Poppy and Bar on the stump with him—the only one missing was Millie the dog. George had everything going for him . . . and he lost. By 19 points! The voters dumped the Bush coronation processional right over into the ditch.

George's campaign strategist, Karl Rove, put a spin on the

Bush defeat that sums up their respect for the democratic process: Too many people voted, he explained. Thank you, Herr Rove.

Indeed, New Hampshire produced a record turnout as independents, mavericks, reformers, young people, old cynics, and hordes of other "unexpected" voters showed up for the sheer enjoyment of giving the cozy, corrupt, insider system a swift McCain kick in the ass. They didn't care whether he could ultimately win the nomination—they had a statement to make. Meanwhile, the national political and moneyed Establishments (excuse the redundancy) had lined up en masse behind Bush's presumed nomination, and they were slack-jawed at this unhappy turn of events. Who were these people, they wondered anxiously? Tom Korologos, a powerhouse Washington lobbyist, told the *Los Angeles Times* that he had visited the Senate cloakroom after Bush's New Hampshire comeuppance: "Their faces were drawn. They were apoplectic."

Not to worry, though, for the political operatives and money boys had the system wired for the long haul. Unlike in New Hampshire, the rules of voting in most of the primaries to come had been written by party apparatchiks to preclude any unexpected citizens from getting into the voting booths, and the schedule of primaries had been stacked to favor an Establishment-backed, heavily financed anointed one. That Establishment closed ranks quickly behind its boy, Bush, to stomp the McCain insurgency. Senator McCain was soon to learn that he was in the wrong party for grassroots rebellion. The day after New Hampshire, Senate majority leader Trent Lott sent forth the official Republican word, like a papal edict: "It is an important fact to consider that an overwhelming number of senators endorse and support George W. Bush."

For his part, George abruptly shucked his "Governor Compassionate" cloak and went snarling into the South Carolina primary as a raw, right-wing, Jesus-loving, Establishment-hugging, bottom-feeding Republican. He accused labor-loving, liberal-leaning, minority-tinged outsiders of using McCain to "hijack" the Republican primaries and deny him his rightful role as nominee, and he even resorted to an appearance at the racist Bob Jones University to howl at the moon, wink at the GOP's constituency of intolerance, and rally them to save his candidacy. It worked. He won South Carolina handily, then focused on March's "Super Tuesday" powerball primaries in New York, California, and Ohio, where money can buy massive amounts of media and out-muscle the McCains of the world.

Bush's muscle men were up to the challenge, willing to go beyond the call of duty (and the intent of law) to protect their investment. For example, just prior to Super Tuesday, a blitz of television ads mysteriously appeared attacking McCain's environmental record, covering him with a coat of slime. The ads also gushed about Bush, putting such a gleam on the governor's environmental record that you might have thought he was the natural-born son of John Muir and Rachel Carson. "Republicans care about clean air. So does Governor Bush" intoned the deep-voiced announcer, concluding with this whopper: "Governor Bush: Leading so each day dawns brighter." We Texans nearly choked on our morning jalapeño juice when we heard this broadside, for our beloved state has attained the rank of Number One in the country for dirty air, and Houston had just passed Los Angeles as the city boasting the worst air pollution in America. Bush's environmental record was so ugly he couldn't get it clean if we gave him a jumbo can of Comet and a wire brush . . . but there he was on the TV, looking like the poster boy for Earth Day.

The mystery of the scurrilous "Bush clean–McCain filthy" ads was: who shelled out the $2.5 million to air them? "There is no connection between my campaign and this ad," said the governor, with a straight face. The legally required tag line merely said the ads were financed by "Republicans for Clean Air." Aside from the oxymoronic aspect of the name, who was behind this group? Someone Bush knew quite well: Sam Wyly of Dallas. Sam and his brother Charles simply list their occupations as "investors," but they are billionaires, owning oil wells, the Bonanza Steakhouse chain, a hedge fund, a software company, the Michael's chain of craft stores . . . and more. They also own a chunk of G.W. Bush & Co., for they were the third highest donors to his gubernatorial campaigns ($210,000), and they were among his biggest fundraisers for the 2000 election.

The law says that an individual can give only $1,000 to a candidate for president. But Wyly had just written $2.5 million in checks to boost his buddy Bush's candidacy. The loophole here is that an independent group can spend an unlimited amount on "issue ads," as long as it does not coordinate the ads with any candidate. Republicans for Clean Air, however, was not even a group, for it had a membership of one—Sam Wyly. As for its independence, RCA was created by Wyly only a few days before the Super Tuesday primary with no other purpose but to help rescue Bush from McCain, and he hired media consultants with Bush connections to prepare and place the spots. "It's everything I've been fighting against," McCain moaned. "Two million dollars in the last few days can make a difference in a race that's in a statistical dead heat." McCain lost New York, California, and Ohio.

These sleazeball ads were tantamount to an illegal campaign contribution to Bush, but the governor willingly played the crooked game, doing anything it takes to get the money and win. As Mark Twain said, "Virtue has never been as respectable as money." Bush refused to condemn either the ad's distortions (i.e., lies) or their financing, nor would he acknowledge that they made a mockery of any concept of political integrity. Confronted directly by the fact that it was his personal pal, political crony, and big-bucks financial backer, Sam, who put the ads up, George said: "I had no idea."

TWEEDLEDUMB AND TWEEDLEDUMBER

Richard Lederer, a writer with a wonderful wit, also is a collector of odd tidbits that he finds in newspapers and elsewhere. He has published several items from the "corrections" columns of various newspapers, including this: "Our paper carried the notice last week that Mr. Oscar Hoffnagle is a defective on the police force. This is a typographical error. Mr. Hoffnagle is, of course, a detective on the police farce."

A two-party system that produces a "choice" of Gore v. Bush, Dull and Dullard, is defective and a farce. It was painful to watch these two scamper around the country for a year claiming to be "just folks" and "for the people." Neither has a clue what it's like for a family to try to make ends meet on barely $30,000 a year, which is the economic neighborhood of a majority of Americans today. Both Al and George are sons of privilege whose idea of hardscrabble is to run out of vowels. They never had to work a drudge shift or worry about making rent, getting good health care, paying bills . . . or getting ahead in life.

It's unusual in a presidential race for *both* the Democrat and Republican to hail from the ruling class, yet voters in 2000 had a choice of two political princes following parallel paths of social advantage toward the White House. Gore is the firstborn son and namesake of a U.S. senator, and Bush is the firstborn son and namesake of a president (as well as the grandson of U.S. Senator Prescott Bush of Connecticut, a descendant of another former president, Franklin Pierce, and has ancestry tracking back to Britain's royals). While Bush is from a far wealthier family than Gore's, both have had all the benefits that money brings, growing up in a world of comfort and connections.

In their campaigns, of course, the candidates downplayed the advantages of their birthright, preferring to dwell at length on the salt-of-the-earth values they say they absorbed as boys growing up in what they describe as Norman Rockwell-like homeplaces—a farm outside Carthage, Tennessee, for Al; the West Texas oil town of Midland for George. Each candidate even has tales of boys being boys, with little Georgie, as his parents called him, engaging in the fine art of catching frogs, putting lit firecrackers down their throats, throwing them into the air, and gleefully watching them blow up; Gore's animal of choice was the chicken, which he says he could hypnotize: "I learned to do that as a kid. I really did." So there was your choice: a frog exploder or a chicken hypnotizer. Draw from these childhood habits whatever conclusions you want about either man's psychological fitness for office.

Bush talks of his roots among the hard-working oil families of West Texas ("I would say people, if they want to understand me, need to understand Midland") and Gore talks of learning "how to plow a steep hillside with a team of mules [and] how to clear three acres of heavily wooded forest with a double-bladed axe." Two regular Joes. But wait! Midland isn't a town of oil roughnecks—West Texas oil workers and their families live in Odessa, one county over from George's town of Midland, which is where the bankers and bosses live. Daddy Bush himself was heir to a New England fortune, and he had his own oil company based in Midland. Plus, little George was a bit different from the average West Texas local in that he summered in the luxury of his family's manor on Walker's Point, which juts jauntily into the Atlantic from Kennebunkport, Maine, and he enjoyed visits at the manor of his mother's wealthy parents in Rye, New York. As for Al Gore's upbringing on the farm in Tennessee, he mostly was raised in the Fairfax hotel on embassy row in Washington, D.C., and while he often reminisced during the campaign about swimming in the Caney Fork River that runs alongside the farm, much of his childhood swimming was done in the members-only pool of the U.S. Senate.

Also, not a lot of regular Joes go to private schools, as Al did at exclusive St. Alban's in Washington, where numerous of the political elites send their kids. His fellow students dubbed him "Prince Al." Bush, who almost incessantly cites his attendance at San Jacinto Junior High in Midland as proof of his commonality with plain folks, doesn't like to mention that he left Midland at age thirteen, after spending only the seventh grade in the hallowed halls of old S.J.J.H. The family moved to a big house in an upscale neighborhood in Houston, where Big George planned to launch his political career, and where Little George was enrolled not in public schools with the folks, but in the tony Kincaid Academy, finishing junior high with people of similar stations in life. After Kincaid, George was spirited off to New England, where he entered, as Daddy had before him, Phillips Academy in Andover, a silk-stocking prep school that specializes in making sure that the offspring of wealth are securely positioned on the well-oiled escalator to inherited success.

But an upscale upbringing is not enough to explain Al's and George's fealties to the rich and powerful. After all, this is America, where the handicap of privilege need not bar anyone from becoming a useful citizen. It can be overcome, even by those entering the political realm, if only they have the gumption and internal fortitude to do it (Eleanor and Franklin Roosevelt being a couple of handy role models here). Serving private interests over the public interest is a choice, and these two presidential aspirants willingly and eagerly made that choice right from the start of their careers. Rather than use their birth advantages to buck the system on behalf of those who get trampled by it, they joined in solidarity with their brothers and sisters who are similarly advantaged, realizing that they could move up by buddying up with business executives, investment bankers, Washington lobbyists, and other money players who could be valuable to them personally and politically.

GORE FITS IN

The Colonial golf tournament held annually at the Colonial Country Club in Fort Worth is a classic that draws all the top players . . . except for one: Tiger Woods. He says he'd like to be there because it's played on a great course and has lots of golf history attached to it, but he now bypasses the event because it's called the *MasterCard* Colonial. Not that he has anything against corporate sponsors, since he's loaded with them himself. But Tiger points out that one of his main sponsors is the American Express card, so "It would be tough for me to come to Colonial." He notes that if he won there he would inadvertently be promoting MasterCard, "and that would be detrimental to my relationship with American Express."

Al Gore, Jr., knows how Tiger feels, for he's got a similar problem. He wants to be there for working families, the environment, family farmers, and all—but that would be detrimental to his relationship with his sponsors (which include American Express and so many other brand names that he'd look like a NASCAR driver if they expected him to wear their logos).

Like Bill Clinton, Gore is a fellow who, in his heart, wants to be with the people. He comes from good populist stock, too—while his father eventually amassed enough wealth to assure that his son would go to exclusive schools and be put on the easy path to financial and political success, Al Senior had grown up poor in Possum Hollow, Tennessee, and he rose to become a decidedly maverick senator. The senior Gore was willing to confront the power elites of his day as he battled for laboring people, tenant farmers, and others, and he also took major political risks on the big fights, opposing the Vietnam War and refusing to sign Strom Thurmond's infamous Southern Manifesto.

But Al Junior is hardly a chip off that old block of in-your-face populism. Far from it—his own mom, Pauline, has described her second child as "a born conformist." Unfortunately, that fits him like a black suit on an undertaker. As he has confirmed from childhood all the way through his vice presidential years, this is not someone who's comfortable coloring outside the lines, much less challenging the corporate order.

He also stayed strictly inside the corporate-drawn lines as he methodically moved through Election 2000, even though some Goreheads wanted us to think that, deep down, Al might possibly be a Democrat. They whispered that he could blossom into some combination of William Jennings Bryan, FDR, and Al Gore, Sr., now that he was finally in a position to free himself from the Wall Street money shackles that bound the Clinton presidency. Yeah, and Dan Quayle is a closet member of the Mensa Society. Anyone who thinks Gore is about to leap out in a pair of tights and a red cape to become The People's Champion needs (1) to get professional help if you really fantasize about Al Gore in tights, and (2) to explain why he spent such an inordinate amount of time in the company of Rattner, Tisch, & Kramer. This is not a firm, but three individuals, although they acted as a sort of political brokerage firm on Wall Street, peddling Gore as their sole commodity. Steve Rattner is chief executive of the investment banking

house Lazard Frères; Jonathan Tisch is scion of the multibillionaire Tisch family, with major holdings that include everything from Loews hotels to the New York Giants; and Orin
Kramer owns the megabucks money-management firm of
Kramer Spellman.

These three gentlemen of the Street became Al's best pals
during the three years leading up to his 2000 presidential run,
touting him as hot political stock and working furtively to
bring him into the inner sanctums of America's most powerful
brokers, bankers, and bond dealers. RT&K's objective was not
merely to introduce him to the conservative (and genetically
Republican) world of these high-level money changers but to
have them really get to know Al, trust him, teach him, and—
dare I say it?—bond with him. According to the *Washington
Post,* the trio of Rattner, Tisch, and Kramer put together dozens
of what they refer to as "cultivational" meetings between Gore
and a Who's Who of America's financial heavies, including top
executives from Goldman Sachs, Lehman Brothers, J.P. Morgan, Citigroup, AIG, and Bankers Trust. Gore courted Wall
Street's money mavens like a boar in heat. He lunched in Manhattan hotels with them, held tête-à-têtes with them in his
Executive Office Building hideaway, had breakfast brainstorm-
ing sessions with them in Washington and New York, brought
them in for White House coffees (some people just never
learn), and even threw three intimate Christmas parties at the
vice president's mansion in 1997 especially to host his new
Street buddies and their spouses. "He sees it as his job," said
Rattner, admiring Gore's wooing of Wall Street givers. "He is
very focused, very disciplined."

The bonding was complete. Rattner, Tisch, and Kramer har-
vested bales of campaign dollars from the fertile fields of Wall
Street to fuel Gore's presidential candidacy, getting checks from
executives at Goldman Sachs, Citigroup, Morgan Stanley, Merrill Lynch, Lehman Brothers, and many more firms eager to buy
a chunk of stock in Al. Just from their own firms and from

their personal pockets, Rattner put $106,000 into Gore, Tisch added $336,000 for the veep, and Kramer was in for $102,000. Check by check, event by event, private meeting by private meeting, Gore steadily forged and fitted the links of his own Wall Street shackles. What he got out of this, of course, was a reliable flow of political money from some of the deepest pockets in the country. What did they get? A good boy. One who was well trained, properly grateful, eager to have their continuing approval, and a born conformist. For example, to demonstrate that he was an attentive student in all those tutorials he got in RT&K's cultivational meetings, the Gore2000 model toned down considerably the enviro-protecto persona that only a few years ago was his political hallmark. Instead, he emphasized a remarkably Republican-like approach that advocated balancing any environmental action with the absolute need to assure that America's "good business climate" (including stock prices of polluters) is not harmed in any way. I mean, we're all concerned about the global climate, right, so why shouldn't the *business* climate be a natural environmental concern? As Al himself put it, "I believe that anybody who aspires to lead this nation in the twenty-first century needs to be fully conversant with the business environment." Save the Dow, man.

Al's focus was on campaign check writers. Jon Corzine, then CEO of Goldman Sachs, was one of those check writers, as well as one of Gore's tutors. He had a cup of coffee and an introductory one-on-one session with him in 1998, later telling *Washington Post* reporter Ianthe Jeanne Dugan: "The Vice President has tried to understand how the global economy works from the eyes of someone sitting in Wall Street."

Swell. When's the last time Gore tried to understand how the global economy works from the eyes of someone on your street? But, then, unlike Mr. Corzine, you and your Goldman Sachs colleagues hadn't written more than $86,750 worth of checks to him, have you? To keep Gore from getting his streets confused, his pals Rattner, Tisch, and Kramer continued during the campaign to surround him with the right kind of people. Various Wall Street executives regularly conferred with him behind closed doors to explain global financial issues and to counsel him on his economic policies ("Don't touch that Dow!")—and they even vetted some of his speeches. Holy Popalorum! VET HIS SPEECHES? What are the working stiffs, dirt farmers, and other regular folks of America to make of a Democrat who meekly submits his thoughts and words for pre-delivery approval to plutocrats ensconced high in their Towers of Mammon, smugly looking down on the American people?

Gore strategists offered a convoluted political rationalization for this Republican-like behavior, explaining that Wall Street itself is sort of "populistic" now that so many Internet-browsing, Starbucks-sipping Americans are, like, you know, really into the market in a third millennium kind of way, and they see CEOs as celebrity studs, so seeing Big Al rubbing shoulders with them really has its own grassrootsy appeal. Really. None other than Roger Altman, the New York invest-ment banker who first introduced Bill Clinton to Wall Street and later helped shape Clinton's elitist economic policies as deputy treasury secretary, embraced both Gore and his "Smart-Politics" identification with wealth. As Altman told *Post* reporter Dugan: "With a third of American households invested in Wall Street, and mushrooming millionaires made there, Wall Street is more important than ever."

Not that Gore means any harm to us nonmushrooming mil-lionaires or to the two-thirds of us who are not immersed in the thrill of the Dow, but—hey—he'd taken the money and kissed the devil square on the lips, so what did you expect him to do?

MONEY MAN. Gore was destined to run for president, not by fate, but by family expectation. "We raised him for it," his father once said, and Al always has been the dutiful son, doing his homework, applying himself diligently, working harder than anyone else, learning from mistakes, striving, seeking to please. A *New York Times* profile notes that even as a nine-year-old kid at 4-H camp, Al would impress the adults with his work ethic, going so far as to *request* the hated kitchen duty." He was the only camper I ever had volunteer for K-P," said the camp director.

Some forty years later, the dutiful, diligent, political Gore was still impressing the adults, showing an unnatural willingness to handle the odious tasks of campaign fundraising. In the *Washington Post*, Ceci Connolly has written that the very first thing Gore did in July of 1992, when Clinton tapped him to be his running mate, was not to have a party with family and friends, but to hit the phones and shake the money tree he had painstakingly nurtured during the past few years. Within twenty-four hours of accepting Clinton's offer, he delivered $1 million in soft money for the campaign. "It was symbolic," says Gore's former staff director: "He wanted to do his part." And when it came time to put some serious money together for the Clinton-Gore '96 reelection campaign, Al was eager to do even more than his part, enthusiastically dialing for dollars. Connolly reports that in a November 1995 meeting with top campaign fundraisers, Gore said, "Count me in on the calls," and he was so eager to please that he complained that the president was down to make about twenty money calls, while he'd only been assigned ten. "Is it possible to do a reallocation for me to take more of the events and calls?" he asked.

Being Gore, of course he was meticulous in accounting for his fundraising production. In a memo for Clinton, the vice president sounded like a shoe salesman submitting his slips to get his monthly commission and bonus: "I did three events this week which were projected to raise $650,000, and under rigorous accounting, actually raised $800,000. For the month, Tipper and I were supposed to do $1.1 million, and it looks like we will be closer to $1.3 million."

It's not that Gore enjoys the K-P duty of raising money, but enjoyment is beside the point for him. In his view, it's what is required to succeed: "If he can internalize the need to do it, he will just suck it up and do it and take satisfaction in a job well done," a former aide told Connolly. Don't whine, don't shirk your duty, just dial, dial, dial that telephone, and when you reach a target on your call list, remember to touch all the bases (spouse's name, how are the kids, thanks again for that event in Aspen), then don't flinch from the purpose of your call, seal the deal: "I've been tasked with raising $2 million and you're on my list," the *Post* reports him saying bluntly at the crucial moment of a call. While other politicians duck and dodge at this moment, Gore is known as an excellent "closer," a fund-raiser's dream. Tony Coelho, a former member of Congress, investment banker, and lobbyist who has raised a barnful of corporate bucks for Democrats, gets a little misty-eyed when he speaks of Gore-the-Money-Man: "He has gotten in the fields and worked with the rest of us," he told Connolly, as though describing a heroic general who got down in the trenches with his troops. "It shows he's a real player in political circles."

Al's personal political mantra is: "It's the money, stupid." In his 1988 bid for the presidential nomination, he was outspent, enduring a humbling loss, and was left holding a $2 million debt. Never again, he vowed. Do what is necessary to get the money. Immediately after that loss, Gore began building the internal team of lobbyists, Wall Streeters, and corporate executives who would propel him to his November 7 date with destiny. Gore's political circle essentially had become a corporate circle, as documented in detail by the Center for Public Integrity in its excellent book *The Buying of the President 2000*.

CAMPAIGN CHAIRMAN. In May of '99, **Tony Coelho** took the helm of Gore's campaign. This is the gent who, as head of the Democrats' congressional fundraising arm in 1981, became the primary architect of the party's shift out of working-class streets and into corporate suites. Abruptly leaving Congress in '89 after an exposé of his financial dealings with a Beverly Hills S&L, Coelho hopped up to a Wall Street investment house where he made a personal fortune (he now owns five homes around the world), and he also became a paid board member for a dozen corporations, including cable-TV giant TCI, the global funeral conglomerate SCI, and the gambling empire Circus Circus. Because of internal conflicts and health problems, Tony left Gore Inc. in May 2000, turning over the chairmanship to **William Daley**, a man who has spent a lifetime merging Democratic Party politics into the boardroom. A highly paid corporate lawyer and lobbyist from Chicago, Daley is a master practitioner of what Windy City insiders refer to as "pinstripe patronage," the linking of political power to money power for mutual profit. Daley, who has been described by longtime political observer Doug Ireland as "a walking conflict of interest and behind-the-scenes deal-maker who leaves few fingerprints," harnessed corporate money to his brother's winning mayoral bid in '89, then raised mucho moolah from the same sources for Clinton-Gore in '92. In late '93, he was called to Washington to pull Clinton's fat out of the fire (a heavy load, indeed) on the NAFTA vote, which was going down because of broad public suspicion (later confirmed by experience) that NAFTA would give the Shafta to most people. People be damned, Daley rallied the CEOs and lobbyists to ram the trade scam through Congress. In '96, he became Clinton's Commerce secretary, functioning there as an on-call escort service for any and every corporation wanting to move investment dollars, factories, jobs, and technology out of America. He was also the engineer in charge of railroading Wall Street's infamous China bill through Congress in May of last year—a bill that 80 percent of Americans opposed. Never mind that Daley had become the highly visible symbol of this legislative mugging of both the public interest and public will, openly operating on behalf of Motorola, Boeing, Microsoft, General Motors, and other corporate pushers of the China deal—just days after the vote, Gore added insult to injury by hoisting Daley to the top position in his campaign for all the world to see. In fairness to Gore, though, wrapping this ultimate symbol of corporatist politics around him did have a kind of confessional honesty to it—sort of like a prostitute wearing pink hot pants to church.

CAMPAIGN STAFF. While the nuts and bolts of running a presidential campaign generally fall to longtime political opera- tives, even Gore's operatives tended to be corporate, including **Carter Eskew**, who came to the campaign from the PR firm BSMG Worldwide, where he'd undertaken such dirty jobs as helping the tobacco industry buff its stained image, directing the ad campaign for the corporate front USA-NAFTA, and developing media for big broadcasting conglomerates that wanted to rip off the public by not paying for the privilege of using our airwaves for their digital broadcasts; lobbyist **Michael Whouley**, who previously had lobbied the vice presi- dent on behalf of such clients as Northwest Airlines, Master- Card, and Visa; **Michael Berman**, of the Republican-led lobbying outfit called the Duberstein Group, where he lobbied for a whole corral of corporate clients, including General Motors, Time Warner, National Cable Television Association, CSX, and the HMO trade association; and **Marcia Hale**, who hailed from Monsanto, where her job was to try to force Euro- pean nations and Japan to swallow genetically engineered food products made from Monsanto's altered seeds without labeling them as the Frankenfoods they are.

THE GORE-TECHS. Gore might not have invented the Inter- net, but he sure got in on the ground floor of Internet politics, surrounding himself with a cadre of top tech execs who've guided his Internet and technology policies, which (duh!) turn out to be exuberantly in favor of the execs and against the inter- ests of consumers, high-tech workers, and citizen's privacy. Yes, they really do refer to themselves as the Gore-Techs, and they include **Marc Andreessen**, co-founder of Netscape (now part of America Online), an original G-T member and Gore fundraiser; **Brook Byers**, a Silicon Valley financier who helped tutor the VP on tax and budget issues that have richly benefited him and his clients; **John Doerr**, a guru of the Valley who, as a venture capitalist, helped launch such successes as Intuit, Netscape, and Sun Microsystems, and has put ideas in Al's head and hundreds of thousands of Silicon dollars into his pocket; **David Shaw**, a Wall Street financier and major Gore money man who specializes in the use of technology in education, and who got a plum assignment in 1997 as chair of a presidential panel on educational technology, which just happened to issue an official recommendation that 5 percent of all public-school funds in America be set aside for buying and implementing educational technologies; and **Jerry Yang**, CEO of Yahoo!, who has helped the vice president reach a "correct" understanding of the economics of the Internet.

OLD PALS. These are the people closest to Gore, who've been with him for years and have his ear regularly on the total range of policy issues, helping him to frame his overall perspective and worldview: **Peter Knight** is Al's most trusted aide, long-time confidant, chief fundraiser, and unofficial consigliere who has cashed in big time as a well-connected lobbyist for such corporate luminaries as Lockheed Martin, Bell Atlantic, Disney, and Schering-Plough. **Tom Downey** is Al's best friend, having served as a New York Congress critter with Gore in the mid-seventies, when he was hell-bent to reform the corrupt money system in Washington (now, he is the corrupt system, shoveling corporate money into the coffers of lawmakers—and presidential candidates—while lobbying for the likes of Microsoft, Merck & Co., Met-Life, National Cable Television Association, and Time Warner). **Roy Neel** is an old Gore hand and friend, having been his telecommunications staffer before becoming head lobbyist for U.S. Telecom, the Washington shop of the

regional Bell Telephone companies. **Tony Podesta** is a longtime
Goreite who has parlayed his White House connections (his
brother, John, was Clinton's chief of staff) into a hot lobbying
career peddling influence for CBS, Novartis, Time Warner, Viacom, and the drug manufacturers association, among many others. **Jack Quinn**, Gore's chief of staff as vice president,
changed hats in 1997 to do lobbying chores for the likes of Bell
Atlantic, Intel, SBC Communications, and Viacom.

THE BOARD OF DIRECTORS. Gore had become so comfy in
the boardroom that he created his own board of directors. It
was self-selecting and even "democratic," in a strictly pluto-
cratic way—you could've been on it, too. All you had to do was
give or raise more than $100,000 for Al's presidential quest.
Among those who did were: **Mitchell Berger**, a corporate
lawyer who handles legal chores for S&Ls, banks, energy corporations, polluters, foreign governments, multinational corporations, and others, having spent a decade at the
influence-peddling shop of Patton Boggs in Washington before
opening his own corporate practice in Florida in the mid-
nineties. **Norm Brownstein**, a wheeler-dealer lawyer and
influence peddler based in Denver, where he has a golden
Rolodex of corporate clients (ranging from McDonalds to
United Airlines to the Denver Broncos), though he mainly
operates at the national level, having spent so much time at the
Capitol and delivered so much campaign cash that Ted
Kennedy calls him the "101st senator." **J. Shelby Bryan**, CEO
of ICG Communications, a burgeoning telecommunications
empire that provides telephone and Internet services across the
country. **Alvaro Cifuentes**, a corporate lawyer now in service
to the many-tentacled lobbying/legal firm of Verner Liipfert in
Washington, who has had a client list of such stellar names as
Borden, Digital, Hyatt, Kodak, Panasonic, Sunoco, and Xerox.
Terry McAuliffe, the Clinton golfing buddy, peripatetic deal-
maker, and Herculean fund-raiser who lifted a mountain of

corporate cash ($275 million by his count) into assorted Clinton-Gore pockets, and who now sits on ten corporate boards, chairs a home-building outfit financed by Republican billionaire Carl Lindner (the Chiquita banana baron), and is a New York investment banker. **Sumner Redstone**, the billionaire CEO of the media giant Viacom, which has within its corporate fortress such properties as the CBS network, Infinity radio, MTV, Showtime, Paramount Pictures, Blockbuster video stores, and Simon & Schuster—as well as 1,300 movie screens, probably in a theater near you. **Haim Saban**, CEO of Fox Kids Worldwide, the number one purveyor of children's television in America, whose top show, appropriately enough, is *Mighty Morphin Power Rangers*. **Alan Solomont**, an occasional Bill Clinton jogging partner and a nursing-home poobah, whose ADS Group is one of the largest chains in the Northeast, and who unabashedly has mixed his multimillion-dollar fundraising for Clinton and Gore with successful lobbying efforts to get the administration to "relax" government regulation of nursing homes.

GETTING GORED. "The real McCoy" wasn't. This old American idiom that denotes something genuine is derived from a renowned 1890s boxer from Indiana named Kid McCoy. In the days before boxers wore gloves and fights had a limited number of rounds, the Kid would crisscross the country, fighting all comers and beating each of them. He was so good, so popular, and such a money draw that a crop of imitators soon sprang up, all claiming to be Kid McCoy. In 1899, however, the Kid himself fought a twenty-round slugfest in which he endured three broken ribs, yet still won. Reporting on the fight, the *San Francisco Examiner* blared in a headline: "Now You've Seen The Real McCoy!" Only, the kid's real name was Norman Selby.

So who is Al Gore? Alas, not the real McCoy . . . not Norman Selby. Instead of the fighter that he has claimed to be on a

range of people's issues, Kid Gore tends to throw in the towel
early, take the money, and run. Consider, for example, the issue
that supposedly defines Al: environmentalism. The Rush
Limbaugh-breaths of the hard-right media foamed at the mouth
and ran around in circles throughout the 2000 campaign, yelp-
ing about how Gore was the reincarnation of Vlad the Impaler
on environmental issues, such an extremist that his secret
agenda was to destroy the economy and force everyone to eat
tofu, ride bicycles, and wear Birkenstocks. I don't know what
kind of wild mushrooms those yelpers were snacking on, but
Al's idea of extremism is to wear a plaid shirt. Nonetheless, he
does have a sincere concern about Earth's ecology, and he certainly talked a great game of green: "We must make the rescue
of the environment the central organizing principle for civilization," he wrote in his thoughtful 1992 book, *Earth in the Balance*. "The environment is much more than a policy position to
me," he declared in a 1999 speech. "It is a profoundly moral
obligation."

But, as actress Rosalind Russell once said, "politics makes
strange bedclothes," and while Al wore a cloak of green, he
had sewn large pockets inside it to store campaign funds
slipped to him by oil, chemical, development, timber, mining,
agribusiness, and other polluting interests. From the first days
of the Clinton-Gore administration, Mr. Environmentalism
began sniffing the money and backing off, refusing to throw
any hard punches at the polluters. Gore's own performance as
vice president was so feeble that people who had suffered from
his actions or inactions took to attending his staged campaign
events last year and shouting out to him: "Read your book!"

East Liverpool, Ohio, haunts Gore, but not as much as he
and Waste Technologies Industries haunt the people who live
there. The town, located on the Ohio River along the state's
eastern border, is home to some 13,000 folks . . . and one
humongous toxic waste incinerator. The WTI waste burner,
now owned by a Swiss corporation, is one of the largest in the

world. Locals and environmental experts say this facility never should have been built there, for it violates five of the eight no-nos that EPA uses to reject a hazardous waste site as "inappropriate." WTI's incinerator—located only 320 feet from homes and 1,100 feet from East Elementary School, where 400 children attend classes and play in the schoolyard—burns 63,000 tons a year of highly toxic chemicals, heavy metals, and other deadly, cancer-causing materials, emitting toxic gases and particles from its smokestack day in and day out.

In a *60 Minutes* report about the dangers of the incinerator, the local school superintendent was asked if there was any consideration of how to protect the school kids of East Elementary in case an "incident" at the plant spewed toxic emissions at them. The superintendent replied that the plan was to rush the children into the school cafeteria and "after we have them in there, to try to seal it as tightly as possible." "With what?" the *60 Minutes* correspondent inquired. "You'd use duct tape, I suppose."

If the people have no defense except duct tape when WTI's belching behemoth disgorges toxics into the air, don't even think about a flood. The plant is situated right on the banks of the Ohio, and the entire town of East Liverpool is in the river's flood plain, offering a dandy chance for lethal incinerator waste to saturate the area, not to mention that cities downstream draw their drinking water from this river. In addition, the incinerator sits above two aquifers, one of which is the only source of drinking water in the area other than the Ohio River.

Flashback to July 19, 1992: Beleaguered opponents of WTI's project were overjoyed this day because Captain Courageous had arrived in the person of Al Gore, Jr. At the time, the project still had no federal permit to operate or even to conduct a "test burn" that it was required to pass before the company could get an operating permit. Campaigning in the area, Gore spoke up for the people: "The very idea of putting it in a flood plain, you know, it's just unbelievable to me. I'll tell you this, a Clinton-

Gore administration is going to give you an environmental presidency to deal with these problems. We'll be on your side for a change." To the delight of these good people, Al and Bill were elected that November, and only a month later the incoming veep boosted their hopes again by reiterating his staunch stance for environmental sanity: "Serious questions concerning the safety of an East Liverpool, Ohio, hazardous waste incinerator must be answered before the plant may begin operation," he declared in a December 7 press statement. "The new Clinton-Gore administration would not issue the plant a test burn permit until . . . all questions concerning the compliance with state and federal law have been answered." Period.

Hoorahs and hosannahs for the Great Goreski, the man who stared down WTI and saved the children! Except that he didn't. Once he was sworn in, only six weeks after his bold December press release, the fearless defender of the folks and the environment turned out to be the one who blinked, suddenly mumbling that there was nothing he could do to stop the permitting process, so sorry, hope no one dies, good-bye. As he retreated, Gore lobbed the blame back to outgoing Bush officials, asserting that in a dastardly last-minute decision, they had given WTI the go-ahead it needed. "Our hands are tied," sighed a spokeswoman for the shiny new vice president, who no longer made himself available to talk about the matter.

But in a thorough (and thoroughly damning) investigative story last year about Al's phenomenal disappearing act from East Liverpool, Jake Tapper of the Internet mag *Salon*, wrote that Gore was hardly the helpless public official he purported to be. Tapper noted that the Clinton-Gore team had not hesitated to overturn other eleventh-hour Bush maneuvers, and he also reported that the rush to judgment on this decision might not have been by Bush officials alone—that a top Gore enviro staffer, Katie McGinty, had told the Bush officials to go ahead with the WTI test-burn permit. Ms. McGinty says she can't remember the conversation.

Her role aside, what about this? In March, two months after the Clinton-Gore inauguration, WTI conducted its test burn . . . AND FAILED! Wouldn't this have been a neat time for a certain environmentally macho vice president to assert himself? This was no minor technical failure, either—the test showed excess emissions of carbon tetrachloride (causes liver cancer), mercury (a neurotoxin that damages people's central nervous system), and polychlorinated dibenzodioxins (a super-nasty that a Boston University expert described to Tapper as "one of the most severe toxic chemicals ever created by humans, causing birth defects, cancer, immunological suppression, and cardiovascular problems"). But Al, he just stayed real still. So, on April 6, WTI received its EPA operating permit, which made it, as Tapper wrote, "the first hazardous-waste incinerator in history to be allowed to run despite having failed a test burn." In fact, EPA did not publicly acknowledge that the corporation had failed the test until six days *after* the permit was granted.

Meanwhile, Greenpeace and others filed suit to stop the incinerator from firing up. This time, at last, the Clinton-Gore team sprang into action. On the wrong side. Administration lawyers were dispatched to help WTI and the EPA battle the citizen groups, and Janet Reno's Justice Department even testified in court on WTI's behalf. While writing his article last year, Tapper tried to get a comment from the Gore-for-President campaign on how he could claim to have done his best for these people when his own administration had schlepped briefcases to court in support of the corporation that was endangering their community and their lives: "A Gore campaign spokesman referred me to the vice president's office," Tapper reported. "The office referred me to the EPA. EPA spokesman Tim Fields . . . says he didn't work for the EPA at the time, so he couldn't comment. When asked for someone who could comment, the EPA never called me back."

In the seven years since Gore took a dive, Waste Technologies Industries has been incinerating away, even though it has recorded thirty-four fires, had five explosions, experienced twenty-seven other "release incidents," and incurred state fines for what the *New York Times* referred to as "violations of air monitoring requirements." How bureaucratically genteel that phrase is. Less genteel is the stark picture of the townspeople's health. A 1997 state study found that the people of East Liverpool have "strikingly higher" rates of cancer deaths than elsewhere in the state and nation (40.25 percent higher than the national average). Tapper dug out more health information, reporting that the small city has a startling incidence of male breast cancer, as well as an uncommon incidence of very aggressive breast cancer in young women. It's also uncommon for a town of 13,000 to have two little boys, one two years old, the other about three, suffering from rare eye tumors, both of whom have had to have eyes removed. Another study found that the incidence of children with mercury in their urine more than doubled within six months of the incinerator getting its operating permit.

Yes, this is an old industrial town of steel and pottery factories, so there is more than one source of pollution, but the very best you can say about adding a cancer machine to the mix is that it was less than helpful. Notice that no WTI executives or board members live anywhere near it. As for the health of those who do live there, more studies are needed, say the authorities. But the incinerator doesn't wait on studies—it keeps on chugging.

Why did Al disappear? The money boys got to him. Coming into office in January of '93, both Clinton and Gore were engulfed by Wall Street insiders, corporate chieftains, lobbyists, and their own "wise advisers" inside the White House—the latter category being composed of such corporate stalwarts as treasury secretary Lloyd Bentsen, Robert Rubin of Goldman Sachs (later to become Treasury secretary), and Robert Altman, also of Goldman Sachs (a firm that later ranked in the top five of Gore's presidential donors). All of these insider voices were whispering to Bill and Al that their populist campaign oratory about such things as raising the minimum wage above poverty, developing an American industrial policy—and making the environment "the central organizing principle for civilization"—was sweet, but now it was time to get serious and work on the agenda of the corporate campaign funders who had paid for the dance.

Specifically, Al was seen by this triumvirate of elders as way too green, and they did not think it helpful to have him running with the rabble in places such as East Liverpool, making loud noises about yanking corporate operating permits. Such talk was scaring the waste product out of Wall Street financiers who already were jittery about the new administration. Al didn't want to be responsible for a Wall Street panic, did he? Besides, the Street had some money in play in East Liverpool. Morgan Guaranty Trust was getting nice fees for handling $128 million in construction financing for WTI's waste burner. The financing was being provided by Stephens, an Arkansas-based financial conglomerate owned by Jackson T. Stephens, who happened to have close ties to Clinton. How close? Stephens raised more than $100,000 for Bill's presidential run and had provided a $3.5 million line of credit for the '92 campaign. With this new information provided to the always obedient son, Gore turned a different shade of green, and he was no longer in touch with his old friends back in Ohio.

"I'm so angry I'm shaking," Terri Swearingen told Jake Tapper. She's a nurse who lives only two miles from WTI's facility, and she's been turned into a citizen activist by it. "Al Gore was supposed to be the environmental hero," she says, "but meanwhile I've got a toxic-waste incinerator in my backyard."

Mystery writer Raymond Chandler once observed, "It is not a fragrant world." Despite an entire gallery of photo ops featuring Gore in an Eddie Bauer shirt announcing his determination to defend the sweet purity of a beach or Bambi or some other natural wonder, Al's World is not so fragrant either. The stench of money and politics overpowers his best intentions. East Liverpool is hardly the only dark stain on Gore's green cloak:

- On October 21, 1999, gearing up his campaign, he made a flat-out scouts' honor, no-wobble, 100 percent-guaranteed, cross-my-heart-and-hope-to-die pledge to end oil drilling off the California coast: "I will take the most sweeping steps in our history to protect our oceans and coastal waters from offshore oil drilling. I will make sure that there is no new oil leasing off the coasts of California and Florida. And then I will go much further: I will do everything in my power to make sure that there is no new drilling . . . even in areas already leased for drilling by previous administrations." *The very next month*, the Clinton-Gore administration granted oil company requests to extend thirty-six drilling leases in California coastal waters. Oil companies were $2 million donors to Gore and the Democratic Party for the 2000 election.
- In 1992, candidate Gore pledged that the new administration would be a ferocious defender of America's vanishing wetlands. Yet with direct subsidies and lax EPA enforcement, the administration has encouraged the sugar industry to continue destroying the Everglades. Among the sugar daddies, Alfonso Fanjul and his Flo-Sun sugar empire in the Everglades have sweetened Clinton and Gore's various money pockets with more than $300,000 in contributions (so valued was Fanjul that Clinton took a phone call from him in the Oval Office while being serviced by Monica Lewinsky). Also, despite Al's pledge, another 500 acres of sensitive New Jersey wetlands are set to be destroyed by an upscale shopping center and entertainment complex to be built atop them by the Mills Corporation. Various federal agencies opposed the deal, but the Council on Environmental Quality, which was closely attached to VP Gore, brokered the dirty deal for Mills. Less than a week later, contributions totaling $43,000 came to the Gore 2000 cam-

paign fund from the grateful folks at Mills. "There is certainly no connection between anyone's contributions and the administration's work on this," said a Gore spokesman. Perhaps. But it's curious that the money had been solicited from company executives by Gore bagman Peter Knight while the deal was being brokered.

- In 1996, as part of his "reinventing government" flimflam, Gore achieved what Nixon and Reagan could not get Congress to sit still for: privatizing the Navy's strategic oil reserve, known as Elk Hills. This huge oil field near Bakersfield, California, literally is black gold, and the industry had drooled over it for decades, just as environmentalists had fought to prevent its ecology-destroying development. It was the largest privatization of federal property in United States history. The winning bidder in the sell-off was Occidental Petroleum. Just coincidentally, Al and Occidental go waaaay back. Indeed, the major source of the wealth amassed by Gore's father came from his long relationship with the company and its legendary chairman, Armand Hammer. Gore has extended the familial ties to Occidental Petroleum, presently owning about a million dollars' worth of the company's stock, and also enjoying a unique neighborly relationship to the corporation. Adjacent to the Gore's bucolic old family farm back home in Tennessee, right along the Caney Fork River that Al talks of so wistfully, he owns yet another farm that he prefers not to talk of at all. It is less bucolic but far more profitable than the homeplace. This chunk of farmland is rich in zinc, and it was sold to Al in 1973 under a sweetheart transaction by Armand Hammer. "Mr. Green" turns out to be a zinc miner! As a by-product, he also turns out to be a polluter—some environmentalists say that runoff from the mine is getting into his beloved Caney Fork. Gore draws annual zinc royalties that have totalled some $500,000 since he acquired the land from Occidental, and he has mined more than half a million dollars in campaign funds from Occidental since he became vice president—including a $50,000 donation that came after one of Al's infamous telephone solicitations from the White House, and another $100,000 wad that rolled in after Occidental's CEO had enjoyed two nights in the Lincoln bedroom. These cozy connections caused industry eyes to roll when it was announced that Occidental had won the bidding on Elk Hills. Writing in *The Nation*, Alexander Cockburn reports that the company was viewed as a bankruptcy waiting to happen until it got its hands on this sensationally profitable oil reserve. Normally, the Department of Energy would decide whether a national asset like Elk Hills, the military's largest strategic fuel reserve, should be sold off. Instead, Cockburn writes, Gore arranged for a private consulting firm named ICF Kaiser International to make this assessment. Guess who was chairman of ICF Kaiser? Al's old pal Tony Coelho. "Oh, ye cynics," wail Gore staffers, asserting that Occidental's good fortune on Elk Hills was all on the up and up. Interestingly, though, the Energy Department has refused to release documents pertaining to the deal.

Again and again on environmental issues, Gore has deferred to money—to Appalachian coal companies, to Florida developers, to oil drillers in Alaska, to timber giants in national forests, to Occidental Petroleum (again) in Colombia. He also deferred to money in his campaign (which is the one time Gore and Clinton usually remember to at least try sounding like Democrats), relegating pollution issues to the back burner. Here's a cause that has his name on it, that the broad public actually cares about. Never mind that he doesn't really walk the walk, he could have talked the talk and hammered Bush, who is as defenseless on environmental issues as an armadillo wandering out on the interstate. But Gore wouldn't even be a rhetorical advocate, fearing that he might give a case of those bad ol' jitters to his contributors. As one Goreite snapped when the *New York Times* inquired about why Al was AWOL on this issue: "He's not running for president as Mr. Greenjeans."

He didn't run as a Joe Lunchbucket Democrat either, choosing more upscale suburbanites as his target constituency and softpedaling the pocketbook issues that could have ignited the laborers, clerks, cab drivers, and other working stiffs that make up America's majority. However, in fairness to Gore, there was one economic issue where he did prove wrong those who say there's not a dime's worth of difference between the two parties. The real difference was shown in 1999 when Gore's Democrats in Congress battled with Bush's Republicans over an increase in the minimum wage. The GOP, wanting to show a bit more of a compassionate face in the election year, decided to suspend its usual parvanimity on this issue and support a great, big, whopping one-dollar uptick in America's minimum hourly pay—*provided* that this generosity be phased in over a three-year period. In other words, Bush's party was offering a gross increase (read that as you will) of only $33\frac{1}{3}$ cents a year—don't forget that fraction of a penny, you'll need it. At the end of three years, the hourly minimum would stand at—do you want to be a millionaire?— $6.15. That's an annual income of about $12,000 for full-time work. Poverty pay.

"The shame of it all," thundered Gore's party, doing its best imitation of John L. Lewis and demanding that more be done for America's lowest-paid workers in this period of conspicuous prosperity. So the Democrats countered with their own proposal. It also would raise the minimum by a buck to the $6.15 poverty level—but by jiminy, they would phase in theirs over a *two-year* period. Fifty cents a year. So there you have it: there is precisely $16\frac{2}{3}$-cents worth of difference between the two parties.

Like Clinton, Gore is a "New Democrat," which is a Republican who dresses in work clothes at election time. It was Al who insisted vehemently inside the White House in 1993 that

Clinton should abandon any effort to put labor and environmental standards into the NAFTA deal. It was Al whose "reinventing   government"   initiatives   included   removing
government poultry inspectors from the unbelievably gross
chicken processing facilities of such giants as Tyson and Gold
Kist, instead letting the corporations inspect themselves;
according to an investigative report by Cox Newspapers last
year, this "reinvention" has resulted in some 25 percent of the
tens of thousands of birds coming out of a Gold Kist plant
each day being contaminated with tumors, pus, sores, infec-
tions, and other diseases, yet under Gore's self-regulation
scheme the corporation is not obligated to do anything about
selling the bad birds to us. It was Al who made a special trip
back to Washington from a 1999 campaign jaunt so he could
be in the Senate to cast a tie-breaking vote against steel workers who were seeking legislation to stop Russia, Japan, and
other nations from dumping their steel into our markets, artifi-
cially depressing prices here and destroying the jobs of more
than 100,000 steel workers. It was Al who expressed a fervent
desire to see Alan Greenspan reappointed to a *fourth* term as
the head of America's central bank, from whence the dour
banker labors relentlessly to jack up stock values for big
investors while holding down wages for workers. It was Al . . .
well, the list is long of Gore's siding with corporate interests
over people.

Al's idea of boldness was to choose as his VP nominee Senator
Joe Lieberman—another "Nuevo Demo" who is a champion of
NAFTA/WTO trade scams, who favors Star Wars and an even
more bloated Pentagon budget, who fought in the Congress to
protect HMOs from being sued when they injure or kill
patients, who balks at a minimum wage that raises people
above the poverty level, who favors privatizing Social Security
for the benefit of Wall Street . . . and who just as easily could
have been George W. Bush's vice presidential choice. Far from

bold, Gore's choice of Lieberman was perfectly safe, comforting the contributors who always come first with him.

Gore means well, but he'll never act on it, because whenever his good intentions clash with the moneyed interests, as they must at a presidential level, he's a money man. Remember, the opposite of courage is not cowardice—it's conformity.

BEHIND THE SHRUB

Last summer, talent agents in Hollywood and New York received a casting notice for what was called a "reality-based" television ad. The client was the Bush presidential campaign, and it was seeking actors and actresses to appear in the ad as "a wide range of assorted, real-looking people." Instead of going into the streets and talking with people, the campaign hired thespians to play the roles of "everyday people on the street."

George W. Bush's life, like his ad, has been reality-based, rather than real. Despite the campaign's careful scripting of his background, this is not a man who's ever done anything to merit running for mayor of a small city, much less president. He has not moved up through achievements, but through his family name and connections. This is why, in Texas, he's been dubbed "Shrub"—the guy doesn't even measure up to a Bush.

This embarrassing fact gnaws terribly at George. "I think I'm asked that all the time," Bush bristled last June when Nicholas Kristoff of the *New York Times* raised the matter that most rankles him. In response, Bush mimicked the interviewer, dropping his voice and posing the damning question himself: "Would you be standing here as presidential candidate if your name were George Smith?" Then he snapped out his answer: "Well, you know, it's not George Smith. It is George Bush. And how did it influence? I have no idea."

No idea? No one can be that obtuse, that self-deceiving, so totally lacking in introspection. Maybe he just forgot what it has meant to him to be a Bush heir, or maybe he was sniffing too much of the ink on his own press releases. Let's help George reflect a bit on how, just maybe, being named Bush rather than Smith might have "influenced," as he puts it:

- **SCHOOL**. Had he been named Smith, George's mediocre-to-poor record in junior high school would have prevented him from entering the highly selective Phillips Academy, one of the top prep schools in the country. But inadequate grades were no bar to a Bush. Not only did his family name (and wealth) provide this exceptional leg up early in life, but being a Bush also rescued him from the poor grades he received once he got to Phillips. George could muster only a C average there, and he also did poorly on his college entrance exams—yet, like magic, the hard-to-crack doors of prestigious Yale University swung wide for the Bush boy. Yale doesn't take a lot of C students—indeed, George's counselor at Phillips tried to deter him from even applying there, since he knew George didn't have the grades to make it. But George was banking on influence, not merit. Daddy Bush was a Yale grad, and Grandaddy Bush was not only an alumnus, but also on the Yale board of trustees. George *Smith* would not have been allowed to matriculate at Yale, but George Bush was welcomed with open arms (the spawn of rich white families being the one American minority that continues to have an aggressive affirmative action program working on their behalf).
- **VIETNAM**. Coming out of college in the 1960s was a dicey experience for young men of draft age, for you were quite likely to be sucked up in the draft and find yourself suddenly in the horrors of the Vietnam jungles, where more than 53,000 Americans were killed. But there was a middle way between actually going to war and illegally dodging the draft. If you could get one of the coveted spots in the National Guard, you would have it both ways: you'd be in

the military, but you almost certainly would not have to
leave the safety of the good ol' U.S. of A. This was the path
George W. wanted. But how to get in? There were only two
or three vacancies in the Texas Air National Guard when
he applied in 1968, and thousands of Mr. Smiths were in
line ahead of him. Bush states flatly that neither he nor his
father, who was a congressman at the time, asked for any
special favors. But he's conning us with that slick response.
He knows very well that when you're in the swirl of
wealth, you don't need to be so crude as to ask for your
own favors. That's what family connections are for. Sid
Adger was the connection in this case. A prominent businessman and political player in Houston (where he was
known affectionately by his peers as "The King"), Adger
was a personal buddy of the elder Bush, lived in the same
neighborhood, sent his kids to Kincaid, too, and belonged
to the same private clubs. Sid Adger placed the call that
moved George to the top of the National Guard list. The
call went to Ben Barnes, who was speaker of the Texas
House at the time and a close political ally of Brigadier
General James Rose, the head of the Texas guard unit.
Barnes passed on the name to General Rose, who later told
a legislator friend that he had just "put that Republican
congressman from Houston's son in the Air Guard." Thus,
Bush was allowed to spend his war years as a pilot, defending Houston from the Viet Cong. It's simply the way business is done for the privileged—Bush's unit also included
the sons of two other men of wealth and political prominence: former Texas governor John Connally and former
U.S. senator Lloyd Bentsen. If Mr. Smith's daddy had been
connected, he could've gotten into the guard, too, instead
of becoming a statistic in Vietnam. Asked directly by the
Dallas Morning News whether Sid Adger intervened on his
behalf, Bush merely shrugged the matter off by saying, "I
have no idea."

- **BUSINESS.** Bush long coveted an image as a West Texas oilman, which Daddy had been, but after eleven years, millions of lost dollars, and three different companies (all of
which went into the ditch), even he threw his hands up in
exasperation and said, "I'm all name and no money." The
boy just never had much of a head for business and he kept
failing, even though investors kept throwing money at
him—something they would not have done for a George
Smith. Bush could not even have gotten started on his
"Giant" fantasy except for family ties. In 1979, when he
launched his first oil company, called Arbusto (the Spanish
word for Bush), it was his well-connected uncle Jonathan
who shook the tree for investors. Out came a Who's Who of
corporate and political big shots—a most unusual line-up
behind a little nothing of an oil startup in West Texas. The
Washington Post documented $140,000 from Lewis
Lehrman, the New York drugstore magnate and former
GOP gubernatorial candidate; $100,000 from E.F. Hutton's
honcho, George Ball; $100,000 from George Ohrstrom, heir
to one of Virginia's largest fortunes; $93,000 from William
Draper III, a California venture capitalist who later was a
top Reagan administration official; and $79,000 from John
Macomber, CEO of Celenese, who would later serve in the
Bush administration. In drilling for oil, George missed more
than he hit, and Arbusto soon was being called "Bust-o" in
oil circles. Most of the big shots lost money on George—"I
think I ended up getting back 20 cents on the dollar," one of
them moaned to the *Post*. Next, two wealthy investors out of
Cincinnati stepped forward to salvage George's oil mess for
a couple of years, ensconcing him as CEO of their explo-
ration firm, Spectrum 7, and using him as "a drawing card"
to entice more investors. Bush's name again drew capital,
but no luck, and Spectrum rolled toward the ditch, too.
Once again, though, a white knight appeared. In 1986,
Harken Oil & Gas, owned by a New York group, liked

George's star power and bailed him out of financial disaster, acquiring both Spectrum and him. Instead of CEO, this time George was simply given $300,000 in Harken stock and paid $120,000 a year to sit as a high-profile member of the board of directors. Four years later, Bush finally escaped the oil business, but not without lingering suspicions that he once again had profited from privileged information gained by his insider connections. On June 22, 1990, he sold all of his Harken stock for a nice personal profit of $835,000. Just eight days later, Harken's audit committee reported that the company had suffered huge losses, soon causing its stock price to plummet. Maybe George just got lucky. Or maybe not, since he happened to serve on the audit committee that reported the losses! When asked later if he had sold his stock because he knew bad news was coming, Bush said he "had no idea" the audit report would be filled with red ink.

BUSH PLAYS BALL. While he was a flop in school and a failure in business, everyone agrees that George W. is a world-class success at one thing: schmoozing. He could shoot the shit for an hour with a stump, and both he and the stump would feel good about it afterward. Even in his dismal business days, he'd hit the country clubs and bars at night, becoming palaver pals with people who could help him later. Along the way, he gained nicknames like "Boosto" and "The Bombastic Bushkin"—testaments to his comradery. Another thing that can be said about Bush is that he's nothing if not loyal—you help him, he'll help you. That's a positive in friendships; in politics, though, it can take another name: cronyism. And when you realize that practically all of George's friends are from the corporate world, you've pretty much defined his governing philosophy: corporate cronyism.

Meet one of George's special cronies: Richard Rainwater. He's little known outside the rarefied world of high finance, but to those denizens he's considered a financial wizard and a skilled corporate deal-maker. Having been a bright Wall Streeter at Goldman Sachs, then having made a bundle handling investments for the gabillionaire Bass family of Fort Worth, he subsequently amassed his own portly portfolio, now owning such properties as Pioneer oil company, the then huge Columbia/HCA Healthcare; the luxurious Canyon Ranch resorts, and the sprawling Crescent Real Estate empire, which has billions invested in high-rise office buildings, golf courses, and other developments. He's also into casinos, costume jewelry, health-food restaurants, and a joint venture with the Chinese called Richina (Richard, rich, China . . . get it? Cute). Bottom line is he now ranks among the one hundred richest people in America, with a net worth in the neighborhood of a billion and a half bucks.

Along the way to that posh neighborhood, he got cozy with the president's boy, who had been hanging around the White House, mucking in his father's 1988 presidential campaign (where he earned yet another nickname from the political and policy pros there: "Junior." It was not a term of respect). Bush was fortyish by now and, despite a family trust fund, he had not made it into the big-money leagues, where you're not merely a son of wealth, but MR. RICH. To flower, even the smallest bush needs to be properly watered, and Rainwater was just the shower that Junior needed to gain real wealth and attain that "successful businessman" image he so desperately wanted.

Rainwater doesn't publicly discuss his financial favors for Bush, merely saying that "George Bush happens to be one of about 100 people that can make the statement that their involvement with Richard Rainwater has had a very positive effect on their wealth." How modest. George doesn't just "happen to be" one of the many—he was openly positioning himself to run for governor of the state (something he wanted to do in 1990, but Republican Party leaders dismissed him, saying he'd never "done anything"). Rainwater could use a governor (and a president), for many of his businesses depend on government contracts and favors. As for the "very positive effect" that Rainwater has had on Bush's bottom line, even that is an understatement. The majority—nay, the vast bulk—of the sudden wealth that George amassed in the past decade has flowed directly from real estate investments, oil deals, and other business schemes that the billionaire arranged for the budding politician. Bush had to do practically nothing to gain these millions. He even got a "Hillary Deal," an immaculate investment like the $1,000 cattle-futures buy that magically returned a thousandfold to her while Bill was governor. In 1991, George was told to put $385 into a Rainwater group that provided consulting services to a national auto-loan company. Three years later—abracadabra!—Bush pulled $45,512 out of Richard's rabbit hat—about a 1,200 percent return, and George didn't even have to do any consulting.

By far the sweetest Bush connection to Rainwater was the purchase and subsequent sale of the Texas Rangers baseball team. In 1989, Rainwater, Dallas financier Edward "Rusty" Rose III, and Cincinnati financier William O. DeWitt Jr. (who had been Bush's partner in Spectrum 7) were the heavy hitters in a partnership that bought the Rangers for $86 million. They brought Bush into the deal, too. Even though he put up a relatively insignificant $600,000 (mostly borrowed from United Bank of Midland, where he had served as a director), George was named "managing partner," a title he shared with Rusty Rose, who actually ran the business. George's role was to schmooze with politicians, money people, and others whose help the team owners needed. He was the team's designated mouth, the guy with the star-quality family name who could open doors.

The job was perfect for the affable George, for it involved no heavy lifting—mental or physical—and it paid well: $200,000 a year. So in his four-plus years as MP, before resigning to run for governor in 1994, Bush was more than able to cover his $600,000 investment in the team, thanks to the generous paycheck his multimillionaire partners stuffed in his pocket each year for acting as the Rangers' front man. He got something else, too—a high-profile position guaranteed to give him extensive media coverage. He milked this opportunity for all it was worth, and then some, regularly getting his picture made with team stars, signing baseballs in the stands for Rangers fans, and, at the sight of any TV camera, hiking his pants leg to show off his cowboy boots with a red-white-and-blue Texas Rangers logo tooled into the leather. Class will always out.

He attended every home game, sitting right down front in the owner's box, acting as though he was *the* owner. He even had his own baseball card printed with his picture and "stats." The whole "managing partner" shtick bestowed on him something he'd not been able to get on his own: an aura of business legitimacy. He clung to it like a drunk grasping his last quart of beer. While giving *Houston Chronicle* reporter R.G. Ratcliffe a tour of the Rangers' stadium just prior to announcing for governor, Bush waved his arm around and claimed the entire enterprise as his own: "When all those people in Austin say " 'He ain't never done anything,' well, this is it."

It's true that the worth of the franchise appreciated richly during George W.'s tenure, but not because of any managerial acumen in the executive suite (and, alas, certainly not because of the team's sad-sack performance on the field during those years). Rather, it was because of a generous dose of corporate welfare from local taxpayers. In 1991, Bush and partners pulled off the old "Build-us-a-new-stadium-you-yokels-or-we'll-move-the-whole-kit-and-kaboodle-to-East-Beelzebub-and-leave-you-with-nothing" heist on local officials. Thus was born the lovely "ballpark at Arlington," costing taxpayers $150 million or so, paid for by imposing a half-cent hike in the always popular sales tax.

Perhaps I should not be so quick to jump on the partners

and compliant local pols for devising such a regressive financing scheme, for it might well have been an act of civic-minded generosity on their part. Since your low-income citizens and average working stiffs can no longer afford to go to the games, due to the jacked-up price of admission to the joint, hitting them for half a penny every time they spend a dollar elsewhere in Arlington gives them a way to participate and share in the pride of "owning" the Rangers. Imagine the warm glow they must feel when driving past the majestic stadium alongside I-30, knowing that their every purchase that day—from diapers to beer—will send a few more of their pennies, nickels, and dimes to the Rainwater-Bush partnership.

One other telling tidbit about George W. is wrapped up in his stadium years. As reported by Robert Bryce in the *Texas Observer*, candidate Bush campaigned in '94 on the tried-and-true oratorical chestnut that government power should never be allowed to stomp on people's private property rights. "I understand full well the value of private property," he assured a group of stuffed shirts at a business gathering just before the election, adding, "I will do everything I can to defend the power of private property and property rights when I am governor of this state." He also said, "The best way to allocate resources in our society is through the marketplace. Not through a governing elite."

I'll bet the Curtis Mathes family wishes it could have been there to hear the governor-to-be lecturing on the proper role of government. Until 1991, they owned thirteen acres of land next to the proposed new ballpark at Arlington—acres the Rangers' brass, including MP Bush, desperately wanted. In April of that year, the team hired lobbyists to push a special bill through the legislature creating a quasi-governmental group that would serve as the legal entity for obtaining their field of dreams. Called the Arlington Sports Facilities Development Authority, it handled land acquisition and other often untidy tasks associated with building a ballpark for the

Rangers. This new authority promptly offered the Mathes family $817,000 for their thirteen choice acres, which was only $4 million less than the land was judged to be worth. Naturally, the family refused to sell. The team had prepared for this inconvenience, however, having quietly tucked into the authority's founding legislation a small provision that granted to it the power of condemnation. So—BAM!—the Rangers' owners simply seized the Mathes land by eminent domain, using their specially created authority (the governing elite) to pay way less than market price and allocate the family's private resources to themselves. In the process, Bush and cohorts stomped property rights flatter than a baby toad on a rainy country road.

The Mathes family sued and was awarded $5 million by a jury. Good luck collecting a dime from the Bush team, however—they claimed that the judgment was not against them (even though they are the ones who engineered the seizure of the land) but against the Arlington Sports Facilities Development Authority: "The sports authority has to pay that," a Rangers spokesman curtly said. For years, the Rangers dillied and dallied, keeping the Mathes family from getting either their land or their money. Finally, after Bush and partners sold the team, the new owners paid the judgment.

Add the confiscated Mathes property to the $150 million that Arlington taxpayers contributed to the team, and suddenly the value of the Rangers franchise had nearly tripled.

When Bush moved into the governor's mansion in 1995 (a move assisted by a $100,000 campaign donation from Rainwater), he made quite a public show of putting his financial holdings into a blind trust. What he didn't publicize, though, was that he left one of his assets out of the trust: the baseball team. This omission let the governor stay informed and involved when Rainwater and the other partners negotiated the sale of the Rangers franchise for $250 million in 1998—the deal that finally elevated George into the class of MR. RICH.

He was paid $2.7 million for his minority share of the sale

price—more than a 400 percent return on his investment. But Rainwater et al. took better care of their gubernatorial partner than that, awarding him what the Cajuns of southeast Texas refer to as a "lagniappe"—a little something extra. In a Cajun restaurant, the lagniappe might be a small plate of andouille sausage or some extra shrimp for your étouffée, but in Bush's case it was a "bonus payment" of $12.2 million. So, the sitting governor of the great state of Texas, with eyes wide open on an insider crony deal left outside his blind trust, was handed nearly $15 million from the sale—a 2,400 percent profit on the $600,000 he had put up just eight years earlier.

The partners were not merely being generous, they were being grateful. In Bush's first term in office, his former business associates have found state government a most welcoming and profitable place. As documented by reporter Ratcliffe of the *Chronicle*, old Bush buddy Rainwater has been first in line at the government trough, enjoying such favors as:

- Being allowed to buy three office buildings from the state Teacher's Retirement System at bargain-basement rates, including one sold so cheaply to Rainwater's realty firm that the state-administered trust fund for teachers lost $44 million on the deal.
- Having the state fund that manages money for Texas universities and public school systems invest nearly $20 million in the stock of his Crescent Real Estate company.
- A Bush veto of a Patient Protection Act that could have affected profits for Rainwater's already troubled Columbia/HCA Healthcare chain of hospitals and HMOs by requiring more care, instituting a better appeals process for doctors and patients, and prohibiting financial incentives that limit care.
- A Bush-backed tax plan that ultimately failed but would have cut some $2.5 million in annual taxes on commercial properties that Rainwater owns in various Texas cities.

- A $10 million windfall for Crescent Real Estate from a sports-arena financing bill signed into law by Bush in 1997; six months later, Crescent's president put $11,000 into Bush's political fund.
- A million-dollar gusher for Rainwater's oil company, generated by the governor in 1999 when he declared that his top priority for the legislative session was to pass an "emergency" cut of $45 million in the state's oil tax in order to "help small producers"; Bush rejected an amendment to restrict the cut to the small oil operators he had invoked, and billionaire Rainwater became the number one recipient of Bush's special tax break.

THEM THAT GIVE, GET. Throughout the 2000 campaign, George W. kept saying that he would do for the country what he'd done for Texas . . . and that is not a threat to be taken lightly. Even by Texas's bottom-feeding standards of "doin' bidness" from the governor's office, Bush's two terms were distinguished by the creativity and sheer volume of the favors he delivered to his corporate campaign contributors.

Take ALCOA, Amoco, ARCO, Enron, Champion International, Dow Chemical, Enserch, Exxon, International Paper, PG&E, Tenneco, Texaco, and Union Carbide. These were among a favored group of thirty-eight major Texas air polluters that had pumped more than half a million dollars into George's gubernatorial fund. They were a favored group because they were exempt from the state's 1971 clean air law, having weaseled through a polluter's loophole that exempted their old factories, utilities, and other smokestack operations that existed prior to passage of the law. These were known as "grandfathered" facilities. By the mid-nineties these filthy grandfathers were happily spewing out nearly a million tons of toxic contaminants per year, making them accountable for more than a third of the total industrial air pollution in Texas, which could boast of being first in America in such toxic pollution.

Even Texas legislators—notoriously obsequious to corporate power—were choking on this loophole, and momentum was quickly building at the Capitol to bring these grandfathered corporations under the law. "Holy smoke!" shouted the CEOs in unison, and off they scampered to Austin to see George. The governor, ever compassionate, got downright teary-eyed as he listened to the plight of these contributor-polluters, and he promptly put his top environmental policy man on the task of easing the corporate pain. This led to a series of secret meetings between the industries, the governor's office, and the state's pollution control officials—meetings convened at the invitation of Exxon and Marathon Oil. (I suppose I don't have to tell you that the corporate conveners saw no need to ask any outsiders, like clean-air advocates, to join the secret sessions.)

About twenty companies were on the governor's clandestine "Grandfathered Emissions Workgroup." They knew the political heat was on (a quarter-million kids went to schools located next to their polluting plants, and the parents were agitating) and that lawmakers would have to take some action in the 1999 legislative session. The group's goal was to deflect the enthusiasm for reform.

Jim Kennedy, DuPont's point man in the work group, wrote an internal memo to his higher-ups, describing the meeting at which the group's legislative proposal was discussed. Appropriately, the group gathered at the Exxon Building in Houston. Kennedy reported that Exxon, Amoco, and Marathon had written a concept paper for legislation that Bush would rubber-stamp and have introduced: "The belief was clearly communicated at the meeting that this industry group was going to be in the leadership role in transforming the concepts into a program that would be approved by the governor's office." The Exxon/Amoco/Marathon concept, which Bush ultimately did embrace in his '99 legislative proposal, was a gem of pure shuck and jive, appearing to do something about all those tons of toxics without requiring the companies to *do* a damned thing. As Kennedy put it in his DuPont memo: "The concept paper has no 'meat' with respect to actual emissions reductions."

Bush's bill, which he and the corporate lobbyists wrangled through the legislature (lobbyist fees topped $2.5 million— enough money to unscrew the Capitol dome), carried the kind of Orwellian title that Republicans seem to enjoy sticking on really bad bills: "CARE—Clean Air Responsibility Enterprise." The legislation calls on the corporations to put modern pollution controls on their grandfathered plants. It does not, however, *require* them to do so. It's no more than an invitation for these gross polluters to join CARE and *voluntarily* cut back some of those nasties they're sending into the air, the neighborhoods, the schoolyards, the homes, and the lungs of millions of Texans. There is no punishment whatsoever for those that simply decline the governor's polite invitation. So far, more than 90 percent of the big polluters have said "No thanks" to Bush's CARE program, and 97 percent of the grandfathered air pollution continues unabated.

Another giver who got a lot from Governor Generous is Kenneth Lay, CEO of Enron, the global energy, telecommunications, and trading corporation based in Houston. In April of 2000, Bush and Lay cozied up at the opening-day game of the Houston Astros baseball team, which had just moved into a brand-new, very cozy ballpark. Area taxpayers had ponied up $175 million to finance this stadium for the private owners, but it was not named "Houston Taxpayers Stadium" or "Joe Fan Ball Park." No, no—it's called "Enron Field," since Lay spent a few million of his conglomerate's cash to buy the "naming rights" to the stadium, letting him use the public facility as his private billboard. Enron gets to deduct these millions from its income tax as a cost of doing business, letting you and me further subsidize the privatization of a public asset. Lay even got the privilege of throwing out the first pitch of the first game in the new stadium. Money doesn't just talk . . . it delivers!

This is a corporate-public fusion that seems perfectly natural to George W. Bush—a comfort zone, even. He was not the slightest bit embarrassed that Kenneth Lay used opening night at the Astros stadium to hold a private party for the Republican presidential candidate. Membership has its privileges. Why shouldn't public facilities, public monies, public office, public trust be deployed for the private gain of your pals? And there is no doubt that Bush and Lay are pals. Lay funneled more money into George's gubernatorial runs than any other source—in excess of $400,000. In turn, the governor gratefully pursued public policies to benefit Enron, including pushing through an energy deregulation bill tailored to fit the company's energy expansion plans; passing a law making it much harder for ordinary citizens to win judgments when giant corporations do them harm—a bill championed by Lay and Enron lobbyists; and trying, but failing, to ram through a property tax reform that Enron helped to write—a "reform" that would have favored capital-intensive energy companies and would have delivered a nice $9 million a year tax cut for Lay's company. George also has personally run errands for Ken, including calling, at Lay's request, the governor of Pennsylvania to help Enron break into the energy market there. Asked by the *New York Times* about his tight relationship with George, Lay offered an odd disclaimer: "No member of the Bush family has ever been on the Enron payroll."

Why pay a guy who, for free, is willing to open the public cookie jar to you? This explains why CEOs who've done business with George in Texas were not merely on his presidential bandwagon, they were out front pulling the damn thing, running alongside to grease its wheels with thousand-dollar bills, and generally doing anything and everything they could to roll this munificent fellow into the White House, where he could do even more for them.

Backing Bush is just good business. For example, Sam and Charles, the wily Wyly brothers who were behind the $2.5 million sneak-attack ads that trashed John McCain and boosted Bush to victory on Super Tuesday, were doing nothing but boosting their own investment in a proven stock. Their $210,000 in contributions had helped Bush get to the governor's office, from whence he produced a sweet return for them. Prior to Bush, the University of Texas's multibillion-dollar trust fund was invested by state employees. George, whose appointees control the fund, chose to privatize much of this investment function, and the Wyly brothers quickly found themselves with a lucrative contract from the state to handle $96 million from the UT fund. Conveniently, they had just set up the Maverick Capital Fund of Dallas, and it received the contract, which pays the Wylys $960,000 in fees each year to invest the public money, plus 20 percent of any profits made on the investments.

THE PIONEERS. As Bush freely admits, he's not a bookish kind of guy. Asked by reporters to name the books that he cherished from his childhood, he listed *The Very Hungry Caterpillar*. It was written the year after he graduated from Yale.

Far more worrisome than having a politician who doesn't read, however, is to have one who so carefully keeps another kind of book: the money book, a ledger of exactly who gave exactly how much to his election fund. In public, Bush was demure about the record-shattering $100 million that he amassed, preferring to speak of average contribution levels ($240) and to tell anecdotes of the folded and worn twenty-dollar bills he got from little people—"I'm humbled to have their support," the hundred-million-dollar man would say.

Of course, you don't raise that kind of money from $20 or $240 check writers, nor do you raise it by hoping that your better-off supporters will individually get attacks of civic altruism and mail in $1,000 apiece (which legally is the most any one person can give). Rather, you raise it courtesy of special interests that collect and deliver sackfuls of $1,000 checks to

you, and that's exactly how George W. Bush has always oper-
ated. For his 2000 presidential run, he dubbed his group of
elite sackers the "Pioneers." These were CEOs and corporate
lobbyists, more than 200 strong, and to achieve Pioneer rank,
each one had to deliver more than $100,000 to the campaign.
They did this by leaning on junior executives, clients, suppliers,
golfing chums, country club companions, brothers-in-law, and
others in their concentric circles to mail $1,000 checks to the
Bushites.

But if these checks were individually pouring into campaign
headquarters, how would Bush know which Pioneer to credit?
Aha! This is where George's true bookishness comes out. Each
Pioneer was assigned an ID number (sort of like the PIN you
use to access ATM machines), which each of "their" donors
was instructed to write on their checks. Thus, the bean coun-
ters in Bush's fundraising boiler room would not only deposit
each check, but also credit the account of the lobbyist or CEO
who generated it. Whenever one's account topped $100,000,
that sacker became a Pioneer—sort of like a college fraternity
initiation in which a chosen pledge becomes a "brother" in the
secret order of GWB.

Kenneth Lay is a Pioneer. He sent a personal letter to Enron
managers in 1999, urging them to give the max to Bush. Covering his butt legally, Lay's letter noted, "In no way is this [solici-
tation] a condition of employment or continued employment at
Enron." But executives could read the handwriting on their
checks, and $50,000 promptly flowed from them to Bush, each
check bearing Lay's BIN (Bush Identification Number). And if
one Pioneer curries favor, why not double your corporate
impact with a second one—Richard Kinder, Enron's former
president, also is a "made guy" with the Bush bandwagon. By
midsummer of 2000, the Enron account was the largest among
the Bush Pioneers, with Lay and Kinder credited with
$983,309 in checks delivered. In addition, the CEO and his
company also had run a pipeline of soft money into the Repub-

lican party, pumping in $742,000 to advance their candidate's election chances. Lay himself became a Republican "Regent"— a platinum level of party royalty who pledge $250,000 a year to the Grand Old Party. And, just to garnish the plate, Lay plunked down another $250,000 in corporate funds to be listed as a "Silver Benefactor" at Bush's nominating convention last summer in Philadelphia. The company was putting so much time and effort into buying Bush that it caused some Enron executives to squirm at the excess and unseemliness of it all: "The wholehearted endorsement of Governor Bush, and the brazen use of the corporate machinery to ensure his election, seems distasteful," one higher-up told the *New York Times*. Understandably, this exec insisted on anonymity.

But Lay's corporate largesse had nothing to do with being a Republican, and it certainly had nothing to do with "supporting good government," "being involved in the democratic process," or any of the other civic-sounding, high-minded rationales that big givers mouth in public. Rather, it had everything to do with bending government policies to the corporate will. A June 15 internal memo soliciting money from Enron executives for the company PAC fell into the hands of the *New York Times*, which reported its contents: "Enron faces numerous legal and regulatory challenges . . . including taxation of electronic commerce, restructuring of the electric industry, international trade legislation, regulation of power plants and oil pipelines, and a variety of environmental and tax issues." The *Times* noted that this was no casual, give-what-you-can solicitation, for the memo declared that the company wanted a million dollars in the PAC for the fall elections, and it even detailed the level of "voluntary" contributions Enron executives were expected to make, ranging from $500 for low-level managers to $5,000 for those at the top levels.

Bush and Enron have a long, symbiotic relationship, like a cowbird to a cow, and it's been very profitable for both, so it's unsurprising that Lay would want to move it to even greener pastures. It's one thing to have a Texas governor giving you a helping hand, but it's like a free trip to a Disney Corporate-world to have a president going to bat for you. As the *New York Times* observed, "Enron lobbies on so many issues in Congress that it takes twenty-six pages for it to list them all on federal disclosure forms."

Since Bush is such a big baseball buff, think of the Pioneers as star players on his campaign ball team, which we'll nick-name the "Big Green Machine." Last summer, the watchdog group Texans for Public Justice issued a terrific packet of Bush League trading cards for the Pioneers, providing the photo, playing position, key stats, and career highlights for each of the top players, labeling the group the Sultans of Clout. Ken Lay's card, for example, dubbed him the team's career MVP—Most Valuable Patron—owing to his multimillion-dollar delivery of campaign cash for Team Bush's 1994, 1998, and 2000 runs.

Then there's the player card for all-American utility infielder **Tom Kuhn**, chief Washington lobbyist for the nation's electric utility industry. Besides the love of the game, Kuhn was playing for a multibillion-dollar pot of gold that his clients would get if he could hit a White House home run. They want federal legislation to force America's electric ratepayers to have to eat the massive losses that utilities incurred when they made a bad gamble in the 1970s on expen-sive nuclear power. As governor, Bush had signed off on just such a deal for utility companies in Texas, leaving Lone Star ratepayers now holding the bag for the industry's nuclear mis-takes. By playing ball with the Pioneers, Kuhn was trying to work himself into position to hit a similar home run for all other utility executives.

Playing far right field was **Hank Greenberg**—not the Hall-of-Fame baseball player of the same name, but the CEO of American International Group, a global financial conglomerate. Hank is a major underwriter of the right-wing Heritage Foun-dation and has been a longtime Bush Leaguer, going back to the 1980s when Daddy Bush owned the franchise. AIG is a regular dipper into the snuff can of corporate welfare, using the Overseas Private Investment Corporation to underwrite its foreign financial flings. The elder Bush even took Greenberg with him on a road trip to Asia in 1992, giving the AIG boss valuable playing time with top leaders there.

Pitching talent for the team included relief specialist **Frederick Webber**. He's the go-to lobbyist for the Chemical Manufacturers Association (though he's a much traveled player in the influence-peddling game, having previously pitched to Congress on behalf of the S&L, soft drink, and electric utility industries). Webber signed up with the Pioneers because he likes to play "Bush rules" ball, where corporate compliance with regulation is strictly voluntary. Also pitching for the team was curveball artist **Charles Cawley**, the honcho of MBNA bank, one of the country's most potent hurlers of credit cards at consumers (if your mailbox is not crammed with credit card come-ons from MBNA, your zip code must be in Antarctica, though it's said that many penguins have gotten credit cards from this bank). Cawley and company were ranked number two in hard-money deliveries to George W.'s White House bid, also mixing in more than $475,000 in soft-money deliveries. If the team wins the pennant, MBNA will get a president who can't spell u-s-u-r-y. Knuckleballer **Charles Wyly**, of the tricky Wyly brothers, was a Pioneer pitcher, too, not only throwing the hard stuff, but also pitching in more than $500,000 in soft money for the team. The Wylys were hoping to compile a record impressive enough to win some bonus money from a Bush presidency for their energy, investment, and other enterprises.

Support personnel for Team Bush came from people like super scout **Joe Allen**, top lobbyist at the heavy-hitting firm of Vinson & Elkins, which lobbies for such clients as Enron, Shell Oil, and Halliburton (the minor-league team of Bush veep Dick Cheney). Allen scouts out other money sources for Bush, reportedly keeping a secret ledger known inside the firm as the "Mystic Book," tracking which partners and clients give to which politicians, and how much is delivered. Vinson & Elkins led the Bush League in slugging percentage last year, with Allen and two other partners becoming Pioneers. Calling the play-by-play for Pioneer games were broadcast moguls **Tom and Steve Hicks**, whose Clear Channel Communications makes them the owners of some 465 radio stations in America, far more than any other corporation. Tom is the fellow who bought the Rangers baseball team from Bush and partners in 1995, generously shelling out the $12 million "bonus" that made George a rich man. Tom is also the fellow who pushed the governor to privatize the handling of the University of Texas endowment fund, creating a private board that was chaired by (guess who?) Tom, and it just happened to dole out UT's money to investment firms connected to (guess who again?) Tom and George W. himself. With a business empire dependent on favorable rulings from such federal entities as the FCC, FTC, and SEC, the Hicks duo bought their way into the Pioneers in the hope of continuing to call the plays from inside a Bush White House.

You can't have a ballgame without junk food, so *Tim Hammonds* volunteered to raise food-industry funds for the Pioneers. He's the lead lobbyist for big supermarket chains that have a beef with the federal government's stricter meat inspection regulations, which are intended to slow the spread of deadly E. coli contamination of America's meat supply. By putting Tim on the team, the industry was hoping it would ultimately get to play by those "Bushball Rules" of voluntary regulation. Good luck on your ballpark hot dog—Bush's do-it-yourself style of regulation could result in a new lyric for fans singing the old seventh-inning-stretch song: "Take me out to the ball game/ Take me out to the crowd/ Buy me some peanuts and E. coli/ I don't care if I ever get back. . . . "

The Pioneer scheme is the largest money-bundling operation

ever undertaken in American politics, dwarfing Bill Clinton's efforts and rivaling Richard Nixon's in the sheer audacity of its corporate appeal. Of the $100 million that Bush sacked up for his nomination, *more than a fourth of it* is known to have come from the 226 people that have been identified as Pioneers. However, the actual percentage of Pioneer money is conservatively estimated to be more like *two-thirds* of Bush's total. This is because (1) many of that group (such as Ken Lay) raised much more than $100,000 each, and (2) the Bush campaign has admitted that some 400 people—not just 226—signed up to be Pioneers. Despite having his meticulous in-house money-tracking system, and despite having said again and again that he believes complete public disclosure is the best approach to campaign finance reform, Bush refused to release the names of all 400 of his money sackers or the amounts each one hauled to the table. Thanks to the digging of Texans for Public Justice, though, we know that, in addition to the names already mentioned, Pioneers who got their $100,000-plus tickets punched for admittance to the inner chambers of a Bush administration include executives and lobbyists for such very special interests as AT&T, American General, Amway, Arthur Andersen, Bank of America, Blue Cross–Blue Shield, Boston Capital Partners, Credit Suisse, CSX Transportation, Embassy Suites, Enterprise Rent-a-Car, First Bank & Trust, First Energy, Flo-Sun sugar, Genentech, Goldman Sachs, Hill & Knowlton, Hollywood Park Racetrack, Huizenga Holdings (AutoNation, National, and Alamo rental cars, etc.), J.P. Morgan, Johnson & Johnson, Lockheed Martin, MassMutual Life-Insurance, Occidental Chemical, Paine Webber, Pilot, Philip Morris, Reliant Energy, Seagram's, U.S. Sugar, and U.S. Trust Co.

Most notable on the list of Bush fundraisers is the heavy presence of lobbyists—a glaring oddity for a man who kept trying to project an image as the "outsider" in the presidential context. Contrasting himself with McCain in the primaries, then with Gore in the general election, George would tighten up his twang and declare that he was "the only candidate without a Washington, D.C., zip code." Then he'd get that little smirky look that told us he was quite pleased with himself. It was a snappy one-liner, but it was silly and really didn't work for him, since everyone knows he's a rich son-of-a-Bush whose daddy is a walking résumé of inside-the-Beltway power connections—Congressman, chair of the National Republican party, ambassador to China, head of the CIA, vice president and president of the entire U.S. of A., for chrissake! And while George W. didn't have a home in Washington in 2000, as both McCain and Gore did, guess who had the most donors with D.C. zip codes? Bingo! And guess who even hired Maria Cino, a veteran Washington lobbyist for United Airlines and other corporate clients, to be the director of his presidential campaign? Bingo!

"It's time to clean up the toxic environment in Washington," boomed Mr. Outsider in April of 2000. He delivered this not at an environmental gathering or campaign finance reform rally, but at a GOP fund-raising gala in the nation's capital. As he spoke, apparently oblivious to the hypocrisy of his own words, he was looking out from the podium at a sea of tuxedoed corporate lobbyists who collectively had just plunked down millions of dollars to be there, munching on horseradish-crusted filet of red snapper and winking at each other while George went on about cleaning up the capital city. Of course, Bush was pointing his finger at the Washington of Clinton and Gore, but he literally was standing in the midst of the city's true toxic environment. If he had wanted to point at someone responsible for the toxic stench, Dirk Van Dongen was right there next to him. Dirk is the head lobbyist for the country's big wholesalers, and he was in charge of channeling the toxic flow of lobbyists' cash into this evening's record-setting, $21.3 million event. Or, he could've pointed to Wayne Berman, a Bush Pioneer and a $100,000 donor to this event, who lobbies for Philip Morris, Paine Webber, Flo-Sun sugar, and a passel of other big favor seekers; or he could have pointed to Haley Barbour, the former Republican party chairman who has used his GOP Capitol Hill connections to reach superlobbyist status, representing such golden clients as all of the major tobacco companies, Bell South, CBS, Microsoft, and Charles Schwab; or Bush could have pointed to hundreds of other Gucci-clad denizens of K Street who swarmed the hall that night bearing corrupt political money and piling it at his feet.

Beltway lobbyists were turning out for Bush because they knew that, far from upsetting the business-as-usual arrangements inside the capitol's corridors of power, he was one of them and would advance their agendas. These consummate insiders had even taken the unprecedented step of rallying behind Bush's candidacy nearly a year earlier. In July 1999, about sixteen lobbyists for industry-wide trade associations convened for an intimate, closed-door dinner at the ornate headquarters of the U.S. Chamber of Commerce, barely a block from the White House. Tom Kuhn, the electric utilities' man, had convened the group. According to the *Washington Post*, which rooted out the story, lobbyists for the oil, automobile, supermarket, timber, chemical, and other industries rose one by one after dinner to pledge their industry's fealty (and money) to the corporate crusade to ensconce Bush in the Oval Office. Fred Webber of the chemical manufacturers was reported to have been downright passionate when he spoke, praising the governor's "hands-off style of regulation," and a chemical company executive later confirmed to the *Post* that his whole industry was wildly enthusiastic for Bush: "We see him as someone we can work with" on the environment. "We want to do things voluntarily." Joining in the after-dinner testimonials was Red Cavaney of the American Petroleum Institute, using understatement to tell why Big Oil is so big on Bush: "Our industry is intimately familiar with him, and we've found him to be very approachable." Then came Tim Hammonds, of the supermarket lobby, expressing confidence that Bush "would please the food industry by dismantling Clinton-era workplace safety regulations."

Remember that the one quality Bush prizes most in politics is loyalty, and a Who's Who of Washington insiders were with George from the start, staying true to him throughout the campaign. In May of 2000, Bush quietly added a half-dozen registered K-Streeters to his campaign as political advisers—a group that collectively had billed $34 million in fees the previous year to influence our government on behalf of America Online, Bristol-Myers Squibb, the HMO trade group, Microsoft, Philip Morris, and Time Warner, among others. The corporate enthusiasm for Bush's candidacy was offered with every indication and expectation that a Bush White House would reciprocate the loyalty. As an elated Kuhn told the *Post* fifteen months before the election: "It's a very, very broad cross section of industries" backing Bush. "From international trade to the service industries to retail, I think people are very, very excited."

And if the corporate people weren't excited enough by George alone, imagine the almost orgasmic ecstasy on K Street and Wall Street when Bush announced Dick Cheney as his veep choice! Instead of choosing a politician who's merely owned by the CEOs, Bush said, what the hey, and put a CEO directly on his ticket. Eliminate the middleman! It's the penultimate corporatization of the White House. Cheney is a guy who has drunk deeply from the golden cup of corporate cronyism. As secretary of defense for Daddy Bush, he not only oversaw the Gulf War against nasty Saddam Hussein of Iraq, but he also doled out hundreds of billions of dollars in Pentagon handouts to such corporate welfare recipients as . . . well, Halliburton, the very corporation that he would head after leaving Bush the Elder, and from which he would be plucked by Bush the Younger—coming full circle in Washington's wonderful world of the revolving door.

At Halliburton, one of the world's largest oilfield service and construction companies (it also owns Brown & Root and

Dresser Industries), CEO Cheney was quick to put his Pentagon procurement knowledge and contacts to work, zooming the company from number seventy-three on the Defense Department's list of money recipients to number eighteen. Thanks to Dick, Halliburton doubled its take in federal contracts, bringing in $2.3 billion in taxpayer largesse during his tenure, plus $1.5 billion in federal loan subsidies. Not coincidentally, he also doubled the corporation's lobbying expenditures and greatly increased its campaign contributions (by the way, the company loaded nearly $300,000 onto the Bush 2000 bandwagon).

In addition to milking his old chums at the Pentagon, Dick had many useful pals in foreign governments as a result of his dealings with assorted potentates during the Gulf War. As one industry analyst told *USA Today*, before Cheney came aboard, Halliburton executives "would fly over [to Arab nations] and meet some third cousin twice removed. Now they meet the king of the country." Connections count. Today, 70 percent of the company's business is outside the U.S.A. Among the foreign contracts that Halliburton gained during Cheney's tenure were two with Baghdad. That's right, the guy who oversaw the destruction of Iraq's oil production capability in 1991 subsequently did business with that old nasty Saddam to help rebuild the country's oil production capability!

Cheney is fully immersed in the corporate culture. As CEO, he presided over a major downsizing in 1999 that slashed the jobs of 10,000 Halliburton workers and reduced medical benefits for retirees, while continuing to draw his own multimillion-dollar pay and get full benefits. In 1999, his paycheck totalled $26.4 million (not counting $280,000 he received as a board member of Procter & Gamble, EDS, and Union Pacific). And when he resigned to join the Bush ticket, Halliburton gave him a sweet $20 million farewell package. This was such a gross public relations stinker, however, that Cheney was rushed out for a press conference on September 1 to announce that he was going to forfeit $3.9 million worth of stock options he had been given by the company. This sounded like a noble gesture, but still he was getting a $16 million golden parachute. Actually, though, it turns out he was getting much more. Cheney failed to mention that just four days before his press conference, he quietly cashed in a big chunk of Halliburton stock he previously had been given by the board of directors—a move that put a tidy $20.6 million profit in his pocket. That brought his farewell haul to some $36 million, but even that's not all, for he still holds about $11 million more in stock that Hallibuton had given to him. It's just the way things work in Cheney's cozy world of crony deals between corporate and public officials. He was the perfect V.P. choice for Bush, the perfect embodiment of Bush's own perception of how things ought to work.

George's upbringing, business experience, gubernatorial record, money ties, vice-presidential choice, and corporate *essence* tell us all we need to know about who he is and who he'd serve as president. This is why it was knee-slapping hilarious to watch him run around the country last year, squawking about how "I'm a reformer. A reformer with results." Sheesh. George W. Bush is to reform what Colonel Sanders is to animal rights activism.

NICE GUYS

In the 2000 race, both Gore and Bush hoped that you wouldn't notice, much less take it personally, that their allegiance is to the moneyed elite. Neither has any ill will toward the workaday majority—it's just business. They're certainly not venal in their practice of special interest politics. Indeed, the public relations people of both parties considered candidates Gore and Bush to have been terrific political products for today's increasingly upscale political market. Product analysts saw Gore as a spin-off brand of the generally popular Clinton Inc., while George W. was an extension of the long-established Bush family brand. They come across as smooth, family-friendly, safe, comfortable, richly appointed, roomy, with plush leather interiors and superior sound systems—each one a Lexus of status quo politics.

I can't say that I really know Al Gore, though I've talked with him a few times, but I can tell you that he's an awfully nice guy. It's true that he's duller than televised bowling, but he's certainly a sincere fellow and seems to have a fine family. He told us that economic growth is the key to helping everyone, that our fabulous prosperity must be continued (though we simply must do more to help poor people share in it), that he's deeply concerned about America's children, that education is a top priority with him, that we need a businesslike approach to protecting our environment for future generations, that family and quality-of-life issues matter personally to him, and that he believes America will be greater than ever as we cross into the twenty-first century together. "Practical Idealism," he called it.

I don't know George W. Bush personally, but by all accounts he's an awfully nice guy. It's true that he's not the brightest puppy in the litter, but he's certainly a sincere fellow and seems to have a real nice family. He told us that economic growth is the key to helping everyone, that our fabulous prosperity must be continued (though we simply must do more to help poor people share in it), that he's deeply concerned about American children, that education is a top priority with him, that we need a businesslike approach to protecting our environment for future generations, that family and quality-of-life issues matter personally to him, and that he believes America will be greater than ever as we cross into the twenty-first century together. "Compassionate Conservatism," he called it.

Old Mr. Powerbroker watched George W. Bush swing with his slow roundhouse right of Compassionate Conservatism, then watched Al Gore counterpunch with his feeble left jab of Practical Idealism, and he just laughed and laughed, not caring one whit whether Compassionate Practicality, Conservative Idealism, or any combination thereof won—because he owned both of these pugs. Among the corporations that invested at least $100,000 in both the Bush and Gore races are:

AFLAC
Air Transport Association
America Online
American Airlines
American Express
American Financial Group
American Gas Association
American International
　Group
Anheuser-Busch
ARCO
AT&T
Bechtel
BellSouth
Blue Cross/Blue Shield
Boeing
Bond Market Association
BP Amoco
Bristol-Myers Squibb
Cellular Telecom Industry
　Association
Chevron
Citigroup
Coca-Cola
Dominion Resources

Edison Electric Institute
Enron
Ernst & Young
Federal Express
GAF
General Dynamics
Global Crossing
International Game
　Technology
Limited
Lockhead Martin
Loews
MBNA America Bank
Merrill Lynch
Metabolife International
MGM Grand
Microsoft
Mirage Resorts
National Association of Chain
　Drug Stores
National Association of
　Homebuilders
Northwest Airlines
Ocean Spray
Paine Webber

Pfizer

PG&E

Prudential

Rite Aid

SBC Communications

Schering-Plough

Seagram

Securities Industry
    Association

Sprint

Teligent

Union Pacific

United Airlines

US Airways

US West

Verizon

Walt Disney

CLINTON'S LAST ERECTION

As the great Mexican revolutionary Pancho Villa lay dying, he suddenly realized his followers would expect some memorable last words from him. But his final breath was quickly upon him, and he hadn't prepared for the moment, so Villa passed into history with this desperate utterance: "Don't let it end like this! Tell them I said something."

Alas, poor Bill Clinton's eight-year presidency has gasped to a close, and you can hear him pleading at the end: "Tell them I *did* something." For most of his two terms, Clinton fretted over his "legacy" rather than doing what it takes to create one. For example, this was the guy who boldly decided in 1997 to join Abraham Lincoln and Lyndon Johnson in addressing the great hurt of racism in our society. His race initiative, crowed the president's team of cock-a-doodle-dooers, would be "The Legacy." Indeed, it was an opportunity for greatness, a matter worthy of Herculean presidential effort. And Clinton, having grown up in the mire of Arkansas's racial divide and been governor there for years, already knew the problems. As a modern son of the South he was perfectly positioned to go beyond a rehashing of problems and delve into solutions, quite possibly achieving some genuine measure of progress. What a way to step into the history books.

It was no small task—legacy building never is. It requires whacking the bastards right in the face, spending enormous amounts of presidential capital, taking hard political risks, and confronting the power structure of America—all things that Lincoln and LBJ did. Clinton, too, started strong, launching his initiative with a gusher of eloquence about what he termed America's "constant curse." But rhetoric was all we got—turn on Clinton's spigot, and he's all foam, no beer. His boldest "action" was to appoint a study commission. He did attend a couple of hoked-up, town hall–style meetings on the subject, including one ill-conceived evening with sports figures that was broadcast on ESPN, but he didn't spend a nickel of political capital.

After meandering around the country talking about the issue for a couple of years, the commission finally sputtered to an end, and in 1999 Clinton announced the conclusion of the whole pathetic exercise—he created a new and shiny bit of bureaucracy called (cue the trumpets): "White House Office on the President's Initiative for One America."

All you need to know about the importance of this office in Washington's hierarchy of power is that it did not have cabinet-level status, it was not a separate agency, and it did not report to the president, vice president, attorney general, chief of staff, or even Buddy, the presidential pooch. Instead, it was headed by the deputy director of the office of public liaison. The *deputy* director! Presumably he reported to the actual, full-fledged director of the office of public liaison, who I understand *did* report to Buddy.

So our pantheon of presidential race healers proudly boasts Lincoln with his Emancipation Proclamation, Johnson with his Voting Rights Act . . . and now Clinton with his WHOOPIFOA. Legacy-wise, he would have been better off if he'd just led America in a one-time, nationally broadcast sing-along of all ninety-seven verses of "Kumbaya."

But every president is remembered for *something*. In college, the textbook for my American history class had photographs or drawings of the various presidents scattered through it, complete with a three- or four-sentence caption describing their major accomplishments in office. I recall that the captions were quite spare for the line of decidedly undistinguished presidents during the robber baron days, extending roughly between Lincoln and the trust-busting T.R. at the turn of the century. Under the photo of one of these mediocre to miserable presidents (it might have been Rutherford B. Hayes or Chester A. Arthur) was a one-line caption noting that "the White House was wired for electricity" during his administration.

I thought of that president's lame claim to fame one day late in Clinton's first term. By then, he had already scuttled practically all of his major campaign pledges, including promises that he would produce good jobs at good wages, raise the minimum wage so no one who works full-time lives in poverty, provide health coverage for all, and stop any international trade deal that failed to protect workers or the environment. Clinton, who says he often dreams of being remembered as another FDR, was facing a fate of not being remembered at all, much like Hayes and Arthur. Then, in 1995, came a proud announcement from Clinton's office that "the White House has been wired for the Internet."

He would have been stuck with this as his epitaph, except that soon afterward he was overcome by his renowned lust, which ultimately led him to make the indelible and infamous mark for which he'll always be remembered—and I don't mean the mess on the dress. Clinton's most ardent and damaging presidential passion was not for Monica but for money.

From mid-1995 forward, he amassed a monument of corrupt, corporate campaign monies—hundreds of millions of dollars that, if stacked together, would thrust higher into the capital sky than the Washington Monument itself—Clinton's final erection.

Particularly harmful was his innovative and tireless pursuit of "soft money," a category that is just as pornographic (politically speaking) as it sounds. This is unregulated money, in terms of where it comes from and how much of it can be given by one source. You see, corporations themselves are forbidden to contribute to candidates or political action committees—and the executives and lobbyists of corporations are limited to giving no more than $1,000 each to candidates, while their PACs are limited to giving $5,000. Running around collecting these "small" checks was not building a big enough political war chest fast enough to satisfy the cash-hungry Clinton campaign operatives in the spring of '95. If only they could uncap the deep well of corporate funds, from which they could draw $100,000, $500,000, even a million dollars at a time. Then late one night, from a cubicle somewhere in a Washington basement, someone shouted, "Eureka! Voilà! Bonanza! Bingo! Come to Papa!"—and the soft-money loophole was found.

CLINTON CHANGES THE MONEY RULES

It's not that the Clintonites were the first or only ones to use soft money for their own political purposes—that honor must fall to the GOP, which seems genetically programmed to sniff out a dollar bill, no matter where it's tucked. (Senator George Voinovich, Republican of Ohio, could be the poster boy for this genetic proclivity—his press secretary confirms that Voinovich once stepped up to a urinal, looked down, spotted a penny in it, reached into the urinal to snare the coin, rinsed it off, and put it in his pocket.) Republican leaders have been hauling bags of soft money into their coffers since at least 1991. But they lacked the vision of what could be done with this money ... and the audacity that Clinton and his campaign showed in going after it.

Ironically, soft money was designed to help political parties return some small measure of importance to "people-politics." Instead of financing campaigns, this money is supposed to develop grassroots networks and to talk about *issues* with voters. Corporations can give directly to these efforts (though relatively few did before 1995), and there is no limit on how much can be donated. The only proviso is that the money cannot go to a candidate, nor can it be spent in coordination with, much less under the direction of, a candidate's campaign. Pure in concept, this little flower was about to be violated on a massive scale by Bill Clinton.

Dick Morris, the well-known low-life political hack and sucker of prostitutes' toes, was Clinton's guru back then, and he says it was the prim Erskine Bowles, a corporate chieftain who later became Clinton's chief of staff, who first told him about "something called issue advocacy advertising." The deal was that they could raise truckloads of corporate soft money through the Democratic National Committee, then have the DNC spend it on an early blitz of image advertising to promote the president's reelection. Clinton himself was wildly enthusiastic about this shell game, grinning like a pig that had finally found a way into the corn bin. You can even see him grinning and talking about the plan on tape, thanks to Sherry Jones, producer of a Bill Moyers television documentary called *Washington's Other Scandal*. She got her hands on a grainy videotape made with a camcorder by someone at a Clinton fundraiser in Washington's swank Hay-Adams Hotel. There was Bill, sipping fine wine and schmoozing with a roomful of suits who had given a ton of soft money to the DNC, candidly telling them about the scam they were running:

CLINTON: It means that we can finance this campaign in 1995 so I don't have to worry about it in 1996. So this is a brilliant thing that they have done, this plan that you have participated in.

He tells them that soft-money contributions like theirs have already bought ads in key markets—ads paid for by the Democratic party, but touting him:

TV COMMERCIAL: As Americans, there are some things we do simply and solely because they are moral, right, and good. . . . The Republicans are wrong to want to cut Medicare benefits. And President Clinton is right to protect Medicare. . . .

The president confides to them that the DNC soft-money commercials have been a big boost to his reelection chances:

CLINTON: The lead that I enjoy today in the public opinion polls is about one-third due to that advertising and the fact that we have been able to shape the debates in that way. And it makes a huge difference.

By raising the money through the DNC, he tells his Hay-Adams coconspirators, he is also able to skirt the legal limit on the total amount his campaign can spend:

CLINTON: We realized that we could run these ads through the Democratic party, which means that we can raise money in twenty- and fifty- and hundred-thousand-dollar lots, so we didn't have to do it all in thousand dollars and run down my . . . you know, what I can spend, which is limited by law. So that's what we've done.

This discovery by Clinton and his clever boys produced a watershed change in the way presidential elections are financed, and it turned him into the most indefatigable, prodigious, and shameless money hustler in American history—and I'm counting Nixon. They did not merely find a loophole in our nation's campaign funding laws, they took an earth auger and bored a hole through the whole damned book, then shredded the pages, burned the shreds, and buried the ashes in the Rose Garden during a lunar eclipse, howling deliriously as they sacked up unprecedented sums of money piled in front of them by corporate executives, Wall Street speculators, con artists, international schemers, hapless and naive tribal leaders, manipulative Chinese generals, and even a few clueless Buddhist nuns—all of whom were shelling out big bucks because the word was on the street: The White House is in play again. Clinton's personal hustle would make Willy Loman wince—partly in envy of his energy, partly in disgust at his tactics. The President of the United States turned the Lincoln bedroom into a one-nighter flophouse, created a "Day at the White House" theme park for big donors, converted the historic map room into the Koffee-Klatch-for-Kash Kafé (532 people slurped a cup-a-joe there in '95 and '96, leaving an average tip of $50,000 each), put John Huang in both the Commerce Department and the DNC to handle the China franchise, personally dialed for dollars from the Oval Office (did he use his cigar, one wonders, to punch out the numbers?), and generally engaged in political obscenities with wild and reckless abandon, making the Monica dalliance seem like an almost sweet flirtation. Since 1995, Clinton has raised more than $145 million in soft money.

The money, of course, has not been given altruistically. You might give $100 or even $1,000 because you believe in what so-and-so is trying to do—but you give $100,000 because of what so-and-so can do for *you*. These are, after all, mostly bottom-line-minded corporate executives who are putting up the money, so from the start of Clinton's carny-barker come-on, contributors had expectations, and they were not often disappointed. From launching a banana war with Europe on behalf of $500,000 donor Carl Lindner of Chiquita to arranging a billion-dollar technology deal with the Chinese for $455,000 donor Bernard Schwartz of Loral, cash to Clinton became a good business investment. There have been no shortage of eager givers, all of whom are thrilled to have this side door into the White House opened exclusively for cash customers.

Clinton's people saw nothing wrong with this. Truman

Arnold, an oilman and longtime Clinton financier from Texarkana, was moved into the DNC in 1995, handpicked by the president himself to set up the soft-money scheme. Arnold told Jane Mayer of *The New Yorker:* "I've been in sales all my life. It's a bit like romance. You go to dinner, and if everything feels right, you proceed to the good-night kiss—or the Lincoln Bedroom."

Clinton money operative Harold Ickes was asked by Bill Moyers a direct question about the president's personal awareness and concern about the slippery ethical slope he was on.

MOYERS: Did he raise a moral question?
ICKES: He did not. He wanted to know whether it was legal. His order to me was, "It's got to be legal." And it was legal.

Nonsense. The White House's soft-money scheme was not the slightest bit legal, much less ethical. Aside from raising what amounts to bribery funds, Clinton and team flagrantly violated the absolute proviso that any expenditure of soft money must be kept at arm's length from the candidates. God doesn't make arms this short:

1. The Clintonites raised millions in soft money from July of '95 to July of '96, properly storing the funds at the DNC.
2. During this same period, the DNC distributed $18 million of this money to the Democratic party organization in each of twelve large states, so those organizations could run "issue ads" to educate the public; so far, so good, but then it starts to get funky.
3. All twelve state parties sent the money they received from the DNC right back to Washington—all of it posted to two national media firms that just happened to be handling the Clinton-Gore reelection campaign; for example, on August 22, 1995, the DNC sent $30,376 to the Florida Democratic

Party and THAT SAME DAY the Florida party shipped
$30,376 to the Clinton-Gore advertising firms in
Washington.

4. These two firms designed and produced the exact same
"issue ads" for each of the twelve states; the firms also
decided which stations would run the ads and at what
times in the various states; then, Clinton's two media firms
paid for the chosen air times in each state (even Mussolini
didn't pay this much attention to the details of making the
trains run on time).

5. The ads that ran were not generic party ads or issue ads—
they were "Bill-Clinton-is-the-best-thing-since-twist-off-
caps" ads, and "Bob-Dole-is-the-cause-of-halitosis-and-
genital-warts" ads; whether you agree with either of these
views or not (I personally doubt the genital wart claim,
but . . .), they clearly were not meant to be broadcast
under the sponsorship of soft money; but there they were.

Yet, Ickes called this "legal," not only when asked by Moyers but also when pressed by prosecutors. So did Bill Clinton,
Al Gore, Don Fowler (then the chairman of the DNC), and all
the president's men. Riddle: How many legs does a dog have
if you count its tail as a leg? Answer: Four. Calling a tail a leg
doesn't make it one.

Common Cause, the watchdog of political corruption, traced
practically every dime of this soft money's amazing ride along
the financial loop-the-loop from the local TV stations to the
Washington ad agencies to the state parties and back to the
DNC. The organization's muckrakers determined that the entire
effort was directed from the White House (Clinton himself was
involved in designing the content of the ads). The DNC and
state parties played zero role—except to launder the money. As
Common Cause put it, "These are not technical violations of the
campaign finance laws. This is not pushing the envelope to take
advantage of loopholes in the law. What is at issue here are

massive illegal schemes [in which the Clinton campaign] knowingly and willfully violated federal election laws."

So, why are none of these characters in the federal pokey?
Because Bob Dole did it too. He got a later start, but once he
saw what Bill and the boys were up to, he decided Republicans
could violate the law just as flagrantly as Democrats, so in 1996
he did the exact same thing. He raised $8.8 million in soft
money to pay for his "issue ads," ran the money through the
Republican National Committee, which disbursed the money to
state Republican parties, which funneled the funds directly
back to the two ad agencies handling the Dole campaign, which
then designed, produced, targeted, and paid for the ads.

In a pathetic effort to claim that these were not "candidate
ads" per se, both campaigns have pointed to the legal nicety that
they were careful not to include the punch line of "Vote for Me
for President." But in a candid moment, Dole himself winkingly
conceded the patent absurdity of this legal distinction: "It never
says that I am running for president, though I hope that is fairly
obvious since I'm the only one in the picture."

Neither party wants to stop the soft-money merry-go-round
for obvious reasons, so even though they both periodically
express high indignation that the soft-money law is being
grossly violated and should be eliminated, it's still there. In
the Congress of 1997 and '98, the Republicans had five different committees chasing Clinton's soft-money outrages, but for
all their huffing and puffing they were not about to blow down
the house built of corrupt political money, because they were
inside it, too. Even His Oily Eminence, Representative Henry
Hyde, threatened loudly for a while that he would add soft
money to his Clinton impeachment charges, but his threat was
as hollow as the charge itself was meritorious. Chairman
Hyde's feigned indignation at fundraising excesses was rendered hilariously hypocritical when, at one point in the hearings, it was noticed that he kept switching out gavels, giving a
single rap with one, handing it to an aide who then handed

him another to make the second rap, and so on. Apparently, Republican fundraising officials had hit on the bright idea that these "100 Percent Authentic Impeachment Gavels Actually Used by Chairman Hyde in the Historic Proceedings Against William Jefferson Clinton" would make nifty premiums to attract major campaign donors.

Every Republican investigation into Clinton's money mess fizzled because, first, the public hooted at the chutzpah of money-drenched Republicans getting all pious about campaign-finance corruption—this is the party of Nixon, after all, and the party that has clubbed to death every reform measure that has raised its tiny head inside Congress. Second, GOP fund-raising operatives and nervous Republican presidential aspirants wanted the investigators to just "shut the hell up" and stop shooting at Clinton on this issue because they knew that they could get caught in the crossfire and, worst of all, the Golden Goose could be killed.

CLINTON *TALKS* REFORM

When Clinton first ran for president in 1992, his campaign manifesto offered this poignant piece of political rhetoric (WARNING! Certain readers might feel a sudden need for Pepto-Bismol after reading the following; it is only one sentence, but be prepared): "On the streets where statesmen once strolled, a never-ending stream of money now changes hands—tying the hands of those elected to lead." Once elected, the rhetoric continued to roll—in his first inaugural address the president pledged to "reform our politics so that power and privilege no longer shout down the voice of the people." Great stuff. So great that he made it a regular refrain in his annual State of the Union addresses. Every January, like a drunk making yet another New Year's resolution to swear off the booze, Clinton has stood before Congress with his pockets full of corrupt money, but with his heart filled with the gospel of reform:

> **1993:** "I am asking the United States Congress to pass a real campaign reform bill this year." (*Cheers*)

> **1994:** "I also must now call on you to [pass] tough and meaningful campaign finance reform and lobby reform legislation this year." (*Cheers*)

> **1995:** "We should also curb the role of big money in elections. . . . This year, let's give the folks at home something to cheer about." (*Cheers*)

> **1996:** "Now I challenge Congress to go further—to curb special interest influence in politics by passing the first truly bipartisan campaign reform bill in a generation." (*Cheers*)

> **1997:** "Let's work together to write bipartisan campaign finance reform into law . . . by the day we celebrate the birth of our democracy—July the Fourth." (*Cheers*)

> **1998:** "I ask you to strengthen our democracy and pass campaign finance reform this year." (*Cheers*)

> **1999:** "Now, we must work to renew our national community as well for the twenty-first century . . . [by passing] the bipartisan campaign finance reform legislation." (*Cheers*)

> **2000:** "I ask you to pass campaign finance reform." (*Cheers*)

Problem is, like that drunk on New Year's Day, he never really wanted reform and never pushed it. Even in his first two years when Democrats controlled the Congress, he made no effort to pass a bill, and thereafter he grew ever more addicted to high-dollar fundraising.

Besides, the last glimmer of hope that the two parties might ever do something about their corruption already had been snuffed out. The chance for them to act came on June 11, 1995, in Claremont, New Hampshire. In a rare happenstance, Clinton and then speaker Newt Gingrich appeared together at a town hall confab, answering questions from the audience. Local citizen Frank MacConnell made national news that day by rising and asking the two of them to clean up Washington by stopping big-money political contributions. Right then and there, Clinton and The Newt impulsively pledged to go to work on it and shook hands on the deal—a handshake that ran on every TV news broadcast on every front page in America. It seemed to be such a genuine moment, so filled with promise, that the audience burst into heartfelt huzzahs. Mr. MacConnell later said that he and others dared to hope that "the handshake seen 'round the world" symbolized the start of a new age in which "a politician's word could still mean something." But Clinton and Gingrich never met again to discuss the topic, and within a month, Clinton was squirreled away in the White House with Dick Morris, plotting their soft-money subterfuge of our election laws. A year and a half later, just before Clinton defeated Dole in a campaign distinguished only by the fact that it burst through the bottom hatches of political hell to wallow in a squalid and horrendous new level of money corruption, Frank MacConnell passed away.

NO LIMITS, NO FEAR

Raw political cynicism is Clinton's lasting legacy. By his careless use of soft money, he has authorized all future presidential and congressional candidates to disregard the law and treat public office as a commodity to be retailed for unlimited sums of campaign money. It turns the political clock back to the utterly corrupt days of Nixon, who literally kept wads of corporate cash stashed around the White House. One of those stashes included $25,000 from Archer Daniels Midland CEO Dwayne Andreas—money used to pay the Watergate burglars. A quarter of a century later, there was Bill Clinton with his 1996 unregulated stash of political money, including $295,000 from Andreas. In case you think anything has changed, Andreas and ADM put at least $200,000 into both the Bush and Gore runs last year.

Oh, the soft-money prohibitions still are on the books, but they're now like one of those quirky old laws that occasionally pop up in news features: "A 1913 Iowa statute makes it illegal, even today, for a farmer to be naked in the cow barn at milking time."

There was a chance to clamp the lid (if not the cuffs) on those who so openly broke the law in 1996, both in the Clinton and Dole campaigns. To their credit, the gutsy staff auditors of the Federal Elections Commission tried to do just that, concluding that Clinton's campaign spent $46 million more than was legal and that the Dole campaign was $17 million outside the law—nearly all of which had been spent on their bogus "issue advocacy advertising." The auditors were gutsy because their bosses, the six FEC commissioners, are political appointees (three appointed by the Democrats, three by the Republicans). The commissioners are appointed to prevent trouble for the parties, not cause it, and they've shown that they'd sooner try sandpapering a bobcat's butt than to stand in the way of the free flow of this illegal money into the coffers of their parties.

Unhappy to see this ugliness suddenly surface and be dumped in their laps, the commissioners were angrier at their auditors than at the outlaws. When the report hit the media, David Mason, who had been an aide to Republican leader Trent Lott before being named to the FEC, snapped: "It's a virtual certainty that these things won't be adopted." He was right. A week later, the commissioners voted 6–0 against any punishment for the Clinton and Dole campaigns.

This left Janet Reno as the last sheriff in Dodge. The attorney general's office had subpoenaed an early draft of the FEC auditors' report and was considering whether its charges warranted the appointment of an independent counsel to investigate Clinton's unlawful spending. Since she had proven to be a mighty slow draw on other Clinton-Gore fundraising violations, there were very low expectations that General Reno would do anything this time, and she actually underperformed on the expectations. Just before Christmas of '98, Reno delivered a nice stocking stuffer for Clinton, ruling that there should be no further legal inquiries into his soft-money sleight of hand because there was "clear and convincing evidence that the President . . . lacked the criminal intent to violate the law."

Huh?

Clinton was known to have been intimately involved in the whole scam—raising the money for it, developing the ad strategy, critiquing and changing the content of the ads themselves. The law plainly says that a candidate can't do this. What part of "can't" had the lawyer-president not understood? Maybe Reno discovered that Clinton had said "KingsX" or had his fingers crossed behind his back while plotting with Morris, or that he hadn't inhaled the whole time. But, no, it was nothing so logical as that. Her ruling was that (follow the bouncing ball here) (1) while the president might have violated the law, (2) he didn't *intend* any violation, as proven by the fact that (3) his lawyers told him his actions were legal, so (4) he "lacked the criminal intent," and (5) *ergo, ipso facto, habeas corpus delicti, and dipsy doodle,* Bill Clinton can walk.

The new legal standard on soft money, then, is that candidates may violate the law with impunity as long as their lawyers tell them it's OK. And every lawyer will say it's OK, because the Clinton precedent now exists, having been sanctioned by the FEC and the Justice Department.

BEELZEBUB'S BUZZWORDS

Being a glossary of political corruption, consisting of words and phrases, from *A* to *Z*, actually used by the buyers and sellers of political influence in these modern times . . .

ACCESS, n. The yellow brick road. It leads straight into the back rooms of Washington. Access is what the buyers of political favors profess to be purchasing from the sellers, as in: *Our contribution to the senator merely reflects our desire to have access to the legislative process.* Buying access is distinguished from bribery chiefly by the fact that the latter officially has been declared illegal, while the former is still at large. Despite protestations by political pettifoggers, experience teaches that there is no practical difference between buying an official's action and buying exclusive access to the official. *Slang*: Greasing the skids. "There is no question—if you give a lot of money, you will get a lot of access," a satisfied executive told the *New York Times* after his corporation had given $500,000 to the GOP. "All you have to do is send in the check." Many citizens are unaware that access is for sale, so out of ignorance they don't bid.

ASK, THE, n. The key moment. After all the wine has been drunk and the dancing done, finally comes The Ask, the naming of a specific price; e.g., *The chairman has the material you wanted him to see on that tax problem, Bob, and he hopes you'll* *consider donating fifty and raising another fifty.* Also called "The Pucker."

BAIT, n. Officeholders and candidates. To hook a major donor, the bait is offered in many forms: *We can arrange a private meeting for you with the speaker;* or, *The president will be golfing at Windswept on the 25th and there's an opening in his foursome;* or, *The senator hopes you might sit at his table at the fundraiser.* All bait opportunities are based on market price and availability. Overnights in the Lincoln bedroom and appearances in Buddhist temples have been discontinued for the 2000 season.

BREAKFAST CLUB, n. A well-appointed den of self-appointed thieves. On Capitol Hill, a breakfast club is organized around a powerful lawmaker who meets periodically in a private and swank setting with a group of lobbyists and other big contributors for a convivial discussion of their legislative needs. (The discussion is discreetly referred to as "platter chatter," as in: *Oh, nothing happened—we just had breakfast and some platter chatter.*) When the chatter is done and the last bit of sausage swallowed, an envelope is slipped into the hands of the lawmaker, who later discovers to his or her delighted surprise that it is filled with checks; e.g., when Representative Dennis Hastert ascended to the speaker's chair in 1999, he immediately instituted a regimen of breakfasting every couple of weeks with a different lobbying firm and their clients; they would devour eggs, talk legislation, and fatten the speaker by $20,000 to $100,000 each time; as a Hastert aide put it, "Dennis likes to do breakfast."

BUNDLING, v. To get close, but not go all the way. Corporations cannot give money directly to a presidential or congressional candidate, which frustrates many CEOs who miss the old days. Hence, the artful dodge of bundling. Since corporate executives (plus their wives and children) can each write

$1,000 checks to candidates, the CEO simply collects, say, a hundred of these individual checks from those in the executive suite of Great Big Global Corporation Inc., bundles them together with a tasteful gold ribbon, and personally hands them to the candidate in the name of the company: *George, here's a hundred grand we've bundled for you at GBGC—don't forget us now, you hear?* Technically, the law is not violated, and the corporation and candidate both get what they want.

CLEAN ROOM, n. (sometimes preceded by "ethically"). A legally sanitized place for raising bribery funds by telephone. The law is prudish about money calls being made from such hallowed sanctuaries as the Capitol, congressional offices, and the White House. (Oops, a couple of slipups there by Clinton and Gore, but see what a fuss it caused, and besides, there was "no controlling legal authority," according to the vice president, and Janet Reno gave him an official kiss on his boo-boo, so it's all better now.) To avoid calling donors from their congressional offices, lawmakers can dart one block away to either the Republican Club or the Democratic Club, where dozens of fully equipped small offices, cynically referred to as "clean rooms," are available for members to do their daily telephone solicitations of special-interest money givers. Both clubs provide showers for the more fastidious members.

CLOSER, n. The one who does The Ask (see above). Usually, the closer is not the candidate but a campaign official who is brought in to do the dirty work of asking a potential contributor for a certain amount of cash; some candidates, like Al Gore, are exceptions: "He's an excellent closer," a Gore confidant says. *Colloquial:* One who seals the deal.

CONCIERGE, n. (also, the "arranger," the "fixer," the "handler," the "contact"). Each major donor to either the Democratic or Republican parties is assigned a staffer in that party's Washington office who serves as their personal, governmental-affairs concierge. Is your legislation hung up in subcommittee, do you want to get on a trade mission to China, is a regulator bothering you? Call your concierge.

CONSULTANT, n. (usually preceded by an adjective, such as "fundraising," "media," "polling," "issue," "speech"). The lowest life form in politics. Also, the highest paid. "Consultants" is the correct answer to one of today's oft-asked questions: *Why do campaigns suck?*

CONDUITING, v. Playing traffic cop on the yellow brick road. Many industry associations give very little money directly to candidates, but they steer truckloads of it to politicians they favor by calling on member companies to send in checks made out to the chosen ones. The checks are then packaged (see "bundling") and conduited to the candidates by the association. There is no limit on how much can be conduited to a candidate, and conduiters claim to provide a service for donors who need guidance; a sort of *Political Bribery for Dummies* approach.

DAISY CHAIN, n. A cooperative effort to weave flowers into links, as innocent girls do in the early summer, gaily linking daisies into beautiful chains. The difference here is that the "daisies" are dollars, the "girls" are lobbyists, and "innocence" was deflowered long ago. To raise a lot of money in a hurry for a candidate, a group of lobbyists will set a goal of, say, $2 million in one month. Then they rush into the money fields, quickly plucking checks from their clients and other interested parties. They link these checks, one by one, into what is called a daisy chain for the candidate.

DONOR, n. One who gives to get; a political investor; the most valued citizen in today's political system.

DOUBLE DONOR, n. Companies that give without the burden of ideology or political passion, concerned purely with making certain that no matter who wins, they win; a nirvana achieved by the fact that they contribute generously to both candidates in a race and/or to both parties; e.g., more than a hundred companies gave at least $100,000 to each party for the 2000 election. *Informal:* In some circles, the Double Donor is referred to as "double crosser" or, more colloquially, as "chickenshit."

FACE TIME, n. A rare and prized commodity, now mostly for sale. The chance to sit face-to-face—constituent to congressmember—for maybe a half hour or more to talk about a particular issue of concern is about as unlikely for regular citizens (i.e., *noncontributors*) as coming face-to-face with a talking pig. It is, however, an opportunity that grows more likely in direct proportion to the amount of money brought to the trough; as a notoriously whorish Texas state senator used to say, "Write your problem on the back of a check for me, then we'll talk."

FLOPHOUSE, n. see *Lincoln bedroom*.

FUNDRAISER, n. The organizer of the bribery.

GOOD GOVERNMENT, n. The altruistic objective of big givers, so long as good government is defined as government good for them; e.g., the chief lobbyist for the giant energy firm Enron, explaining her corporation's $50,000 donation to George W. Bush's 1999 gubernatorial inaugural bash, said: "We clearly never expect to receive anything other than good government as a result of any kind of contribution we make." Subsequently, one of Governor Bush's good government priorities in the '99 legislative session was to pass an electricity deregulation bill pushed by Enron. It passed. Good government happens.

HOUND-DOG, v. *Slang,* to sniff out and pursue new or reluctant contributors, like a hound dog after game; to have an instinct for the hunt, as in: *He hound-dogged that rabbit right out of the bushes when no one else even knew it was there.*

IN COMPLIANCE, v. The first resort of scoundrels. The blissful state of being legally covered when accepting obvious bribes; e.g., when the Republican congressional leadership killed anti-smoking legislation the day after the Republican party took $220,000 from tobacco companies in 1998, reporters were assured that the transaction was "in compliance with all the ethics rules." Alert citizens will note that those who proclaim the loudest to be in compliance with the rules are those who write the rules.

INTERESTED MONEY, n. The golden goose of the political sys-tem. Potential donors who need particular political favors are the biggest, fastest-growing, and most reliable category of big-money donations: "Both parties go through donor lists to find people with particular concerns at stake in the legislative process or the executive branch, and they go out and hit them up," a GOP fundraiser confessed to *USA Today.* Synonym: *bribery funds.*

KISS, v. To score: *We kissed Exxon today.*

LEADERSHIP PAC, n. The legalized slush fund of a powerful politician.

LEVERAGE YOUR VOICE, v. Euphemism for "money talks, bull-shit walks": Representative Ellen Tauscher, telling *Roll Call* about the sudden flood of political money now surging out of Silicon Valley high-tech corporations, explained: "I think clearly it is important to be able to establish yourself as to how the political process works. I think that they understand that this is part of the process and that they want to leverage their voices." Synonym: *pay to play*.

LINCOLN BEDROOM, n. See *flophouse*.

MAINTENANCE, v. Taking care of big donors. Both national parties keep skilled mechanics available twenty-four hours a day, seven days a week, including road service. "Preventive maintenance" includes keeping donors well oiled with high-level phone calls, greasing any governmental problem they have, and periodically bringing them in to Washington to check their engine pressure and give them special briefings; e.g., former senator Lloyd Bentsen used to hold a monthly breakfast open only to those who gave $10,000 or more, and former senator Rudy Boschwitz issued special blue stamps to his contributors so his staff would expedite their mail. "High maintenance": donors who demand lots of attention. *Slang:* whiners.

MATING DANCE, n. The cooing, wooing, flourishing of feathers, prancing, and dancing performed by political candidates in front of possible contributors; often done in flocks, where several contributors are assembled for, say, a cocktail reception, when several candidates join them and proceed to strut their stuff, hoping for one or more matches.

MEMBER, n. A first-class citizen. Membership in the high-donor clubs of either party puts you in the skybox of American politics. Democrats have their "Jefferson Trust" ($100,000-plus) and their "Chairman's Circle" for givers of $500,000 and up, while Republicans have their gold-card "Team 100" ($100,000 and up) and their platinum-card "Regents" ($1 million over four years). Membership definitely has its privileges—e.g., a GOP fund-raiser explained to an undercover MSNBC reporter that while they can't guarantee private meetings with key lawmakers, the party will always try to set one up whenever a major donor needs it, adding: "I've never heard of a Team 100 member being denied a meeting."

MENU, n. The price list for access. The parties have become so flagrant in their disdain for even the appearance of ethical propriety that they have published brochures that offer specific access for specific levels of giving—from $5,000 photo ops with the vice president and $25,000 skeet shoots with GOP committee chairmen to $10,000 private work sessions with committee staff and $100,000 Florida retreats with senior White House staffers. "We had a brochure from the GOP, and we virtually copied the format," said the DNC's 1996 soft-money coordinator to *The New Yorker*. "I wanted some sort of consistency to [the pricing of access]. I didn't want the people in L.A. to get better access than the oil jobbers in Texas."

NO QUID PRO QUO, n. As low as it gets. The final defense politicians offer for accepting corruption funds from corporations is that there was no explicit promise to deliver a goodie for a gift: *"The lobbyist asked for no quid pro quo," said the chairman, "and I promised none."* This lowers the ethical bar to ground zero. *Anecdote*: The Texas legislature consistently shortchanges poor people so badly that the Lone Star state regularly ranks number forty-nine in various measurements of basic human decency, usually positioning us barely ahead of Mississippi; beleaguered progressives in our state are, therefore, reduced to being proud we're not dead last, cheering heartily, *Thank God for Mississippi!* This is now the sad standard of national political ethics—*thank God he never came right out and promised a quid pro quo!*

REPUBLICAN/DEMOCRAT, n. The two-faced mask of evil intentions worn by most lobbyists, all corporations, and too many politicians: *I am neither Republican nor Democrat, but both.* Like Beelzebub himself, this is a creature that can take many forms but serves only one interest: his own. *Slang:* Republicrat.

ROLODEXES, n. Money people with networks of money people
and a willingness to work them. The Rolodexes are the prize
catches of all major campaigns, for they are peers of the big
givers, they speak the native tongue and know the secret
handshakes, and they can harvest checks faster than a John
Deere haybaler: "You could care less about a guy who can give
$100,000," said the former finance coordinator for Bill Clin-
ton—it's the individuals who can work their Rolodexes to tap
dozens of others for twenty-five, fifty, or a hundred thousand
dollars each who truly matter. Shopping center mogul Mel
Sembler for George W. Bush, superlobbyist Peter Knight for Al
Gore, real estate baron Ted Welch for Lamar Alexander, Gate-
way lobbyist John Heubusch for Elizabeth Dole, AIG honcho
Hank Greenberg for John McCain—these are a few of the big-
league Rolodexes in the 2000 presidential campaigns. Another
Bush Rolodex, Christopher Burnham, who heads a Wall Street
investment firm, says, "I am absolutely enthused about this. I
have called my Christmas card list, my professional list, my
own political lists from fundraising over five campaigns. When
I get through with that I'll turn to the phone book."

SEASON TICKET HOLDER, n. The Brahmans of the political
caste. Both parties now have an ultimate pedestal for super-
givers who put more than $250,000 a year into their respective
cups, though it is the Republicans who designated theirs the
Season Ticket Holders. *Origin:* It seems that the GOP's weekend getaways for donors and politicians at Aspen, Palm Beach,
and elsewhere were becoming so overrun with the riffraff
who contribute only $100,000 each that your true elites were
finding these events "crowded" and difficult to get quality face
time with the politicians; thus was born, in 1996, the Season
Ticket Holder class, with members awarded carte-blanche
access to the party's top officeholders and granted entree to

the most intimate gatherings with GOP politicians. Those with their tickets punched are also said to hold "season passes," as in: *Make time this morning for me to see the gentleman from Philip Morris, for he's got a season pass.*

STROKING DOLLARS, v. The political art of wooing major donors, stroking their egos, and eventually stroking dollars from them for a campaign. Commonly practiced by candidates at gatherings of the GOP's "Team 100" or the Democrat's "Team 2000," where numerous stroking opportunities presented themselves. *Archaic*: wining and dining. *Regional*: In parts of the South, candidates refer to themselves as pickpockets, as in: *I've got to go to that black-tie dinner in Houston and pick a few pockets.*

UNILATERAL DISARMAMENT, n. The ultimate dodge, used most often by Democrats, to avoid any slowdown in the fundraising arms race, as in: *I strongly support campaign finance reform, but the other side is raising millions, and you can't expect us to unilaterally disarm, so we're going to keep raising the big money, too.* It is a version of "The devil made me do it." The disarmament dodge ignores other choices, from emphasizing low-dollar fundraising to pushing for public financing; e.g., Senator Russ Feingold of Wisconsin, a reformer running for reelection in 1998, did not disarm, but did have the integrity to deescalate, refusing to use soft money and imposing a spending limit on his campaign; his Republican opponent was forced by this stand to deescalate, too, though he didn't go nearly as far; the result was that Feingold was significantly outspent, yet he won anyway, in big part because of voter appreciation for his effort to restrain the whoring for dollars. Back in Washington, Feingold's reward was to be reviled by his own Democratic colleagues for showing them up.

VACUUMING, v. Going far beyond a candidate's or party's

usual base of donors to try gathering contributions from interests they really don't know. Vacuuming can find some real treasures, but it can also find some real problems, as in: *The casino boys ought to like my tax-incentive plan, so let's run our vacuum through Las Vegas and see what we pick up.*

WHORE, n. A term of endearment among insiders; a politician who engages in promiscuous legislative intercourse with a donor for money. While politicians never want to be called a whore in public, they often refer to each other as such in private as praise for being a successful fundraiser, as in: *Why you old whore, I heard you scored a big one with Globex International!*

ZIPS, THE, n. The most bountiful hunting grounds for bagging campaign contributions by presidential and high-profile congressional candidates. In order, the top-ten most lucrative zip codes, based on total amount of money given, are: 10021 and 10022 (New York, NY), 90210 (Beverly Hills, CA), 10017 (New York, NY), 20008 and 20007 (Washington, D.C.), 10128 (New York, NY), 33480 (Palm Beach, FL), 10028 (New York, NY), and 90067 (Century City, CA). The five Manhattan zip codes run contiguously up the posh East Side of the city, from Forty-sixth Street to Ninety-sixth, stretching from Fifth Avenue to the East River—these are the penthouses of the clans that run Wall Street. The two Washington zip codes are the Georgetown and Rock Creek Park neighborhoods, where the top lobbyists dwell; fundraising consultants refer to these prestigious addresses simply as The Zips, as in: *My candidate is having good luck in The Zips.*

PLUTOCRACY IS NOT GOVERNMENT BY A FAR-OFF PLANET

Ask someone to name a bizarre Texas billionaire and chances are Ross Perot's name will pop out.

Ah, how short our national memory is. On the scale of billionaire bonkerdom, Perot is barely a 1 when compared to the perfect 10 of Mr. H. L. Hunt, a Dallas oilman, who was ridiculously rich, severely right-wing, and nuttier than a hundred-pound sack of goobers. He was a billionaire back when that was unusual, in the 1950s and 1960s, and he was given to such egomaniacal tendencies as living in a mansion that was a replica of Mount Vernon—only, to put the father of our country in his place, H. L.'s was built a wee bit bigger.

How right-wing was he? Start with the John Birch Society and keep moving out there, *way out there,* to the point where you could call Dwight D. Eisenhower a tool of the communist conspiracy. Hunt went that far, and farther, using his *Life Line* radio program to make his daily dump into the intellectual discourse of the time. (I used to hear his program as a teenager growing up in Denison, north of Dallas and a lot closer to Earth than whatever planet Hunt was beaming from.) But the apogee of H. L.'s strange political odyssey came with the 1960 publication of *Alpaca,* a novel that he personally penned to set forth his utopian vision for the governance and safekeeping of America. The essence of his utopia was that the richer you are, the more votes you would get. Seemed only fair to him. In this transparently self-serving vision, Hunt himself would have outvoted all of the people of the Corn Belt, South Side Chicago, both Dakotas, and Duval County, Texas.

Alas, poor H. L. couldn't get anyone to take him seriously at the time. Yet, the spawn of his genius is with us today in the form of a political system that does indeed allow a few corporations, lobbyists, and superwealthy individuals a much larger vote than all other Americans combined. In today's *Alpacian* system, money is the ballot that counts and the people who vote with money are the citizens who matter. STAND BACK, BAR CHART COMING THROUGH! These things are usually so tooth-grindingly wonkish that they can cause your fillings to pop out, but the disparity between those who are treated as serious political players and the rest of us is so extreme that it cries out for a graphic, so here it is, ready or not:

PERCENTAGE OF THE AMERICAN PEOPLE WHO DONATE MONEY TO NATIONAL POLITICAL CANDIDATES

Donate $0	████████████████████████ 96%
Donate up to $200	███ 4%
Donate $200 to $1,000	▌ .09%
Donate $1,000 to $10,000	╎ .05%
Donate $10,000 to $100,000	← (Need magnifying glass) .002%
Donate $100,000 or more	← (Need Hubble telescope) .0001%

Source: Center for Responsive Politics (www.opensecrets.org)

Since it takes at least a three-zero donation for your name to get noticed by presidential candidates or top congressional officials (and four zeroes to get any attention paid to your political concerns), the arithmetic of today's politics is pretty straightforward: 99.9 percent of us are invisible and irrelevant to those who run the game, and the real "majority" is the one-twentieth of 1 percent who put $1,000 and up into it. We're talking about only 136,000 people in a nation of 270 million.

Richard and Helen DeVos of Grand Rapids, Michigan, are among this moneyed "majority," ranking in the very top echelon. These two are the founders of Amway, the direct-sales powerhouse that peddles everything from Nestlé to Wonderbras through a network of in-home sales reps. *Mother Jones* magazine reports that in April of 1997, Richard and Helen each wrote $500,000 checks to the Republican National Committee, instantly crowning them as the party's largest individual soft-money donors and, of course, making them much beloved, celebrated, consulted, and pampered by Newt Gingrich, Trent Lott, and other cooing party officials. But the DeVoses were not parting with a million cool ones simply to express their love for the GOP or the free-enterprise system. No, no, Nanette—three months after their checks were written, Newt and Trent teamed up in a closed door, eleventh-hour tax-writing session to slip a little ol' amendment into the massive 1997 tax bill. Provision C, section XI, reads: "Modification of passive foreign investment company provisions to eliminate overlap with subpart F and to allow market-to-market election, and to modify asset measurement rule." Abracadabra and hocus pocus! This arcane provision gave Amway a special annual tax break worth at least $19 million. The Amway amendment also can be used by a couple of other corporations, but Amway lobbyists admit that they engineered the loophole. There had been no consideration of this giveaway in either the House or Senate—no debate, no votes, not even a bill. Newt and Trent simply arranged to sneak it into the bill in the dark of night—a little "thank you" for Richard and Helen, courtesy of us taxpayers.

Mother Jones also found that "Kissing Bob" Packwood, the sexual harasser and former senator who fell so far from grace that he became a lobbyist, had been hired by Amway shortly after the million-dollar DeVos donation to the GOP. His job was to grease the skids for the tax break with his former colleagues. Conveniently, one of Packwood's former staffers had moved over to become Lott's staff counsel for tax issues, so the deal was sealed quickly. To prevent a flare-up from the Clinton administration, Amway lobbyist Roger Mentz, a former Treasury official, was dispatched to work his magic on his former colleagues, which he did, getting them to put Treasury on record as "not opposed" to the break. Since it was known inside the White House that this was one that both Gingrich and Lott wanted, Clinton didn't fight them, signing the tax bill without excising the Amway giveaway, which he could have done by exercising the line-item veto that was available to him at the time.

The DeVos family continues to be big-time benefactors of the GOP, keeping up payments on their private parcel of "democracy." As daughter-in-law Betsy DeVos put it in an op-ed that ran in *Roll Call,* "I know a little something about soft money, as my family is the largest single contributor of soft money to the national Republican Party. I have decided, however, to stop taking offense at the suggestion that we are buying influence. Now I simply concede the point. They are right. We do expect some things in return." What things? Specifically, she wrote, "We expect a return on our investment." Score one for candor. Betsy also said, "We expect a good and honest government." Well, the DeVoses seem to have bought one "honest" enough to give them a nineteen-to-one return on their million-dollar investment. She calls that "good" government—you might call it "corrupt."

The DeVoses, joined by a few hundred other individual money givers (and getters) and by a who's who of brand-name corporations that give (and get) even more, have risen to become America's ruling class as we turn the calendar to a new millennium. Individuals such as Bernard Schwartz (Loral Space & Communications), who personally gave $736,000 in 2000; Carl Lindner (Chiquita Brands), who gave $837,000; and Jon

Corzine (Goldman Sachs), who gave $366,000, are among the reigning nobles, as are such corporate barons as Union Pacific ($1.2 million in 2000), RJR Nabisco ($717,000), FedEx ($1.6 million), Lockheed Martin ($1.7 million), Bell Atlantic ($2.9 million), UPS ($2.4 million), Travelers Group ($2.9 million), AT&T ($3.8 million), and Philip Morris ($2.1 million).

"Money has come to be the moving power in American politics," said Senator William E. Borah back in 1926. A progressive Republican (*dinosaurus republicus progressus*—extinct circa 1980), Senator Borah of Idaho continued: "Some years ago, politicians got into the habit of seeking contributions from men of great wealth. . . . It was inevitable, if the large sums were to be given, that large sums would have to be returned in some way. Hence, money and politicians joined forces, and money has its say in shaping legislation and in administering the laws of the country. . . . It is a fearful national evil and will in the end, if not controlled, destroy the government of the people and substitute, therefore, a government of the few— the few who have sufficient money with which to buy the government."

In Borah's time, it was the likes of Andrew Mellon, the imperious multimillionaire banker, who reigned. Not only did money men like him buy the government of the day, but Mellon himself was ensconced as secretary of the treasury for *three* consecutive Republican administrations—those of Harding, Coolidge, and Hoover. He was there (as Robert Rubin of Goldman Sachs has been in the Clinton-Gore years) to ensure that the nation's governmental policies enrich the elites, even when such policies wreak havoc on workers, farmers, and everyday Americans. In Mellon's case, the myopic policy of upper-class enrichment led to the farm depression beginning in the 1920s and ultimately to the Great Depression that engulfed the entire country.

Three-quarters of a century later, we are living again under the "fearful national evil" that Borah spoke of, with modern-day Mellons controlling both our politics and our government, merrily enriching themselves at the expense of the many while blithely declaring that these are the best of times and that our democracy is sound. Bullfeathers. America's democracy has been buried in a stinking heap of bribery money, and people know it. Polls consistently find that the vast majority of Americans—75 to 90 percent, depending on the question— believe that their voice doesn't matter, that politicians do what their big contributors want rather than what ordinary voters want, and that neither party is interested in them. They believe this for the best of reasons: It's true! Look at our corporatized health-care system, at our butt-kissing corporate-driven policy toward China, at job-sucking trade deals like NAFTA, at the rubber-stamping of megamergers leading to price-gouging cartels in everything from banking to drugs, at the promotion of factory farms over farm families, at the selling of America's sovereignty to the World Trade Organization, at our tax laws that reward speculators and punish workers, at Wall Street's grab for the people's Social Security funds, at the push to allow corporate manipulation of the very genetics of our food supply, at the accelerated poisoning of our air and water, at the gorging of weapons manufacturers with ever larger piles of our tax dollars, at . . . well, at practically the entire agenda of both the White House and the Congress.

Washington and their Wall Street cohorts might think they're fooling the people, but they're fooling themselves if they think the people don't see what's going on. Humor columnist Phil Proctor tells of a first-grade teacher who gave her class the first part of some well-known proverbs, then asked them to fill in the rest. To the biblical adage "As you shall make your bed, so shall you . . ." a student responded, "mess it up." Out of the mouths of babes, huh? Indeed, the economic and political elites have made their corrupt bed and messed it up for the great majority of people. In this momentous year of 2001, the United States is no longer a democracy but a *plutocracy*. As former speaker of the house Jim Wright puts it, plutocracy is not government by a far-off planet. It is government of, by, and for the wealthy. Today, a million dollars easily outpolls a million voters—and wouldn't that cause H. L. Hunt to bust out in a great big grin?

Some would say that "plutocracy" is not quite expressive enough to describe what we have. So here's a selection that you might find more apt:

> **Diabolracy: government by devils.**
>
> **Pornacracy: government by prostitutes (also, Strumpetocracy).**
>
> **Foolocracy: government by . . . well, it's obvious.**
>
> **Kakistocracy (my favorite): government by the worst people in society.**

Last year's presidential and congressional elections had the usual kaleidoscope of BPE's—Big Political Events: the primaries, the national conventions, the debates, the cacophony of the TV campaign, and the drama of election night itself. But guess what? Even before the Iowa caucuses in January when the first votes of Election 2000 were cast, IT WAS ALREADY OVER!

OK, still up for grabs was which personality would get to sit in the big chair with the Presidential Seal on it and which party would have a congressional majority. But already decided was the basic issue of who government will serve, with the status quo assured on middle-class job loss, trade scams, environmental gradualism, mergers, corporate welfare, biotech insanity, campaign-finance corruption, and the other policies that most affect Americans at the kitchen-table level.

Last year's election was reduced to personalities rather than policies because the policy election—the *real* election—

was held the year before, 1999, in the corporate suites and the living rooms of the rich. Any and all presidential candidates who had banked the money it takes to have a real shot at winning were vetted in 1999 by these privileged few, meaning the candidates' views on all the kitchen-table issues had been pretailored to get the money—a tailoring that lacks much subtlety, essentially coming down to this obsequious pledge: "I [name of candidate] will put your financial interests above all others, and I will do nothing without clearing it with you first." It's a pledge that's also expressed more colloquially as "You da Man!"

Sure, we still got to vote, but the moneyed interests are the ones who had *chosen our choices*. For example, Goldman Sachs and its executives put thousands and thousands of dollars into Al Gore's campaign. And into George Bush's. And into John McCain's. And into Bill Bradley's. No matter who won, Goldman Sachs was going to have a friend in the White House—and probably will get at least one of its own executives appointed to a key administrative position, from which to keep an eye on the company's political investment.

By purchasing candidates wholesale, Goldman Sachs and the other plutocrats guaranteed a campaign that was much ado about nothing, with the debate restricted to *social issues* such as abortion, *hokey issues* such as who can downsize government the most (while hypocritically lavishing ever more wasteful spending on the Pentagon, the antidrug war, and corporate welfare—hypocrisy being a valued trait in recent U.S. presidents), *local issues* such as zoning, school tests, and traffic jams, and *nonissues* such as which candidates can be the most pious about never ever even thinking about doing cigar tricks with White House interns.

THE CONVENTIONS:
A TWO-FOR-ONE SALE

"**M**y strengths are not [in] being a legislative titan. My strengths are not [in] being taken that seriously on the substance side. My strengths are my youth, my energy . . . my family name, my connections."

—*Representative Patrick Kennedy, chairman of the Democrats' congressional fundraising arm, speaking at a June 2000 event in Cherry Hill, New Jersey*

You know that "the times they are a-changing" when the son of Ted Kennedy has become a bright star within his party, not because he's the present-day embodiment of the Kennedy family's political passion for economic fairness and social justice, but solely because he raised more campaign cash from corporate interests for the 2000 election than any Democratic money sacker in congressional history. Patrick is part of the supercharged, twin-engine, legalized bribery machine that both the Democratic and Republican parties have become, and his little Cherry Hill confession speaks volumes about the extent to which America's treasured democratic process has been turned on its head, with both parties celebrating connections over substance, money over people.

If there were any doubts about the money-soaked vacuousness of Election 2000, they were erased last summer in Philadelphia and Los Angeles, where the Republicans and Democrats respectively gathered for their national nominating conventions. Of course, there really was nothing to do at these confabs, since the nominees had been chosen months before and the frothy, say-nothing platforms already were locked in place. Delegates—supposedly the agents of grassroots democracy—had no role except as colorful props for the television cameras. The absence of any real action and the Disneylike "Showtime!" presentations from the two podiums led the major networks to cut coverage to a minimum, complaining that there was "nothing happening."

Wait a minute. Nothing happening? Nothing except *the outright selling of our government in an orgy of corrupt corporate cash that bought unlimited favors from the whores of Washington who were hauled to the conventions by the two parties to service the buyers.* Wouldn't that have made good television?

The doings on the podium and the convention floor, where the networks stayed tightly focused, were irrelevant to the shaping of our nation's public policies, but up in the corporate skyboxes, behind the velvet ropes stretched across the doors of posh restaurants, out at the members-only golf clubs, inside the suites atop the luxury hotels, and in other secluded venues in Philly and Los Angeles, the money powers were rubbing up against the political powers in ways that pervert all public policy to the satisfaction of the money powers. The Republican and Democratic conventions no longer serve a public purpose (even though each received $13 million from us taxpayers to put on their show). Aside from giving the establishment parties a free shot at propagandizing a prime-time TV audience, these quadrennial gatherings now serve the strictly private purposes of lobbyists and CEOs, who conveniently have all the key Congress critters, administration officials, and political operatives corralled for a week with no distractions, nowhere for them to go, and nothing to do but schmooze. As one lobbyist confided to Richard Whittle of the *Dallas Morning News*, "Just imagine one big reception. You can get to spend a lot of quality time with members of Congress. It's just amazing how much time you've got them cornered. That's why lobbyists go."

The GOP presented a touchie-feelie, "We-are-the-world" convention program under the mushy slogan, "Prosperity with a purpose." Behind the scenes, though, the clear purpose was to advance the party's own prosperity by selling its leadership, its agenda, and the convention itself to corporate johns: AIG, AT&T, Verizon, Blue Cross/Blue Shield, DaimlerChrysler, Enron, General Motors, Global Crossing, Hewlett-Packard, Microsoft, Motorola, PepsiCo, Philip Morris, Prudential, SmithKline Beecham, Union Pacific, Unisys, and US Airways were among more than thirty official corporate sponsors of the convention, putting up $100,000 to $1 million each. This got them not only a good time and gobs of general good will from grateful Republican officials, but their top executives and lobbyists were also given extra-special face time with George W. Bush, Dick Cheney, and the party's congressional leadership.

Not to be outdone, the Democrats sold their leaders, agenda, and convention, too. Interestingly, prior to convening in Los Angeles, the Democratic party brought members of the Gabrieleno/Tongva Tribe, the first known inhabitants of what is now Los Angeles, to the convention hall for a blessing ceremony, which officials said was intended to reflect the party's "commitment to its core principles of inclusion, access, and opportunity." None of the tribe's members however, were included in, given access to, or afforded the opportunity to enjoy private tête-à-têtes with Al Gore, Joe Lieberman, and the party's congressional leadership, as were such $100,000-to-$1 million convention sponsors as: AIG, AT&T, Bank of America, Boeing, Chevron, DaimlerChrysler, Ernst & Young, General Motors, Global Crossing, Hewlett-Packard, Lockheed Martin, Microsoft,

SunAmerica, Transamerica, United Airlines, UPS, and Waste Management.

From direct subsidies to regulatory loopholes, all of these corporations are seeking governmental favors from the leaders of the two parties they now officially sponsor. "Certainly there is an overarching government affairs objective to our involvement in the political process, and this is certainly a part of that," admitted a Microsoft spokesman when asked about his company's $1 million sponsorship of both conventions. If you, like me, are alarmed that such million-dollar "involvements" are choking the process, you'll not be happy to learn that you and I also have to subsidize the choking, for Microsoft et al. are awarded a tax deduction for their sponsorship money.

Sponsorship orgies, however, were the tamest of the money games that corporations played with the two parties during their convention weeks. Especially rank were the bashes various unabashed companies threw for certain lawmakers, each of whom just happened to oversee the legislative agenda of the host company. For example, Representative Billy Tauzin, the Louisiana Republican who is in line to become chairman of the mighty Commerce committee, was fêted at a Mardi Gras Night in Philadelphia. Revelers snacked on fried alligator, jambalaya, and suckling pig, while enjoying free booze and shaking their booties to the tunes of Bourbon Street musicians imported for the lavish affair. The tab: more than half-a-million bucks. For a party! No problem, it was cheerfully picked up by thirty-three corporations with a long list of pending business before the Commerce committee. Among the gifts for attendees at Billy's ball were silver coins imprinted with the names of five of the hosts: America Online, BellSouth, American Insurance Association, United Distillers and Vintners, and . . . NBC! Funny, I don't recall any NBC coverage of this soiree.

Two weeks later, there was a similar bacchanalia called Mardi Gras Goes Hollywood, this time honoring Senator John Breaux, a Louisiana Democrat (sort of). Guess who is a powerful member of the Senate Commerce committee? John! One of the Louisiana musicians brought in for the high jinks was Big Bad Voodoo Daddy—an appropriately named choice for a party celebrating a senator who clearly has his mojo working with the corporate crowd. For $25,000 each, companies not only were listed as hosts, but also got a seat at an intimate lunch with Breaux, as well as a spot on his very own float in the Mardi Gras parade that was part of this opulent party held in Paramount Studios. More than twenty corporations, all with legislative itches that Breaux can scratch, put up the money to get down with John during his Hollywood moment.

So many parties, so little time. Among them: Senate leader **Trent Lott** had a "LottHop" featuring American Bandstand impresario Dick Clark—all attendees received dandy yellow tote bags emblazoned with the logos of Lott's sponsors, including AT&T, International Paper, Lockheed Martin, and U.S. Tobacco; Democratic Representative **John Dingell**, ranking member of the Commerce committee, had a House of Blues blowout, paid for by the nuclear, gas, mining, and electric utility industries; George W. Bush's chief economic advisor, **Larry Lindsey**, was treated to a brunch by General Motors, which happens to employ Lindsey as a consultant, as well as having him on the board of one of its subsidiaries (asked by the *New York Times* if it was appropriate for the auto giant to sponsor him, Larry seemed genuinely surprised by the question and said, "It's a natural thing to do"); Senator **Jeff Bingaman** of New Mexico, who is top Democrat on the Energy committee, was celebrated by Enron, the global energy giant that is George W. Bush's top money giver and also is lobbying furiously for a federal energy deregulation bill that would mean billions for the company—"We want to make sure Mr. Bingaman knows what our position is," said an Enron man; the odious Representative **Tom DeLay**, Republican Whip in the House, had several corporate-funded events in Philly, including a "Friends of Tom DeLay" golf tournament—must've been hard to get up a foursome for that; **The Blue Dog Democrats** (aka Worthless Old Hounds) are a kennel of Republicanlike lawmakers, and they showed their true colors not only by being treated to a blue-themed party on the Santa Monica Pier (drinks dyed blue, blue corndogs, blue carpet covering the boardwalk, etc.), but also by having a gaggle of blue-ribbon Republican givers pay $50,000 each to sponsor the dogs, including the NRA, Philip Morris, Raytheon, and U.S. Tobacco; and Representative **Mark Foley**, the Florida Republican who heads his party's Entertainment Industry Task Force, which develops GOP media policies, was the honoree of a whoop-de-do paid for by (who else?) the media barons, including Time Warner (CNN), Viacom (CBS), News Corp. (Fox), and Disney (ABC)—did you see any of these networks cover this interesting conflict of interest?

Not only were these unholy shivarees conflicts of interest, but they also would seem to conflict with Congress's own ethics rules. Isn't there a gift ban that says a member cannot accept any gift worth more than $50 from a corporation or lobbyist? Yes, but remember, where there's smoke . . . there are sure to be mirrors. Congress writes its own rules, after all, and it cleverly wrote a little loophole into the gift ban that says a lawmaker can accept the gift of, say, a half-million-dollar party thrown in his or her honor so long as the corporate hosts invite at least twenty-five people who are not lawmakers and as long as those invitees are drawn from an entire industry, not just from one company. Slick, huh? And this is the same Congress that expressed outrage at Bill Clinton's infamous parsing of legalities when he said: "It depends on what 'is' is."

Lawmakers drove truckloads of cash through this loophole at both conventions. Indeed, for his Mardi Gras Goes Hollywood event, Senator Breaux even went out of his way to point out this ethics law escape clause when he solicited corporations for sponsorships: "Special exceptions to various ethics rules allow corporations to offer hospitality and [to] stage events that otherwise might be prohibited or limited by state or federal codes," he wrote coquettishly. It was like putting a giant, blinking neon sign on the Ethics Highway saying, "Loophole, Next Exit . . . Loophole, Next Exit. . . ."

One difference between the two conventions was that the Republicans were not at all red-faced about the flagrant prostitution they engaged in, while the Democrats tried to be demure, pretending that they were simply running an escort service.

In Philadelphia, for example, Union Pacific ran temporary railroad tracks next to the convention hall, then rolled in a special "heritage" train described by the **Dallas Morning News** as "thirty air-conditioned, elegantly appointed dining, lounge, and sleeping cars." This rolling bordello was open at all hours, with selected members of Congress invited to come in for breakfasts, brunches, lunches, cocktails, receptions, dinners . . . or just to lounge around. The corporate chairman and ten lobbyists were on board to keep company with the lawmakers. A Union Pacific vice president told the *News* that the congressional "guests" would be entertained, then they would get down to business: "When you're sitting, breaking bread, you have a conversation: 'You know that bill we've got going? Well, here's what you ought to know about it.'" They even had golf carts to run the "guests" back and forth between the convention hall and the train.

Democrats had just as many events with their corporate donors, yet they insisted that in no way were these to be called fundraisers. Instead, convention officials instructed the media that the proper phrase was (believe it or not): "donor servicing" events. Terry McAuliffe, the convention organizer (and the Energizer Bunny of Clinton-Gore fundraising), told the *New York Times* that the corporate checks for the assorted schmooze-fests in Los Angeles had been delivered prior to the convention. Therefore, explained McAuliffe, since no money actually changed hands at the events, it's technically improper to call them fundraisers. The party is merely servicing its donors,

Terry told us. Yeah . . . like Heidi Fleischman serviced the clients of her "Hollywood Madam" escort ring.

On Tuesday morning of convention week in Philadelphia, Ruth Conniff of *Progressive* magazine caught one of those juicy, joyous moments when the mask is ripped off this corrupt system. The scene was a $1,000-a-plate breakfast for Majority Leader Trent Lott at the swank Four Seasons hotel. Republican political heavies mixed contentedly with corporate lobbyists, secure in their cozy seclusion, when suddenly they were confronted by what Conniff describes as "a bikini-clad hooker with a Miss Liberty hat and a pair of thigh-high fishnet stockings stuffed with dollar bills." The "hooker" (actually Jessica Parsley of Rainforest Action Network) and two other women began chanting at the startled clique of insiders: "Trent Lott's a corporate whore, We won't take no more." Four Seasons staff rushed to push the outsiders from the room, quickly closing the glass doors behind them. Conniff writes that as the women were hustled out, "Miss Liberty blew kisses and waved through the glass at the gawking breakfast goers."

Don't you think Miss Liberty would have made a perfect guest for Ted Koppel's *Nightline* that Tuesday? Instead, Ted recycled some talking puffheads of the media to tell us rubes what we should think about Laura Bush's convention speech, Dick Cheney's contribution to the ticket, the latest poll numbers, or some such. Amazingly, the Mr. Bigs of the media still wonder why their convention ratings are so low and their credibility is barely a notch above that of politicians.

Meanwhile, the two parties continue to express bewilderment about why a majority of the American people refuse to vote for either of them, even in presidential years. Luckily, we have no less a political theorist than Dan Quayle to respond to any confusion on this point: "A low voter turnout is an indication of fewer and fewer people going to the polls," Danbo explained a few years ago. It must be true, as I've been told, that if you stand close enough to Dan, you can hear the ocean.

You could dismiss his tomfoolery, except that he's not that much more ludicrous than the others. This is why, when presented a choice of Al Gore and George W. Bush on election day, millions of Americans say: "Oh, hell, I need to work on my car."

YOU DON'T MATTER

POLITICAL PASSIONS FLARE

Monroe County, KS.—The campaign culminated in a bloody tragedy at Clarendon Saturday afternoon. The candidates were to speak and a great crowd had gathered. The debate became heated and one of the partisans, Wm. Walls of Holly Grove, attempted to strike one Dillard. But Dillard pulled his gun and shot Walls, who fell to his knees, pulled his revolver and shot Dillard twice, after which Walls fell back dead.

The mob rushed in on Dillard, but his friends surrounded him and, with pistols and knives, declared their intention to defend him. Sheriff Robinson attempted to arrest Dillard, but was shot in the thigh. The mob then closed in on Dillard and beat him terribly. A stray bullet killed a spectator. Dillard was finally spirited away, and the mob is after him.

—News dispatch, c. 1890s

Now *that's* politics. Imagine getting worked up enough to have a fistfight, much less a shoot-out, over any of the platitudes and pabulum being put out by the Bush or Gore campaigns. I mean, do your neck hairs bristle when Shrub Bush scorches the hustings with such incendiary rhetoric as "I believe all public policy should encourage strong families"? Does your blood rise and your fists ball when Al Gore issues his clarion call for an "N11 National Traffic Hotline"?

Politics should matter. I know that's a radical thought, perhaps hopelessly idealistic in this age of carefully calculated political centrism, when the money backers demand candidates who are inoffensive (especially inoffensive to money interests), and when the army of consultants that directs every campaign insists that the way to win is not to lose. So both parties are scuttling cautiously along the pollster-tested center line like a couple of sand crabs, going sideways for fear of being perceived as either moving forward or backward.

Of course the Republican presidential nominee didn't thump the tub about the class war being waged against the middle class and poor folks by America's moneyed establishment—but neither did the Democratic nominee. *Of course* the Republican didn't storm Wall Street's barricades of privilege to assail the greed of corporate downsizing and outsourcing of American jobs—and neither did the Democrat. *Of course* the Republican didn't stand on the steps of the Capitol to decry the thievery of America's democracy by Gucci-wearing, PAC-peddling, Binaca-breathed corporate lobbyists—nor did the Democrat.

What a difference a generation makes. I can imagine teenagers today, as they come of voting age, gawking in disbelief as their parents tell them that there actually was a time when a Democratic presidential nominee was a species discernibly different from the Republican, when the Democrat was not skittish about kicking corporate ass, and when the Democratic party didn't need a consulting firm to figure out who it was for . . . and who it was against. This is a party with a heroic history of siding unequivocally with the common people against the bastards, a party that once even voted by a 4-to-1 margin at its national convention to disown any political candidate within its own ranks "who is the representative of or under obligation to J. Pierpont Morgan . . . or any other member of the privilege-hunting and favor-seeking class."

Today, the Democratic party itself, as well as its top candidates, *boast* of being under obligation to Morgan—or, more specifically, to J. P. Morgan Inc. and Morgan Stanley, the two Wall Street firms spawned by old J. Pierpont. Democrats go shamelessly and often into these houses of greed, obsequiously seeking campaign funds in a straight-up exchange for their populist principles and constituency. Al Gore, Bill Bradley, and the Democratic party bagged some $250,000 from the two Morgan firms for the 2000 election.

This is an appalling perversion of everything that is *important* about the Democratic party. If William Jennings Bryan were alive to see this, his eyeballs would explode and his hair would burst into flame! He would note, correctly so, that the party's only reason for existence is to serve those who want to challenge the haughty rule of Morgan Inc. and the other members of the privilege-hunting, favor-seeking class. It's fine for the J. P. Morgans to have one party, but if the Democrats, too, are inside the houses of Wall Street, where does this leave the vast majority of us who are outsiders?

Since Labor Day of 1996, it's been my good luck to be able to spend two hours every weekday talking with the American people on my call-in radio show, *Hightower's Chat & Chew*. With cohost Susan DeMarco, piano player Floyd Domino, and our occasional guests at the Round Table inside Threadgill's World Headquarters (the legendary Austin restaurant from which we sling our radio signal and our B.S. coast to coast), I've had a steady stream of feedback from folks about what's going on where they live, far away from Wall Street.

I know, talk-radio listeners are said to be a bunch of know-nothing right-wingers spewing thirty-two flavors of pure dittohead venom, but that's not been our experience at all.

The American majority that's being stomped on by Wall Street and pissed on by Washington wants a politics with meaning and passion, one that's worth getting embroiled in a fistfight. These folks want a politics that rallies them, in the stirring words of FDR in 1932, to join in a "crusade to return America to its own people." That would be a politics that would bring hordes of people to the polls. But in the politics of the two-party duopoly, people don't matter.

Steve Sovern found that out a few years ago when he ran for Congress from Cedar Rapids, Iowa. A Democrat, he was a promising candidate with a terrific group of volunteers and an enthusiastic base of support. The party brought him to Washington for a two-day candidate's workshop put on by the Democratic Congressional Campaign Committee. Steve says he was excited to be among some seventy other grade-A Democratic candidates attending this how-to-win workshop: "I looked forward to returning to Cedar Rapids filled with ideas, ideals, issues, and inspiration." He came to the meeting all bright-eyed and bushy-tailed with his notepad and tape recorder, ready to absorb all the wisdom the party could offer.

"Understand how the game is played," offered a big-time media consultant as the workshop opened. "Game?" thought Steve, as it quietly dawned on him that this might not be about ideals and issues. "Money drives this town," intoned a DCCC staffer, followed by another consultant who informed the budding members of Congress: "You have to sell yourself to Washington first," by which he meant the lobbyists who control the PAC funds. Representative Peter Hoagland, then a lawmaker from Nebraska, came in to assure the group that "raising campaign money from Washington PACs is much easier than from individuals because it's a business relationship." Steve's eyes squinted as he thought, "Business relationship?" The DCCC staffer clarified the point, in case any of the seventy innocents didn't get it: "These people are paid to give you money. You have to *do* certain things, but they *want* to give you money."

What if you don't want to take their filthy lucre, which Steve did not? Congressman Hoagland: "Some of you may be under pressure to repudiate PACs. I strongly suggest you not take the hook. Restrain yourself, don't let zeal for reform influence you." Hmmm, thought Steve: "Let lobbyists' money influence you, but not zeal for reform?"

To put theory into practice, day two of the workshop began with a "mating dance" brunch. The DCCC invited a flock of PAC directors to eat croissants and look over the seventy congressional prospects, who in turn were expected to preen, strut, and do whatever it takes to mate monetarily with the PACs. Steve reports that the candidates wore blue name tags, while the PACs sported red ones. Representative Beryl Anthony of Arkansas led the dance, informing the candidates that the assembled PAC directors were their friends, that PACs represent "little people." Steve says, "I saw the Phillips Petroleum PAC representative smile with approval. I wondered if he was representative of the 'little people' to whom Anthony referred." The congressman then urged the PAC reps to visit with each of the candidates while they were in town, because he was sure the money interests would find matches among the lawmakers-to-be that will "make your board of directors proud of you."

Left out of the equation, said Steve, "were the people I sought to represent." Instead, all the instruction was on raising money and hiring Washington consultants to run their congressional campaigns. "You can't hire local people—forget it!" bellowed a PAC director. Congressman Hoagland underscored the point: "[You] must hire world-class people and not local people. *That's why you have to raise a lot of money.*"

Don't even mess with volunteers, the eager candidates were told by a PAC director: "They can't do polling, radio, direct mail, or TV." Steve was stunned: "At the moment he spoke, my campaign had scores of volunteers who still believed in a government 'of the people,' phoning neighbors to talk about the campaign and issues that concerned them. Other volunteers were stuffing and stamping envelopes for a direct-mail response to those concerns."

At this point, he had absorbed all the cynical, manipulative, money-driven expertise he could stand, so he rose to his feet and told them so, pointing out that what they were telling the candidates is exactly what people hate about politics, that this approach is a dangerous turnoff to turnout, and that it ought to be Democrats who lead the crusade to end the kind of politics they were being coached at this workshop to use. Steve says, "There was an uncomfortable silence after my comments." Then a PAC director said: "Well, I guess we don't have to worry about contributing to *that* campaign." There was a spattering of nervous laughter, then the workshop proceeded as though nothing had happened.

Sure enough, the PACs did not contribute. Steve says he was even cut from the DCCC mailing list after the workshop, no longer sent any issue papers or legislative updates. Instead, the Washington money, expertise, and even DCCC staff went to another Democrat who had already lost twice in this congressional district but was willing to "play the game." With his Washington lobbyists' PAC money, the two-time loser was able to overwhelm Steve in the primary, then proceeded to lose for a third time to the Republican in the fall.

FIRST, KILL ALL THE CONSULTANTS

Here they come, tromp-tromp-tromping over the horizon, the mercenary army of professional political consultants, now more than thirty-five thousand strong! They are coldly efficient at what they do, and they control practically every campaign in America, from city council to president.

Of course, political consultants have been around since politicians first popped up. The earliest recorded evidence of these creatures was Quintus Cicero's tract, the *Handbook of Electioneering,* which he wrote to guide the 63 B.C. campaign of his famous orating brother, Marcus Tullius Cicero, who was seeking a consulship to Rome at the time. (However, some date the craft much farther back, crediting the snake that advised Eve with being the first consultant—which shows what trouble they can cause.) Only recently, though, have these political pros become so pervasive and dominant. Whereas electioneering even twenty-five years ago was handled by the candidate, a campaign manager, a press secretary, maybe two or three other paid staffers, and a host of committed volunteers, today there are paid specialists to run every aspect of the campaign:

Strategic planner	**Debate simulator/coach**
Campaign director	**Telemarketer**
Staff manager	**Delegate counter**
High-dollar fundraiser	**Speechwriter**
Low-dollar fundraiser	**Radio ad producer**
Event planner	**TV ad producer**
Scheduling coordinator	**Radio/TV time buyer**
Poll-question writer	**Direct-mail writer**
Poll taker	**Direct-mail list buyer**
Focus-group coordinator	**Media relations director**
Voter targeting director	**Travel aide**
Weasel coordinator (just kidding)	**Opposition-research director**
Field-staff director	**Issue-development director**
Dress and color adviser (not kidding)	**Get out the vote director**

More than fifty separate job categories exist for political professionals—including consultants who specialize in finding and selecting candidates to run for particular offices. Yes, it has come to this low ebb: Consultants choose the candidates! It will not surprise you, I'm sure, to learn that their chief criterion in choosing a "good candidate" is that the person have an aptitude for fund raising—gotta keep the army fed. And it's a hungry army—one survey found that of the $542 million spent by all congressional candidates in a recent general election, $248 million of it went to these hired guns. There is so much paid staff that just keeping in touch is a problem—one of the odder artifacts unearthed when sifting through the statistical rubble of Bob Dole's 1996 presidential organization was this: He spent $14,000 on beepers.

The impact of this mercenary invasion of American democracy has been devastating, reducing elections to computerized, cynical exercises in which the people are irrelevant, and such niceties as issues, ethics, and the future of the nation are beside the point.

Candidates don't need their own core beliefs, or goals for America, when their handlers can provide market-tested beliefs and goals for them based on the results of an electioneering mechanism called the focus group. Borrowed from Madison Avenue, this process involves bringing a dozen or so voters into a room for a few hours of professionally structured conversation around such profound political questions as: "If George W. Bush were an animal, what would he be?" Miles Benson of Newhouse News Service sat through some focus groups last year and reports that participants "are hooked to computers and handed a device with a dial to twist to register the intensity of their reactions, positive or negative. These responses are displayed instantly as trend lines on a graph, with a computer isolating the effects of various words and ideas and showing precise differences in the reactions of Democrats, Republicans, and independents." Benson writes that consultants watch the group while hiding behind see-through mirrors, recording facial expressions and body language. Out of this voyeuristic exercise come the candidates' campaign themes ("Prosperity with a Purpose" or "You Ain't Seen Nothing Yet"), positions on issues, their phrases for attacking opponents, and other manipulative language designed to sell product A over product B. This is why so many candidates come off sounding like a breath of hot air.

The official creed of consultants is: Whatever It Takes! The point is to win. Period. Consultants live and die on their won-lost record, so distortions, innuendos, outright lies, dirty tricks, spying, negative ads, gay-baiting, hate mailings, and so forth are just part of the accepted weaponry of modern campaigns. As a consultant once told me, "We always stand on principle. And stand on it and stand on it, so it won't ever rise up and get in our way."

The most common weapon in the consultant's arsenal is the attack ad, which we've all seen and learned to loathe. Humorist Dave Barry explained these in a column last year: "In America, the only way you can get elected to high office is to hire expensive consultants who conduct expensive polls to find out what the voters think, and then, having found out that the voters think that all politicians are slime, make expensive TV commercials wherein you show a hideously unflattering photograph of your opponent and have a snarling announcer say something like: 'Harvey Hackenslit would have you believe that he has never eaten live human babies. Who's he trying to fool?'"

A preacher in the Methodist church I attended as a boy used to teach us kids that "you don't make your house any prettier by burning down your neighbor's." Apparently, consultants attended a different church, for negative campaigning—going after their opponents with lies, hammers, tongs, blowtorches, chain saws, and nuclear explosives, all designed to pervert positions and burn down reputations—is considered a legitimate part of the game.

I've had my own political house singed. When I ran for reelection as state ag commish in 1990, a last-minute negative TV ad smeared me . . . and hurt me. It came from my GOP challenger, whose campaign was being coordinated by Karl Rove, a fellow who served last year as consultant-in-chief on the George W. Bush presidential bandwagon. The ad showed a flag burner torching Old Glory and tossing it on the ground to burn. The camera panned in on the flag, then, arising out of the flames came my picture, along with the somber voice of a narrator declaring that Jim Hightower supports flag burners. I did not, but the impact on voters was visceral and damaging—

"My God," I could hear the viewers muttering to themselves, "I kind of liked ol' Hightower, but I had no idea he was a flag burner."

A 1998 poll of two hundred political consultants found nearly unanimous agreement that they found nothing wrong with such negative campaigning. Syndicated political columnist David Broder reports on an article written by two consultants with a firm called Campaign Performance Group: "Fear, anger, envy, indignation, and shame are powerful emotions in the political arena. . . . Go the distance. . . . Negative campaigning is rarely pretty. Sometimes it doesn't feel very good either. But once you've made the decision to inform the voters of your opponent's shortcomings, stick to your guns. . . . Remember, you're playing to win."

Then there are dirty tricks, which range from sophomoric pranks (like the "black fax," which involves faxing black paper to an opponent's fax machine in the wee hours when no one's around, thereby burning out their ink cartridge and filling their fax room with a pile of black paper) to the dangerous. Years ago, my friend José Angel Gutiérrez led a third-party insurgency to defeat the old Anglo power structure in Zavala County, Texas. Angel himself became county judge—a mighty powerful position in Texas, controlling road money, patronage, and a lot more. At reelection time, though, he kept coming across rattlesnakes in the most unusual places—like his desk drawer, his mailbox, and his wastebasket.

Once known as backroom hatchet men, today's consultants are as out front and as quoted as the candidates, sometimes more so, taking credit for everything from the campaign's strategy to the candidate's speeches. They've become media stars—which tells us all we need to know about the vacuousness both of politics and of our country's celebrity system. Case in point: Dick Morris, who has no credibility and nothing to say, yet says it over and over again on national television yakety-yak shows. He's the party-hopping consultant who has no ethical problem with having been a gunslinger for Bill Clinton, then for Trent Lott, then back to Clinton, whom he coached on how to become more Republican than Bob Dole in his '96 reelection bid. The whorish Morris fell into complete personal and professional disgrace that year after his ongoing affair with a Washington prostitute of the sexual variety was exposed. She told the media that he revealed White House secrets to her while sucking her toes in a $400-a-night hotel. That's kinky on several levels. Yet, like a bad tamale, this gasbag keeps coming back—he got a book contract, writes a newspaper column, was on TV more often than Lucianne Goldberg (herself a former GOP dirty-tricks consultant) during the Monica Lewinsky unpleasantness, and still today is a sought-after television commentator, actually asked to give the public his insights into the ethics of other political players.

This would be inexplicable, except that it's not unusual. The media has bought wholly into the consultantization of our politics, reporting on the game rather than the substance, so it routinely interviews consultants in lieu of candidates, it evaluates the relative "seriousness" of candidates based on which set of consultants they hire, it relies on consultants as primary background sources for its election coverage, and it reports straight-faced the polls and political spin of consultants.

There's a term that applies to the media's tedious and essentially empty coverage of America's elections: teptology. It means boringly detailed discourses on trivial subjects. That's what we get when the media bothers to cover elections at all, which increasingly they don't. Rocky Mountain Media Watch, a fine watchdog group that monitors the decline in electoral coverage, analyzed 128 newscasts by local television in twenty-five states just before the '98 elections. Viewers were four times more likely to see a paid political ad than a news story about the campaigns. A third of the newscasts carried not a single political story. The three major networks were just as sorry—

from Labor Day to Election Day in '98 they carried only 72 campaign stories (down from 268 four years earlier). In that same period, the nets carried 426 Monica Lewinsky stories.

This is the same media that runs editorials on Election Day chastising candidates for not talking more about issues and scolding people for not paying more attention and not turning out to vote.

The system is strictly an insider game in which the media and consultants not only know each other, they *are* each other—media types routinely cross the street to become consultants or campaign staffers, while consultants and staffers just as routinely cross the other way to become the media. Bob Beckel, for example, was a hired gun brought in to direct Walter Mondale's 1984 run for president against Ronald Reagan, a lamentable effort that resulted in Mondale winning only his home state of Minnesota. Shortly afterward, however, Beckel had his own political TV show! My friend and longtime political reporter Ken Bode said to Beckel, "Geez, Bob, imagine if you'd won two states—they would've given you your own network." Our laughter has now turned into reality, not for Beckel, but for Roger Ailes, the former GOP and Reagan operative-for-hire who has been ensconced by Rupert Murdoch to run the news division of Fox Television Network.

Those in this political class have turned politics into mechanics, turning off voters who would be a lot more interested if an election was about policies that might improve their lives. But, hey, shout the pros to the American majority: This is not about you! We don't even want you voting, because you're not in our databases, and when you vote the results are unpredictable and . . . well, messy.

It's the dirty little secret of today's money-and-consultant-based politics that a low voter turnout is desirable. This is because consultants for both parties maintain massive databases of voting records for every U.S. household. They know who in the household has voted, how often they've voted, how they're inclined to vote, and what their hot-button issues are. Since most people have been turned off by politics and government, and therefore don't often vote, the focus of campaigns is on the few who most regularly go to the polls—including union members, pro-choice women, and environmentalists for Democrats; antitaxers, antiabortion stalwarts, NRA members, and the extreme religious right for Republicans.

These "voters who really matter," in the parlance of the political pros, are the domain of get-out-the-vote consultants. They pore over miles of computer printouts, targeting their core constituencies as well as the persuadables and the swing voters. The *Wall Street Journal* reports that they are assisted in this narrowing of the political focus by specially designed computer programs with names like "Turnout Advantage," "Smart Select," and "Vote Predictor." As a Democratic GOTV specialist told the *Journal,* "You're trying to sort out the grass from the weeds, collect the most data and figure out how many voters you can get out of these little clusters."

To help motivate their targeted "base," both parties play legislative games in Washington, forcing votes on what are called "hand-grenade issues" that won't pass but will provide electoral ammunition. Republicans, for example, keep returning to so-called partial-birth abortion bans, prayer in the schools, abolition of the income tax, a constitutional amendment against flag burning, and piffles like majority leader Trent Lott's "Ten Commandments Defense Act" (don't ask).

With their key voters identified, the consultants then apply the mechanics of GOTV, including phone banks, targeted mailings, phone banks, door drops, phone banks, absentee-voting and early-voting drives, phone banks, rides to the polls, phone banks, voting-day checkoff lists, and more phone banks. The calls can be annoying. A Republican in Palos Verdes, California, fed up with all the GOTV calls to her in the

'98 election, proposed in a letter to the *Los Angeles Times* that political operatives be banned from telephoning without prior written consent from the voter: "I got five calls a day for a week, then one evening a call every three minutes for an hour and a half—and my number is unlisted!" At least she was wanted—unlike the majority.

In case you're under any delusion that this will all go away, I'm sorry to report that the consulting industry is so entrenched that it has its own magazine (*Campaigns & Elections*), its own Grammy-style awards (the "Pollie"), and—horrors—its own PR/lobbying organization, called the American Association of Political Consultants. Based on Capitol Hill (where else?), AAPC's mission statement lists such goals as "enhancing the political process and improving public confidence in the American political system," and "reaching out to involve and educate young people in the art of political consultation and in the benefits it brings to the practice of democracy."

Please AAPC, back off. Leave our young people alone. Do not molest them any further with your obscene talk about any benefits that this bloodsucking coven of consultants brings to our democracy.

If AAPC is not a clear sign to you that the ideal of citizen government is headed straight to hell in a consultant's rocket-powered alligator briefcase, be forewarned that there's something called the Graduate School of Political Management at George Washington University. "Professional campaigning is a multi-billion dollar business, which is becoming increasingly sophisticated and technology driven," enthuses the GSPM Website, apparently oblivious to the fact most Americans find this a deplorable development that needs to be fought, not taught. Nonetheless, they are churning out a whole new generation of political professionals (pol pros) bearing master's degrees that proclaim them to be proficient at subverting democracy. Among the socially useful jobs that the GSPM girds its students to perform are campaign manager, fund-raiser, lobbyist, and corporate public affairs officer. Classes include "campaign advertising and promotion," "issues management," "managing government relations," "lobbying the budget process," and "executive fundraising."

Gosh, think how great this country might have been if— instead of Jefferson, Paine, Washington, Madison, and the other citizens who came up with all that "We the People" stuff—there had been some GSPMA degree-holders to do the job for us.

THE NONEOFTHEABOVES

In the nineteenth century, British economist Walter Bagehot said: "The cure for admiring the House of Lords is to go and look at it."

The American majority has taken a long, hard look at the Democrat-Republican, two-party house of cards—and they are cured. You'd never know this, though, by listening to or reading the establishment media's farcical coverage of election results. "America Moves to the Right," screamed a headline the day after Newt Gingrich's Republicans won control of Congress in 1994; "New Conservative Tide," announced another; "Voters Endorse Newt's Contract," asserted still another. But look out! Only four years later, voters were stampeding again: "America Seeks Middle," "A Move to Moderation," "Voters Choose Centrism" blared headlines the day after the 1998 congressional elections.

Boy, the people must be exhausted after having dashed so far to the right, then turned right around and bolted en masse back to the center. One could get tennis-neck watching the electorate dart back and forth—except that about 94 percent of folks didn't dart anywhere.

Let's do the math (it's only one paragraph, so you can do it,

I know you can; come on, let's try). First, the Republicans. In 1994, about 22 percent of eligible voters went Republican in Newt's "big sweep"; in 1998, about 18 percent of voters went Republican; so, only 4 percent of eligible voters darted from the GOP. Did they dart to the Democrats? No. In 1994, about 19 percent of eligible voters went Democratic; in 1998, about 17 percent of voters went Democratic; so, even though the media pitched the '98 election as a "Democratic comeback" against Newt, they actually lost 2 percent of eligible voters from their column. In addition, third-party candidates got about 1 percent of the vote in both years: Therefore, the media-induced image of electoral masses surging here and there comes down to only 6 percent of eligible voters going anywhere.

Now, here's THE BIG STORY missing from the media's election coverage: The fastest-growing party in America is not the Republicans or the Democrats but the NOTA party—the *Noneoftheabove* party. All those numbers in the paragraph above come down to the startling fact that 58 percent of voters in 1994 could not stomach getting in the polling booth with either party, while in 1998, the Noneoftheabovers had grown to 64 percent. Need a chart to visualize all these numbers? Here:

PERCENTAGE OF ELIGIBLE VOTERS WHO VOTED, BY PARTY

Year	Republican Party	Democratic Party	Third Parties	NOTA Party (*i.e.*, did not vote)
1994	22%	19%	1%	58%
1998	18%	17%	1%	64%
SHIFT	−4%	−2%	same	+6%

Source: Curtis Gans, Committee for the Study of the American Electorate.

In 1964, I got some 760 votes in a race for student body president at the University of North Texas. That was about 10 percent of the students in the school, and I thought, sheesh, how embarrassing. And I was the *winner!* But these days we're electing national lawmakers and governors on margins almost as low as my collegiate election. Consider "Shrub's Story." The upwardly mobile Texas governor was reelected in '98 by what was hailed nationwide as a "breathtaking landslide," with Texas voters "overwhelmingly" endorsing his political management of the state. Instantly, he was propelled into the front ranks of presidential aspirants, based on this demonstration that he is "a formidable vote-getter."

Unmentioned was the fact that the turnout in his election was a dismal 26 percent—lowest in the nation. He ran against a Democratic party that had essentially abandoned its own gubernatorial nominee. Roughly 16 percent of eligible voters is all that George W. Bush could muster to stand with him. It's not so much that he increased the usual vote that Republican candidates for governor can count on, but that the Democrats had collapsed, unable to draw more than about 8 percent of the eligible to vote for them.

Bush was not alone among politicos in the last election who claimed to be exhilarated but were really just breathing their own exhaust fumes. "Democrats Exult in Broad Victory," declared the *Los Angeles Times* after the party cut into the GOP majority in Congress. Yet, the Republicans still controlled the House and Senate, and the Democrats actually had a lower percentage of voters going with them in '98 than in '94. Worse, the party-of-the-people continued to sag with its natural constituency of working-class folks—it only led Republicans among voters with a high school degree by two percentage points, and it lost among voters with some college but not a four-year degree. This is not happy news for Dems at all, since Americans with less than a four-year degree comprise 75 percent of all adults. Indeed, the party's only significant gain was among voters with incomes of more than $75,000 a year—a pool that includes less than 5 percent of the people. How many brains does it take to figure out you dive in the deep end rather than the shallow?

The media—clueless to the bone—hailed the '98 national vote as the public's demand for don't-rock-the-boat centrism. Again, the *Los Angeles Times*: "The nation's voters are looking for moderation...." Really? Then what was that Jesse "the Body" Ventura thing in Minnesota all about? Whatever you think of Ventura since his '98 election, it's clear that the people who put this pink-boa-wearing, shaved-head, kick-ass professional wrestler and Reform Party upstart in the guv's chair had something other than moderation in mind. But the political pros and media pundits gawked at him like he was a billy goat in a tutu: "This is the most bizarre result of the evening," gasped the election analyst at CNN.

Compared to what? Strom Thurmond and Jesse Helms still sitting in the U.S. Senate, despite being dead for years? A cockroach like Bob Barr and a purse-lipped, pucker-assed prude like Bill McCallom getting reelected to the Congress? Indeed, how about the fact that special-interest money gives incumbents such an advantage that house members are *four times more likely to die in office* than to be defeated? Isn't that bizarre?

Since Jesse wasn't a product of the money/consultant system, however, the media simply couldn't fathom his rise to high office. "Ventura's plain talk and populist ideas brought a near-stampede to the polls, many of whom told exit pollsters they voted only because 'Jesse' was in the race," marveled a *Los Angeles Times* election analyst, adding in befuddlement, "How exactly Ventura managed this is still being dissected." Managed? Dissected? Hello, pundit, please call home after your next orbit around Mars. The point is that Ventura *didn't* manage it—it's who he is, and dissecting that is like dissecting humor. More media: "Setting himself as outside the mainstream, he nonetheless came across as an 'Everyman' and had broad appeal across class and party lines." Good grief, get a grip. "Everyman" *is* outside the mainstream, at least as it's defined by those who draw the class and party lines. One more: "He effectively presented himself as a contrast to politics as usual." He didn't "present himself" as a contrast—he *was* a contrast!

Because he was unmanaged and outside the mainstream, not only did he win, but Minnesota's turnout was the highest in the nation at 60 percent. Ventura was especially strong with young people, blue-collar and Democratic voters, and mad-as-hellers who had not voted in years.

Jesse's election was the most publicized voter rebellion of '98, but hardly the only one. If you want a contrast to politicians-as-usual, you couldn't do better than Fred, a seventy-nine-year-old retired dairy farmer in Vermont. Fred Tuttle decided to run for the Republican nomination to the U.S. Senate against one Jack McMullen. The Vermonters who voted for Fred were definitely making a statement against today's politics of cynicism, which McMullen represented perfectly.

McMullen is a multimillionaire Boston consultant who decided he would buy himself a Senate seat, so he registered his Vermont vacation home as his new permanent residence in 1997, garnered the support of the state's GOP establishment, and set out to defeat incumbent senator Pat Leahy. Of course, to get to Leahy, he first had to hop the hurdle of the September '98 Republican primary, but Jack was spending $300,000 of his own money on the primary, airing a blitzkrieg of television and radio ads and running an all-out modern campaign designed by the best pros—so he was confident. Besides, his only opponent was some old coot in overalls.

Tuttle, who wears a cap that says "Fred" on it, had already had fifteen seconds of fame, having been the main character in an independent film called *Man with a Plan* (still available on video), written and directed by his neighbor, John O'Brien. In the film, Fred's character gets tired of being a broke dairy farmer and decides to run for Congress, because the job pays well. His motto is "I've spent my whole life in the barn, now I want to be in the House," and he has a bumper sticker on his manure spreader that proclaims: "Spread Fred."

Meanwhile, back in real life, Fred and his filmmaker neighbor were upset that a Massachusetts millionaire was prancing into their state with an overdose of cash and arrogance. To twit this twit (and to gin up a bit of publicity about their movie), they decide to enter Fred in the primary against McMullen. To make a wonderful story short, Fred caught on — and "Spread Fred" bumper stickers became a cry of Vermont rebellion against today's whole sick system of politics. Tuttle spent only $216 on his campaign — $16 for the filing fee, and $200 to rent Porta Potties. The portable toilets were an unexpected, out-of-pocket expense necessitated when a crowd of two hundred people showed up for Fred's "Nickel-a-Plate" fundraising dinner at his farm. Come election day, Fred drubbed McMullen, 55 percent to 45 percent.

He's not in the Senate, because . . . well, basically he endorsed Leahy, saying the senator was a good man doing a good job. Besides, Fred said, "I can't go to Washington, D.C. Too many people down there."

The cognoscenti don't like to talk about it, but centrism, moderation, middle-of-the-road, and status quo generally get a swift kick in the butt whenever people get a sense that their votes can matter, when an ax handle is put in their hands to smash the machine. Jesse and Fred were part of this recurring political phenomenon in 1998, but there were plenty of other ax handles available, too, thanks to ballot initiatives.

- Voters in Arizona and Massachusetts gave a resounding YES! to *public* financing of their state elections, crimping the power of corporations to buy government policies. (Arizona's initiative even included a tax on lobbyists to help pay for the public election fund.)
- By a stunning 66 percent margin, the electorate in Wash-

ington State said YES! to a "living wage" initiative that
effectively sets the wage floor there at $6.50 an hour, even
indexing it to inflation.

- In Colorado, an initiative to regulate the massive (and mas-
sively polluting) corporate hog factories that are stinking up
the place pulled a YES! from 64 percent of the voters;
South Dakota went even farther to stop the spread of these
corporate stinkers, with 59 percent of the voters there saying YES! to a constitutional amendment that flat-out bans
them from the state.

- In open defiance of the loopy national drug czar and of
demagoguing politicians who are denying the medical use of
marijuana even to terminally ill patients, voters in Alaska,
Arizona, Nevada, Oregon, Washington State, and the District of Columbia said a great big YES! to initiatives authorizing marijuana for medical cases in their jurisdictions.

Then there's Newport, Maine. Desiree Davis, thirtysome-
thing, enjoyed mowing her lawn topless. But neighbor Mary
Thompson didn't like it, so she collected 125 signatures to put
the issue on the November '98 ballot. A spirited public discourse ensued, including the printing by Desiree's mother of
T-shirts declaring the wearer to be an "Official Member of the
Topless Lawn Mower's Club." (Yes, if you were really a topless
mower member you would not be wearing a T-shirt, but it's
the political statement that matters here.) The debate was
held, the vote was taken, and Newport went on record 775 to
283 to let it all hang out when mowing your yard. No reports
yet as to whether tourism is up in Newport during mowing
season.

Now comes Election 2000, a space odyssey so far out that
even Stanley Kubrick would have had a hard time imagining
it. Fueled by an unprecedented level of corrupting cash, the
Republican and Democratic candidates disconnected themselves from the body politic and accelerated away from us at

approximately the speed of light, creating a deep and dark divide between what the people want from politics and what they got.

The result was not so much an election process as it was a burlesque. In an article ridiculing an "election" for the district legislature in Beijing, China, the *Chicago Tribune* reported that "candidates had been selected in advance behind closed doors—ensuring a satisfactory result regardless of who was chosen. Even the candidates seemed somewhat nonchalant about the process. [One] said he wasn't sure exactly what entity he was running for or even for how long he would serve. 'If I get elected, I'm sure I'll find out, and I'll let you know.' If elected [he] said his goal is to 'represent the people's will.' But he acknowledged he didn't know what the will of the people was."

This farcical Chinese election, though, was not that much farther out than our own space odyssey. Most of our candidates, too, are selected in advance behind closed doors, ensuring "a satisfactory result" for the moneyed interests that do the selecting, no matter which ones ultimately are chosen in the formal balloting. While our candidates generally do know what office they're seeking, most are as lost as their Chinese counterparts on what the will of the people might be.

In a way, our current system is more cynical than that of the Chinese, for it is much more widely hyped, providing all the trappings of a democratic process, yet withholding the substance. In 2000, we got campaigning out the kazoo—bunting everywhere, cheering supporters artfully arranged at every campaign stop, caucuses and primaries, nominating speeches, balloons and confetti, nonstop polling, an assault of ads, televised debates (do all you can to exclude third parties), campaign slogans and throbbing theme songs, an overdose of punditry, and of course Election Day itself—even as the system drew the ring of actual participation tighter and tighter around a closed circle of special interests. Issues of consequence to ordinary folks were ignored, deliberately avoided by tacit agreement of the two parties, or crassly used as ad fodder by candidates who will do nothing about them once in office, further trivializing the debate and putting more mock in demockracy.

An example of this mockery came our way in last year's congressional election when both parties conspired to keep an explosive issue away from voters. The issue surfaced on the floor of Congress in 1999 when Dennis Hastert, the Republican Speaker of the House, suddenly rose on his hind legs to make an appeal to help a group of American people that he said were suffering economic distress. He called for federal financial assistance, noting that these people have kids to support: "I am not crying crocodile tears, but they need to be able to have a life and provide for their families. They need to have a modest increase in their salary," the Speaker implored. Was Dennis experiencing a hot flash of compassionate conservatism for minimum wage workers, or maybe for the low-ranking U.S. soldiers who are so poorly paid they have had to go on food stamps? No. His impassioned plea was for members of Congress, including himself! He was pitching for a congressional pay hike, and he was so persuasive that members said, "OK," and voted to grant themselves a $4,600-a-year raise, elevating their annual pay to $141,300. This was done with no public hearings, with virtually no debate, and with the full complicity of the leader of the House Democrats, Dick Gephardt.

Having done it in '99, the Hastert-Gephardt duo thought, why not do it again in 2000 (raising your own pay, as you might imagine, can be habit-forming). So they did, this time by $3,800 a year. Again, no hearings, no debate. The party leaders agreed to a code of silence—"This is a member's issue," declared one of Gephardt's top advisers to an inquiring reporter from *Roll Call,* saying flatly, "We won't talk about it." The majority of Americans who have seen their own incomes fail to keep pace with inflation, might disagree that using their tax dollars to boost the pay of lawmakers is "a member's issue." But, just as the people were not consulted or allowed to comment prior to the two pay hikes, neither were they given a chance to express themselves politically after the deed was done. This is because both parties swore a blood oath not to make the raises an issue in the November elections, because "it usually is unpopular with voters."

This insidious system begs for ridicule. In January 1999, as part of the hype for his gubernatorial inauguration, which his consultants carefully orchestrated as a prelude to the formation of his presidential exploratory committee, George W. Bush included a pitch to the politically significant Latino voters by adding this slogan to his ceremonial banners: "*Juntos Podemos*," which translates as "Together We Can." Unfortunately, the *Houston Chronicle* reported it as "*Juntos Pedemos*," which translates loosely as "We fart together." For many Americans, Latino or otherwise, that's a fair summation of what today's political system delivers.

"I won't vote," Manuel González told the *New York Times*. A superintendent at a store called Sunny Fruits and Vegetables in the Bronx, Manuel speaks for the multitudes when he says, "Doesn't count anyway—the politicians do what they like. It's not a people's country. It's a money country."

Tragically for America, Manuel is right. He can vote for Bushgorebradleymccainforbesadnauseam and nothing in his life will change. I happen to think he *should* vote—go third party, write in Daffy Duck, anything to show that he's there, that he casts an American's protest against the two-party con, that he won't be run out of the voting booth by the bastards— yet, there's no denying the angry truth of his statement: The politicians do what they like . . . it's a money country.

What kind of "election" is it that does not address, much less treat, the needs and aspirations of the millions and millions of Manuels who, after all, *are* America? What kind of democracy is it that can be perfectly satisfied, even glad, that Manuel won't vote? Indeed, despite there being an open presidential seat, despite the control of Congress being up for grabs, despite this being the first election of the third millennium—more Americans bowled in 2000 than showed up to vote in the national balloting. The covenient wisdom of the conventionalists is that the masses simply don't care, or that they're a bunch of louts who *shouldn't* be voting, or that they're just happy with the job the Establishment parties are doing. The "happy" theory is the current favorite of the pundits and editorial writers of the corporate media, and all I can say to them is, if your IQ ever reaches fifty . . . sell!

The good news is that whenever and wherever people can find ax handles like Jesse and Fred—when they find an election in which they matter and can make a difference—they jump on it like a hungry grackle on a grasshopper. These periodic and scattered rebellions are the makings of a larger and very important progressive movement that is growing stronger, becoming more organized, and getting both more focused and energetic each year as the Powers That Be continue to distance themselves politically and economically from the majority. Like all democratic movements in our country's history (from the founding itself on through the abolitionists, populists, wobblies, suffragists, labor, civil rights, and others), this has been a long time coming, and it still will be a long time building. As usual when democracy is on the move, there are more naysayers than waymakers, more clingers to the status quo than risk-takers (even among progressive activists), and the media fiefdoms view it all with their usual clueless disdain, though mostly they ignore it or simply are too far removed from the people to get it. Nonetheless, a new politics is coming because it must, and it's already visible in such outcroppings as the stunning Seattle Tea Party in 1999 (when the haughty WTO got a hearty dose of citizen agitation), the inspiring Students Against Sweatshops movement that's on the march and winning victories on campuses across the country, the successful living wage campaigns being waged in city after city, the surging opposition to genetically manipulated Frankenfoods, the Internet rebellion against the corporate and governmental assault on our right to privacy—and in the rise in third-party energy.

RALPH

Michael Moore, the perpetual burr under the saddle of the comfortable set, said last year that "Bush and Gore make me wanna Ralph." Millions of voters did exactly that, as Ralph Nader's Green party candidacy offered not only a choice beyond Bush and Gore (the dreary and the drab, as Ralph put it), but also the first real chance in more than a decade to make a progressive break from the corporatist reign of the two-party duopoly. In explaining his decision to run, the legendary citizen's champion put right up front the "feelings of powerlessness and the withdrawal of massive numbers of Americans from both civic and political arenas," noting that "big business has been colliding with American democracy and democracy has been losing." He fumed that citizens are being treated as "a backdrop for political maneuvering by big business," and he declared, "It is necessary to launch a sustained effort to wrest control of our democracy from the corporate government and restore it to the political government under the control of citizens."

This was not the launching of a campaign, but of a political crusade. It was focused not merely on issues (though Nader is a walking-talking database of issues), but on the core matter of democracy itself, asking the fundamental question: "Who the hell's going to be in charge here—global corporate profiteers, or We the People?" The answer to this, Ralph said, had to come from "a fresh political movement" arising from the grassroots efforts of the people themselves, describing it as "a green plant pushing up between the two fossil parties." He urged that people use his presidential run to start building a new political channel for the long haul, advancing the cause in 2000 by establishing the presence of what he called a blue-green alliance, strengthening its national voter base, electing progressives to local and state offices, and developing the pool of organizers and other political talent.

Nader's campaign was not about getting him to the White House (he certainly spent no time measuring drapes and looking at color swatches for couches in the Oval Office), but it was about positioning progressives to be a real and independent political force to be reckoned with in campaigns to come, rather than continuing as a pitiable supplicant to the Republican leaders of the Democratic party. Ralph's run was bigger than a single presidential campaign, bigger than the Green party, bigger than Ralph—it was the start of a political coalescing for a disparate populist coalition that has been aggressive and effective on a range of progressive issues, but has had no unifying political focus and no political home of its own. Ralph had the personal commitment, the credibility, the *cojones*, and, yes, even the celebrity it takes to rally people for such a momentous undertaking, offering America's disaffected, disenfranchised voters the chance to create their own politics, to create choices they could be *for*, rather than always voting against, or having to settle for the evil of two lessers (as Dave Dellinger put it years ago)—or, worst of all, not voting at all. This is Politics with a capital P, and ultimately it is the only way to win.

Besides, it's fun! Nader surprised himself and all of us who've known him for years by actually enjoying campaigning. By June of 2000 he had traveled to all 50 states, raising issues, hope, and hell. Wherever he went, he would stand with locals on a picket line, at a homeless shelter, in an inner-city church, in front of a toxic waste incinerator, at a protest against a corporate hog factory—celebrating the phenomenal progressive struggles that local folks everywhere are making, linking their efffort to the larger, now global battle against runaway corporate power. "This country has more problems than it deserves," he would say of the manifest injustices of corporate power in every community he visited, "and more solutions than it uses," he would add, beaming at the gathering of creative, gutsy citizens fighting those injustices.

He was not running *for* the people, but *with* them, insisting in every locality that they had to do the heavy lifting, that they also had to run, not just him. "A basic function of leadership is to generate more leaders, not more followers," he said in a novel twist to politics-as-usual, which glorifies followers and reduces audiences to applause machines. Asked at one stop what people could do to help his campaign, he told them not to wait for headquarters to produce a list for them, but to come up with their own ideas, their own materials, their own unique ways to reach people and spread the word. Hearing this, one lady went out and produced her own Nader bumper stickers: "Vote for a *real person* for president!"

In addition, Ralph used the concept of fundraisers to put the people back at the center of politics. While he certainly held fundraisers (the money raised locally stayed with the local people to finance their grassroots organizing), he also held campaign *time*-raisers. "Who here will volunteer four hours a week?" he'd ask people at an event, passing out time-raiser pledge cards for people to sign. It was a way to value people, and it produced tangible results; raising 10,000 hours in a community will have a greater impact than raising $10,000. Nader's time-raisers produced millions of dollars worth of campaign activity that Bush and Gore had to spend their corporate loot to buy.

Every effort was made by the status quoers to quash this insurgency—including calls placed by Gore henchmen to some prominent Nader supporters urging that they back off.

* * *

To minimize the reach of Nader, as well as of Pat Buchanan and any other third-party nuisances, the hokey National Commission on Presidential Debates (supposedly an independent body established to govern the televised debates, but actually a corporate-funded front group of Republican and Democratic leaders dedicated to the perpetuation of the two-party duopoly) was dispatched to keep them from participating—even though two-thirds of the public told pollsters they wanted to hear both Nader and Buchanan in the debates.

Then there was the MasterCard moment. When Ralph ran a cheeky and very effective television ad last summer, corporate power took out its sledgehammer. The 30-second spot, created by irreverent adman Bill Hillsman, who had gained renown for his off beat ads for Senator Paul Wellstone and Governor Jesse Ventura, was a parody on MasterCard's "priceless" ad. Over video footage of Bush and Gore at swank events, the announcer said: "Grilled tenderloin for fundraiser . . . $1,000 a plate. Campaign ads filled with half-truths . . . $10 million. Promises made to special interest groups . . . over $10 billion. Finding out the truth . . . priceless." Then it switched to shots of a crusading Nader, with the announcer saying: "There are some things money can't buy. Without Ralph Nader in the presidential debates, the truth will come in last," and the ad directed viewers to the campaign's Website to help open the debates. The response from viewers was phenomenal, and the response from MasterCard International was, well, priceless. The financial giant sued Nader for $5 million, claiming copyright infringement. Oh, the irony! MasterCard, which had lobbied hard in the past for legal restrictions to prevent its own wronged customers from suing it, suddenly was at the courthouse with a bevy of corporate lawyers suing America's consumer champion. Nader responded that the corporation was taking its name "Master" too literally. He told them to lighten up and reread the First Amendment, which protects parody as free speech. MasterCard's "priceless" ads had been used in dozens of other parodies (there's an entire Website dedicated to them), yet the corporate jefes singled out Ralph's parody to go after with its legal beagles. It was a raw attempt to keep him off the air, even with paid advertising.

Of course, the corporate media weighed in against Nader with almost comically overwrought editorials and columns. One know-nothing columnist, James Lileks, took a hatchet to Nader, claiming that Ralph's Green party platform contained all sorts of damned-near-communistic ideas. He said he'd found the platform on a Website. Unfortunately for this "journalist," he got the wrong Website. There are two Green party organizations—the one whose nomination Ralph accepted, and the much smaller one that columnist Lileks found while surfing on the fringes of the Web. In his rush to vilify, Lileks had not bothered contacting the Nader campaign, which could have saved him from tripping over his own hatchet.

Leave it to the *New York Times*, the official voice of The Way Things Are, to take the most sweeping whack at Ralph, which it did in a June editorial. The *Times* editorialists huffed from on high that Mr. Nader was off on a "misguided crusade," which, of course, signaled to every anti-Establishment citizen that Ralph must be right on target. Nonetheless, the paper chastised Nader for "engaging in a self-indulgent exercise"—never mind that Ralph is the least self-indulgent person on the political planet. How more self-indulgent can you get than, say, George W. Bush's entire life, or than the totally self-interested corporate powers that bought the agendas of the Big Two parties? Then the *Times* went from huffing to puffing, decreeing that "there is no driving logic for a third-party candidacy this year" and that "the public deserves to see the major party candidates compete on an uncluttered playing field." Oh, I see now—Ralph, his supporters, and his issues are "clutter." It's good to be clear on how we're viewed by the cognoscenti from their perches of power. As for the paper's curious notion that "the public deserves" to have been left alone with Bush-Gore in 2000, I agree with progressive columnist Norman Solomon who asked, "What did we do to deserve this?"

From the vantage point of Labor Day 2000, which is when I am writing this, it is impossible to know how Nader's candidacy will fare on Election Day, two months hence. Early signs are positive—big crowds, genuine enthusiasm, strong support from a long list of mavericks and progressive risk takers (from Michael Moore to Granny D, Barbara Ehrenreich to Willie Nelson, Susan Sarandon to Randall Robinson, Studs Terkel to Bonnie Raitt, Ben Cohen to Linda Ronstadt), 8 percent in national polls (double digits in California, New York, Oregon, Michigan), some decent media coverage, terrific response to direct mail fundraising, on the ballot in 44 states, etc. Yet giant unknowns persist—can he get into any of the debates with Bush and Gore, will the activist students rally 'round and take up the electoral cause, will on-the-fence leaders of some of the national progressive organizations suck it up and get into the fray ("I love Ralph, but, gosh, I don't want to make Gore's people mad," whimpered one tiger who had gotten his start with Nader), will the disgruntled Jesse-Ventura-sort-of-disgruntled voters be able to find Ralph in the media coverage of the general election, and—a big one—will rank-and-file progressives who're sincerely worried that supporting Ralph might help elect Bush be willing to break free from the two-party trap this time and join Nader on the political offensive—or will they decide that the better part of valor is to stay hunkered down on the defensive, knowing that nothing good will happen, but hoping that nothing too bad will happen either?

Well, Ralph can't win, is the negative cry. Thank the gods that faint hearts like these did not deter others from trying to win in the dark days prior to 1776, or when the suffragists first stepped forth to be received with raucous ridicule (none of the big three suffragist leaders—Elizabeth Cady Stanton,

Susan B. Anthony, and Lucretia Mott—lived to cast a vote), or when other democrats stood up in our rich history. It's politically childish to expect to "win" in your first foray, if by winning you only count putting Nader in the presidency (though in 1860, in a four-way race, the six-year-old Republican party got into the White House with Lincoln, who took 39 percent of the vote). The point is to make a start, make progress. There's a child's riddle that asks: How do you get a rhinoceros to the top of an oak tree? Answer: Sit it on an acorn and wait. In 2000, Nader at least planted a political acorn to begin lifting the progressive movement up toward the top.

Nader's candidacy aside, America's democracy has turned dangerously dysfunctional. Whether or not the Noneoftheabove majority finds Ralph, it will not be dammed up for long—like floodwaters, it will find outlets. This is *the* political story of the millennium, not Bush, Gore, or whoever. Noneoftheabovers are the largest, fastest-growing, and most important political force in our nation. But where will they go? They are nonideological and multiideological (sometimes in the same person), and they've been somewhere between intrigued and inspired by an odd-bedfellow range of recent political rebels, from Nader to Jesse Ventura, Jerry Brown to Ross Perot, Jesse Jackson to Pat Buchanan. They are a populist force with the power to realign the old right-to-left theoretical configuration of politics, supplanting it with a more vital (and radical) top-to-bottom real-life politics based on people's desire to take their country back from an aloof and arrogant power structure (often referred to colloquially and collectively as "The Assholes").

Two things for sure: (1) This mass will move; and (2) it will be messy. It will not move as one body, certainly not at first, but the anger and aspirations of so many cannot be contained, so the most dramatic and defining political events in the opening decade of the new century will flow from efforts by Noneoftheabovers to assert themselves. It will be messy because there is no road map for a flood—it cuts new channels, over-flows boundaries, and swamps old structures. So far, it has been breaking out in spurts and rivulets, such as assorted third parties, maverick campaigns, and the term-limits movement.

But here's another messy reality that warrants reflection by those elites who imagine there will be no price to pay for having stiffed the majority, both politically and economically, lo these many years: The ballot is not the only form of political expression. For example, meet the militia. Yes, yes, it's considered politically proper to dismiss this skulking movement as a collection of paranoid gun kooks, zoned-out survivalists, and raw racists—but it's also politically stupid to dismiss such an explosive movement out of hand. The kooks, survivalists, and racists are there all right, yet the rank-and-file of many militias is made up of people we know . . . or once knew. They're the family farmers of the eighties and nineties who were suckered by governmental policies that got them way overextended on farm credit while at the same time pushing massive overproduction that busted their crop prices, then allowed the bankers and hustlers to waltz in and merrily rip their land, livelihood, and pride from them. They are also former U.S. autoworkers who saw Washington wink while General Motors dumped seventy-three thousand of them on the trash heap of global greed in the late eighties and early nineties, while simultaneously creating approximately seventy-three thousand jobs in Mexico, Brazil, China, and other wage-busting outposts.

These were middle-class people who did what the system asks: be skilled and productive, work hard, be loyal, have a family, fight your country's wars, go to church, obey the laws . . . go vote. They'd earned a slice of the pie, working up to $30,000 to $40,000 a year. Then, from far away, some incomprehensible force suddenly reached down their throats, grabbed 'em by the balls, and yanked their whole beings inside-out. Where was the system, they wondered, that had told them that if they followed the straight and narrow they'd live the American Dream? The system was over on the side, smirking at them and coddling the brutes who'd done the yanking. What does either party have to say to these roughed-up, bedrock Americans? Where was either Clinton or Bush in '92, or Clinton or Dole in '96, as hundreds of thousands of them were getting stomped? Silence. Also in 2000, Bush and Gore seemed unaware that these people are still out there. "Oh, yeah," they might have said if pressed, "I remember something on television some years ago about a farm crisis and some downsizings." Where did they think these people went? They didn't think about them at all. These are America's disappeared.

But they *are* there, and if no one is beating a political path to their doors, it need not be a surprise that they'll try to forge their own political paths, even if that means arming themselves for . . . what? Who knows, but there it is. This is what is at stake when the majority is shunted aside by the two-party system to become Noneoftheabovers. The populist movement is upon us as both the Republicans and Democrats narrow their attention even tighter on the affluent minority. But will this populism break out as a progressive and inclusive movement, as is possible? Or will it turn ugly, devolving into a reactionary, insular, bitter, brutish, and ultimately self-consuming rage, which is also possible?

At present, there is a huge hole in America that has to be filled. The top 20 percent of Americans—who own 96 percent of all stocks and bonds, who have 85 percent of all the net worth, who made 89 percent of all the gains in the stock market run-up of the nineties—now own the two big political parties. There has to be something for the 80 percent of Americans. Just as a shadow is not something, but the lack of something; just as loneliness and hunger are not something, but the lack of something; neither is Noneoftheabove something. It is the lack of a political say in America. If this pent-up majority is not to turn ugly, a new politics has to be forged that opens a broad new channel so these good people have a real say in the way things are being run and the way things are being shaped for the future. Ordinary people have to matter again.

GO, GRANNY, GO!

Bo Pilgrim is a big-time chicken processor in East Texas, but he wasn't known to the average Texan until 1989, when he committed such a faux pas inside our state Capitol that he was widely excoriated in the media as a political embarrassment. Now you've really got to go some to rise to the level of "embarrassment" in Texas politics, where we often elect embarrassments to high office just for their amusement value (I'll not stoop to naming any names here, but someone with the initials P.H.I.L.G.R.A.M.M. qualifies).

Bo earned his niche in the Lone Star Hall of Embarrassments during the state senate's consideration of a worker's compensation bill that he did not want to see passed, for he feared it could take a dime or two from his chicken-plucking profits. So, just two days before the noble senators were to vote, and while they were debating the bill, Mr. Pilgrim went to Austin to put in his two-cents worth, just as any ordinary citizen might. Only his wasn't two cents. He stood in a corner just off the senate floor, signaling first to one senator then to another, calling them over one by one to have a brief word with him. Then he would put a $10,000 campaign check into their hands, along with some materials about the legislation.

During the day, as the debate droned on, Pilgrim disbursed nine $10,000 checks, all to senators who had been identified as swing votes on the issue. One senator rejected Bo's offering outright, and another spoiled the party by not only returning his check promptly, but also blowing the whistle, which led to quite a press scramble to have the other bribees explain themselves. One already had rushed to the bank and deposited his! Another said with a forced smile that, Golly, he didn't even realize there was a check in all those materials he'd been given by Mr. Pilgrim. And another, when asked if the contribution seemed unseemly, responded: "Unseemly . . . that's in the eye of the beholder." He kept the money.

The fun part of such audacious bribery is that it's not illegal! Texas being Texas, our legislators have never been strong for interfering in the free flow of money into their pockets, so Pilgrim's check-waving routine was technically legal. Still, it was tacky, and the news about Bo and his Little Bo-Peeps set off a full round of indignant editorials and stern scoldings by the media and assorted Establishmentarians. However, the real embarrassment was not that money had changed hands over a legislative vote, but that it had been handled so sloppily. "Goodgodamighty," bellowed the professional lobbyists privately. "Don't this Pilgrim boy know how to play the game? You deliver the check before or after the vote, you dummy, *not during it*, and damn sure not on the floor of the senate with God and the Associated Press watching the whole damned deal go down. We need to take up a collection and buy Bo a brain cell." All in all, it was an edifying moment in Texas civics for the schoolchildren of our state.

The embarrassment of Bo Pilgrim came back to me in early January 1999, when I first heard about quite another kind of pilgrim. Doris Haddock is her name, known to her family and now to countless numbers of us who have been touched by her great spirit, as Granny D.

At eighty-nine years of age, she embarked on an extraordinary pilgrimage. Beginning New Year's Day of that year at the Rose Bowl Parade in Pasadena, California, she set out to walk the entire breadth of this great country, all thirty-two hundred miles of it, to the nation's capital. This was not a fitness feat she was striving for, but a political feat of prodigious proportions. Her mission was nothing less than to put a stop to today's uptown Bo Pilgrims—the slick, suave, sophisticated versions of the chicken plucker, the ones in the corporate suites and lobbying offices who are using their checkbooks to buy legislation, too, and—through their massive soft-money contributions, PACs, bundled checks, and other devices—to drown out the voice of the people in American politics. "Call me crazy, call me God-sent," proclaimed this feisty octogenarian as she began her cross-country journey, "but I am on a crusade to create a groundswell for campaign finance reform, to eliminate the cancer of corporate money that's killing our democracy."

At least a few thought she was crazy—and they were in her own family! Actually, her two children, eight grandchildren, and eleven great-grandchildren ranged from supportive to enthusiastic about this idea of hers, but there was a natural concern that it was quixotic and not all that safe. Still, they knew and trusted her, they knew her seriousness, so they helped her do it. "I believe the people who make progress for us are crazed. You can't send an eighty-nine-year-old woman into the desert without thinking that," her son Jim told the Los Angeles *Daily News*. "But there's a difference between crazy and insane," he said.

Bingo! Thomas Paine was a crazy. Sojourner Truth and Frederick Douglass, too. Mary Helen Lease ("The Kansas Pythoness") and "Sockless Jerry" Simpson of the great populist movement, Eugene Debs and Mother Jones of labor—crazies, one and all. Yet these and so many, many more are the ones who've stretched the reach of our democracy, not the presidents, tycoons, and other "Great Men" of the time, nearly all of whom have fought ferociously to suppress the free thinkers, iconoclasts, political mavericks, visionaries, organizers, and other democrats—like Granny D.

Who is this lady? A widow who has lived a long time in

Dublin, New Hampshire, population fourteen hundred. She was a secretary and office manager for a shoe company before retiring some years ago. She is informed and well-spoken, polite, patient, and respectful of others. But don't mistake politeness for meekness—after all, this is the "Live Free or Die" state, and Doris Haddock always has been a reformer, and often an agitator. In the 1930s she performed one-woman feminist plays, so you know she's not afraid to speak her mind.

In 1960 she took on her first national crusade. It was against an insane scheme by Edward Teller, father of the H-bomb, to use thermonuclear weapons to (hold your breath now) dig canals. Like the Panama Canal, only he figured nuclear blasting could reengineer the landscape all over the planet. All he needed was a chance to show his stuff. Through her church, Doris and her husband, Jim, learned that Teller had targeted a place that, ironically, was named Point Hope, way up in northwest Alaska, inside the Arctic Circle. It was a remote village of poor and powerless Eskimos, and Teller planned to demonstrate the efficacy of his nuclear relandscaping dream by detonating six bombs to create an artificial harbor there. Never mind that the Eskimos wanted neither the harbor nor the radiation that would result.

Doris was determined that this brilliant idiot had to be stopped. With Jim, five other people, and a really big dog crammed into a VW minibus, she took off for Point Hope. This is a terrific tale (check the 1993 book *The Firecracker Boys* by Dan O'Neill), but I'll flip to the ending for you: Doris and her hardy band of Volkswagen activists succeeded in stopping Teller after a three-year campaign that went all the way to JFK in the White House—a result that no one outside her group would've thought possible. Granny D might be idealistic, but she's no naïf when it comes to taking on the system.

Why walk? Because of Jack Kerouac, Willie Nelson, Mildred Norman, and an old man on the road. And because she doesn't have much time left. In January 1998, not long after her best friend had died, Doris was being driven by her son to see her sister in Florida. Along the way, in a melancholy mood, she noticed an old man standing by the highway as they roared past. He was "wearing a black watch cap and a full-length Macintosh, leaning against his cane," she later wrote in a personal remembrance. "He was miles and miles from any town or house. 'What's he doing way out here?' I asked my son, Jim. 'He's on the road again, mother,' he replied." She and Jim then talked for a while about the road, about Kerouac's book and Willie's song. "It occurred to me that I should go on the road for the political issue I cared most about: campaign reform." This had been her crusade recently in Dublin, where she had been speaking out and getting signatures for Common Cause's petition drive to pressure Congress on the issue. "I looked at my son as he drove us along," she writes, "and I knew I was about to change our lives when I spoke. I told him that I would walk across the U.S. for campaign finance reform. I said I would talk about how our democracy is being purchased from underneath us. I would help round up votes for reform in Congress."

"Oh, boy," sighed Jim.

Shortly after, Jim went from sighing to coaching, realizing that his mother was determined to do it and had to be prepared. To walk across America in a year required doing 10 miles a day. So she began training on the streets and hills of Dublin, working her way up to 10 miles while carrying a 25-pound backpack. What a sight! Then eighty-eight, five feet tall, stooped a bit from the years—she would walk and walk, sometimes spending the night sleeping on the ground, getting used to spending a year on the road. She learned about another remarkable woman, named Mildred Norman, who had walked seven times across the country during the McCarthy period and the Cold War, talking about the need for peace. Mildred began each of her treks by walking in the Rose

Bowl Parade, but when the parade stopped, she just kept going. Her plan was simple—walk until given shelter, fast until given food. The simplicity of it appealed to Doris, so she adopted this basic plan.

Working with an auto club, she mapped out a route, which a geologist acquaintance revised to avoid the cold and any steep climbs. Jim got airline tickets to fly them to L.A., and daughter Betty got a cell phone for her. She decided she needed a road name, too, and she chose Granny D, which one of her granddaughters always had called her. She was ready.

On Christmas day, she and Jim flew nonstop to the West Coast. She had a window seat and gazed out on America for five hours. "It is a very large place we have here," she said to herself.

Staying in Santa Monica, she went down to the beach, because she wanted to wade a bit in the Pacific waters. As she did, she thought, "I'm going to walk over to the East and put my feet in the Atlantic." It was a calming way to simplify the enormity of what lay just ahead. There were a lot of people on the beach that morning, so she decided to practice her technique for getting signatures on her petitions. It was her plan as she traversed the country to sign up as many ordinary Americans as possible on a simple, straightforward petition. "We the People of the United States Beseech Our Government to Enact With All Speed Meaningful Campaign Finance Reform." The petitions would put the lie to the claim by pundits and politicians that the people don't care about reforming the corrupt system. But as she stood there, offering her petitions, no one stopped. "An old woman at the beach is evidently quite easy to walk by," she later wrote—"but they were all polite."

A young woman who had been watching came over and asked Granny what reform meant to her. She explained, and the woman sighed, then offered a bit of advice. She said she thought at first that Granny D was talking about a local issue, so people weren't sure what it was about. "Add the word *national,"* she advised. "Say national campaign finance reform, and people will get it immediately." Sure enough, the extra word was all that was needed. People stopped to sign, and the helpful young woman stayed on for a while as Granny's barker: "This woman is walking across the United States for national campaign finance reform. Support her by signing her petition." It was the first of countless encounters with the wonderful people of America who do indeed care very much about reform and would lend helping hands to Granny D for the next fourteen months. On January 1, she put on her special reinforced corset for her back, her hiking boots with steel supports, her orange vest proclaiming "Granny D—Pilgrim for Campaign Finance Reform," her backpack, and her floppy, broadbrimmed straw hat—then she followed the Parade of Roses along its route until it ended at Sierra Madre Boulevard . . . and Granny kept going east.

She was never alone. Stepping out of Los Angeles with her the first day was Ken Hechler, himself eighty-four years old. Once a speechwriter for Harry Truman, Hechler is a terrific, hell-raising political leader and reformer from West Virginia, having served as its representative in Congress and presently serving as its secretary of state. He had seen a brief item about Doris Haddock's intention to walk for reform, and he decided to help her—he has walked with her for some stretch of the road in every state. Ken also was running for Congress in 2000—"If Granny can walk at eighty-nine, I can run at eighty-four," he told me.

Common Cause also adopted Granny, notifying its membership all along the route that she was headed their way. So Common Causers were there at the start—Ralph and Maria Langley, a retired couple from Upland, California, who showed up in their Cadillac to escort her across the state and into the Mojave Desert. They would drive alongside her as she walked in the mornings, then drive ahead of her while she rested in the afternoons to alert the media and local officials in the next town that "Granny Is Coming!" It was hard traveling at first, for the press coverage was sparse, the helpers few in number (though strong in energy and heart), and the road was ever so long. "At some level, I thought the whole thing was ridiculous," Doris confided.

But things quickly picked up as people heard about her. That's all it took—let people know that some woman is on the road fighting the Washington bribe artists, and they'll say, "Where do I sign up?" The first big media break was Michael Coit's article in the Los Angeles *Daily News*, which went on the AP wire and put Granny's trek on the national radar. That's how I learned about her. My *Chat & Chew* radio talk show began on January 14 to have a weekly chat with Granny D, usually via her trusty cell phone, and we've continued with her for the whole trip. Not only was she a delight for our listeners, but they were thrilled to learn that she would be passing through their town, and they turned out to welcome her, walk with her, put her up for the night, buy her a hot meal, arrange for her to speak to local groups, circulate her petitions, and generally be a part of this gutsy lady's pilgrimage.

The routine was for her to be up and out early (6 A.M. in the summer months, to try beating the worst of the heat), walk the 10 miles of the day (taking rests as she needed them), mark the spot where she left off, then be driven by volunteers for a lunch, nap, event, or whatever people had arranged for her in a nearby town. After an overnight in a home, B&B, motel, or the best deal she could get, she'd be driven out to her marker the next morning to start another 10-mile leg. No fudging for Granny—her odometer is true.

What a trip. Cars, pickups, and eighteen-wheelers would honk at her little group; some would stop to sign the petition or join the troupe for a while; "Go, Granny, Go!" became the common greeting; mayors and high school bands would meet her at the city limits; parents brought their children out to walk with her; town after town proclaimed "Granny D Day";

she got enough keys to the city to start a locksmith shop; she was welcomed into a Tucson biker bar (where she was told that the word would be spread among bikers to keep an eye out for her on the road and assure her safe passage); she lectured at colleges, rode in rodeo processions, threw out the first pitch in a minor league baseball game, spoke from the steps of state Capitols, got blown down a couple of times by the wind in West Texas, did innumerable interviews, and, among other sights, she saw a rattlesnake.

Not all snakes are in the wild, though. Some are in the U.S. Senate. One of the most fun moments came early in the journey, in front of the Phoenix office of Senator Jon Kyl. This Republican has been a vituperative voice against reforming the corrupt money system, and Granny D wanted to have a public discussion with him about it—not a formal debate or staged confrontation, but a civil and civic conversation. An hour would be nice, but less would be acceptable too. Arizona Common Cause tried for weeks to set up a meeting, but the senator's schedule was just awfully tight, don't you know, what with him being so very, very busy with many, many important matters demanding his attention . . . and garbage like that. Yet Granny kept coming, 10 miles a day, getting closer and closer to Phoenix, and getting more media attention the closer she got. Finally she was there, and hastily word was sent to her that the senator could spare ten minutes for a private hello in his office. No deal, said our crusader, sending word back that she would arrive at his front door, with the media present, and invite him to come out. She and the local media arrived, and our *Chat & Chew* radio crew also took our national audience live to the action via the cell phone—but no Jon. We imagined him not only locked inside his inner office with the lights out, but also hiding under his desk. "I think he's afraid of Granny," our champion said with a smile so impish that it could be seen on radio.

A side note to the Kyl episode: Common Cause alerted my

radio producer that the ABC, CBS, and NBC affiliates in Phoenix were not intending to cover her arrival on the senator's doorstep, since he had said he wasn't going to appear. Hello, Pulitzer Prize committee, has news judgment been outlawed in Arizona? Here's a money-drenched senator hiding in his own office from a little old lady who wandered in off the desert so she could ask him to give reform a chance. Wouldn't viewers find Kyl's hide-and-seek behavior amusing, odd, silly, impolite . . . *newsworthy*? We gave out the phone numbers of all three network affiliates in Phoenix and unleashed our radio audience to call them. The stations all came, and they ran the story on that night's news. Sometimes people have to free the "free press" from itself.

Granny just kept going. Dallas was her halfway point, and a local reporter, Jacquielynn Floyd of the *Morning News,* joined her for one morning's walk:

A morning with Doris offers instruction in determination, endurance, and passion for a cause. More than anything, it demonstrates just how far 10 miles is. . . . We were a jolly little parade when we set out from a Mobil station; Doris, her support van, a few hardy tagalongs, and a police car with flashing lights. Well-wishers honked and waved; one man showed up with a bouquet of flowers as a send-off. . . . And so we walked merrily along the first few miles, waving to bystanders. . . . Part of the party peeled off after mile four, and some took a break to ride in the van. . . . Between miles six and seven, I turned kind of queasy, doubtless because of the whopping dose of caffeine it had taken to get out of bed at 4 A.M. . . . By mile eight, my dogs were barking fiercely, and I secretly marveled that the human body could excrete so much sweat. Doris never complained— she never does, her entourage says—so I kept my mouth shut. Mile nine felt like a forced march at bayonet point.

Nobody but Doris had the energy left to lift a hand and wave.... We collapsed gratefully at the 10-mile mark.... I was footsore and exhausted, but proud of making the whole hike. But on Saturday morning, I'll be fast asleep. Doris will be on the road again.

The real story is not her march, but her message, and the fact that it resonates so clearly with such a broad majority of Americans. The need for reform really doesn't take much explaining, whether talking before a local chamber of commerce crowd, in a union hall, on a college campus, in a church, or with folks sitting in a booth at a café. Also, Granny says it so plainly—asked by a reporter what kept her moving, she replied, "I have eleven great-grandchildren, and I want them to grow up in a democracy." At that Tucson biker bar that embraced Granny, the manager (known simply as Kuzzton, and who is going to ask him if that's his first, last, or nickname?) said that he's not surprised that she could come in there and strike up a conversation with the regulars about something supposedly so boring as campaign financing: "Most of the customers know that issue real well. It seems like it takes too much money to get elected, and a regular person can't do that."

Not that everyone sends Granny hugs. Her Website (still operative at www.grannyd.com) has drawn some unpleasant communications from assorted boneheads, but the polite New Englander is more than a match for them:

BONEHEAD #1: You are a fraud. Your Website is a fraud. Al Gore, Bill Clinton, Bill Bradley, and you are all frauds.

GRANNY D: Thank you for taking time to write to me. Sometimes when I get up in the morning I indeed wish that I were a fraud! But my old muscles and bones tell me that I am the real thing.

BONEHEAD #2: [You are] a leftist.

GRANNY D: Yesterday I was a leftist, but this morning I was a rightist, because the traffic was safer there. Tomorrow, we'll see.

BONEHEAD #3: Get lost!

GRANNY D: Thank you for your brief note. If you knew how many wrong turns I take, you would be cheered no end.

Granny turned 90 the day she entered Harpers Ferry, West Virginia, and about a month later, February 28, 2000, she arrived at Arlington National Cemetery, right across the Potomac from Washington, D.C. She had invited me to join her there, and I jumped at the chance, for it meant I could be part of her triumphant entry into the Capital City, reporting live via the trusty cell phone to my national radio audience that eagerly had followed her across country. The next morning, Leap Day, with a troop (or troupe) of about 500 others who had come as far away as Alaska to make the last leg with Doris, we crossed Memorial Bridge into Washington, pausing briefly at the Lincoln Memorial for Granny to say a few words from the steps, looking east up the long national mall to her final destination, the U.S. Capitol. Rather than going directly there, though, the entourage detoured north to go by the White House, striding on past the U.S. Chamber of Commerce headquarters, over to Farragut Square (where Granny and I gave hell-raising speeches), then we turned east again, going straight up K Street, otherwise known as Gucci Gulch, ground zero for Washington's corporate lobbyists, the home of the very corruption Granny is fighting. More and more people joined our progression as we walked, and we soon stretched for several blocks, chanting as we went ("hey, hey, ho, ho, corporate money's got to go," and so forth), with Granny up front, cheerfully pressing forward (periodically she would turn solicitously to me to ask if I was OK—am *I* OK? I'm not 90 and I haven't walked 3,199 miles! But yes, I'm OK). As we trudged up Capitol Hill itself, we were joined by a flock of reform-supporting senators and representatives, and there was a festive spirit in the air. We looped around the north end of the nation's Capitol building and came into view of the east steps, from which presidents give their inaugural speeches, and from which Granny would speak. There we beheld a wonderful sight: Spilling down the steps and across the vast parking area in front were some 4,000 people, come from all over the country to join Doris Haddock, a citizen from Dublin, New Hampshire, at the conclusion of her long, momentous, and joyous journey.

Then we heard Doris, a 90-year-old great-grandmother, reach to her full five-foot height and admonish the powerful for the arrogance of their assertion that Americans "don't care" about Washington's refusal to stop the money corruption in our capital. "Along my 3,000 miles through the heart of America, which I made to disprove your lie, did I meet anyone who thought that their voice as an equal citizen now counts for much in the corrupt halls of Washington? No, I did not. Did I meet anyone who felt anger or pain over this? I did indeed, and I watched them shake with rage sometimes when they spoke, and I saw tears well up in their eyes. The people I met along my way have given me messages to deliver here. The messages are many, written with old and young hands of every color, and yet the messages are the same. They are this: Shame on you who raise untold millions of dollars in exchange for public policy. Shame on you, senators and congressmen, who have turned this headquarters of a great and self-governing people into a bawdy house."

Not everybody was moved. On the day of Granny's arrival, Senator Mitch McConnell of Kentucky, the gauche drum major of congressional corruption, snickered that campaign finance reform "ranks along with static cling on the list of issues that Americans don't think much about." In a gesture of his generous spirit, Mitch said that he would award Granny D "a foot massager" for her heroic efforts. Granny responded: "Senator McConnell has the anatomy all wrong. He doesn't understand where he gives us pain." Equally out to lunch (probably with a

lobbyist) was Senator Trent Lott, the Republican majority
leader, who said of Granny's feat, "She could do more for
future generations if she'd deal with issues that really affect
people's lives every day." Thank you, Professor Lott, for that
little lesson in civics. This from a senator who, when asked by
a reporter at an opulent resort getaway for $100,000 givers to
the GOP if he thought it was right for moneyed interests to be
able to buy such exclusive access to top lawmakers, responded:
"I think for them to have the opportunity to do that is the
American way."

Doris didn't retire, as she certainly had earned the right to
do, after her cross-country achievement. She continues to crisscross the country (though now by plane) to join citizens anywhere who are standing up to the corruption. Only two
months after her Leap Day speech, she was back at the Capitol, this time going inside the building with 31 other folks.
They were not a tour group come to gape at the paintings and
statues of Great Americans that line the corridors of this
"citadel of democracy"—they had come to *practice* democracy.
Doris had accompanied a "democracy brigade," one of several
organized in the past year or so by a creative, purposeful, and
courageous group called Alliance for Democracy that, among
other activities, practices nonviolent civil disobedience to confront the autocratic and avaricious forces in our society.

Doris's brigade went into the historic rotunda, under the
very dome of democracy, and there she did something outrageous: She proceeded to read aloud from the Declaration of
Independence. "We hold these truths to be self-evident . . .
unalienable rights . . . Life, Liberty, and the pursuit of Happiness . . . Governments are instituted . . . deriving their just
powers from the consent of the governed . . . whenever any
form of government becomes destructive of these ends, it is the
Right of the People to alter or abolish it," she read, as Mitch
McConnell's and Trent Lott's Capitol police moved in to stop
her from reading further, twisting her arms behind her back,

cuffing her tightly, pushing her and her 31 compatriots out of the Capitol and into a paddy wagon, hauling them to the station to be booked, fingerprinted, photographed, and put in jail.

Think of the irony: Under the laws written by our congressional leaders a corporate lobbyist can meet a lawmaker in the rotunda and hand over a $100,000 check, even while that lawmaker is considering legislation to benefit the lobbyist's client. That's legal. But it is *illegal* for a citizen of the United States to read the Declaration of Independence out loud in that same rotunda.

A month later, Granny and group's transgression came before Chief Judge Eugene Hamilton of the D.C. federal court, and she made a statement there worthy of Patrick Henry and Sojourner Truth: "Your Honor, the old woman who stands before you was arrested for reading the Declaration of Independence in America's Capitol building. I did not raise my voice to do so and I blocked no hall. . . . I was reading to make the point that we must declare our independence from the corrupting bonds of big money in our election campaigns. And so I was reading these very words when my hands were pulled behind me and bound. . . . Your Honor, it is now your turn to be part of this arrest. If your concern is that we might have interfered with the visitor's right to a meaningful tour of their Capitol, I tell you that we helped them have a more meaningful one. If your concern is that we might have been blocking the halls of our government, let me assure you . . . that they are blocked by the shameless sale of public policy to campaign contributors. . . . If Attorney General Janet Reno would properly enforce the federal bribery statute, we would see lobbyists and elected officials dragged from the Capitol building and the White House, their wrists tied, not ours. I would be home in New Hampshire, happily applauding the television news as my government cleaned its own house. In my 90 years, this is the first time I have been arrested. I risk my good name. . . . But, Your Honor, some of us do not have much power, except to put our bodies in the way of injustice. . . . So I am here today while others block the halls with their corruption. . . . But if it is a crime to read the Declaration of Independence in our great hall, then I am guilty."

Indeed, it is a crime. So, as absurd as it is, she and her hardy band were deemed "guilty," subject to as much as six months in jail and a $500 fine. However, in rendering the verdict, Judge Hamilton said to the defendants: "As you know, the strength of our great country lies in its Constitution and her laws and in her courts. But more fundamentally, the strength of our great country lies in the resolve of her citizens to stand up for what is right when the masses are silent. And, unfortunately, it becomes the lot of the few, sometimes like yourselves, to stand up for what's right . . . because not always does the law move so fast and so judiciously as to always be right. But given the resolve of the citizens of this great country, in time however slowly, the law will catch up eventually. So it becomes my lot to apply the law as it is at this time. Perhaps not as it should be, but as it is. With every confidence that, to the extent that it is lacking in righteousness, it will reach that point eventually, given the resolve of her citizens to make it right."

He assessed no jail time, no fine, and even reduced the usual $50 administrative fee for each defendant to $10. After the court session, Judge Hamilton met privately in his chambers with Doris, gave her a hug, and told her to "take care, because it is people like you who will help us reach our destiny." Some of his clerks were in tears.

In the better world that Doris Haddock is doing so much to build, she would not be arrested at the behest of petite royalists such as Mitch McConnell and Trent Lott. Rather, she would be brought inside the House chamber, escorted up to the speaker's podium, and from there be asked to speak to a joint session of Congress in a nationally televised address. I know what she would say, because she has said it again and again from sea to shining sea, and I've never heard a better speech in my life, delivered with such honest passion. Here is the speech, only slightly condensed, as she deliverd it in 1999 to the national convention of the Reform party in Dearborn, Michigan:

Ladies and Gentlemen,

I have been involved in reform fights through most of my adult life, but I have saved the most important for last.

It is my belief that a worthy American ought to be able to run for a public office without having to sell his or her soul to the corporations or the unions in order to become a candidate. Fundraising muscle should not be the measure of a candidate—ideas, character, track record, leadership skills: those ought to be the measures of our leaders.

It is my belief that the hundreds of thousands of our dead, buried in rows upon rows in our national cemeteries, sacrificed their lives for the democracy of a free people, not for what we have today. It is up to each of us right now to see that these boys and girls did not die in vain.

With the support of my dear children, grandchildren, and great-grandchildren, I began my trek and I will see it through. I am doing it to bring attention to the fact that ordinary Americans like me care desperately about the condition of our government and the need for campaign finance reform.

I have traveled as a pilgrim, and Americans have taken care of me through each of my eighteen hundred miles. If you knew, as I know from these last seven months, what a sweet and decent nation we live in, you would be all the more determined to raise it out of this time of trouble— this sewer of greed and cash that we have slipped into.

Friends, I have walked through a land where the middle class, the foundation of our democracy, stands nearly in ruins. Main streets have given way to superstores. Towns have died. Family farms, family businesses, and local owners have given way to absentee owners and a local population of underpaid clerks and collection agents. People are so stressed in their household economies, and in the personal relationships that depend on family economics, that they have little time for participation in the governance of their communities or of their nation. They struggle daily in mazes and treadmills of corporate design and inhumane intent. They dearly believe their opinions matter, but they don't believe their voice counts.

They tell me that the control of their government has been given over to commercial interests. They cheer me on, sometimes in tears, but they wonder if we will ever again be a self-governing people, a free people.

With the middle class so purposefully destroyed—its assets plundered by an elite minority—it should not surprise us that the war chests of presidential candidates are grotesquely overflowing. . . . The privileged elite intend to elect those who have helped them achieve this theft and who will help them preserve their position of advantage. That is what accounts for the avalanche of $1,000 checks into presidential campaigns.

Walk through [any] city and mark the doors of the families who cannot afford to give $1,000 to a presidential candidate or to a senator or two. For those who live behind these millions of doors we do not have a democracy, but an emergency—a crisis that deeply threatens our future as a free people.

The thousands of Americans I have met are discouraged, but they are not defeated—nor will they ever be. They know that the government and the social order presently do not represent their interests and are not within their control—that American democracy is nearly a fiction. But the flame of freedom that no longer burns in public, burns securely in their longing hearts.

It is said that democracy is not something we have, but

something we do. But right now, we cannot do it because we cannot speak. We are shouted down by the bullhorns of big money. It is money with no manners for democracy, and it must be escorted from the room.

While wealth has always influenced our politics, what is new is the increasing concentration of wealth and the widening divide between the political interests of the common people and the political interests of the very wealthy who are now able to buy our willing leaders wholesale. The wealthy elite used to steal what they needed and it hardly affected the rest of us. Now they have the power to take everything for themselves, laying waste to our communities, our culture, our environment, and our lives, and they are doing it.

What villainy allows this political condition? The twin viral ideas that money is speech and that corporations are people. If money is speech, then those with more money have more speech, and that idea is antithetical to democracy. It makes us no longer equal citizens.

Business corporations are not people. They are protective associations that we, the people, allow to be chartered for business purposes on the condition that they will behave.

We must look to whether we can still afford, as a people and as a planet, to give these little monsters a birth certificate but no proper upbringing, no set of expectations, no consequences for antisocial behavior.

We are simply tired of the damage they do, and we are tired of cleaning up after them. If they are to be allowed to exist—and they are indeed important to us—they must agree to be responsible for their own activities, start to finish, without requiring public dollars to be used to clean their rooms up after them. The era of corporate irresponsibility must be ended immediately, particularly in regard to the degradation of our political and cultural and natural environments, while we still have the power to act. Parents know that there comes a time when infantile behavior persists, but the child is too large to do much with. We Americans still can act in regard to the corporations we have given birth to, but not by much of an advantage. Our advantage will evaporate early in the twenty-first century if we do not act soon.

Friends, does it matter if it is Rupert Murdoch or Michael Eisner, instead of Marshall Tito or Nikita Khrushchev, who owns everything and decides everything for us, even if, through the stock exchange, we all have a powerless piece of this new mass collective? The soul of democracy is diversity, not concentration. Diversity requires the human scale, not monstrous scale.

General Eisenhower said, "Pessimism never won any battle." He was right. Pessimism visualizes defeat. What we visualize, we bring forth. Carl Sandburg wrote: "Nothing happens unless first a dream."

To the reformers, then: Learn optimism if you would have the endurance to succeed, and endurance is required.

Where to find optimism? Well, I have found it for you out on the road, and I give it to you now. It is this:

I give you the Americans I have met. Without exception, they deeply love the idea of America. It is an image they carry in their hearts. It is a dream they are willing to sacrifice their lives for. Many of them do. There is no separating this image of democracy from their longing for personal freedom for themselves, their family, their friends. To the extent that our government is not our own, we are not free people. We feel a heavy oppression in our lives because we have lost hold of this thing, this self-governance, that is rightfully ours because it is our dream and our history. But the spirit of freedom is strong in the American soul, and it is the source of our optimism and joy, because it will always overcome its oppressors.

On the road so far, these Americans have taken me into

their homes and fed me at their tables—shown me the children for whom they sacrifice their working lives and for whom they pray for a free and gentle democracy. And I will tell you that I am with them.

Yes, it is a long road ahead. But what nation can look at their neighbors with such pride as can we? Who thinks they can stand in the way of our need to be free, to manage our own government, to be a force for good in the world, to protect our children and our land, to sweep away before us anyone who tries to turn our sacred institutions of civic freedom to their greedy purposes?

On the road so far, I have seen a great nation. I have felt it hugging my shoulders, shaking my hand, cheering from across the way. I am so in love with it.

Thank you all.

ELECTION 2000: EPILOGUE

Politics can be a humbling pursuit, as I learned at the very start of my first run for statewide office in Texas. To gather a full head of steam, I decided to announce my candidacy a year before the election, scheduling a series of events in a half-dozen cities. In San Antonio, my campaign planning committee thought it would be an excellent idea to launch our local effort with a noontime rally at La Villita, the historic "old town" section of the city. Located alongside San Antonio's popular River-walk, smack in the center of the busy downtown, La Villita includes a plaza that can hold a couple hundred people—perfect for our rally and a perfect setting for media shots.

On the appointed day, I flew expectantly to San Antonio, was driven triumphantly to La Villita, and strode cockily into the plaza, where I was greeted by a teeming crowd of . . . eight. Eight people! There were twelve people on my planning committee! The only thing that saved me from total humiliation was that no one from the media came either. Never again would I bill any of my political events as a rally.

Just as I couldn't call eight people a "rally," neither can we call what happened last November 7th an "election," not in any meaningful sense. Instead, Election 2000 was precisely what I predicted it would be in the first edition of this book, written in the summer of '99 as BushGoreBradleyMcCain-ForbesDoleKeyesQuayleHatchAlexanderetal were just gearing up their presidential campaigns: "a money-soaked, corporate-driven, issue-avoiding, made-for-television snoozer, completely unconnected to real life." Sheesh. I hate it when I'm right about these things.

An election is not worthy of the noble democratic connotation the word carries unless it offers a legitimate possibility for a free people to choose among policy directions. Cicero said it plainly 2,000 years ago: "Freedom is *participation* in power." Most Americans today are not fooled into thinking that their presidential ballot delivers any participation in power for them. They know that they could vote till the cows come home, but choosing either a Gore or a Bush won't bend national policies away from servicing the elites toward serving the many. Either way, Big Money wins, for neither candidate presents a different direction.

This is the opposite of what we're being told by the official sources. The full peerage of the American establishment pumped its hype machine full tilt throughout 2000 to convince us that what we were witnessing was democracy incarnate, a glorious example of freedom in action, with the two-party system delivering what various media outlets proclaimed to be "high drama," "clear choice," and "the most dramatic election in U.S. history." Drama? Choice? Gore *v.* Bush was like choosing between Miller Lite and Bud Light—either way, mighty weak beer.

On big issues of national importance (and of genuine significance to regular people), Gore and Bush either agreed on their positions or agreed not to raise the issues at all. Among the taboo topics delicately sidestepped by both candidates:

- The job-busting reality of NAFTA, WTO, and other acronyms of global corporate greed.
- Wage stagnation, ever-lengthening work hours, and declining middle-class opportunities for most American citizens.

* CEOs fattening themselves while ceaselessly downsizing their workforces, not only in manufacturing industries, but also in service, high-tech, and other industries said to be our job future.
* The increasing corporatization of health care, which not only excludes 43 million Americans, but effectively shoves many millions more into shoddy, unaffordable HMOs.
* The ongoing (though largely unreported) farm crisis, with more than 100 American farmers being forced out of business each and every day.
* The crushing corporate squeeze on local pharmacies, bookstores, car dealers, travel agencies, and other independent businesses.
* Steadily rising tuition and fees at both public and private colleges, pricing most families out of higher education opportunities.
* Merger-mania that's shrinking jobs, consumer choice, and service while simultaneously raising prices in practically every business sector, from banks to telephones.
* The wholesale invasion of our privacy, not only by government, but especially by our employers, credit card companies, banks, and other corporate snoops.
* The genetic contamination of our food supply by Monsanto, DuPont, and other profiteers that collude with Washington to avoid having to prove that their altered products are safe for long-term human consumption.
* A critical shortage in most cities of apartments and houses that working-class people can afford.
* The continuing theft of our right to self-government by corporate executives and lobbyists who use their campaign contributions to control the governmental agenda and lock out ordinary citizens.

As for drama, hark back to the second presidential debate. If you watched it (and not many did—it drew the second-lowest viewership in the history of TV debates, barely outdrawing the Clinton-Dole boreoff in 1996), you would have been hard-pressed to figure out that Gore and Bush were running against each other. *Forty times* in this so-called debate, the candidates said to each other, in so many words, "I agree with you." Even milquetoast moderator Jim Lehrer finally asked in exasperation: "Is there any difference?" You could almost hear the clicks of TV remote controls switching channels in unison from coast to coast as Gore responded, "I haven't heard a big difference in the last few exchanges," and as Bush replied, "Well, I think it's hard to tell."

When they did disagree on kitchen-table issues that might have captured people's imagination, their differences were obscure, lacking any discernible distinction or visceral connection to most of the electorate. Both candidates went on tediously, for example, about the arcane details of their respective health-care proposals, but the public couldn't find themselves in either plan. This is because both were offering minimalist reforms, with neither coming close to providing the broad and bold coverage that the majority has said again and again it wants: health protection for every single American, especially for all children. Also, both were careful to channel their meek and miserly reforms through the existing network of corrupt, bureaucratic, autocratic, and avaricious HMOs and insurance giants. You might as well try throwing a lamb chop past a wolf as to try getting reform through these outfits. People could have been engaged and excited by a proposal for universal health coverage that would bypass these corporate middlemen and reunite us patients with our doctors, but Gore and Bush were too tightly tied to the campaign funds of these very middlemen to allow a whisper of such corporate heresy.

Instead, the major party nominees mostly gave us a silly noncampaign, treating voters as consumers of phony political events designed and test-marketed to entertain and distract attention from anything real. Gore planted that Big Wet Kiss on Tipper at the Democratic convention, wowing the media, so Bush responded by going on *Oprah!* and planting a smack on her cheek. Bush traded jokes with Leno, so Gore went on *Regis* and hypnotized a chicken—Ha! Top that, Bush-boy!

Sure, they *posed* as champions of the middle class. In September, Bush took to declaring that he had "real plans for real people." Like an irritating parrot that knows only one line, George W. kept repeating this as though if he said it enough, maybe someone would buy it: "Squawk . . . real plans for real people . . . Squawk . . . ." This from a guy whose idea of middle class is a family with only one Lexus in the driveway. Gore was no more convincing in his pose as working-class hero. In August, he went skittering across the rust belt on a widely ballyhooed Working Families Tour, promising to fight the money powers on behalf of "those who need a champion." Yet even as he spoke, he had at his side the Clinton administration's inhouse Wall Streeter, former Treasury secretary Robert Rubin, who had spent his entire Washington tenure doing everything he could to hold down worker's wages. This amounted to a huge stage wink at the corporate powers, assuring them that Al's sudden spurt of quasi-populist rhetoric was nothing for them to worry about, for it was *just* rhetoric—Rubin still had a firm grip on economic policy. If there was any doubt about the symbolism of Rubin's presence, Gore dispelled it by proudly and loudly trumpeting that the Wall Street man was the architect of his campaign's ten-year blueprint for the nation's economy. For working stiffs, this was like being told that Captain Hook would be in charge of their prostate exams.

Given this dismal performance, how can anyone be surprised that politics has become a mass turnoff? Throughout Election 2000, Harvard's "Vanishing Voter Project" conducted weekly surveys to track the public's thoughts on the process. The surveys consistently found that even among those inclined to vote, more than 60 percent of the people agreed that "Politics in America is generally pretty disgusting." In a post-election *New York Times* op-ed piece, project director Thomas Patterson wrote that "there was no week in which more Americans thought the campaign had been exciting rather than boring. Even in the final week, the margin in favor of 'boring' was 48 percent to 28 percent." In only a fourth of the weeks did people find the presidential campaign informative, and in two-thirds of the weeks people found it "discouraging." In the final week of the election, 75 percent of people said candidates "will say almost anything to get themselves elected," and 80 percent agree that the big campaign donors "have too much influence."

The only real buzz in the whole Gore-Bush face-off came after election day, when the whole country awakened to learn about dimpled, pregnant, and hanging chads—the byproducts of messy voting machines in Florida. At last, here was political DRAMA! The candidates had lacked either charisma or issues to ignite the countryside, but now we had procedure to excite us. Wow. It's a sign of how sad the race was that the star of 2000 was not Al or George . . . but chad. Nonetheless, a hungry media was on the story like buzzards on roadkill. Whether the country was to get Bud Light or Miller Lite in the White House depended on a few hundred wayward votes in Florida, and each blip in the recount tallies, each interim court decision, each bit of spin by the two campaigns was treated as Big Honking Breaking News that was exhaustively covered as though something had actually happened (perhaps the zenith of media absurdity came when a Florida judge commanded that all 1.1 million Palm Beach County ballots be transferred to Tallahassee for court examination, and a Ryder truck was rented to haul them there on November 30, prompting CNN, apparently a little slap-happy by then, to put a camera crew on a helicopter, follow the truck, and provide live coverage of the entire trip—that's right, *seven hours* of a truck toodling down the highway, a live shot broken only by CNN commentators and analysts periodically remarking on the momentousness of what we were witnessing, and by repeated video shots taken early that morning of men loading the ballots into the Ryder rental!).

Assorted pipe-smoking pundits even exclaimed that the thin vote divide constituted "a crisis for American democracy." This was not a view widely shared by the people themselves, who continued to arise each morning, have a cup of coffee, and go to work as usual. Like following a baseball championship series, people were cognizant of the hullaballoo in Florida, rolling their eyes at some of the shenanigans, but not treating the outcome as something that would make any actual difference in their lives, much less viewing it as a crisis.

AMERICA'S DISCARDED VOTERS

Meanwhile, the pipe-smoking pundits didn't give a puff about a far wider electoral divide that actually does pose a crisis for our democracy: *the missing 100 million ballots.*

These were the uncast votes of almost HALF of the American electorate, who chose not to enter the polls on election day largely because they feel they've been cast out of the process by a vacuous, cynical, and elitist political system that no longer gives a damn about their needs and aspirations. These mostly are middle- and low-income folks making less than $50,000 a year. While the media did innumerable interviews with a handful of elderly, Jewish voters in Palm Beach who had inadvertently punched Pat Buchanan's number on their infamous butterfly ballots, this massive bloc of 100 million-plus, working-class, nonvoters has virtually been ignored by the media. One exception was a fine article in October by *New York Times* reporter Rick Bragg. He had traveled to Cross City, Florida, a hardworking town on the state's Gulf Coast, where he found that, on the scale of pleasant choices in life,

Gore and Bush ranked right down there with a root canal.

With the election only three weeks away, local folks told Bragg they were turned off by both candidates: "I don't think they think about people like us," said 41-year-old Cindy Lamb, who runs the combination Chevron station and Greyhound bus stop. "Maybe if they had ever lived in a two-bedroom trailer it would be different," Cindy said. "I don't think either one of those men running for president has ever had to worry about where their next paychecks are coming from."

People in Cross City, like most people across the country, live paycheck to paycheck, and they're aware that it was Democrat Gore who was the insider pushing so hard for NAFTA, which has shut down factories and taken good-paying jobs beyond their reach. Aundray Dogain, at 31, is a shift manager at the local McDonald's where she fights the heat, grease, body aches, and low pay of fast-food work. "They both look the same to me," she said of the Gore-Bush choice, adding pointedly that no matter which one ascends to the presidency, "my life won't change."

Tracy Hunt, 25, is a manger at the Hardee's restaurant, and he echoed Aundray's take on the two candidates: "It doesn't really matter. That's the harsh reality." He noted with disgust that both had crowed about being for working families like his, but Tracy wasn't buying it, because he'd heard it all before: "They say they care. This is just to get in. This time next year, it'll be a different ballgame."

As a punctuation point to the widening chasm between political land and reality land, Cindy Lamb looked at her station's gas pumps and said: "Yesterday, gas went up to $1.61 from $1.59. Those guys don't worry about things like that, but it's a lot."

People like Cindy, Aundray, and Tracy—the under-$50,000 crowd—make up nearly 80 percent of the U.S. population, yet exit polls on November 7 found that for the first time they've fallen to less than half of the voting population. As the "New

Democrats" (embodied by Clinton, Gore, and Lieberman) have jerked the Democratic party out from under this core populist constituency, pursuing the money and adopting the agenda of the corporate and investor elites, the core constituency has—big surprise!—steadily dropped away from the polls. In 1992, the under-$50,000 crowd made up 63 percent of voters. In 1996, after Clinton and Gore had relentlessly and very publicly pushed NAFTA, the WTO, and other Wall Street policies for four years, the under-$50,000 crowd dropped to 52 percent of voters. After four more years of income stagnation and decline for these families under the regime of the Clinton-Gore "New Democrats," the under-$50,000 crowd dropped this year to only 47 percent of voters. At the same time, those who are prospering under the Wall Street boom, cheered on by the policies of both the Republican and Democratic leadership, have become ever more enthusiastic voters. In 1996, voters with incomes above $100,000 (about three percent of the population), made up nine percent of the turnout; this year, they were 15 percent of the turnout. This rising income skew among voters causes both parties to push more policies that favor the affluent minority, which causes an even greater turnoff for the majority, which causes fewer of them to vote, which causes both parties to push more policies . . . well, you can see the downward spiral we're in. This is especially damaging to the Democrats, since these nonvoters are Franklin Roosevelt/Harry Truman/John Kennedy/Lyndon Johnson people—natural constituents for an ungelded, unRepublicanized Democratic party.

The pundits have puffed all kinds of smoke at us about the "legitimacy" of the new president, based on the Florida count, recounts, noncounts, and court cases. But no matter whether Bush or Gore staggered into the presidency, neither could make even a cosmetic claim to being the people's choice, for the one clear result of this dismal election was that *Americans didn't want either of them*. The close popular and electoral votes were not a reflection of evenly divided support, but of which guy people would vote to throw off the island first. Both "won" this negative contest. Let's do the math:

- 52 percent of eligible voters either did not vote or voted for third-party candidates.
- Among the 48 percent of Americans who cast ballots for Bush or Gore, there was an even split, giving each roughly 24 percent of eligible voters.
- But wait—a good half of these voters were not actually for the candidate they checked on their ballots, but rather were voting *against* the other guy.

This means that neither Bush nor Gore could muster the support of more than 12 percent of the electorate. *There* is the illegitimacy of the election process, and *there* is the crisis for our democracy.

How did the Democratic party establishment deal with this crisis of legitimacy and its own declining numbers? By blaming Ralph Nader. Partisans wailed that Ralph denied Gore the few hundred votes he needed to prevail on election night. Indeed, Nader polled some 95,000 votes in Florida, which prompted New York socialite and Hillary Clinton money-man Harry Evans, to blurt angrily, "I want to kill Ralph Nader."

Hold your horses, please. Ralph was not the message—he was only the messenger. The politicos and pundits were ignoring another set of election statistics in Florida that were way more revealing about the core weakness of the corporate Democrats. I'm grateful to Tim Wise, a Nashville-based writer and activist who dug into the Florida tallies and exit polls to find some stunning results that refute the "Ralph Did It" assault. The numbers show that Gore was the problem, not Nader. Start with two constituent groups that Democratic nominees usually win in the Sunshine State:

1. Seniors. By a 51–47 percent margin, Gore lost the over-65 vote in Florida. Bush got 67,000 more senior votes than Gore did. Had Gore simply broken even with this constituency, he would have won on the 7th.
2. White Women. This group typically votes Democrat in Florida, or splits evenly. Gore lost them to Bush by 53–44 percent. Had he gotten 50 percent of these votes, he'd have added 65,000 votes to his total—plenty enough to have put the state in his column election night.

Now it gets really ugly for the Gore campaign, for there are two other Florida constituencies that cost them more votes than Nader did. First, **Democrats**. Yes, Democrats! Nader only drew 24,000 Democrats to his cause, yet *308,000 Democrats voted for Bush*. Hello. If Gore had taken even one percent of these Democrats from Bush, Ralph's votes wouldn't have mattered. Second, **Liberals**. Good grief! Gore lost 191,000 self-described liberals to Bush, compared to less than 34,000 libs who voted for Nader.

Why would Democrats and liberals vote for (gag) Bush? Some Democrats were likely so appalled by Clinton's personal behavior and Gore's fundraising escapades that they flipped all the way to Bush, while others found no defining economic difference between Gore and Bush, so they voted on the basis of George W.'s (false) claim to be the integrity candidate. Some liberals noted that Bush actually has proposed less of an increase in the Pentagon's already bloated budget than Gore did, and some were so angered by the vice-president's atrocious record of selling out working families, environmentalists, and farmers that they wanted to give him the double whammy of taking a vote from him and giving it to Bush. In any event, Gore failed to close the deal with these voters—a fact that has nothing to do with Nader.

Election 2000 should not have been close. George W. was a laughably weak candidate—he is seriously IQ-impaired, his performance as governor was a joke, he was on the wrong side of public opinion on practically every economic issue, he was perversely proud to be the polluter's candidate, he was shamelessly without principle, he had the snide demeanor of a rich man's son, he reeked of special interest money . . . and the list goes on. Can you imagine what Lyndon Johnson, for example, would have done to this boy? He'd have swallowed him whole like a hush puppy and said, "Thank you, that was yummy, I think I'll have another."

All it would have taken was a real-life Democrat. But if Democrats continue to put forth weak-kneed corpora-crats, they'll continue to lose Cindy, Aundray, Tracy, and the rest of the party's natural constituency that now does not vote or votes in third-party protest. Instead of scrambling for a few hundred squirrelly votes in problematic precincts in Florida or elsewhere, why not light the political fire of 100 million votes now not being contested?

GOOD NEWS

In South Austin, just a few blocks from my home, there's a great, refurbished-but-still-inexpensive motel that personifies the laid-back, nonconformist spirit of our city. The Austin Motel's attitude is put front and center on its marquee facing South Congress Avenue, proudly declaring to the traveling public:

NO ADDITIVES

NO PRESERVATIVES

CORPORATE-FREE SINCE 1938.

For those of us who long for a politics that can make such an authentic declaration, we need look no further than the American grassroots, which is, after all, right in front of us.

An unadulterated, corporate-free politics is building where it matters most, locally, and it's spreading all across the country. This movement scored important and inspirational victories in 2000 that are models of progressive strength, giving us building blocks for the next time, and the next time, and the next time. Naturally, the corporate media ignored these victories.

CLEAN ELECTIONS. In the midst of the muck and mire of a money-swamped national election, an extraordinary flower was blooming in Maine and Arizona. These are two of the four states that already have passed initiatives providing for public financing of their legislative and statewide elections. Holy Moly, cry the opponents of publicly financed elections, why in the world would we want to give some of our tax dollars to politicians? Yoo-hoo . . . we already give ALL of our tax dollars to politicians. Under today's private, pay-to-play system of financing elections, the politicians who get elected by special interest money divvy up our tax monies to the fat-cat contributors who put them in office. For contributors, this system offers a deal that's just too good to turn down. Business 101 teaches that anytime you can put in a dime and take out a dollar, grab it! In the case of a state legislature, say, corporate donors gladly put up a few hundred thousand dollars to put their chosen ones in office, then in turn these legislators dole out millions of dollars in subsidies, tax loopholes, regulatory favors, and other governmental goodies to the donors.

If we're ever to get politicians to serve public need rather than private greed, we've got to eliminate this legalized bribery, and the cleanest, most effective way to do it is to provide public funds for all candidates of all parties who show a minimal level of popular support. By publicly financing election campaigns, we get the corrupting money out of the system, save billions of dollars in tax-paid giveaways now being funneled to private donors, and take back our political process from the bagmen. Plus, we can do it on the cheap! For less than $5 per taxpayer per election year, we can finance all the candidates.

But we also get an extra-special bonus with public financing—regular people can run for office again. By creating this common pool of public campaign funds, a school teacher, plumber, organic farmer, homemaker, restaurant owner, laborer, student, or anyone else (you!) can gain access to compete against the incumbents, without having to sell out his or her principles. Meet some people who took this route in 2000, running for state offices in Maine and Arizona, the first two states to make their public campaign funds available to candidates:

- Deborrah Simpson, a waitress and single mom living in Auburn, Maine, had never run for office, but Deb qualified for access to the state's Clean Elections fund, and took on an "old boy" Democrat in the primary for a state legislative seat. Unburdened of the need to waste time fund-raising, she knocked on nearly every door in the district, and defeated her established political opponent by 87 votes. In the general election, she faced the brother of the fellow who had held the seat for six years, but despite his name recognition and financial backing, Deb won by 250 votes.

- Marilyn Canavan, 68, a longtime advocate of campaign reform, had never run for office because she couldn't stomach the thought of dialing for dollars. But with public financing available, she ran, defeating Republican and independent party rivals who were financed by special interests. "It is a good feeling knowing I don't owe anything to anybody except my constituents," she beamed.

- Jay Blanchard, an education professor, was the first Arizonan to receive Clean Election money, using it to run a grassroots campaign and win a state senate seat. Running in a heavily Republican district, Democrat Blanchard was up against the powerful House speaker, Jeff Groscost, who was expecting to "ascend" to the senate, propelled by more than $100,000 in business backing. Blanchard had $27,000 in public funding, which as he said, "doesn't level the playing field, but it gets you on the playing field." In his case, being there was crucial, for a budget scandal blew up in the speaker's face, allowing Blanchard to trounce him. Had public financing been unavailable to Blanchard, he would not have run, Groscost would have been unopposed, and angry voters would have had nowhere to turn when the scandal broke.

- Henry Camarot got fed up with blowhard Barbara Blewster, a Republican from a toney Prescott district. Blewster's forte was making breathtakingly stupid and bigoted statements about minorities, yet she kept getting elected with the support of moneyed interests who don't care about bigotry as long as she delivers for them. They backed her again this time, but Camarot defeated her despite being outspent by $50,000. He notes that he would not have challenged such a heavily financed incumbent had it not been for the Clean Election system, which gave him a fighting chance.

Public financing is like getting a new transmission, a supercharged fuel injection system, and a lube job for our sputtering, clogged-up election system. This is blood-pumping reform—reform that matters, opening up the process and changing the dynamics of government. In Maine, there was a 40 percent increase in contested primaries; more women ran for office than ever before; almost half of the races had at least one "clean" candidate; the new system was used by first-timers who previously felt shut out, incumbents tired of the money chase, Democrats, Republicans, and independents; over half of the clean candidates won. In the legislature alone, a third of Maine's house members now have no ties to special-interest money and half of the senate is free of such corrupting money ties. Likewise in Arizona (despite a court fight that delayed implementation of the Clean Elections law and deterred many who had planned to use it), 60 candidates used the public fund in 2000, and 16 were elected, including 12 of the 60 house members, two senators, and two of the three members of the powerful Arizona Corporation Commission.

So effective is the Clean Election system that the money powers are doing all they can to crush it. Last November, initiatives for public financing were defeated in Missouri, where Anheuser-Busch, Hallmark Cards, Kansas City Power & Light, and the Missouri Association of Realtors poured hundreds of thousands of dollars into an anti reform campaign, and in Oregon, where a gaggle of corporate lobbyists financed a high-dollar media blitz that distorted the meaning of public financing, saying that it was designed to fund "extremist" candidates. In a state with 26 ballot initiatives, many of them hotly contested, Oregon reform forces were buried in a deluge of money, distortion, and lack of focus. The good news is that among voters who did know what the initiatives in both Oregon and Missouri would do, there was very strong support. Even better news is that reform forces already are organizing in both states—and elsewhere—for cleaning up the system. Again, public financing works, which is why it will be aggressively opposed by regressive forces, but this is also why it will be increasingly demanded by the public . . . and ultimately will prevail.

JUST SAYING NO TO THE DRUG WAR. One of the important realignment issues for American politics is the wasteful, fraud-ridden, money-sucking, liberty-invading, anti-privacy, minority-oppressing drug war that is so beloved by Bush, Gore, and the full leadership of both parties—and so detested by conservatives, libertarians, populists, liberals, and other people of common sense. In November, the people pounded the tinhorn generals of drug-war repression, winning sweeping victories in five states that held votes to free people from the loopiness of these so-called warriors. Two more states, Colorado and Nevada, joined the six that already have authorized seriously ill people to use marijuana for medical purposes under a doctor's guidance. The U.S. "Drug Czar," General Barry McCaffrey foamed at the mouth against both of these initiatives, but 54 percent of Coloradans said "yes" and 65 percent of those radical Nevadans approved.

Two other states, Oregon and Utah, rose up to stop the notorious "assets forfeiture" outrage used by national, state, and local cops in the name of fighting drugs. This dictum comes right out of the playbook of King George III and other tyrants, authorizing police to seize cars, cash, homes, and other property of people who happen to be in the vicinity of a drug investigation—even if they are not charged with a crime, much less convicted. Tens of millions of dollars are reaped annually by police authorities, who are allowed to keep the seized assets of even innocent citizens. No longer can cops do it in Oregon, though, where 66 percent of voters said "get outta here," requiring that a citizen first has to be convicted of a crime involving their property before the property can be grabbed. Even then, the seized loot goes not to the gendarmes, but to drug treatment programs. Meanwhile, in hard-core, conservative, Morman Utah, the vote was even more emphatic, with 69 percent favoring the initiative to require a crime before any forfeiture takes place, and with all seized-property proceeds going to the state's school fund.

The most significant turnaround in drug policy came with Proposition 36 in California, which at least begins to treat drug addiction (just as we do with nicotine and alcohol addiction) as a health problem, not as a jailable crime. It allocates $120 million a year to drug treatment options, including not only medical programs, but also job and literacy training and family counseling. This initiative is projected to divert 24,000 nonviolent drug users and 12,000 parole violators from jail to treatment each year, saving taxpayers more than $125 million in annual prison costs and $475 million in new prison construction. This helps explain why 61 percent of California voters supported Prop 36—a bigger percentage than Al Gore got.

Then there's the decriminalization issue. In Mendocino County, up in Northern California's "Golden Herb" district, 58 percent of voters rallied to decriminalize marijuana growing— Measure G provided that any adult can grow 25 marijuana plants for personal use. In an act of civic chutzpah, the measure also directs the county sheriff and prosecutor to make marijuana crimes their LAST priority, and it directs county officials to seek an end to state and federal marijuana laws. OK, you say, that's Crazy California—but what about Alaska? Having already okayed medical use of marijuana, this supposedly conservative state had Measure 5 on the ballot, which not only would have decriminalized marijuana use by adults, but also would have granted amnesties to people previously convicted of nonviolent marijuana "crimes." It went further. Measure 5 would have appointed a state panel to consider reparations for those who've been harmed by marijuana prohibition. Yes, it failed . . . but 40 percent of voters were for it!

The citizens are way ahead of the politicians on the need to rein in the authoritarian zealots who are trampling liberties, destroying lives, denying treatment to dying and suffering people, and profiteering in the name of fighting drugs. With last year's sweeping victories, 17 out of 19 reform initiatives have passed around the country in the last four years.

LIVING WAGE. 2000 was a very good year for proponents of restoring some fundamental fairness to America's wage scale, with Denver, San Fernando, Omaha, Toledo, Alexandria, Cleveland, St. Louis, San Francisco, Eau Claire (county), Berkeley, and Santa Cruz raising to 53 the number of places adopting a "living wage" standard. This rapidly spreading grassroots phenomenon is grounded in the proposition that full-time work ought to lift employees above the poverty level and provide basic health-care coverage. But the greatest victory last year was a "negative win" in Santa Monica, where voters absolutely stomped on an *anti*–living wage initiative.

With a cynicism deeper and darker than the Pacific Ocean's Mariana Trench, luxury hotel owners in this Southern California beach city attempted to dupe voters with a corporate stealth campaign that would have outlawed living wage laws affecting them. In an Orwellian example of doublespeak, the hoteliers called themselves "Santa Monicans for a Living Wage," and put forth Measure KK that would require corporations receiving city contracts to pay their employees $8.32 an hour. The deception in this corporate-backed maneuver (they hired signature gatherers to sneak their initiative onto the November ballot) is that while the hotels receive millions of dollars worth of city-financed benefits, they don't have any direct city contracts, so they would be exempt. Only 62 employees in all of Santa Monica would have been affected by KK! Meanwhile, inside the language of the initiative was a provision that would have blocked the city council from enacting any broader ordinance covering the booming hotels and upscale restaurants along Santa Monica's two-mile coastline.

Leading the charge was the posh Loew's Santa Monica Beach Hotel—a property owned by one of Al Gore's top money men, Jonathan Tisch of New York. The Loew's operation pumped $325,000 into Measure KK, with another $350,000 coming from the Edward Thomas Companies, owners of the exclusive Shutters on the Beach and Casa Del Mar hotels. In all, the tourist titans who profit on the backs of low-wage workers put a million bucks into pulling off this voter scam.

Real living-wage proponents were caught off guard, but once they were aware of the corporate end run, they jumped all over KK. "What it ended up doing in the end," said one grassroots leader, "was pissing off the community." Even though they were outspent five to one, they launched a one-on-one campaign to talk personally with 16,000 voters. "What we're aiming for is a resounding 'no,' something so definite that no other big business in the country will use this tactic," said Madeline Janis-Aparicio, local leader of the people's forces on this issue. Not only did the people succeed, they routed the forces of greed so thoroughly that the corporate coalition quietly "suspended activities" of KK a week before the election. Ultimately, nearly eight out of ten Santa Monicans said no to the initiative, the trickery, and the profiteers. "It was meant to dupe the regular people and they felt insulted by it," said local union leader Rene Talbott. "It's just mean-spirited. You don't need to have profit with exploitation."

WINNERS. We can take heart, too, from hundreds of victories won by hard-charging, unabashed progressives running for local and state seats, as well as such congressional successes as populist champion Lane Evans in Illinois, Rush Holt in New Jersey, Marcy Kaptur in Ohio, Rick Larson in Washington, Betty McCollum in Minnesota, Hilda Solis in East Los Angeles, and David We in Oregon.

Third parties gained strength, too, with New York State's scrappy upstart, the Working Families Party, having a great day on November 7. Despite having ballot confusion that makes Florida's SNAFUs look smooth, despite having their voting-line levers mysteriously broken on scores of voting machines, and despite having some of their poll workers harassed and even arrested on election day—the WFP drew more than 100,000 New Yorkers to their party's line. This is double what they had in '98, their first year on the ballot, and it raises Working Families to the fourth largest political party in the Empire State.

Greens also bloomed with the election of all sorts of local officials across the country, including city council members in places like Arkansas, California, Hawaii, and Wyoming, as well as assorted school board members, county trustees, parks commissioners, and even a Soil and Water commissioner in Des Moines.

In all of these burgeoning efforts for insurgent Democrats, the New Party, Working Families, Greens, the Labor Party, state and local initiatives, and other determined rebellions against politics as usual, there is a new pool of exciting candidates, experienced and trained organizers, fresh political advocates, and renewed civic energy. Here is our strength, gaining ground mostly below the media's radar, raising real issues and steadily advancing a new politics of substance and passion. At the level of two-party presidential politics, Election 2000 was an empty and alienating exercise, but the giant is starting to stir, and the possibility of having a national election that matters is not as far off as the Powers That Be would have us believe. Keep agitating.

PART TWO

SOME SAY WE NEED A THIRD PARTY, I WISH WE HAD A SECOND ONE

SOME SAY WE NEED A THIRD PARTY, I WISH WE HAD A SECOND ONE

Tolstoy's dying words reportedly were: "I don't understand what I'm supposed to do."

It occurred to me that maybe this is the problem with the Democratic party—it's been so long since its leaders actually included the *demo* portion of the party in their thinking that they've forgotten how. Not that it would seem all that difficult, but sometimes even the obvious needs addressing. For example, *Funny Times,* one of the most useful newspapers of our age, recently compiled a list of instructions that can be found on various packages and products, including these treasures:

- On a frozen dinner box: "Serving suggestion: Defrost."
- On the package for an iron: "Do not iron clothes on body."
- On a packet of peanuts: "Open packet and eat contents."
- On a helmet-mounted mirror for bicyclists: "Remember: Objects in the mirror are actually behind you."
- On a camera: "This camera only works when there is film inside."
- On a chain saw: "Do not attempt to stop chain with your hands."

Equally obvious would be a how-to instruction for building a real *Demo*-cratic party: "To have a people's party, go to the people." *Not just to the bean sprout eaters, but to the snuff dippers as well,* talking about the gut-level issues of economic fairness and social justice. For example, working people *are* overtaxed—the income tax is the least of it for most folks, who are socked again and again by grossly regressive federal payroll taxes, state and local taxes of all sorts, ever increasing sales taxes, and more and more "fees" attached to everything from plane tickets to using a national park. It's not enough just to complain that Republican tax cuts are a giveaway to their fat-cat contributors (which they are), for that doesn't do anything for the working stiffs who really need the tax relief. How about going to the people with a real populist tax-cutting program for the middle class, including a proposal to stop taxing work (wages), instead taxing international currency speculation and short-term stock market transactions?

What about the fact that the genetic manipulators, led by Monsanto, have messed with our food supply and with Mother Nature in a massive and most alarming way, and that our watchdog agencies have conspired with the manipulators to hide it from us? This would make a lively campaign issue, and it's a growing national concern that would allow a people's party to get on the side of the people. And while we're at it, why not start talking about the American government's dirty little wars—like its destructive, money-gobbling drug war that's been an embarrassing failure at stopping the flow of drugs but is spectacularly successful at stomping on people's liberties; or the war against the family farm, using both the actions and inactions of government to squeeze efficient, productive people off the land; or the war against unions, writing the rules of collective bargaining in such a way that the union-busting tactics of a century ago are back, and legal; or the war on privacy, using "terrorism" and "drugs" as the alarm buttons to allow all levels of police deeper into our personal lives.

These issues are part of the election that *could be* if we had a no-bullshit Democratic party that really wanted to stand up for America's workaday majority, kick Republican butt from coast to coast, and realign American politics for the next century. At the heart of this populist politics is the recognition that there has been a radical and totally undemocratic remaking of our economy in the past few years, deliberately wrenching it to serve the few, then pretending to the many that the changes are the result of immutable forces that have brought a halcyon epoch of prosperity for all. Political leaders of both parties, including Gore and Bush, are full participants in the pretending. But who are they fooling? The wrenchers and pretenders can put all the cologne they want on this skunk, but it won't cover up the stink.

MUGGING THE MIDDLE CLASS

You pay a price for going against your political roots, whether you're the Democratic party . . . or a boy of eight.

That's how old I was when I made my first foray into partisan politics. It was 1952, and a neighbor who ran an insurance agency in my hometown of Denison was a local coordinator for Alan Shivers, a candidate for governor. At this time, Texas literally was a one-party state, with both Democrats and Republicans confusingly (and uncomfortably) residing together inside the Democratic party. Your actual Democrats were backing the crusading people's champion Ralph Yarborough for governor that year, while your faux Democrats (Republicans in hiding) were behind Shivers. A scion of one of the Anglo families that reigned rather brutishly over the old plantation system of the Rio Grande Valley, Shivers was the candidate of the state's financial powers. Members of this money caste later came to be known as Shivercrats. It was not a term of endearment—a ditty from the fifties went:

A buzzard is a dirty bird,
A skunk a stinking cat,
But the dirtiest creature on the earth,
Is a God Damned old Shivercrat.

None of this meant anything to me at eight, though, for my attention was not on politics but on becoming the second baseman for the Tigers, my Little League team. I wouldn't have known Shivers from a five-pound roll of bologna. All I knew was that my insurance agent neighbor was willing to pay me and my brother fifty cents *each* to put some campaign flyers in the screen doors of homes for several blocks around. Since I was paid only twenty-five cents to mow yards, being offered half a buck just to distribute a satchel full of flyers seemed like easy money, even if they were flyers for some guy named Shivers. Only in later years would I learn that he was for the bankers and big shots over the kind of people that made up my own family and most of my town—tenant farmers, railroad workers, small businesspeople, and other working folks. Meanwhile, I had the flyers to get out and baseball to play.

It was an easy job until I came to a certain house on West Crawford Street. I went briskly up the sidewalk toward the high steps that led up to the front porch. It was when I started to take the steps that I first heard the growl. A very deep growl. A very serious growl. Instinctively, I froze, my eyes jerking up to the porch to encounter the biggest sheepdog I've ever seen—and one that was most unhappy to have me intruding on his turf. However, my daddy had taught me that dogs really are afraid of us humans and that I should have no fear of a barking bowser—just look the creature square in the eye and go ahead about my business. Despite a staccato surge of signals from my primitive brain frantically shouting "Run, you little bastard, as fast as your eight-year-old legs can possibly go!" I calmly recalled Daddy's doggie admonition, overruled my brain's primitive impulse, and proceeded to climb the stairs.

My foot had not touched the bottom step before that dog was down on me like a . . . well, like a big dog on a small boy. He knocked me down, bowled me over, sank a couple of teeth into my thigh, and sent me sprawling and squawking all across the yard, spraying Shivers's flyers hither, thither, and yon. Never has one boy scrambled backward so quickly, fleeing to the safety of the street and doing a sort of gimpy-legged half-run, half-hop toward home. I never looked back, having forever abandoned the flyers, the satchel, the fifty-cent payday, *and* Alan Shivers.

Call it what you will, but I sensed in my very being at that moment that the gods were speaking to me: "Jim Hightower, don't you ever again go against your populist roots for money."

Maybe we need a big dog to bite the national Democratic party. Maybe that would cause it to come to its senses and come home to its populist roots. Today's Democratic leadership—from Gore and Lieberman to the DNC—has taken the money and willingly become Shivercrats. As a result, they now compete with Republicans to win a plurality of the minority of relatively well-off Americans who vote. And, to appeal to this minority, they campaign and govern on policies narrowly tailored to benefit the few, ignoring or actually stiffing the many, which further shrinks the Democrats' electoral base and makes them ever more dependent on the money powers, which demand an even narrower focus on their special needs, which . . . well, you see the downward spiral. Amazingly, this suicidal strategy is the product of smart people (too smart by half, maybe) who seem to have lost all traces of street savvy. They're like the fellow who received this less than glowing performance evaluation for his work: "This employee has the full six-pack, but he's missing the little plastic thingy that holds it together."

IF THESE ARE GOOD TIMES, WHY AREN'T I HAVING ONE?

To build a new majority politics means (Oh, the genius of it!) appealing to the majority. Where to start, where to start? One place is with the truth—start talking about the *real* economy. How about admitting what the majority of people already know since they're experiencing it: The middle class is getting mugged.

"Mugged?!" shriek the Perky Purveyors of Perpetually Positive Press about Prosperity. "Sweet Visa and Holy MasterCard, Hightower, don't you listen to the news, don't you know about the leading economic indicators, don't you follow the Dow, don't you feel the *buzz*, don't you know, for God's sake, that Starbucks has opened its two thousandth store—you call that getting mugged?" America is a sea of prosperity, we're assured, and everyone can dip their sterling-silver ladle in it at will. Hasn't *Newsweek* magazine informed us that "pampering is going mainstream," that "massage is now for the masses," and that things are so good for average middle-class folks that their typical day now includes buying a $3 cup of mochaccino coffee on their way to work, getting a $35 pedicure on their lunch break, then stopping by the Sharper Image store on the way home to pick up such self-pampering gadgets as a $249 "private masseuse" back massager. It has. These are the best of times. We know it because we're told it over and over. Check these recent headlines about the economy:

Consumers See Blue Skies Ahead

Dreams Really Do Come True

Go-Go Growth

Misery Just a Memory

How Long Can Americans Keep Splurging?

Why Life In the U.S. Has Never Been Better

A Nearly Perfect Economy

Like a fuzzy blue blanket, this constant overlay of economic superlatives creates a warm feeling of national comfort, a sense that except for the odd poor family all is right in the jolly kingdom of America. The blanket of good news also shields the comfortable from having to address the possibility that there just might be something fundamentally flawed about globalization, conglomeration, outsourcing, and the other processes of economic rapaciousness that are loose on the land. "Who cares if a few people lose their jobs," shrug the PPPPPP, "there are beaucoup jobs out there, Bubba, *if* you really want one, and, besides, all that globalization and whatnot sure seems to be working for everybody else, haven't you been paying attention to the economic reports?" To punctuate the point, they always turn to the one indicator that's been relentlessly perky: the Dow Jones Average.

"WHERE TO NOW, MIGHTY DOW?" This was the Associated Press headline March 30, 1999, when the Dow closed above 10,000 for the first time in history. The media pealed with joy! *USA Today* enthused that "10,000 is more than just a number. . . . It's like Mark McGwire beating the home run record, it's like the calendar turning to the year 2000, it's like McDonald's selling its first billion hamburgers. It's a cultural milestone." A market analyst for Prudential went over the top with the Dow: "It's exciting. It's America. We all should get up and sing 'God Bless America.' " The *New York Times* joined the cheerleading, saying flatly, "The Stock Market surely is America today," which surely is the millennial equivalent of the 1950s comment by GM's chief executive, Charles Wilson, that "What is good for General Motors is good for the country." *USA Today* went even further, elevating

Dowism to the level of a mystical omnipresence, claiming that the whole nation "is riveted to every tick in the market" and "attuned to Wall Street," asserting that as the Dow rises, "a lot of people feel wealthier and inclined to spend more on cars, houses, and other goods."

The story of the Dow's awesome prowess was still reverberating in the media when, lo, it came upon us again, bringing glad tidings to all. Barely a month after topping 10,000 the Mighty Dow blew past 11,000—and once again the media was filled with tales of the nation's euphoria at this blessed event.

There were heretics, here and there, of course. *Newsweek*'s Allan Sloan, for example, termed the Dow Jones average such a hokey indicator of real economic strength that rather than watching worshipfully for it to surpass 10,000 or any other arbitrary height, we should "obsess over something more important. Like why Buffy the Vampire Slayer has blond hair and black eyebrows."

Sloan aside, though, the media and the politicians broadly accept that the market is God and that the Dow is God's own messenger, conveying the Word that when the Dow is up, so is America. Harvard divinity professor Harvey Cox, writing in *Atlantic Monthly*, observed that "current thinking already assigns to The Market a comprehensive wisdom that in the past only gods have known. The Market, we are taught, is able to determine what human needs are, what copper and capital should cost, how much barbers and CEOs should be paid, and how much jet planes, running shoes, and hysterectomies should sell for. But how do we know The Market's will?

"In days of old," Cox continues, "seers entered a trance state and then informed anxious seekers what kind of mood the gods were in. . . . The prophets of Israel repaired to the desert and then returned to announce whether Yahweh was feeling benevolent or wrathful. Today, The Market's fickle will is clarified by daily reports from Wall Street. . . . Thus we can learn on a day-to-day basis that The Market is 'apprehensive,' 'relieved,' 'nervous,' or even at times 'jubilant.' On the basis of this revelation awed adepts make critical decisions about whether to buy or sell. Like one of the devouring gods of old, The Market—aptly embodied in a bull or bear—must be fed and kept happy under all circumstances. True, at times its appetite may seem excessive—a $35 billion bailout here, a $50 billion one there—but the alternative to assuaging its hunger is too terrible to contemplate."

Cox then tells of the power that what I call Dowism holds over our secular leaders of both parties in Washington: "If any government policy vexes The Market, those responsible for the irreverence will be made to suffer. That The Market is not at all displeased by downsizing or a growing income gap, or can be gleeful about the expansion of cigarette sales to Asian young people, should not cause anyone to question its ultimate omniscience. Like Calvin's inscrutable deity, The Market may work in mysterious ways, 'hid from our eyes,' but ultimately it knows best."

Indeed, the theology of Dowism, just as of other religions, is dependent on a hearty dose of faith over reason. Cox quotes an early Christian theologian who remarked: *"Credo quia absurdum est"*—"I believe because it is absurd."

Especially absurd is the new insistence by fervent Dowists that Wall Street has spread to every street, that there has been a miraculous democratization of stock market wealth to the broad populace. Therefore, what's good for the market *really is* good for America. So you've been downsized, so you're among the 80 percent of Americans whose incomes have gone down or barely kept up with inflation in the boom-boom nineties, so you and the spouse are working three or four jobs just to try to stay even—stop your bitching and start counting your stock market blessings.

In a front-page headline, the *New York Times* trumpeted: "Share of Wealth in Stock Holdings Hits 50-Year High." The *Times* had done its own analysis of American household wealth—a measure that counts everything you own, including your house, car, bass boat, clothing, furniture, velvet paintings of dogs playing poker, your collection of those tiny liquor bottles you get on airplanes . . . and your portfolio of stocks and bonds. Good gosh, gushed the *Times*, people's homes are no longer the number one source of their personal wealth; stock market investments are! Strip off those old "Share the Wealth" bumper stickers, for the dream has at last been realized. As the *Times* put it, "The size of their paychecks aside, many Americans are feeling richer as the value of their stock holdings rises. . . . Where skyrocketing real estate prices once provided reassurance to the middle class, soaring stock portfolios now do."

Before you "middle-classers" dash out to buy a $250 bottle of Dom Pérignon to celebrate your newly discovered stock wealth, let's all take a deep breath and stand back from the giddiness for a moment. The *Times* rushed to disseminate the Good News about household wealth without applying the first lesson of journalism, which teaches reporters to answer the six most basic questions in a story: who, what, where, when, why . . . and *huh*? In this case, your household's stock portfolio is averaged with those of Bill Gates, Ted Turner, Warren Buffett, and the other 1 million or so families at the very tippy-top of the economic pyramid. These elites are among the wealthiest 1 percent of Americans and need a special bank vault just to hold their stock certificates. The law of averages is such that if you've got one foot in a bucket of ice and the other in a bucket of boiling water, on average the temperature should be just right for you. Likewise, the *Times* can claim that "average" households now have 28 percent of their wealth in stocks, without noting that most people have NONE of their wealth in stocks.

In one of the weirder incidents involving the zeitgeist of the Dow, one Richard Grasso, the chairman of the New York Stock Exchange, was helicoptered deep into the jungles of southern Colombia in June of 1999 to the village of La Machaca. There he met for an hour and a half with Raul Reyes, one of the top commanders of the powerful rebel group that controls better than a third of that nation. The rebels are pushing for social justice for the vast majority of Colombians who are impoverished, while the elites in Bogotá enjoy the good life of selective capitalism. What an odd meeting—there was Grasso, coming from the very pit of capitalism, still wearing his $150 shirt and the pants of his $1,000 suit (in a gesture to the informality of the occasion, he had tossed his tie and jacket), giving a big *abrazo* to this rebel leader, who was fully decked out in jungle camouflage. They had their conversation and, who knows, maybe even a round of s'mores at the rebel encampment; then Grasso left as quickly as he had come, later telling the *Wall Street Journal* that he and Commander Reyes had "talked about economics, capital markets, and how peace translates into economic opportunity for Colombia." Give Wall Street a Chance, was Grasso's Beatles-esque message: "I gave him a tutorial on what's happened in the U.S. in terms of this democratization of capitalism. One of the messages I wanted to emphasize is how . . . with indirect ownership, literally everybody in America is a stockholder."

★ LITTLE MISS ROSIE SCENARIO ★

If you are wont to believe the rosy economic assessments of today's authoritative voices, consider the following blasts from the past. These quotes show that there is nothing new about power elites who stand in the back of a wagon orating at length about how things are rolling along perfectly, while everyone in the crowd can see that the wheels have fallen off the wagon. Here is a sampling of public statements by the authorities of the day as the Great Depression unfolded.

SCENE ONE. In 1929, stock prices were soaring, media barons were hailing the prosperity of the Roaring Twenties, and the public was assured that there would be nothing but good times ahead:

"The economic condition of the world seems on the verge of a great forward movement."
—Bernard Baruch, American financier, *Financier* magazine, June 1929

"Stocks have reached what looks like a permanently high plateau."
—Irving Fisher, Professor of Economics,
Yale University, October 17, 1929

SCENE TWO. On Thursday, October 24, 1929, panic struck Wall Street as stock values plummeted $6 billion. But not to worry:

"The worst has passed."
—Joint statement by thirty-five of the largest houses on
Wall Street at the close of trading, October 24, 1929

"I see no cause for alarm."
—J. J. Bernet, President, Chesapeake and Ohio Railway,
Friday, October 25, 1929

"I do not look for a recurrence of Thursday."
—M. C. Brush, President of the American International
Corporation, Friday, October 25, 1929

"We feel that fundamentally Wall Street is sound."
—Goodbody and Company, market letter to customers, Friday,
October 25, 1929

SCENE THREE. On Tuesday, October 29, 1929, the bottom fell out of the stock market, hysteria gripped Wall Street, the nation trembled . . . but the authorities still viewed it all through rose-colored glasses:

"[The Wall Street crash] doesn't mean there will be any general or serious business depression."
>—*Business Week,* November 2, 1929

"The end of the decline of the Stock Market will . . . probably not be long, only a few more days at most."
>—Irving Fisher, Professor of Economics,
>Yale University, November 14, 1929

"Financial storm definitely passed."
>—Bernard Baruch, American financier, cablegram
>to Winston Churchill, November 15, 1929

SCENE FOUR. As the weeks and months passed, stock prices continued to plummet, farmers were bankrupted, banks went under, and bread lines stretched for blocks in the cities—yet the authorities pretended nothing bad was happening:

"In most of the cities and towns of this country, this Wall Street panic will have no effect."
>—Paul Block, Block newspaper chain, editorial,
>November 15, 1929

"[1930 will be] a splendid employment year."
>—U.S. Department of Labor, New Year's forecast,
>December 1929

"I see nothing in the present situation that is either menacing or warrants pessimism. . . . I have every confidence that there will be a revival of activity in the spring, and that during this coming year the country will make steady progress."
>—Andrew Mellon, U.S. Secretary of the Treasury,
>December 31, 1929

"Gentlemen, you have come sixty days too late. The depression is over."

  —Herbert Hoover, responding to a delegation requesting a
  public works program to help speed the recovery, June 1930

SCENE FIVE. The ultimate in authoritative prognostication came from the prestigious Harvard Economic Society. Here are some of its determinedly cheery insights offered in the Society's *Weekly Letter* as the depression turned ever more wrathful across the American countryside:

"With the underlying conditions sound, we believe that the recession in general business will be checked shortly and that improvement will set in during the spring months."

        —January 18, 1930

"Since our monetary and credit structure is not only sound but unusually strong . . . there is every prospect that the recovery which we have been expecting will not be long delayed."

        —August 30, 1930

"[R]ecovery will soon be evident."

        —September 20, 1930

"[T]he outlook is for the end of the decline in business during the early part of 1931, and steady . . . revival for the remainder of the year."

        —November 15, 1930

Note: In 1931, the economic squeeze of the depression forced the Harvard Economic Society to suspend publication of the *Weekly Letter.*

SCENE SIX. The depression was in full rage, but some folks still didn't get it:

"These really are good times, but only a few know it. If this period of convalescence through which we have been passing must be spoken of as a depression, it is far and away the finest depression we have ever had."

—Henry Ford, c. 1931

"I don't know anything about any depression."

—J. P. Morgan, Jr., American banker and financier, c. 1931

(Source: Christopher Cerf and Victor Navasky, *The Experts Speak*. Villard Books.)

Señor Reyes—I recommend that you plunge even deeper into the jungle and lock-and-load. Mr. Grasso lies, or (let's be generous) he embellishes like a vinyl-siding salesman. Six out of ten U.S. citizens own no stocks at all—not through a 401(k), a mutual fund, a pension plan, nothing. The Dow might as well be a pink- and purple-polka-dotted cow for all the good it's doing the typical household. And most folks who are "in the market" are barely there. In fact, 89 percent of all stocks are owned by only 10 percent of American households, and nearly half the stocks are owned by those 1 million families who comprise the wealthiest 1 percent of Americans.

Yet, Washington continues to bow before the Dow, with Republicans and Democrats alike proclaiming all of America to be "prosperous" so long as the market's investors are prospering. A rich example of this skewed perspective came to the fore in mid-May of '99 when Treasury Secretary Robert Rubin stepped down as pontiff of the Clinton administration's Dowist economic policies. Another media gush ensued, with adoring paean after paean hailing Rubin as the "Architect of Prosperity" (*New York Times*), and virtually every story cited the tripling of the Dow Jones Average as the high mark of his "wildly successful tenure" (*Washington Post*).

In a farewell Rose Garden ceremony filled with more adoration than the pope usually gets, President Clinton did not praise Rubin simply for his righteous due, which was that he steadfastly fattened the fat no matter what it cost others, but by asserting that Rubin was somehow a populist pontiff. Without so much as an embarrassed twitch, Clinton proclaimed to the assembled media that Rubin had come to Washington "to help me save the middle class." Middle class? Rubin, a money-scavenging investment banker who amassed a $100 million personal fortune at Goldman Sachs before coming to Washington to preserve and extend the wealth of his privileged peers, wouldn't know a middle-classer if he ran over one with his limousine. Apparently oblivious to the irony, Clinton pressed on with his characterization of Rubin's work as an exercise in grassroots economics: "He built a spirit and a belief that we could actually make this economy what it ought to be for our people. That will be his enduring achievement—along with the fact that everybody believed as long as he was secretary of the Treasury nothing bad could happen."

Was *Saturday Night Live* scripting this? Rubin was the guy who fought ferociously to kill any of the jobs initiatives that candidate Clinton had promised in 1992, who promoted high stock prices by encouraging lower wages for middle-class workers, who opposed any significant increases in the minimum wage, who pushed hard for NAFTA and the World Trade Organization, who breakfasted every week with Fed chairman Alan Greenspan and enthusiastically backed his wage-stifling monetary policies, who took billions of tax dollars that could have been used to rebuild America's manufacturing base and instead used them to bail out rich speculators who had made bad gambles in Asia and Latin America, who protected corporate welfare from any budget cuts while whacking away at health and housing programs that benefit working families, and who generally treated the middle class like a fire hydrant in a dog show.

Hanging a final accolade around Rubin's neck, Clinton praised him as "the most effective treasury secretary since Alexander Hamilton." Now this one seems to be a true fit.

Hamilton was the most aristocratic of all the founders, distrusting the common people and advocating that only the "rich and well-born" should govern. As the first treasury secretary, Hamilton insisted that the federal government's role was to protect and promote the interests of the propertied classes, including helping to make their investments profitable. This was no big surprise to those who knew the guy, since he had earlier tried to change Jefferson's three inalienable rights from "Life, Liberty, and the Pursuit of Happiness" to "Life, Liberty, and Property." He and Rubin are soul mates there! Secretary Hamilton also proposed America's first tax plan, putting the burden not on the rich and well-born but on the small farmers. He then goaded President George Washington into amassing an army (bigger than the one he had commanded against the British) to march on the small farmers of the Pennsylvania frontier to put down the "Whiskey Rebellion" that they had mounted against Hamilton's tax.

There was no Dow Jones average during Hamilton's tenure at Treasury, but as in Rubin's tenure the operating principle was that speculators got rich . . . and the commoners got shtooked.

CONSUMER CONFIDENCE INDEX. Another happy statistic has gained prominence in recent years, popping up monthly with the intent of delighting us, much like a jack-in-the-box can cause two-year-olds to squeal with joy when the little clown head pops out. This little clown is called the "Consumer Confidence Index," and it practically always tells us that consumers across America are a happy lot, brimming with confidence about economic conditions and in a mood to spend, spend, spend. Apparently they think we have the gullibility of two-year-olds who think the clown really does live in the box.

Since 1985, the index has been computed and promoted by the very official-sounding Conference Board, and it is now dutifully reported each month by all the media, who treat it as though it is not only something real but also profound, as in this 1999 AP story: "The Conference Board reported today its index of consumer confidence rose 3.2 points to 132.1 in February from a revised 128.9 in January. Consumers were thoroughly pleased with the current economic situation, the report said." Feel better? It's that fuzzy blue blanket again being pulled over any unpleasant economic realities that folks might be experiencing. How can the economy have anything wrong with it if your fellow consumers are so upbeat? Hell, upbeat doesn't say it—they're at 132.1! So if you're feeling maybe a 107.8 or even 67.4, then there must be something wrong with you, Bucko.

What we have here is proof again that the media will report the wildest tales with a straight face as long as there are some decimals involved. Here's the inside skinny on the Consumer Confidence Index:

First, despite its ubiquity and authoritative tone, the index is not the bona fide calculation of any government agency, academic institution, or other independent entity. Rather, The Conference Board Inc. is a private business that is thoroughly dependent on delivering and publicizing monthly reports that please its corporate clients, which include an alphabet full of brand-name marketers, such as Aetna, BankAmerica, Chevron, Dow Chemical, Exxon, Ford, General Electric, Hewlett-Packard, IBM, JCPenney, Kmart, Lockheed Martin, Merrill Lynch, NationsBank, Philip Morris, RJR Nabisco, Sears, Texaco, United Airlines, Wal-Mart, and Xerox.

Basically, the Board is a service company for corporate executives, holding seminars and conferences for them, producing reports, doing management research, organizing executive "networking groups," and the like. Just as the U.S. Chamber of Commerce and other corporate service organizations have an unabashed procorporate agenda, so does the Conference Board, which has no representatives of consumers, workers, or other broad public interests overseeing its work. John Williams, an independent consumer research analyst who is the director of a watchdog organization called the Shadow Bureau of Government Statistics and who produces a no-nonsense newsletter of economic conditions called *Straight Shooter*, says bluntly: "The purpose of the Conference Board is to promote business, and it is dedicated to good news for business."

Second, the index is a lot less authoritative than its tone suggests. Each of its monthly releases to the media carries this notation: "The Consumer Confidence survey is based on a representative sample of 5,000 U.S. households." That's a most impressive number of citizens for the Board's surveyors to talk to each month . . . except that they *don't* talk to the people. The survey is simply a multiple-choice questionnaire that is mailed out to the 5,000 households. Not mentioned in the monthly media releases is the fact that less than half of these households actually respond by the time the index is compiled, so it's really a *completed* survey of more like 2,000 to 2,500 households each month. Still, 2,000 households could make a very valid survey *if* the Board used a representative sample of the U.S. population chosen by the scientific sampling techniques used by professional pollsters. It does not. Instead of mailing the questionnaires to 5,000 homes chosen from all hundred million U.S. households, the 5,000 monthly names are drawn from a preselected pool of less than 700,000 households! January through December, the survey goes out to another 5,000 addresses taken from this same tiny pool—which includes a mere six-tenths of 1 percent of us.

Nor are these 700,000 chosen scientifically. Rather, the Board's surveyors send out assorted direct-mail solicitations asking, in effect, "Anyone out there want to be in our survey pool?" If this strikes you as lacking somewhat in survey-selection professionalism, consider that some of those already in the pool get their golfing partners, their business clients, their brother-in-law Bob, and other acquaintances to jump in, too. No one gets paid to participate, but there are free products to sample from time to time, and there's the thrill of knowing that you're speaking for America, even if you really don't.

Then there's the matter of the questionnaire itself, which is not exactly a penetrating examination of any consumer's basic sense of economic confidence. It asks sixteen questions, nine of which are marketing queries, like what make of car you plan to buy in the next six months, what brand of refrigerator you're likely to purchase, and which airline you plan to fly on your vacation. The other six questions cover general opinions of whether overall business conditions are good, normal, or bad; whether there will be more, the same, or fewer jobs in the next six months; and whether stock prices can be expected to increase or decrease.

That's it. Yet, on the basis of these vague questions, the Conference Board issues not only its firm assertion that America's consumer confidence stands precisely at 132.1, but it also adds such sweeping rhetorical embellishments as "consumers were *thoroughly pleased* with the current economic situation." Apparently, if you torture the statistics long enough, they'll confess to anything.

Even if the Board did not embellish, there is a built-in positive bias to the survey because of the inherent optimism of us Americans. Our immigrant culture ("Seek a new beginning"), our enterprising nature ("I *can* make a silk purse out of a sow's ear"), our frontier spirit ("Go west, young man") all well up to produce an emphatic "Yes!" when we're asked, "Will tomorrow be a better day?" But there's more at work than human optimism in these survey findings—there's also the fact that people's responses to such questions can be influenced by what they are being told by the mass media. If the newspapers and broadcasts are blaring "Zip-a-dee-doo-dah, Zip-a-dee-a/My, oh my, what a wonderful day" over and over, there's a tendency to go down the road humming that tune, too, because you can't get it out of your head. Are business conditions good? Zip-a-dee-doo-dah! Are employment conditions good? Zip-a-dee-a!

Professor David Fan of the University of Minnesota has done a "media climate index," which has been stunningly accurate at predicting the outcomes of consumer confidence surveys—whenever the news is saturated with sunny economic stories, you can count on the confidence index to be almost exactly as radiant. Even in the early years of the depression of the 1930s, when the authorities kept insisting that the overall economy was doing well, people agreed with that assessment, although they were personally devastated. As Studs Terkel revealed in his poignant and magnificent oral history *Hard Times,* folks blamed themselves for losing the farm or being in a bread line, because officialdom said that prosperity abounded in the land, with everyone but YOU (you loser!) being in splendid shape.

Third, at least one industry insider says the Conference Board is a little loosey-goosey with its tabulations. Al Sindlinger, a pioneer of telephone surveys, is the fellow who came up with the very term *consumer confidence* way back in 1928. He conceived of a confidence index as a way of measuring the likelihood of consumer buying. Years ago, he first connected to the Conference Board through a contract he had to supply *Newsweek* with his data. The Board also had an arrangement with the magazine that allowed it access to Sindlinger's weekly survey information, and for a brief while he even furnished data directly to the Board. But he soon quit letting them use his information because, he says, "They always put a spin on it." He says that if his findings showed that confidence was up, the report would be zapped out to the media within hours, but if the numbers were down, they would put the report on hold until more surveying could be done, and they would tell him, "Wait a couple of weeks, something must be wrong with the data." Sindlinger doesn't like what the Board's index has become: "It's no longer a measurement, but a promotion." As a professional, he is particularly appalled by the fact that the board "seasonally adjusts" their data, which he says allows them to rig already dubious numbers. The Board's numbers reflect nothing but people's attitudes or opinions, so Sindlinger asks, "How can an opinion be seasonally adjusted?"

Al Sindlinger continues to do his own consumer analysis, issuing weekly reports to subscribers via his "Sindlinger Fax." His reports offer a kitchen-table perspective of not only how people are feeling but how they're actually *doing*. And these days, Al is not using any glib phrases like consumers being "thoroughly pleased" with the way things are going. While about a third of the people he surveys are indeed bullish about their economic fortunes, he says another third are standing still, and the final third are in the negative. There's the two-thirds majority that's wondering when, if ever, the politicians are going to begin telling the truth about the economy and start fighting for those who are being mugged.

THE FLO CHART

Flo is a waitress at the Dine & Go Diner, where she works an early breakfast shift, six to nine. Then she goes downtown to the law offices of Meager, Wages & Miser, where she's a "legal aide" (much like a plow mule is a "farm aide"), doing grunt work ten to four for a bevy of insurance company lawyers. Ironically, Flo doesn't have insurance. She does have a couple of great kids, though—Kim, twelve, and Zach, seven—and she considers them her real job, though she is stretched mighty thin on time and energy and wishes she was with them more frequently. She's also taking a couple of night courses at the community college, trying to get ahead.

To know how the nation's economy is doing, we don't need to consult some trumped-up confidence index or the ethereal Dow Jones average but the Flo Chart: How's Flo doing? Hers is the heartbeat of America's majority—the 80 percent of folks who are paid less than $50,000 a year, the 60 percent who don't own *any* stocks and bonds, the 75 percent who don't have a university sheepskin hanging on the office wall . . . and the half to two-thirds who aren't voting because neither party is fighting for Flo.

The economic elites try to fool Flo by pointing to the glittering stock market; the media elites try to fool Flo by pointing to their smiley-faced consumer reports; the political elites try to fool Flo by pointing to the 20 million jobs created in the nineties. So why isn't Flo fooled? Because, to determine her economic situation, she analyzes data that the elites ignore. Calculated by universally accepted, scientific survey techniques and seasonally adjusted for inflation, Flo's leading economic indicator is called "Income." Or, in the more technical jargon that she sometimes employs: "How's my in-coming matching up with my out-going?"

When you're alone at your kitchen table doing calculations like that, it's hard to be fooled by a distant chorus telling you you're doing great. Even a few political leaders have figured this out. Representative Jim Traficant, a working-class Democrat from Youngstown, Ohio, offered this pungent economic assessment during a one-minute address from the floor of the U.S. House: "Let us tell it like it is: When you hold this economy to your nosey, this economy does not smell so rosy. If [it's] any consolation to the American workers, I never heard of anyone in America committing suicide by jumping out of a basement window. I yield back all of the propaganda on this great economy." With important exceptions like Traficant, politicians of both parties gloat about America's amazing "job-creating machine," and the media cheerfully parrot industry's claim that so many people are now at work that they can't find applicants for all kinds of jobs, from low-tech hamburger flippers to high-tech computer code writers. For employees and job seekers, however, the issue is not getting a job (Flo has *two)*, but getting a job that offers middle-class basics—decent income, health care, vacation time, and pension. Nor is this merely a crude issue of financial compensation; at the personal, social, and political levels, this is about workaday Americans being valued and getting respect.

You want statistics? Here's one that's as true as they come for measuring prosperity in America, and it's a ticking time bomb inside our champagne-popping, self-satisfied political system: In real dollars, average hourly wages in 1973 were $13.91. Today, they average $13.24. Far from gaining from the "Boom," *American workers are paid less today than when Richard Nixon was president*! We're talking about the income of the majority of our nation's people.

This decline comes at a time when people are busting their butts—working harder, longer, and smarter. Since Nixonian times, the productivity of workers has jumped by a third. Economics 101 teaches that more productivity equals economic gains for all. The *New York Times* continues to mouth this economic platitude: "Only when productivity rises, can incomes and living standards rise for most Americans" it intoned in a 1998 article headlined "Productivity Sets Fast Pace." So—yoo-hoo, *New York Times!*—where's the "rising incomes and living standards" for the mostest of the people? You don't need Economics 101 to do the cognitive analysis of the discrepancy between theory and reality on this one. Anyone who can spell IQ knows that folks are doing more and getting less—at the same time that the Establishment is whooping and hollering about the fact that our overall economic pie is growing at an unprecedented rate and that more wealth is being generated than ever before.

The income drop for working families in these otherwise prosperous times would have been even more precipitous except for two factors. First, the flow of women into the workplace. Median family incomes have not risen since the Nixon years, but they would have plummeted disastrously, since real wages for 80 percent of American men are down. The chief stopgap against total family financial disaster has been that both spouses now work. Even with this, though, families are barely keeping up, much less getting ahead. Economist Lester Thurow reports that since the early seventies, "The proportion of year-around, full-time working wives has doubled for those with children and increased 50 percent for those without children. More female work should be leading to more household income. But it isn't." So Mom and Dad are scrambling to stay middle class, sometimes working a couple of jobs each, yet leaders of both political parties avert their eyes, pretending that this eight-hundred-pound gorilla is not sitting in the corner at the lavish party they're having to celebrate "Boom Times." The only acknowledgment they have given to these families' stress has been to chastise them for not spending enough time with their children. Duh.

The second factor keeping families out of the poorhouse (temporarily) is debt—mostly, debt that is being piled up on those friendly little pieces of plastic that pour into our mailboxes almost daily with the siren phrase, "Preapproved Credit!" printed so boldly on the envelope. Banks offer 4 billion credit cards every year, which is fifteen for every man, woman, and child in the country. About 60 percent of households now owe money on their credit cards, with the average debt being $7,000! If you're only making $25,000–$30,000 a year, that's a heavy load, and it's costing you $1,000 a year just to pay the interest. The result has been a doubling in the 1990s of families filing for personal bankruptcies. Congress is responding to this crisis, though. Not to help the families (you dreamer), but to protect the banks and other credit-card issuers by making it next to impossible for working stiffs to use the bankruptcy laws.

The twenty-five-year decline in the Flo Chart almost exactly tracks the twenty-five-year rise in the Democratic party's fealty to Wall Street money. As the party's congressional, White

House, and campaign officials bonded tighter and tighter with the corporate and financial elites, they distanced themselves further and further from Flo, effectively leaving her with no representation in matters of economic policy. The fact that Flo is being pounded economically is not a case of benign neglect but of the Democrats joining the Republicans to support policies that mug her, stealing her middle-class aspirations by aggressively holding down her income.

Let me be blunt: Low wages are the official policy of the U.S. government. If you're a manufacturer wanting to hold down wages here at home, the government will book you on a trade delegation to Asia, hook you up with a contractor that provides workers for as cheap as a nickel an hour, underwrite your foreign investment, suspend tariffs and quotas so you can ship your cheap-labor products to stores back here, and put out a press release saluting you for joining in a private-public partnership to foster "global competitiveness." If you're a minimum-wage employer, don't worry about any rabble-rousing populism from Democrats—they'll give you a wink as they hold any increases to a level way below poverty. Even at the higher wage levels, if you're a Microsoft, IBM, or Silicon Valley giant and want to put a drag on the salaries of your engineers, programmers, and other high-tech workers, count on the Democrats to join Republicans in helping you import an extra 50,000 or so of these workers each year from Pakistan, Russia, and elsewhere, letting you pay them a third to a half less than U.S. workers, thus busting the American salary scale.

And if wages do show any sign of creeping up, count on Uncle Alan to step in and stomp on them. Alan Greenspan, as chairman of the Federal Reserve Board, is the ruling authority over our nation's monetary policy, and he hates wage increases. You see, if wages rise, they might possibly pinch corporate profits ever so slightly, and this might spook your big Wall Street investors, causing the high-flying stock prices of corporations to slip a notch. Since today's upper-class prosperity is built almost entirely on the bloated prices of those corporate stocks, both parties are determined that nothing should spook those investors, even if this means keeping Flo down. It's really a choice of who you want to help—the few who profit from stock prices, or the many who depend on decent wages. Both parties have made the same choice—Greenspan. First appointed by President Reagan, this Darth Vader of wage earners was reappointed by President Bush, then reappointed twice by President Clinton. He has been the bipartisan hit man on Flo. It's a convoluted process, but essentially Greenspan uses the Fed's power over interest rates to hammer the poor lady, much as some clod might use a sledgehammer to swat a fly. At the slightest hint (even if imagined) that it's possible sometime in the future for wages somewhere to rise even negligibly . . . Greenspan pounces. This guy hunts down wage hikes like Joe McCarthy used to hunt down commies, and he'll use every power the government has to keep working people's paychecks down. Last summer the cold-eyed, pursed-lipped Greenspan openly urged Congress to bring in more immigrants, using them as wage-busters: "I have always thought . . . we should be carefully focused on [what] skilled people from abroad and unskilled people from abroad . . . can contribute to this country. . . . If we can open up our immigration rolls significantly, that will clearly make [wage inflation] less and less of a potential problem."

Add to Washington's wage-busting policies the delight that Wall Street takes in corporate downsizing, and you have a surefire formula for holding wages (and people) down. The politicians who talk so loud and lovingly about America's job-creating machine go mute on the topic of America's job-*destroying* machine, which has been ruthlessly efficient. Challenger, Gray & Christmas is a highly regarded employment firm that tracks job cuts daily, and it reports that companies have been eliminating some 64,000 jobs a month, most of which are the higher-paying jobs that come with health care, pensions, and vacation time. It gets little media coverage, but downsizing in the late nineties has been more rampant than it was in the eighties and early nineties, when it was a major media story and led to Clinton's '92 presidential victory. Remember his slogan, "It's the economy, stupid," and his pledge to create "good jobs at good wages"? Instead, he learned that if he just laid low, like Brer Fox, while corporations punted those jobs, Wall Street investors would cheer lustily and run up the stock price for the companies doing this "streamlining," then the media would focus on the lightning flash of the Dow Jones average, and he would get credit for presiding over a thunderous, stock-driven boom.

Clinton's self-congratulatory claims about job creation and prosperity for all call to mind "Boss Daley," the longtime mayor of Chicago, who once said with a slip of the tongue, "We shall reach greater and greater platitudes of achievement." The president and other politicians have averted their eyes from the massive loss of good middle-class jobs, hoping that if they don't see it, maybe no one else will either. But working families already know all about it, of course, since they know the people being punted . . . and fear they'll be next. Stephanie Schmidt, an economist with the Urban Institute, surprised herself when she did a paper titled "Workers' Beliefs About Their Own Job Security," published in 1999. She had assumed that all the upbeat reports on stock gains and job creation would have just about everyone loaded with optimism. *Newsweek* had even done a cover story called "The Year of the Employee." It went on at great length about "this white hot job market," claiming that people *want* to be fired because they get such "hefty severance packages." Besides, said the magazine, today's lucky job seekers can take their choice of job offers that not only include "stunning pay increases and gold-plated stock options" but also such perks as being allowed to bring your dog to work (complete with company-supplied Milk-Bones).

"It's the revenge of the downsized," *Newsweek* prattled.

But Schmidt found that most working people must not have read that issue of the magazine. Instead, workers today have as much job anxiety—fear of losing their jobs—as in the bad old recessionary days prior to Clinton's election, and they're even more scared that if they lose their current job, they won't find another one as good in terms of pay and benefits. She also found that this insecurity is no longer the burden of blue-collar workers alone but now has permeated the white-collar world as well.

Lest you think such anxiety is mere paranoia, take a peek behind the glowing job-creation numbers that politicians and the media toss around. "Job Growth Remains Strong," blared the headline on an Associated Press story in May of 1999, reporting that 234,000 new jobs had been created the previous month. But what kind of jobs? Not high-paying manufacturing positions—indeed, 29,000 of those had been lost during the month. Instead, the bulk of the additional jobs were in the low-paying service sector, including 18,000 new hires by temporary-help firms, 23,000 in health-care services, and 64,000 in restaurants and bars.

Yet, the public keeps being told not to sweat the loss of America's manufacturing jobs, because the future for the middle class is in high-tech "knowledge jobs," so "cross that bridge to the twenty-first century," as President Clinton said. Al Gore flatly proclaimed that 60 percent of new jobs will require advanced technological skills, and George W. Bush echoed the mantra that the "new economy" means you've got to be a college-educated techie.

But this is just another middle-class mugging. Education analyst Richard Rothstein of the *New York Times* reports that in the next decade, "employers will hire more than three times as many cashiers as engineers. They will need more than twice as many food-counter workers, waiters, and waitresses than all the systems analysts, computer engineers, mathematicians, and database administrators combined." He adds that "we already enroll enough college students to fill foreseeable vacancies in professional fields," yet corporations and their political puppets are deliberately flooding the job market with overeducated workers—a cynical ploy that will turn the middle-class's high-tech future into low-paid work. The real job market is decidedly low-tech. Between now and 2006, according to Clinton's own Bureau of Labor Statistics, the thirty fastest-growing job categories include only seven that require even a bachelor's degree. Most of the other twenty-three jobs are decidedly low-tech, with *more than half of them paying less than $18,000 a year.* Here's the real "middle class" future, ranked in order of the occupations expecting the most job growth:

OCCUPATION	MEDIAN ANNUAL PAY	EDUCATION OR TRAINING REQUIRED
Cashiers	$12,844	Short-term on-the-job training
Registered nurses	$36,244	Associate degree
Salespersons, retail	$19,344	Short-term on-the-job training
Truck drivers	$25,012	Short-term on-the-job training
Home health aides	$15,184	Short-term on-the-job training
Teacher aides and educational assistants	$13,312	Short-term on-the-job training
Nursing aides, orderlies, and attendants	$15,184	Short-term on-the-job training
Receptionists	$17,628	Short-term on-the-job training
Child-care workers	$12,324	Short-term on-the-job training
Clerical supervisors	$28,860	Work experience

and managers		
Marketing and sales worker supervisors	$26,988	Work experience
Maintenance repairers, general utility	$25,220	Long-term on-the-job training
Food counter, fountain, and related workers	$12,116	Short-term on-the-job training
Food preparation workers	$13,728	Short-term on-the-job training
Hand packers and packagers	$16,120	Short-term on-the-job training
Guards	$17,472	Short-term on-the-job training
General office clerks	$19,344	Short-term on-the-job training
Waiters and waitresses	$14,092	Short-term on-the-job training
Adjustment clerks	$21,580	Short-term on-the-job training
Cooks, short order and fast food	$13,728	Short-term on-the-job training
Personal and home care aides	$14,820	Short-term on-the-job training
Food service and lodging managers	$23,816	Work experience
Medical assistants	$22,412	Moderate length on-the-job training

(Source: Bureau of Labor Statistics)

I AIN'T GOT NO HOME IN THIS WORLD ANYMORE

When she was First Lady, Nancy Reagan received a letter from a single mom whose job paid so little she had to use food

stamps to help make ends meet for her family. She was getting
only $27 a week in stamps, which didn't buy a lot of groceries,
but Ronald Reagan was on his high horse at the time railing that
these "handouts" for food should be slashed (even while the
Gipper was also demanding that much fatter handouts to Pentagon weapons contractors be grossly increased—a perverted policy of beating plowshares into swords). The letter writer was
upset by the president's political rant at her expense and
wanted to know directly from the First Lady how she thought a
family could get the nourishment it needed on *less* than $27.
The working mother did get a response, though not one she
could have anticipated: The First Lady sent a White House
recipe for crab-stuffed artichokes. Cost-per-serving: $20.

Her office later claimed there had been a mix-up in the mail
room, but Nancy's "Let them eat stuffed artichokes" incident is
a pretty fair representation of the attitude that Washington has
had ever since the Reagan years, not only toward matters of
poverty but also toward matters of deep concern to millions of
middle-class people—especially those paid under $32,000 a
year, which is roughly half of us. In our Land of Plenty, not
only is this half of Americans caught in a wage squeeze, but
they're also caught in a health-care squeeze (a fourth of them
are without any coverage at all), a pension squeeze (six out of
ten have no pension), and another squeeze that receives almost
no publicity: housing. Since most politicians and the media live
in upscale neighborhoods and have grown oblivious to "how
the other half lives," it would likely surprise them to hear that
schoolteachers, bank tellers, computer programmers, police
officers, secretaries, travel agents, firefighters, hair stylists,
latte-slingers at Starbucks, and others whom they brush by in
their busy lives are unable to afford skyrocketing apartment
rents, much less the purchase price of today's homes.

Indeed, like the wage squeeze, the housing squeeze is
buried in a blizzard of blithesome statistics. "How can you say
the middle class is hard hit, Hightower," asked an incredulous

Pittsburgh caller to my radio talk show, "when the papers are full of stories about people everywhere buying new houses?" He was right about the news coverage: "Sales of new homes rose in November to a record," exulted a 1999 *New York Times* piece. "Low mortgage rates and consumer optimism pushed up sales of new single-family houses. . . . The housing market is on track to register a third consecutive yearly record," the *Times* marveled. But, as Yogi Berra once said, "Half the lies they tell me aren't true," and the full truth behind today's red-hot housing stats is that they hide more than they reveal.

It's true enough that construction abounds—just follow the sounds. From sea to shining sea concrete is being poured, power saws are buzzing, nail guns are going bam-bam-bam, and new homes are being raised like totems to the Gods of Prosperity. If you need a house, just reach out and grab one, since houses aplenty are being built. But this "grab one" attitude reminds me of a series of radio and television ads that Fort Worth oil-well magnate Eddie Chiles ran incessantly in the late seventies. Known as "Mad Eddie" for his right-wing diatribes against Jimmy Carter, his ads closed with this tag line, delivered in a hard Texas twang: "If yew don't own an awl well, git one!"

The problem with "gitting" either an oil well or a house is money. This is where the economic powers clobber the housing-hungry middle class coming and going—most folks have seen no pay hikes coming, even as they've seen housing prices going, going, going . . . right through the roof. For them, the construction boom is just a lot of noise.

Practically all of those power saws and nail guns we hear are at work on expansive and expensive homes for the bankers, lawyers, executives, media managers, and politicians. In Austin, the high-tech boom town where I live, construction is roaring. A recent article, for example, reports that sixty-two more homes are going up in the Costa Bella subdivision. Grab one, if you can—this is a gated subdivision in which the developers require that each house contain at least 5,500 square feet of living space and at least a three-car garage. My entire *block* in south Austin doesn't have that much square footage. Prices go as high as $5 million, though, in fairness, I should note that a mix of economic classes are welcome at Costa Bella; some homes there sell for as little as $750,000. Probably starter houses.

OK, your bankers, bosses, and big shots need housing, too, so we can't begrudge the industry for meeting this market demand. But where is the industry when it comes to the swelling demand for homes priced at $80,000 or under? I'm not talking here about public housing projects or federally subsidized housing (though as the number of the working poor has risen so dramatically in the nineties, and as Washington has whacked funding for housing programs, there's a surging need for this housing, too). Rather, I'm talking about the vaunted marketplace that we're told is so omniscient that it responds to all demand. Well, there's a tidal wave of demand that has built up for modest homes with mortgages that a family making $20–$25–$30,000 a year can afford without having to sell off their kids. Try to find such a house.

Sticking with the Austin example, the city council approved a measure last year to offer a mortgage discount to police officers, firefighters, and paramedics if they buy a home in the city. At present, the very people we entrust with our safety and lives, people who should be a living part of our community, mostly commute from outlying areas, chiefly because housing prices are through the roof. Rodolfo Estrada has been an APD patrol officer for five years. He lives in an apartment in the city but is looking to buy a home for his family. He earns about $39,000 a year, but he says, "I've been looking in the city of Austin, and I've also looked in Hays County [to the south of us]. I'd prefer to stay in the city, but it's so expensive." More than half of Austin's police officers live outside of the city they are sworn to protect, and about half of our firefighters are also out-of-towners.

The rule of thumb is that you can't spend more than 30

percent of your monthly pay on housing and still have enough to cover food, car, and other expenses. Most bankers, however, are even stricter, refusing to grant a mortgage that takes more than 25 percent of your paycheck. For someone making $30,000, this comes to $625 a month. You're going to go house shopping on that?

Forget a new house. Homebuilders today would get a hernia from laughing uncontrollably at you if you came around flashing that kind of money. Hey, they'd say between bursts of guffawing, we'll sell you one of these three-car garages for $625 a month. Of course, the square footage in some of the garages being built would do nicely for the modest-home market, but it's way more profitable for developers to serve the luxury clients, so that's where practically all of them have gone. In the small but growing city of Austin, there are some 350 developers putting up some 10,000 homes a year. Less than 5 percent of these houses, however, are priced below $100,000. Of the 350 developers, only a couple are even trying to build for the rising surge of Austin families who make under $30,000 a year, and they are faced with indifference and outright rejection from the financial community. One who is trying to respond to these families is Haythem Dawlett, a developer who says lenders had zero knowledge about this market and even less interest in serving it. Just to prove that there is a demand, Dawlett and his partners built three model houses with their own funds, then held an open house. They got forty-eight buyers in a single weekend. Those homes got built, but still the lenders and builders hold back, not because these homes aren't profitable, but because they are not mega-profitable like the high-end houses, so this gusher of a market goes begging.

So, you say, I don't have to have a new house, I'll just get a used one. Well, get in line fella. The kind of used home you've got in mind already has someone using it, and even if they're moving out there's a long line of buyers at the doorstep. Since the industry is no longer building this scale of house, the supply of them is so low that even the most modest old houses are being priced way beyond that six-and-a-quarter a month you've got in your pocket, especially if they're in a neighborhood being gentrified, as so many are now that more upscale buyers decide they want to live near downtown rather than out in the scenic hills, the lake region, or other primo spots of ultra-urbia.

Not that *every* old house is priced out of reach. If you're willing to go far enough out, you can find affordable housing around every city. Here in the Austin area, for example, Clyde Puckett will sell his house to you, and the price might be right. Drive about thirteen miles from Austin to the neighboring town of Manor, then go another seven and a half miles northeast from beautiful downtown Manor and there you'll find Puckett's place, just off Hog Eye Road. Local humor writer John Kelso, after hearing so many complaints that housing here has become prohibitively expensive, went looking for affordable and came across Clyde, who's thinking of selling because even Hog Eye Road is getting too crowded for him. He says there are nearby neighbors now, and their dogs make it impossible for him to let his chickens run loose in his yard anymore. Besides, he no longer feels entirely comfortable stepping out on his front porch to take a piss.

His house is what the real estate people might call a "fixer-upper." It's a trailer that he bought twenty-three years ago, plus a wooden structure adjacent to it that is presently filled with trash. "I was tearing it down," says Clyde of the wooden building, "but I ran out of steam." So it's still there, lending a bit of rustic charm and available for whatever creative whimsy the new owner might bring to it. He concedes that the main house—the trailer—could use a new floor, though he's kept it patched up pretty well, including having put a Neighborhood Crime Watch sign over "one of the bad spots." But, he notes proudly, "I don't have a rat or a snake. I got six cats, and they run a tight ship."

The Puckett Place sits on two acres that offer exciting land-scaping opportunities. At the moment, the grounds are graced with an abundance of "yard art," including eight rusting vehi-cles, a pile of used tires, an oil drum, a supermarket basket, an old kitchen sink, and many other fine pieces. "If I didn't live around junk, I don't know what I'd do," Clyde says of his col-lectibles. Much of the junk is inoffensive, though, because it's invisible, covered with weeds that range up to fourteen feet high. "I'm a naturalist," says the keeper of this kingdom. "I think if the good Lord put it out there to grow, give it a chance." Writer Kelso, who took a tour of the place, says there is no pool or hot tub, but there's a sizable low patch near the road with standing water in it, which the realtors would describe as a "natural habitat." Clyde, being more down to earth, simply warns: "Don't fall in this pond, or a bullfrog will eat you."

What will it cost to make all this yours? Clyde says, "I imag-ine I could get $40,000 if I cleaned it up and mowed a little bit."

All right, all right, you scream in frustration, the American dream of home ownership has been put out of my reach, so I'll simply have to settle for renting a place. Good luck. Affordable apartments are becoming a thing of the past, too. Again using Austin as a bellwether, rents have almost doubled here during the nineties and are now averaging nearly $900 a month for a small, two-bedroom apartment—well beyond the budgets of the middle-classers I'm talking about. Damion McKeon, an Austin firefighter earning $30,000 a year, says he can't touch an apartment here: "I would be pretty much scrimping by if I lived in Austin. The rent is astronomical here." Because there are so many people chasing so few apartments, even complexes that the experts refer to by the architectural expression "a dump" are bringing premium prices.

The good news is that apartment construction in Austin is up in the last couple of years. But these are not being built for working stiffs. Of the 4,312 apartment units built in 1998, only 5 percent were moderately priced. Indeed, a bitter irony for the construction crews building these apartments is that they're averaging maybe ten bucks an hour and have a hard time finding anything they can afford to live in. They sure won't live in these new complexes, which are mostly luxury nests for the affluent, including a new category of upscale rentals called "corporate accommodations," catering to those executives needing an in-town place.

Just a couple of blocks from Threadgill's World Headquarters, the great Southern-cooking Mecca from which Susan DeMarco and I broadcast our daily radio program, was a downtown apartment complex named River Woods. It was nothing fancy, but its twelve brick buildings, nestled among a dozen graceful, old live oak trees were plenty pleasant. The cars parked here were mostly American with a lot of miles on them: Malibus, some Ford pickups, a low-slung Camaro, a Jeep, a meter-reader's truck, several vans, a '72 Lincoln Continental, a Mercury Cougar, and two dump trucks. There was no swimming pool, but there were barbecue grills on the balconies, children's toys on the patios, and one apartment with a couple of prized racing pigeons in a cage. River Woods was a place of two- and three-job working families, and they were paying $550 for a two-bedroom apartment. Located on South Congress Avenue within sight of the state capitol building, the complex was the kind that most cities need more of, yet this one no longer exists. It was bulldozed. Last year, Dallas megadeveloper Trammel Crow bought the property, and the Austin newspaper reported excitedly that he was contributing to our downtown's revitalization by razing River Woods to erect some 250 fabulous new luxury apartments going for $1,500 a month and up. Crow's new digs bear the appropriately toney name of Reserve on Congress. Current residents were told to take their Malibus, barbecue grills, and pigeons and kindly fly the coop, get out of the way, vamoose.

Also in downtown Austin is Sixth Street West, a low-cost

apartment complex in a neighborhood that has long prided itself
in its economic and racial diversity. But the boom at the top of
the economic ladder is destroying the diversity. Ruth Granjeno,
her husband, and her two boys, José and Erik, are residents of
the complex, which has 129 units for folks of modest means,
with apartments priced between $350 and $600 a month. She
works as a janitor and is a housecleaner for five nearby families,
plus she is vice president of the PTA for Matthews Elementary,
the school her boys attend, only five blocks away. She has lived
there fourteen years. "This location is safe," Ruth says. "I walk
to work. I walk to the houses I clean. I know everyone." A grocery store, a washateria, a dry cleaner, a drugstore, and other
services are right there in her neighborhood. It is what city living should be for families like hers.

But along comes Royce Gourley Jr. He owns ten apartment complexes in Austin, and in 1999 he added Sixth Street
West to his fiefdom. This is a hot and happening area now,
with antique shops, beaucoup boutiques, sidewalk cafés,
espresso joints, and other wondrous improvements coming to
the neighborhood. So many improvements that families like
Ruth Granjeno's are viewed by developers as low-class eye-
sores who need to be sent packing. Gourley tried to do just
that—one month before school was to start, he started handing out thirty-day eviction notices to Ruth and about twenty
of her neighbors. Think about that. Not only were these families being dumped out of their homes and forced to scram-
ble furiously to find a place before school opened, but their
children also were being booted out of Matthews Elementary
by this developer, since no other affordable housing is available in the Matthews district. "I'm willing to pay $800 for a
two-bedroom apartment," said Ruth, "but there aren't any."
When asked by the *Austin American-Statesman*, Gourley said
he didn't really even know how many families he was boot-
ing, nor would he say what his new, upscale rent structure
would be, but, he snickered, "Obviously, I'm not spending

money over there to keep the units leased at $350 a month."

He didn't snicker long, however, because a coalition of Matthews families and eight tenants, including the Granjenos, sued Gourley for racial discrimination. It seems the tenants he booted out all just happened to be Mexican-American. A judge issued a restraining order against ousting the families that were suing, and that brought Royce galloping to the settlement table. The Granjenos had their rent raised substantially, but they got to stay: "When I thought we had to leave, I cried because I thought we'd lose the school and my friends. Now I'm very satisfied." It does pay to fight the bastards. About a third of the families, however, had already moved out or could not afford the jacked-up rents.

Where were the families of Sixth Street West and River Woods to go? Away. Many ended up like so many other families who find themselves in what the bureaucrats coolly term "inadequate" housing. Dora Johnson knows about such inadequacies. She and her two-year-old daughter live in a two-bedroom Austin apartment, but not alone. Four others are crammed in with them, none able to find apartments with rents they can afford on their own. That's six people trying to get along in two bedrooms, one bathroom, a kitchen, and a living room. The same local paper that hailed Trammel Crow's luxury project reports that it's no longer a matter of poor people being left out but of "working, middle-class citizens [whose] chance of finding an apartment or house that is affordable is more difficult than at any time in Austin's history." Nationally, some 40 percent of renters don't have the income to qualify for the average two-bedroom apartments in their area. What do they do?

- They do what Dora and her little girl are doing—they live with family, friends, co-workers, or strangers, cramming together in small spaces.
- They live in rundown places, often in dangerous areas of town, where the rents are lower (but still expensive—in

Austin; $500 a month has become the low end for a one-bedroom apartment).

- They go to the outer edges of the city, which means they are in slurburbia, facing long commutes to their jobs—Courtney Gentry and her roommate, for example, came to Austin with $500 each to spend on rent, which they hoped would put them in the University of Texas area, near where they worked. "We couldn't find anything," she says, so they're in a complex out in northwest Austin, nowhere near the center of the city, commuting for forty-five minutes in rush hour, and still paying $980 for their apartment.
- Or, they lie about their income or find a manager who'll let them in even though the rent is substantially more than a third of their paycheck, which means they have less to spend on food, medicine, and other needs (70 percent of renters in the United States now pay more than a third of their monthly income on rent).

They make do . . . and stew. They also scorn a political system that doesn't respond to them, doesn't want them, doesn't seem to know them. In a song he titled "I Ain't Got No Home," Woody Guthrie wrote about an everyman of the depression era who is a direct ancestor to today's majority that's been rendered invisible in a culture of wealth and is being ignored by both political parties:

> *I mined in your mines, and I gathered in your corn*
> *I've been working, mister, since the day that I was born*
> *And I worry all the time, like I never did before*
> *Cause I ain't got no home in this world anymore.*
> *Well now I just ramble 'round to see what I can see*
> *This wide wicked world is sure a funny place to be*
> *The gambling man is rich and the working man is poor*
> *And I ain't got no home in this world anymore.*©

How soon we forget our own history—or, rather, how quickly our real history is buried by the Powers That Be in the futile hope that if today's citizens don't know about it, we won't think to rebel in similar fashion. The economic disparities, social dislocations, and political alienations of the twenties and thirties produced a massive upheaval that had the cock-sure capitalism of the time grappling uncertainly with everything from native fascism to homegrown socialism. It was this grassroots rebellion against the Wall Street elites and their corrupted cronies in Washington that finally produced—after angry and bloody battles all across the countryside—the social contract and the middle-class framework of laws that are now being so cavalierly dismantled. Today's economic destruction is being wrought under cover of a media-hyped middle-class prosperity that simply does not exist. It's a suicidal social order that thinks it can push its majority to the edges. It's a stupid political system that has two political parties representing the 20 percent minority, and none standing up for the 80 percent majority. Hush, say those in charge, everything is golden. Let the people eat stuffed artichokes.

FIGHTING THE SIN OF WAGES

There's a comic strip created by Bob Thaves I like entitled "Frank & Ernest"—two disheveled, often beleaguered, somewhat Chaplinesque fellows who live on the hardscrabble side of life yet are always mirthful about the absurdity of the system and of the situation in which they find themselves. One of the strips shows a frazzled Frank at the end of the workweek with his desk still piled high with stacks of paperwork to get done, his wastebasket overflowing, his files a jumble, saying: "I think the only person who ever got his work done by Friday was Robinson Crusoe."

And, as you'll recall, Friday was not actually paid money.

There you have the tension in today's economy for most folks: *mucho* work, *poquito* money. Peek behind the facade of our national prosperity, and you'll see that it's propped up by the working poor who are working diligently in high-rise office buildings, in the celebrated service economy, in the industrial parks of our cities, and elsewhere—people who are there day in and day out doing all the basic chores that keep the system going, yet getting shorted every payday. "You know why they call it 'take-home pay'?" asked a caller to our radio show. "Because that's the only place you can go on it." READER ALERT: STUNNING STATISTIC DEAD AHEAD: Twenty-five percent of the jobs in today's celebrated economy pay a poverty wage! That's 32 million people.

There is very good news, however, for something is being done to lift these wages. Not by Washington (where both parties continue to tinker around with the minimum wage, doing their part to keep it as minimal as possible), but by a grass-roots movement of America's low-wage workers themselves. It's called the *Living Wage* Campaign, and it has spread from Baltimore, which enacted its ordinance in 1994, to forty-six other localities that have already put living wage standards on their books and to dozens of others where campaigns are under way. This is an amazing success story of people taking matters into their own hands, getting organized, and defeating the formidable power structure of city after city, yet you would not know from the arbiters of national news that it is even happening (no doubt they are too busy celebrating the roaring economy in which, as *Money* magazine told us in a 1999 cover story, "Everyone Is Getting Rich").

These campaigns start from a basic principle of justice: Full-time work ought not leave you in wretched poverty. Yet talk with the people on the front lines of poverty—the churches and social workers—and they'll confirm that every city in America is experiencing a crush of working families living in homeless shelters and going to soup kitchens for meals. To fight paycheck impoverishment, the Living Wage movement has begun by targeting corporations that are given contracts and subsidies by local governments. Why should our tax dollars be paid to companies that return only poverty pay to our communities? Annually across the country, for example, billions of dollars worth of tax abatements and taxpayer-financed giveaways are handed out to corporations as lures to get them to build a store here or a factory there. The rationale for the handout is always that it will produce JOBS! But in case after case, the city gets suckered—many of the promised JOBS! are never created, and those that are pay too little for a family to make ends meet. Many billions more of taxpayer dollars are being given through contracts to corporations—build a public swimming pool, provide meals for the jailhouse, handle the city's waste disposal, manage the public parking lots, run the buses, process the payroll, landscape the parks, and all sorts of functions that the city (or county, school district, etc.) used to do but has since privatized. But privatization has meant privation for the people hired by the corporation to do the work.

Here's a radical thought: Our public funds should not depress the wages of our own citizens and be the cause of poverty, which saps the vitality of a city and costs taxpayers even more in social services to the deprived workers. This has been the compelling political message of the Living Wage movement, which has pushed through various initiatives and ordinances requiring that corporate contractors and recipients of corporate subsidies pay a wage that a family can live on, even if it is at a meager level. How much? Every local campaign has developed its own standard, with most using the poverty level for a family of four in their area, which usually puts the wage somewhere between seven and ten dollars an hour. As the movement has gained experience and strength, more of the ordinances also require health care benefits and some paid vacation time.

Los Angeles Times writer Nancy Cleeland wrote in February

1999 about that city's ordinance, putting a face to the techni-calities of it: "Let the academics, politicians, and labor leaders debate the definition of a living wage. For airport janitor José Morales, it means two concrete things—a bed and a car." Working for a private company that has a contract to provide janitorial services at L.A. International Airport, Morales, thirty-six years old, was making $5.45 an hour, which doesn't stretch very far, certainly not in Los Angeles. Cleeland reports that, for housing, "he shared a converted garage with his sis-ter, her husband, and the couple's two young sons. Too poor to buy furniture, they scavenged cardboard boxes from a nearby supermarket and spread them on the floor to make a commu-nal bed." Mr. Morales had to get up at 4 A.M. each day because his only transportation was the city bus system, and it took two hours, including changing buses, to get from his garage to LAX. It was also a two-hour bus ride back to his garage. Twice he was mugged at his corner bus stop.

Now life has picked up a bit for him, thanks to the city's 1997 Living Wage law, which lifted his pay a buck-eighty an hour. It doesn't seem like much, $1.80. A pack of cigarettes costs more, a draft beer is more, a single copy of *Money* maga-zine is more. But it's $3,600 a year for a full-time American worker like José Morales. Admittedly this is not as generous as the $8,400 that members of Congress gave themselves in a cost-of-living pay raise in the last Congress, but it's better than the miserly 50-cent increase that Congress doled out in the minimum wage for 2001. Cleeland writes that the $1.80 boost for Morales "moved him from a chronic state of crisis to a more manageable level of poverty [$7.25 is about $14,500 a year gross income]. He still counts pennies. He still scans the garbage he dumps for discarded treasures. He still considers a rare fast-food meal to be a dining-out experience."

Morales concedes, "The truth is, it's not a very livable wage. But it's a big change for the better." As an active union mem-ber, he will keep organizing and working with others to put more livability in people's paychecks, more fairness in the system. For now, however, the Living Wage victory at least provides what he calls a *salario digno,* for it has meant that he and his extended family could get out of the garage and into a two-bedroom home. It's only 800 square feet; it's not exactly in the 90210 zip code, and it's still mighty cramped with the five of them in there, but it's a real house. And it has a real bed in it—Morales's first purchase was to get the family off of that stack of cardboard. Slowly, they have since been able to add other furniture, including a small dining table. His second purchase was a '93 sedan—so, no more two-hour commute, no more 4 A.M. wake-up, no more bus stop muggings. Another big change was that the L.A. Living Wage law includes health insurance, "and for families," Mr. Morales says simply, "that means a lot."

In my work, I spend a big chunk of time flying around the country. In an airport a few years ago, I noticed for the first time a routine that I've since seen repeated several times in various airports. I saw a custodian making his rounds, gathering the trash that passengers leave strewn about the gate area when they board their plane. I watched him work his way down the concourse from one gate to another, and as he went, he would quickly make a pass along the banks of pay phones between the gates, checking the coin slots to see if anyone had left some change. Maybe it's a compulsion, I thought, or just an amusement (like some sort of custodian's Las Vegas). My assumption was that airport jobs, while not Fat City, were after all city positions and certainly wouldn't be so poorly paid that coin-slot change would count as income.

But that was before realizing just how extensive privatization has become in local governments. In Los Angeles, for example, most of the janitorial jobs—from the airport to the zoo—have been "outsourced," a bit of new economy jargon that means public tasks (and public money) have been farmed out to private interests. This has been sold to voters on the ideological assertion that corporations can run the public's business better than governments can, so just give us the contract and, by Jove, watch us save the taxpayers a bundle! Local politicians, eager to look like budget saviors (even as they take campaign contributions from the contractors), have been more than happy to go along. But the corporation always builds into its contract a juicy profit for itself, incredible salaries for its executives, an advertising budget, and other costs far beyond what a government agency has—so where does it get the "savings"? From José Morales and the janitors I've seen gleaning change from pay phones.

This hidden subsidy for privatization was the genesis of the Living Wage Campaign in L.A., which David Reynolds of Wayne State University has described in an excellent and comprehensive guide he authored with ACORN, the grassroots organizing group, bearing the straightforward title "Living Wage Campaigns: An Activist's Guide to Building the Movement for Economic Justice." In the City of Angels, the campaign began in 1995 with an organizing effort at LAX by two unions (Hotel Employees Restaurant Employees and Service Employees International). During the next several months, more than a hundred Los Angeles organizations joined the grassroots coalition to battle the wage ripoff—from homeless groups to small businesses, from taxpayer groups to churches, from political groups to retirees. It would be an arduous battle against a recalcitrant power structure that included Mayor Richard Riordan and the city's business establishment, which presented itself under the disingenuous name of The Coalition to Keep L.A. Working and snidely referred to the Living Wage proposal as the Job Destruction Ordinance. Their claim was that $7.25 an hour would force the privateers to eliminate the jobs rather than "suffer" the economic blow of paying a higher wage (though who exactly was then going to do the janitorial chores the company had contracted to perform was not addressed—perhaps some junior executives from headquarters). Of great worry also for the corporate crowd was that this ordinance would "only add to the perception that Los Angeles is not business friendly." Oh, great, better that the Morales family sleep on cardboard boxes stacked on a garage floor than that the city be seen as less than embracing to every rapacious contractor that wants to make a killing.

With the mayor in the pocket of the business establishment, the Living Wage advocates had to win not merely a majority of votes on the city council, but a veto-proof supermajority. Reynolds reports that they laid siege to the council, steadily barraging the members with letters, phone calls, faxes, e-mails, and visits. At Thanksgiving 1996, more than a thousand plates arrived in council offices, each one hand-decorated with some illustration of the "challenge" of trying to feed a family on poverty wages. In the Christmas season, a hundred clergy led others to city hall, accompanied by an actor draped in chains and playing the part of Jacob Marley, decrying Mayor Scrooge's opposition to the living wage. In addition, a group of merry carolers went to city hall and nearby restaurants singing carols with lyrics suitably adjusted for the message of the campaign. At LAX itself, low-wage workers like Morales took the media on a tour to highlight their working conditions.

They also kept expanding their coalition—as any janitor knows, the more straws in your broom, the more dirt you can sweep out. To the suprise of the establishment some business leaders supported the coalition, ranging from companies like Bell Industries to retailers like All American Home Center to smaller shops like The Stationery Place. Executives from these firms pointed out that good wages are *pro* business, since they reduce turnover, increase morale, produce better-skilled employees, and improve productivity. They also noted a basic lesson of economics—your workers are your customers. As Henry Ford wrote in 1926, "An underpaid man is a customer reduced in purchasing power. He cannot buy. Business depression is caused by weakened purchasing power. Purchasing power is weakened by uncertainty or insufficiency of income. The cure of business depression is through purchasing power, and the source of purchasing power is wages." These business advocates also raised the point of fair competition—the public subsidy of low-wage contractors undercut those, like themselves, who pursued a high-road business strategy of good wages.

A big breakthrough for the Living Wage advocates came when Protestant, Catholic, and Jewish leaders were organized into Clergy and Laity United for Economic Justice—CLUE. Bringing a moral and theological dimension to the campaign, CLUE leaders prompted discussions of the wage issue in their own congregations, preached of the justice aspect from their pulpits, wrote op-ed pieces, made pilgrimages to city hall, and used their own political contacts to press the issue.

In January, 1997, council members were greeted by a flood of New Year's cards beseeching them to do the right thing. For the next three months, coalition delegations visited the council twice a day, three days a week. They kept reaching out, kept focused, kept pushing—and on March 18, they won a *unanimous* vote for a living wage of $7.25 an hour indexed yearly to inflation increases, with family health benefits, and twelve paid days off each year. Mayor Riordan vetoed it. The city council overrode his veto.

Versions of this success story have been repeated, so far, in:

Alexandria	Detroit	Milwaukee County
Baltimore	Duluth	Minneapolis
Boston	Durham	Multnomah County
Buffalo	Gary	(OR)
Cambridge	Hartford	New Haven
Chicago	Hayward (CA)	New York City
Cleveland	Hudson County (NJ)	Oakland
Cook County (IL)	Jersey City	Omaha
Corvallis	Kankakee County (IL)	Pasadena
Dane County (WI)	Los Angeles County	Portland (OR)
Denver	Madison	San Antonio
Des Moines	Miami-Dade County	San Fernando

San Jose	St. Paul	West Hollywood
Santa Clara County	Toledo	Ypsilanti (MI)
(CA)	Tucson	
Somerville (MA)	Warren	

Key players have been ACORN (which operates the National Living Wage Center); unions such as AFSCME, HERE, and SEIU; an up-and-coming progressive political group called the New Party; the central labor councils in these cities, along with an umbrella labor group called Jobs With Justice; and local churches and interfaith groups like CLUE.

The Living Wage campaigns themselves are only a start, for the wages established still can be achingly low and apply only to the relatively few workers employed by government contractors. But they *are* a start, and an encouragingly strong one, too, delivering tangible benefits for regular folks too long ignored. The effort alone is enormously important, for it is getting thousands of people informed and involved, getting them into the streets, giving them confidence that their activism matters, developing battle-experienced grassroots leaders, and uniting a broad coalition for the long haul. The effort is also generating a phenomenal debate that Washington and Wall Street thought had been suppressed—a debate not only about the working poor, but also about questions of fairness and justice in a society that is being taught to value nothing but predator economics.

The very existence of such a movement—one that is now organized and linked from coast to coast, one that has the moral high road, and one that is actually *moving*—sends a chill through the nation's economic and political powers. It's like the hunter's nightmare, in which someone shouts: "Look out—the rabbit's got the gun!"

RETURN OF
THE ROBBER BARONS

During my political campaigning years, I came to a Zen-like understanding of Ernest Tubb's country-music classic, "There's miles and miles of Texas." Simply getting from here to there, crisscrossing the 262,000 square miles of this huge state, can be daunting to a statewide candidate. (I know that you Alaskans presently claim bragging rights on size, but no one's fooled by all that ice—a little more global warming and the ice will melt, leaving you guys standing on Rhode Island West.)

Of big help to me in my long-distance travels was Air Hightower—the private airplanes that a dozen or so of my supporters owned and would occasionally make available to me. These were not corporate jets with uniformed crews, luxury accommodations, and full meal service, like some of today's presidential candidates have at their disposal, but a collection of rather rudimentary single- and twin-engine prop planes (one literally was a crop duster) that were owned by farmers, lawyers, and other generous souls who volunteered to fly me around. Each of these owners would serve as a crew of one, combining the roles of pilot, navigator, mechanic, flight attendant, troubleshooter, chaplain, beer supplier, and freelance political adviser on our trips together.

Stuff happened. In a 1986 incident, two other politicos and I needed to fly from Austin to Lubbock for an evening political rally and get back the same night. Bob Armstrong, who had been a longtime Democratic officeholder and was then an Austin attorney, volunteered to ferry us out and back, a wearying 700-mile round-trip in a cramped plane. It was eleven or so by the time we returned to the Austin area, and we three passengers, having exercised on the home leg by doing a few twelve-ounce elbow bends, were slumped in our seats napping. Sitting in the front seat next to Bob, I was gradually brought out of my airborne snooze by the sensation of our plane circling again and again in a slow, droning loop around the hills on the city's west side. It seems that Bob's transponder had gone on the fritz. It could receive, but not send, signals, so he was unable to contact the tower to let them know we were approaching for our landing. We could even see the airport, but you can't come in to a public airport without permission, so Bob's theory was just to keep circling until they noticed and contacted us. They didn't.

After twenty minutes of not being noticed, Bob switched to Plan B. We flew to Executive Airpark, a small, private airport about ten miles north of Austin. It was closed for the night; but we landed anyway and taxied up to the double-wide mobile home that served as a terminal. There we executed a high-tech telecommunications maneuver that saved the day— or, in this case, the night. Bob and I hopped out of the plane, I gave him a quarter, and he used the pay phone outside the double-wide to ring up the air traffic controllers in the tower over at Greater Austin International to let them know we were ready to come in. Then we piled back in the plane, took off, got just high enough for the radar to find us, and were brought home at last.

If only there was a political party that would notice that America's majority is going around and around in circles somewhere out in the hills, within sight of the bright lights of prosperity, yet not being brought in. Instead, even the Democrats are zeroed in on the special needs and peculiar whims of the dominant business executives and investors who are rapidly and radically consolidating power within practically every economic sector, affecting the kind of jobs we get, our families' access to quality health care, the prices we pay, the purity of our food and water, the news we're fed, and much more. This reordering of America's (and the globe's) economic structure is being done with no public discussion about whether it's anything we want. Indeed, it's presented as the work of immutable market and technological forces, as though it's been ordained by the Economic Gods. This reminds me of a song by the Austin Lounge Lizards, titled "Jesus Loves Me, but He Can't Stand You"—apparently these economic gods love the executives and investors doing the consolidating, since their fortunes and power are greatly expanded, but they can't stand us, since ours are diminished. Don't worry your fuzzy little heads about it, we're told— watch TV, play golf, go to the mall—it's nothing but progress on its inevitable march into the new millennium. As farmers say, when you find something gooey and stinky on your boots, think bullshit.

There is nothing inevitable, much less beneficent, about the corporate consolidations, downsizings, wealth concentration, and other enormous changes rocking our economic and social order. They are the result of nothing more mystical than brute force and old-fashioned scheming among the power elites. The executives and investors plot with each other, conspire with politicians of both parties, and employ academics and media flaks—all to create the legal framework for their power grab, to implement it, and to devise the buzzwords of conventional wisdom to rationalize it ("global competitiveness" being the current cover-all).

These elites have plenty of precedents in American history for putting a mask of inevitability over the face of avarice. Go into a high school or college history class, and you'll find textbooks that still glorify the nineteenth-century industrialists who "followed their destiny" to build great industrial empires: Jay Gould's railroads, John D. Rockefeller's oil refineries, J. P. Morgan's steel factories. But Gould's empire was built less on entrepreneurial genius than on bribes and fraud; Rockefeller was not a marketer but a ruthless monopolist who lied and cheated to build his $2 billion fortune; and Morgan's U.S. Steel Corporation *became* the steel industry not because of any natural superiority of product or business skill but, as the great historian Howard Zinn puts it, "by closing off competition and maintaining the price at $28 a ton; and by working 200,000 men twelve hours a day for wages that barely kept their families alive."

In his superb book, *A People's History of the United States*, Zinn added, "And so it went, in industry after industry — shrewd, efficient businessmen building empires, choking out competition, maintaining high prices, keeping wages low, using government subsidies." A hundred years after the reign of these Robber Barons, we're back to the future, for Zinn's description is just as apt for Bill Gates, Sanford Weill, Philip Knight, Ron Perelman, Hugh McColl, Michael Eisner, Henry Kravis, and their allied Robber Barons who reign at the dawn of 2000. No less self-centered and ruthless than the Goulds, Rockefellers, and Morgans, these men have engineered today's world of conglomeratization and monopolization, demanding tribute from the rest of us in the form of low wages, high prices, and tax subsidies, while amassing unfathomable personal riches and spinning golden cocoons to isolate themselves from the consequences of their actions.

MERGING, PURGING, AND SPLURGING

When I was about twelve, I decided I should read the Bible from cover to cover. I did fine with the early chapters, which are filled with familiar stories I learned in Sunday school.

Then I came upon Chronicles I and hit the wall of genealogy delineating the royal line of David. Page after page is devoted to such scintillating information as, "Caleb son of Hezron had children by his wife Azubah (and by Jerioth). These were her sons: Jesher, Shobab, and Ardon. When Azubah died, Caleb married Ephrath, who bore him Hur. Hur was the father of Uri, and Uri the father of Bezalel. Later, Hezron lay with the daughter of Makir, the father of Gilead, and she bore him Segrub. Segrub was the father of Jair, who controlled twenty-three towns in Gilead. . . ." And on and on it went. I finally waded through it, reading every "begat," "firstborn," and "bore"— understanding none of it.

It occurs to me that this is the way most people feel when they come upon the seemingly endless list of corporate mergers that are reported almost daily in the business pages of the newspapers. The largest ones might even make front-page news, though there's never any interpretation that would help a reader understand why this is happening and what it means to them: Exxon took over Mobil, and BP got both Amoco and ARCO. Travelers Group, which earlier had consumed Salomon Smith Barney, swallowed Citicorp, thus becoming the gargantuan Citigroup. NationsBank subjugated BankAmerica, not only gaining its assets, but also seizing its name, like some feudal baron might appropriate the coat of arms of a conquered foe. SBC Communications snared Ameritech, Bell Atlantic grabbed GTE and renamed itself Verizon, and AT&T picked off TCI. From Germany, Deutsche Bank reached into Boston and snatched Bankers Trust, while Daimler-Benz reached into Detroit and took away Chrysler.

The urge to merge—the urge of one corporate giant to devour another—was insatiable in the nineties, completely remaking the economic landscape for all of us. The short list above includes but a few of the recent large mergers among corporate baronies. The financial value of 1999's consolidations totaled nearly two trillion buckaroos, which beat the record-setting year of '98, which beat the record-setting year of '97, which beat the record-setting year of '96, which . . . et cetera, all the way back to 1990. And 2000 was expected to set yet another record. The corporate couplings have become so massive that the thesaurus can no longer keep up. "Big" became "giant," which became "huge," which became "gargantuan," which became "mega-mammoth," which will become some worse contortion of the language. When Price Waterhouse, one of the Big Four accounting firms (they were the Big Eight as recently as 1997), merged with another biggie, CoopersLybrand, the subsequent name was too long to get on a letterhead, so it was reduced (along with competition) to the still-cumbersome PricewaterhouseCoopers. My favorite indicator of how far beyond us these behemoths have gotten comes to me when Southwestern Bell, my local phone monopoly (now a *deregulated* monopoly), sends me its monthly bill. Southwestern, which was one of the seven "Baby Bells" created by the 1984 breakup of AT&T, controlled local service in its original territory of Texas, Oklahoma, Kansas, Missouri, and Arkansas until 1996. That year, it reached out and plucked another Baby Bell, Pacific Telesis, giving it control over California and Nevada phone customers, too. Then, in '98, it added a third Baby Bell, Ameritech, to its roster, giving it the customers in Illinois, Indiana, Ohio, Michigan, and Wisconsin. Don't look now, but Ma Bell, as AT&T was derisively referred to prior to the breakup, is being reincarnated as Southwestern Bell, which now defines itself on its bills with this charming slogan: "Your friendly neighborhood global communications company." Lily Tomlin at her satirical best could not top that.

A merger consultant recently told the *Wall Street Journal* that "the whole mentality of corporate America is M&A driven right now." M&A doesn't refer to kinky sex, not exactly, but to the kinky business phenomenon of mergers and acquisitions (it's so common that there's even a magazine called *M&A*,

which some of your better stores keep in plastic wrappers on the top shelf with other XXX-rated material). "If you're not consolidating, you're not in the game," said the consultant.

Hmmm. Game. Did you know you were in a game?

Mergers are a game the barons play at great profit to themselves, yet millions of people who don't even know the game is being played, much less have a say in the rules, end up on the losing end—workers, customers, small businesses, communities, ordinary shareholders, and even the company itself.

WORKERS. Typically, news stories about corporate mergers make no mention of anything so downbeat as job cuts. Instead, there's usually a photo of two gloating CEOs, a statement about how out-of-this-world HUGE the deal is, a cute little anecdote about how the executive duo first came up with the idea of marrying their companies ("We were in the same foursome at the Rolls-Royce Golden Golf Getaway at Platinum Pines last year, and when we both birdied number 7, I said to Jack, 'This could be the start of something big,' and we looked at each other, and both of us knew then . . . "), plus the stories invariably contain a liberal sprinkling of voodoo incantations, such as "synergies," "market compatibilities," and "strategic dynamics," designed to appease skeptical Wall Street analysts about a marriage that otherwise looks about as well thought out as your average $25 quickie wedding in Las Vegas.

Actually, merger stories do include cryptic allusions to job cuts, but you have to know the jargon. Trying to figure out what corporate officials are saying is no easier than deciphering government gobbledygook, since plain English is passé and CorporateSpeak has invaded the language. Consider these gems culled by AP writer Eric Quinones:

"Population Equivalents"—a term used by cellular phone companies to mean "people."

"Mortality Experience"—coined by life insurance companies to denote "death" (an "adverse mortality experience" is the industry's phrase for "more death claims than expected," though the deceased can be forgiven if they think that their own individual mortality experience is adverse).

"Social Expression Product"—the greeting card industry's generic jargon for "birthday card," "get-well card," etc.

So, wink-wink, when a merger is announced, those who know the game know you don't look for some straightforward statement like "jobs by the jillions are being whacked by these bloodsucking curs," but instead you must seek out certain telltale code words: "To build shareholder value, *operating efficiencies* have been identified"; "The merger will result in a *restructuring* of the firm"; and, "Executives intend to pare *structural redundancies* resulting from the acquisition."

Of course, *you* are the "redundancy," if you're one of the hundreds of thousands of employees who have gotten the boot in the past decade after hundreds of major corporations have merged. Unlike the full media treatment given to the merging, the subsequent purging gets little coverage—usually a one-paragraph notice back in the business pages, much like an obituary: "Citigroup to cut 10,400," "Wells Fargo to cut its workforce by 4,600," "America Online plans 1,000 layoffs," and "First Union to cut 5,850 jobs" are a few of the obits that ran in 1999, months after these companies had announced their mergers.

While no one is safe, the employees of the subjugated firm in a takeover feel especially vulnerable, and they often feel betrayed by their own top executives who helped orchestrate the merger. When British Petroleum acquired Amoco in 1998, for example, word soon spread through the corporate grapevine that 6,000 employees would pay the price, and that most of these cuts would be made on the Amoco side. Sir John Browne, BP's steely-eyed, job-whacking CEO, didn't mince words: "We have to get through the harvesting of low-hanging fruit," he said as he eyed the Amoco personnel chart. The *Wall Street Journal* reported that a bit of gallows humor quickly spread down the hallways of Amoco's Chicago headquarters: "What do you call the new CEO? Sir John. Our old CEO? Surrender. Chicago management? Sur-plus." The good news is that Browne didn't slash 6,000 employees. The bad news is that he slashed more than 10,000.

John Challenger of the job-tracking employment firm of Challenger, Gray & Christmas reports that corporations fire at least one out of every nine employees after a merger. If each job loss were marked with a simple white cross in a field, as is done at many battlefield cemeteries, the sight would be staggering, just as the reality is staggering to the families who suffer the loss.

OTHERS. Beyond the immediate impact on jobs, mergers ripple throughout our society, and I don't mean the kind of gentle ripples you get when a pebble is tossed in a pond, but the kind of ripples you'd get by dropping a cement block in a punch bowl. Start with the obvious fact that the whole idea of these massive consolidations is to eliminate competition. Oddly enough, however, CEOs puff themselves up at press conferences and publicly assert that the new jumbo-combo company was created to "improve competitiveness." One wonders whether such vacuousness comes naturally to them or whether they have to practice it. You don't need to be a CEO to see that where there were two, there is now one, and this is not generally a competitive plus for the rest of us.

Take the oil industry, which has recently been rushing to reconstruct Rockefeller. Old John D. put together the Standard Oil Company by hook *and* crook in the 1870s, monopolizing the industry and generally operating in such a tyrannical fashion that the Supreme Court intervened in 1911 to bust his trust into thirty-four companies. Just as a salamander can grow another leg, though, these thirty-four legs have been trying to grow another salamander. The Standard Oil trust has steadily been coming back together in the past few years, especially the biggest parts of it.

- Standard Oil of Ohio (Sohio) and Standard Oil of Indiana (Amoco) have been taken over by British Petroleum, which also is taking over the old Standard Oil's Atlantic Refining Company (ARCO).
- Standard Oil of California (Chevron) has taken over Gulf, and now Chevron itself is in talks to be merged into Royal Dutch Shell, which already has absorbed Texaco.
- Standard Oil of New Jersey (Exxon), the largest U.S. oil company, took over Standard Oil of New York (Mobil), the second largest U.S. oil company.

The $80 billion merger of Exxon and Mobil in late '98 brought the two largest chunks of John D.'s empire back together, creating the world's largest corporation, surpassing General Motors. The two barons, Lee Raymond of Exxon and Lucio Noto of Mobil, had begun their flirtation only six months earlier at a meeting of the American Petroleum Institute (the industry's cozy 'club and lobbying arm), and Raymond spoke grandly at the news conference about his and Noto's selfless motivation in forging the new combine, saying it was simply a matter of wanting "to deliver more value to our shareholders, and our employees, and customers."

Customers and employees, however, saw it for what it was—two giants gaining more control over them. "Rockefeller's Revenge," one consumer group called it, noting that the combination meant that the refineries and stations of the two largest oil companies were no longer in competition on price and service. For employees, the Christmastime merger certainly was a lump of coal. At least 9,000 of them learned they would lose their positions in accounts payable, receiving, finance, information systems, and the other back-office divisions of the two companies. Nor has it been any blessing for hundreds of gasoline dealers who leased their stations from either Exxon or Mobil. The companies often had stations competing across the street from each other. But with the merger, one is gone—and so is the family that ran the place, along with the hired help they had. These are people who never heard of Mr. Raymond or Mr. Noto, but suddenly the impact of a meeting between two corporate autocrats at the American Petroleum Institute has rippled across the country and turned their little corner of the world upside down. Also, the small-business operators who leased from Mobil now find themselves in an Exxon corporate culture, where station rents are up to five times higher than what Mobil charged, and where leases are for three years instead of the ten-year term offered by Mobil. Meanwhile, down in Beaumont, Texas, some 900 workers at Mobil's largest refinery worry that the merger will shut it (and them) down. Exxon has two refineries of its own along this Gulf Coast crescent, so a third one might fit that category of "structural redundancies." Beaumont itself will take a body blow if this refinery is closed. From cafés to car dealers, bars to barbershops, hundreds of other people in the area depend on the good paychecks that those 900 union refinery workers earn.

Like marriages in the heyday of royalty, corporate mergers are not about love or natural affinities; they are pure and simple power arrangements, and the size and reach of them now overwhelm balances of power that such competing social forces as unions, consumers, environmentalists, farmers—even governments—had established since the Robber Baron days of infamy. Here is a sampler of what has been wrought by corporate fiat in just the last three or four years:

- *Health Care.* Met Life, Prudential, New York Life, Travelers, and John Hancock are among the major HMO competitors that were there a moment ago, but are now gone, gulped

down whole as a boa constrictor eats a pig by the likes of
Aetna, Cigna, and Unitedhealth Group. Not only are these
three already the dominant national players in what is now
referred to as the health-care *industry,* but they divide up
the national territory to give them near monopoly power in
city after city, which is where it counts, since most people
don't leave town to go to the doctor. Aetna, which is notorious for squeezing the care out of health care, has captured
40 percent of the Philadelphia market, nearly 60 percent in
several New Jersey cities, and a third in Atlanta, Orlando,
and San Antonio. As Consumers for Quality Care put it in a
letter to antitrust officials, "With greater market share in
key cities and states, Aetna [has] put itself in a position to
offer more patients less coverage for ever higher premiums." Two-thirds of the U.S. market is now in the hands of
the ten largest companies. Already, the consolidated HMO
industry is acting not in competition but in concert—in
1998, the biggest national firms decided virtually on the
same day to dump their Medicare service for rural seniors,
and in 1999 every one of them uniformly hiked premiums
for all of their patients.

- *Environment/Government.* British Petroleum's takeover of
ARCO is also a takeover of the Alaskan economy and environment. In the nineties, five other oil firms pulled out of
Alaska's North Slope, the largest oil field in North America,
turning over their leases to either BP or ARCO, which once
were fierce competitors. But now they are one, giving BP
monopoly control of the Alaskan pipeline, control of nearly
75 percent of the oil in Alaska, and ownership of 80 percent of Alaska's economic base. A state legislator notes
that his homeland has essentially become a colony of the
London-based conglomerate, which can now dictate the
price of oil leaving the state (a price that determines 75
percent of state government revenues), the terms for developing Alaska's untapped natural-gas fields, the wages and

employment conditions for oil workers, and the nature and extent of environmental protection.

- *Food.* Monsanto has spent $8 billion to pluck such seed companies as DeKalb and Asgrow from the competitive field, and Du Pont has snapped up Pioneer Hi-Bred, the country's largest seed company. These two biotech giants now control half of the U.S. market for soybean seeds and more than half of the corn seed market, America's first- and second-largest crops. If you control the seed, you begin to control the crops, the farmers, and food itself, and Monsanto and Du Pont are using their duopoly to do all of that. (Monsanto, for example, has genetically altered the DNA of its seeds so the crops can absorb more of a particular pesticide the company makes.) Meanwhile, Monsanto itself was plucked by the European drug giant Pharmacia. Farmers are also squeezed by the merger-fed growth of middleman monopolies—Cargill, the world's largest privately held corporation and the world's number one grain shipper, took over the shipping operations of Continental Grain, previously the third-largest shipper. Bottom line for grain farmers is that typically they are paid a penny or two a bushel less than they would get if the merger had not happened—which adds up to a loss of more than $2,500 a year for the farmer. As the head of the National Farmers Union puts it, "Mergers and acquisitions in agriculture are occurring—and being approved—at breakneck speed with little regard for the consequences to America's farmers." Attention food shoppers: Do you buy your groceries from Royal Ahold of the Netherlands? No, you say, I shop at the Bi-Lo stores in the Carolinas, Georgia, and Tennessee; at Edwards supermarkets in the New York region; at Tops in upstate New York, Ohio, and Pennsylvania; at Giant in the D.C. area; at Pathmark stores in metropolitan New York and Philadelphia; or at Stop & Shop in New England. All of these, however, have been taken over by Royal Ahold, making it the dominant

food retailer on the eastern seaboard and the fourth largest
in the entire United States.

- *Air Travel.* Deregulation of the airlines, which was supposed to spur competition, instead shrank it, with majors
buying each other while also squeezing out or buying up
the regional and discount companies. Essentially, there are
only six major airlines—American, Continental, Delta,
Northwest, United, and USAir—and they cooperate, rather
than compete, on most routes, dividing up the turf through
their hub system. As Continental's CEO confided in a 1998
industry confab, "American kind of controls Dallas–Fort
Worth and Miami. We've got Newark, Houston, and Cleveland. Delta's got Atlanta. . . ." And so on. To eliminate the
inconvenience of any actual competition, the government
routinely grants immunity from antitrust laws for airlines
that want to "cooperate" (can you spell c-o-n-s-p-i-r-e?) on
prices and schedule. And indeed they do conspire—a rare
glimpse of their price collusion came in the mid-eighties
when court documents revealed a phone conversation
between Robert Crandall, then CEO of American Airlines,
and Howard Putnam, president of a now-defunct airline:

> **CRANDALL:** Yes, I have a suggestion for you. Raise your
> goddamn fares 20 percent. I'll raise mine the next
> morning.
>
> **PUTNAM:** Robert, we . . .
>
> **CRANDALL:** You'll make more money and I will too.
>
> **PUTNAM:** We can't talk about pricing.
>
> **CRANDALL:** Oh, bullshit, Howard. We can talk about any
> goddamn thing we want to talk about.

The further conglomeration of the big six into a big three
or even a big two already is underway. Northwest now
owns more than half of the voting stock in Continental, and
both American and Delta have been maneuvering to grab
Northwest for themselves. Last year, United and US Air
announced that they would become one, a move that would

give the merged giant control of *a third* of the flights in and out of Boston, Baltimore, Los Angeles, New York's La Guardia, and Washington National; half to *two-thirds* of the market in Chicago, Philadelphia, San Francisco, and Washington Dulles; and *three-fourths* of the flights in Charlotte, Denver, and Pittsburgh.

To squeeze it all even tighter, the whole global market of some 200 airlines has already been consolidated into four huge air-travel "alliances" (One World, Atlantic Excellence, Star Alliance, and Wings) that stifle competition, letting them set routes, schedules, and prices—all beyond the reach of any one nation's regulators. *Condé Nast Traveler* cites the chairman of TWA, which doesn't belong to any of the four alliances, as saying that attempting to compete with these airline "cartels" would be "like trying to compete with Standard Oil before it was broken up."

- *Books*. The publishing industry, too, of which I'm a teensy footnote, is succumbing to the tidal wave of conglomeration and consolidation. By 1997, eight publishing octopi had their tentacles around most of the book world: *Bertelsmann* (Bantam, Doubleday, Dell, the Library Guild, etc.); *Viacom* (Simon & Schuster, Pocket Books, Scribner, etc.); *News Corporation* (HarperCollins—Me!); *Time Warner* (Warner Books, Little Brown, Time-Life Books, Book-of-the-Month Club, etc.); *Advance Publications* (Random House, Alfred Knopf, Crown, Ballantine, etc.); *Pearson* (Viking Penguin, Putnam, Dutton, Signet, etc.); *Hearst* (William Morrow, Avon, etc.); and *Holtzbrinck* (Farrar Straus, St. Martin's, Henry Holt, etc.). Three years later, Bertelsmann has grabbed Random House, News Corporation has taken William Morrow and Avon, and Time Warner is moving on Simon & Schuster. The few become fewer, and the choices for writers and readers shrink.
- *Garbage*. Even the humblest of industries is not beyond merger mania, and consolidation in the waste-disposal

world is causing a real mess. As we enter the high-tech millennium, the low-tech world of garbage has fallen to two companies that own most of the landfills and waste collection terminals in the country—Waste Management Inc. and Allied Waste Industries. Built by a series of rapid mergers, these two now control more than half of America's residential, municipal, and industrial solid-waste handling. As they have gained control of market after market, fees have steadily risen, often dramatically. Within weeks of consuming its largest competitor in 1999, for example, Waste Management jacked up its landfill fees by 40 percent. But this is not the only price of waste-disposal monopoly—it is much more profitable for these companies to dump everything in their landfills than to sort out materials for recycling, so the environmental advances that so many cities have made are endangered by the sudden grip that these private firms have gotten on our garbage. Neil Seldman of the Institute for Local Self-Reliance puts it bluntly: "They will use their size to control the bins and trucks and to discourage recycling wherever they can."

WHY IS THIS HAPPENING? Butch Hancock, one of the wonderful singer-songwriters who sprang forth in the 1970s from the unlikely musical soil of Lubbock, Texas, says that he was taught two big lessons growing up in this strait-laced farming town: "One is that God loves you and you're going to burn in hell. The other is that sex is the most awful, dirty thing on the face of the earth and you should save it for someone you love."

With this kind of logic in his background, perhaps Butch is the one to explain why the political system is so benign toward a handful of individuals who are causing so much damage to so many with their merger schemes. It would be one thing if the junior Rockefellers doing the scheming were generating real efficiencies, growth, and value for the companies and their shareholders, but the most embarrassing aspect of their deals is that mostly they don't work—not even in a business sense.

The corporate landscape is littered with the carcasses of mergers that collapsed of their own weight, the victims of executive excess. There's Quaker Oats, the solid purveyor of breakfast cereals and pancake mixes, reaching in 1994 for a snappier image by paying $1.7 billion to grab the cool beverage of the time, Snapple. Just three years later, the goof had proven to be so huge that Quaker unloaded Snapple for $300 million—nearly a billion and a half dollars less than it paid for its prized acquisition. Or, look at First Union, the sixth largest bank in the country, constructed not of granite and sound loans but of mergers, gobbling up such firms as CoreStates Financial and the Money Store, for which it paid too much, boasted too loudly, and managed too poorly. One financial analyst says of First Union, "For years I complained about the prices they paid for acquisitions, but I always said they ran a good bank. But now they're having serious problems running the basic bank—the wheels are coming off the cart."

A textbook case of merger malaise was the 1985 combination of RJ Reynolds with Nabisco, which then was taken over in 1988 by the swashbuckling, junk-bond-wielding investment syndicate of Kohlberg Kravis Roberts. It was the largest deal ever at the time, and it was glorified on Wall Street and in the business media as a bold and sparkling model of what financial engineering could do. Yes, thousands of people would lose their jobs; yes, the company would be saddled with enormous interest payments on the $30 billion KKR borrowed to seize the prize; yes, whole chunks of the prize would have to be sold off to pay the bondholders; and yes, there were a few stuffy analysts who said the match was one made in hell, not in heaven—but, get out of the way, spoilsports, we're talking about geniuses. With money! The geniuses got away with corporate murder—KKR took billions in fees and profits when they sold out in 1991—but regular investors saw their RJR Nabisco stock fall by half, and, by 1999, the company was in such a mess that it split itself apart, leaving Nabisco an independent company again, but a much weaker one than when it was caught up in the grand experiment fourteen years earlier. The same analysts and media that gushed about the deal back then used terms like "a sad saga," "a notorious chapter," "financial ignominy," and "the Debacle" to describe it in 1999. Yet, KKR is still doing deals, and the investment bankers that made hundreds of millions in fees for putting the merger and subsequent takeover together collected even more millions for taking RJR Nabisco apart.

There's a country song entitled "If I Tell You I Love You, Consider Me Drunk." Wall Street expresses a drunken love for just about every merger that comes along by bidding up the stock price of the mergers. Then sobriety sets in. Academic studies abound to show that, after a year or so, most mergers turn ugly as it becomes apparent that they won't deliver promised efficiencies and corporate harmonies, so the stock prices fall and shareholders are stuck with a loser. One study by the corporate accounting firm KPMG found that *less than 20 percent* of mergers produce any benefits for shareholders, and "over half actually destroyed [shareholder] value." The *New York Times* has covered several of these studies, reporting that "most mergers result in stocks that lag behind those of other companies in their industry [and] many mergers result in actual losses for their shareholders"; "most acquisitions fail, academics say, because the post-merger business cannot support the price paid to forge the combination"; and, "the most comprehensive study of conglomerate mergers . . . found that the profitability of acquired companies on average declined."

So who the hell is pushing these hellacious deals? The people sporting the big toothy grins at the press conferences when they're announced: the CEOs of the merging companies and the investment bankers who are paid multimillion-dollar fees to broker the deal. The Wall Street brokers get the least attention, so let's start with them, giving credit where it's due. All the major Wall Street firms have M&A divisions whose job is to encourage companies to merge. Like lobbyists in Washington, M&A agents are on the prowl wherever CEOs gather—whispering, presenting possibilities, advising, urging. There are massive fees to be made, and reputations, too. Being a top-ten M&A broker gets you prestige, bragging rights . . . and more lucrative deals, since CEOs looking to merge want someone who's been around the block a few times. There's even a formal ranking, called the League Tables, that lists Wall Streeters by the dollar value of the mergers they pull off. Top of the list in the last year of League rankings was Goldman Sachs, with 339 deals valued at nearly a trillion dollars. Merrill Lynch was second, followed by Morgan Stanley Dean Witter, Salomon Smith Barney, and Crédit Suisse First Boston (notice for amusement's sake that the last three are themselves products of mergers). The bankers' incentive to push for more consolidations is clear—in the Exxon/Mobil merger, for example, J. P. Morgan for Exxon and Goldman Sachs for Mobil split about $50 million for a few weeks' work.

Not that a lot of pushing is needed. CEOs, who tend to have egos about the size of a supernova, get a jollies-jolt from having their pictures splashed across the front pages of major dailies. The media splash lets them strut around the next Predators' Ball as the baddest merger men in the whole damn country.

Just as some people have to have the biggest, flashiest car on the block, executives develop one-upmanship rivalries. Some say that Edward Crutchfield, Jr., CEO of the Charlotte-based First Union bank, put his empire at risk with too many ill-advised mergers because he was in a pecker-measuring contest with his crosstown rival Hugh McColl, Jr., CEO of Charlotte-based NationsBank. McColl bought Boatman's bank of St. Louis; Crutchfield bought CoreStates Financial; McColl bought Barnett Banks of Florida; Crutchfield bought the Money Store; Crutchfield announced a thirty-story office tower to dominate the Charlotte skyline; McColl announced a forty-five-story skyscraper; Crutchfield then suggested he might erect a hundred-story edifice. Even ineptness seems to be a point of rivalry—just as First Union announced last May that it had suffered heavy financial losses and was toppling over into the ditch, NationsBank announced in the same month that it was staggering with the top-heavy load of its acquisitions, especially its merger with BankAmerica, which turns out to have had a number of land mines in its investment portfolio and to be burdened with out-of-date computer technology. (You would do more checking into the purchase of a $600 used pickup than some of these guys do into a $60 billion bank merger.) As one analyst said of First Union's buying binge: "This is a tale of ego run amok."

It is not simply ego, however, that fuels the executive urge to merge—it is visions of sugarplums dancing in their heads. This is where merging begets splurging. No child's Christmas fantasy can come near the reality of the payday that top executives arrange for themselves when cutting these deals. In November 1998, a double-trunk ad appeared in newspapers. Filling one page was a life-sized head shot of Jürgen Schrempp, CEO of Daimler-Benz, Germany's top auto company. On the opposite page was the well-groomed mug of Robert Eaton, CEO of Chrysler. Linking the two heads was a banner headline proclaiming "Vision Meets Vision." These two "visionaries" had just forged the DaimlerChrysler corporation through a $40 billion amalgamation operating under the new slogan "Expect the extraordinary."

The extraordinary thing in this transaction is that Chrysler's top brass literally turned themselves into gold, whether or not the merger proves to be successful for anyone else. Eaton is the most golden of them all—he got $3.7 million in cash right off the top, $70 million in stock grants, and $149 million worth of shares in the new DaimlerChrysler corporation. It was explained that this $223 million handout to Eaton was needed as incentive to keep him on the job for a couple of years to make sure the transition went smoothly. If he quits or is fired during this period, he would get another $24.4 million—plus, the company even pays the taxes on his golden parachute (and, since paying the taxes is considered compensation that itself is taxable, DaimlerChrysler also would pay Eaton's taxes on the taxes—not a lot is left to chance by these boys). One more sugarplum: The fifty-eight-year-old Eaton was awarded an extra $30,000 *a month* on his pension, bringing him to $1.7 million a year, every year, for the rest of his life. Making sure that none of you more cynical types misunderstood his motivation in selling America's number three car company to the Germans, the visionary Eaton felt compelled to state publicly that this merger was strictly about corporate efficiencies and shareholder value, "and obviously my own personal situation had no bearing whatsoever."

Generous to a fault, Eaton also took care of those below him. Not secretaries or line workers, you understand, but those in the suites adjacent to his: Robert Lutz, a Chrysler vice chairman, got a $62 million package from the merger; Gary Valade, Chrysler's chief financial officer, got $52 million; and Thomas Stallkamp, Chrysler's president, took $50 million.

Likewise, Lou Noto hit a big one. He's the Mobil CEO who peddled his company to Exxon in a deal bigger than the annual economic output of most of the world's countries. A spokesman told the *Wall Street Journal* that Noto pushed the sale solely because "it is in the best interests of the company" and that he "has never made decisions based purely on his own financial gain." Explain that to the 9,000-plus workers fired, who note that Noto's personal gain from the merger was about $16 million, including $7.8 million in severance, $2.1 million in "retention" pay, and $200,000 worth of "other" pay. Also, he gets $5.7 million to cover taxes on his package. In addition, don't forget the $33 million he gets in stock grants and the $12 million coming to him for his shares in Mobil. That's a total of about $66.6 million—clearly the work of the devil.

The quick-buck award goes to Robert Annunziata, who became CEO of Global Crossing two years ago, having been lured to the Bermuda-based telecommunications firm with a $10 million signing bonus, a $5 million low-interest loan to buy company stock, and a three-year employment contract at a million per. He didn't last. Within three *months,* Annunziata sold Global to the regional phone company US West. He gets $135 million from the deal.

And so it goes—Sanford Weill and John Reed, the barons of Travelers and Citicorp taking $26 million each from their merger, which cost 10,400 workers their jobs; Richard Notebaert, who was paid $30 million when Southwestern Bell took over his Ameritech regional phone company, plus a special bonus of $2.5 million for "extra work" related to the merger, not counting $32 million in stock payments; and Frank Newman, whose stewardship of Bankers Trust led to massive losses for the shareholders and layoffs for employees, getting $135 million in his sellout to Deutsche Bank. "The corporate executive maximizes his own welfare first, the company's second," observes economist Walter Adams. "He doesn't ask himself what will the company look like ten years down the road if I negotiate this acquisition."

Lest I give the impression that merger mania produces absolutely no economic benefit outside of the executive suites, I hasten to point out a growth industry that has been spurred by all this M&A activity: sign making. With corporate names changing faster than some traffic lights, sign companies are busy covering the changes. Here in Austin, for example, the people who run the General Neon Sign Company were some of the few citizens who found a silver lining in the takeover of our First State Bank by faraway Norwest Bank. General Neon got the 1998 contract to bring down the blue-and-white signs at thirty-two First State branches, replacing them with the green-and-white emblems of Norwest. Barely a year later, General Neon is bidding to undo all the signage it just completed. Norwest has been acquired by Wells Fargo Bank, you see, and its colors are red and gold.

PIRATES. The poster boy for the merging and purging that is ripping so violently through our society could well be Gerry Cameron, a lesser light on the global corporate marquee, yet one whose actions pretty well sum up this sorry saga of greed.

Cameron was boss hog at U.S. Bancorp, based in Portland, Oregon, until May 1997, when it was announced that the bank was being absorbed by a grasping, national banking empire with the anonymous (and vaguely ominous) name of First Bank System Inc. Shortly after the takeover announcement, "The System's" CEO, John F. Grundhofer, uttered the words that sent a chill through the normally chill-hardy people of Portland: "By eliminating redundancies and increasing efficiency, we can improve service and offer a broader portfolio of products."

"Redundancies." Four thousand Oregonians were to be made redundant by the deal struck between Cameron and Grundhofer—one of the largest mass firings in the state's history. U.S. Bancorp's headquarters building in downtown Portland was to be emptied, with those functions being assumed by the new parent company in Minneapolis. U.S. Bancorp's credit-card processing center was to be shut down, too, with its functions moved to The System's own processing center in Fargo, North Dakota (rentals of the macabre movie *Fargo*, by the way, shot up dramatically in Portland video stores as word of the merger ripped through the city). Did Grundhofer say the firings were designed to "improve service"? Maybe he thought the people of Portland all rode into town on a turnip truck—in addition to 4,000 fewer employees to serve the public, the merger plan included eliminating forty-four branch offices of the bank.

Gerry Cameron did prove to be a stand-up guy for one of U.S. Bancorp's employees, however: himself! The new, merged bank has Grundhofer as president and CEO, but a sly, smiling Cameron sitting next to him as chairman. It's not merely a title he gets—Gerry negotiated a sweetheart package that assures him the same $1.6 million annual salary and bonus he had been getting, a lump-sum payment of $12.4 million (sort of a gratuity for doing the deal), a grant of stock in the new company worth a good $8.6 million, and the payment of the taxes he owes on the entire generous package. Untold millions more were to come to him from profits he would gain by cashing in the stock he held in his old bank. Oh, one more lollipop: a cool million dollars a year for his retirement.

In a special touch of class, Cameron's $12.4 million gratuity was to be handed to him the same day those 4,000 employees were to begin cleaning out their desks.

The workers and their families were not the only ones taking a hit for Cameron's merger maneuver. Other businesses in and around the U.S. Bancorp Tower were also rocked by the sudden blow: The janitorial and cleaning crews, for example, were faced with an uncertain period of empty floors and no work; Your Store, the coffee shop on the ground floor, had an immediate drop in business when Gerry's merger was announced, as did Grampy's, the sandwich shop across the street ("People are scared," Grampy's owner told the *Portland Oregonian*. "They don't know where they're going next"). Higher up in the tower, the law firm and the accounting firm handling the bank's business were looking at their own job cuts; and business at Geranium Lake Flowers, which catered to bank employees, began declining as soon as the bad news hit, with one exception—it had a temporary uptick in orders for sympathy bouquets to be delivered to bank employees who were being fired.

When I hear about such voracious and reckless executives, so willing to enrich themselves at the expense of their co-workers, I find myself enraged and wanting to shout, "You bunch of pirates!" But then I realize that this is unfair. To pirates.

Not to romanticize the buccaneers of the high seas, but they practiced a form of floating democracy that was extraordinary compared to the way other businesses acted in those days . . . or in these days. Writer Bart Jones of AP has reported that pirates voted on such basic issues as whether to attack a particular ship and which direction to sail, and everyone on board got a fair share of the booty. Kenneth Kinkor, a historian who studies pirate records and their shipwrecks, says that the sharing of gains from pirate raids typically paid the captain two shares, the quartermaster one-and-a-half shares, and every crew member one share. By way of illustration, if $100,000 worth of loot was to be split among a ship with a hundred pirates, the captain would get about $2,000, some $1,500 would go to the quartermaster, and the other ninety-eight pirates would get about $1,000 each.

At the time, the captains of merchant ships were getting fifteen times more than the crew, and it was not uncommon for the sailors to get stiffed by the mercantile trading companies, ending up with nothing. Compare those captain-crew spreads to today's corporate captains, who routinely are taking 475 times what the typical "crew member" gets, and who have been regularly abandoning the crew in mergers and massive downsizings.

Pirate society was surprisingly civil in other ways, too. Who provided the first workers' compensation plan? None other than the notorious Captain Kidd, in 1695. It was common, says Kinkor, for pirates to be awarded a handsome disability payment by the captain and crew if they lost an arm or leg in battle, and widows sometimes got payments, too, when pirates were killed. There was even a remarkable level of racial equality—about a third of the pirates were black, mostly former slaves, and they were entitled to the same vote and the same share of the plunder as white crew members. Indeed, Kinkor found records of black pirates being chosen captains by crews that were mostly white. And, while these pillagers certainly could be vicious brutes, Jones reports that "pirates often treated prisoners decently to encourage other ships to surrender rather than fight to the death." (The black skull and crossbones of infamy was not raised as an attack flag but as a warning to surrender—an all-red flag was hoisted to say "here we come.") Jones also notes that "many pirate ships imposed rules such as no smoking below decks after sunset, lights out by eight, no women or boys aboard, and no gambling, which often led to fights."

Piracy, which lasted about fifty years over the late 1600s and early 1700s, was largely a rebellion against the enormous injustices and legalized thievery of the merchant shipping corporations and other respectable men of commerce, so it's not surprising that the maritime revolution offered an onboard social structure more humane than the autocratic and abusive one it was fleeing. Then, as today, the real pirates weren't the ones with eye patches and peg legs.

HAS ANYONE SEEN TEDDY? The massive mergers that are ongoing are the black holes of our economic universe, sucking money and power from everyone around them into the dark-star vortex of the corporate barons who are at the center. Industry after industry is succumbing to this downward swirl of competition that eliminates choice, raises prices, cuts jobs and wages, reduces the quality of service, stifles innovation, and permits tighter corporate control of the political system. The Establishment titillates us with the zing-pop-and-sizzle of computer technology that, we're assured, is breeding change faster than bunnies on Viagra, promising that this change is going to remake our economy and our drab little lives in ways we could not have imagined in the Olden Tymes of, say, 1998. But while they have us gazing numbly into the BillGatesian

Future, they are busy grabbing, whacking, destroying, congloming, and conspiring to remake the global economy in their own private image—which is the image of Rockefeller, Gould, and Morgan. This awesome massing of power is by far the biggest and most threatening development to America's workers, small business, farmers, consumers—and to our democracy—in a century, yet there's not a peep about it from the political system. Neither party has merging and purging on their legislative agenda, nor was it on the 2000 election agenda.

There's a famous political cartoon of Teddy Roosevelt swinging his big club of antitrust, with assorted fat barons splayed at his feet, labeled Railroad Trust, Oil Trust, and so forth. While Roosevelt turned out to be more bluster than action in his trust-busting efforts (he took campaign funds from the very trust builders he was trying to bust, including $150,000 from J. P. Morgan in his 1904 presidential campaign, and he was a softy compared to the true populist challengers of corporate power, such as Wisconsin congressman "Battling Bob" La Follette), he nonetheless used the bully pulpit of his office to rally the public's seething anger at their imperious economic masters and to give the issue of unbridled corporate greed the national prominence it warranted. He did enough to cause steel magnate Henry Clay Frick to utter his famous complaint, "We bought the son of a bitch and then he didn't stay bought."

Modern-day barons have had no such problem with Bill Clinton, who has been perfectly content to stay on the porch and watch the big dogs run right over the middle class, offering not so much as a bark, much less a bite. Imagine Clinton calling Weill, McColl, Kravis, Perelman, Noto, Newman, Cameron, and the rest "the biggest criminals in the country," as Teddy once called Rockefeller and his fellow robbers. Why, that would be unthinkable, since these are people Clinton socializes with, golfs with, invites to formal White House dinners, sends on trade missions to Asia, consults with on both global and domestic economic policies, and, of course, raises money from. In a 1998 interview with the *Wall Street Journal,* Clinton simply shrugged his shoulders when asked about the furious rate of mergers sweeping the economic landscape, saying he thought it was "inevitable." What a giant. Thank God he was not in charge of the fire department.

Yes, there is the widely reported case against Microsoft's anticompetitive practices, pushed by the extraordinary Justice Department prosecutor David Boies to prove that there's at least one tooth left in the old watchdog. But Microsoft is a case of such egregious, arrogant, and stupid monopolistic abuse that even many in the computer industry wanted it brought, and it represents no awakening to the much more damaging and systemic corporate concentrations that are clobbering us in practically every industry. Indeed, Clinton was squeamish and closed-mouthed about the Microsoft unpleasantness, seeming to wish it was not happening on his watch, and certainly not wanting it to prompt a larger political debate.

No sweat there, since Gore and the Democrats pocketed more than $2 million from Microsoft, while Bush and the Republicans also took more than $2 million. So—poof!—the issue simply didn't exist in their 2000 contest. Gore essentially stayed mum on the Microsoft matter, and Bush gave it one of his sly winks, implying there would not be a Microsoft case if the company could just stall it until he got to the White House. On the larger antitrust issue of predatory corporate giants squeezing out competition, both Bush and Gore were more wet noodle than big stick, content to go along with the very Clintonesque approach of defining away the monopoly problem. The Clinton administration devised two novel antitrust theories: One is based on what your definition of "bad" is—if two merging companies can show that their combination will produce efficiencies and profits for them, this internal private "good" can offset the bad that will befall the public, such as lost jobs, less consumer choice, and higher prices. The other unique theory is based on your definition of what "competition" is—it's OK for a merger to eliminate competition today if there is "potential competition" that could, maybe, ought to, possibly might arise somehow, somewhere, sometime in the future. These are transparent ploys that would make old John D. blush, but such is the state of antitrust politics today.

Far from opposing the mating dances of corporate Goliaths, Washington actively encourages them. In 1995, for example, the Pentagon was so pleased that the giant weapons maker Lockheed was going to take over competitor Martin Marietta that it ponied up nearly a billion of our tax dollars to pay for the merger costs, including shelling out some $3 million in a bonus to Lockheed CEO Norman Augustine and $31 million more in bonuses to other top executives who engineered the merger—a combination that cost 19,000 workers their jobs. The government payouts to Augustine and the other executives were orchestrated by then-secretary of defense William Perry and his deputy John Deutch—both of whom had previously been highly compensated consultants to Martin Marietta and had a close personal relationship with Augustine.

(An interesting footnote to this government-induced merger is that one fellow who lost his job as a result of it went away with a big grin on his face: Lamar Alexander—the hapless candidate for the Republican presidential nomination! He had been a well-paid ex-board member. The merged company wanted a smaller board, so it paid Lamar $236,000 for agreeing *not* to serve on the new Lockheed Martin board.)

Washington also lent a helping hand in the 1997 creation of Citigroup, which for the first time since the depression brought a major bank (Citibank) together with a major insurance company (Travelers) and a major brokerage house (Salomon Smith Barney). This convergence of financial enterprises under one roof was hailed by Wall Street as "the future"—a conglomeration that could sell insurance to its banking customers, sell stocks to its insurance customers, and sell banking services to its stock customers. Unfortunately, the massive Citigroup merger was illegal at the time, specifically outlawed by provisions of the Bank Holding Company Act of 1956 and the Glass-Steagall Act of 1933. Bankers, stock speculators, and insurers have been kept apart because periodically one or the other of these three financial branches will step into deep doo-doo and slide toward the abyss of complete collapse. The concept is the same as on a kindergarten playground—you don't tie three kids together, because if one falls, they all go down. If, say, an insurance company is collapsing, it could raid the assets of its bank and brokerage to try to save itself, thus pulling down all three. Better to keep them apart. Yet, there were Citibank, Travelers, and Salomon—joining together.

How could they do this? Because they're By God CITI-GROUP, and the politicians and regulators looked the other way. Ralph Nader reports that Sanford Weill and John Reed, the co-CEOs of Citigroup, met with Federal Reserve chairman Alan Greenspan ten days prior to the announcement of their merger for a secret tête-à-tête to prevent any rude public questioning of their deal by impertinent regulators. Loopholes were found—not loopholes that actually fit this huge merger, but like a rhinoceros squeezing into panty hose, Citigroup was nonetheless squeezed through the available loopholes. Besides, said the winking politicians of both parties, we're planning to "modernize" those fussy old laws so the Citigroup deal will become perfectly legal after the fact. It took three years for the laws to be modernized, yet there stood Citigroup all the while, an outlaw with inside protectors. The one who pushed hardest inside the government for this scam was Robert Rubin, then Treasury secretary. Months after the law passed, Rubin left "public service" to rejoin the private sector. Right, he's now at Citigroup, drawing an estimated $125 million a year.

Imagine you trying this. Let's say you get caught smoking marijuana—a mood-altering product that many expect to be legalized someday. Do you think the country's drug prosecutors would stand by, letting you keep taking tokes by invoking the Weill-Reed defense of "it's gonna be legalized someday, man"? It's more likely that drug czar Barry McCaffrey would kiss Willie Nelson full on the lips at one of Willie's Fourth of July picnics than for that to happen.

The difference between you and the Citigroup executives can be quantified: $1,409,250. That's how much they've funneled into Republican and Democratic coffers in the last two years alone. You can add $25,713,000 to the tally also—that's how much they spent on lobbying fees since '97. (Ironically, one result of the Citigroup merger was a few pink slips for lobbyists. Citibank had twelve Washington lobbyists before the merger, plus having at least two outside lobbying firms on contract, while Travelers and Salomon Smith Barney had two lobbyists and three firms on contract. Now the combined company has a couple fewer lobbyists, but, with its size, an even more powerful impact on legislation and regulation.)

If you were hoping that, perchance, Al Gore, Bill Bradley, George W. Bush, or John McCain would take on Citigroup, you needn't have bothered. They all took campaign contributions from its executives or PACs. Overall, those who are doing the merging, purging, and splurging put millions of dollars into Election 2000, which is why neither party mentioned merging, purging, and splurging—the biggest structural change taking place in our economy.

CEOs WITHOUT A CLUE

A bumper sticker asserts: "It's lonely at the top, but you do eat better."

We should only know. We peasants are rarely allowed even a peek over the walls into the compounds of privilege where America's corporate royalty lives and plays. But I have my sources, so I can offer the following unbelievable-but-true glimpse into the lifestyle and mind-set of those at the very top.

To protect the person who brought this on-the-scene report to me, I've made up names—call him Bob, and call his firm the GlobalGigantica Fund.

GGF is a major Wall Street investment outfit that annually curries a bit of tax-deductible favor with its corporate clients by laying on a lavish three-day golf outing and pig-fest. It's held at someplace like Faraway Shorthills-on-Hudson, one of the posh resorts where demanding executives get the pampering (an old hometown buddy of mine calls it "poodling") that they've come to consider their due. The 1999 GlobalGigantica affair drew an air show's worth of $35–$50 million Gulfstream executive jets to the resort's private landing strip, and each CEO from various brand-name baronies of our country would disembark like a proper potentate, step into a waiting stretch-chariot, and be whisked to his spacious cabaña, there to be afforded all the amenities that money can command.

Nothing surprising so far in our narrative—this is about the level of gross indulgence you might imagine them getting. But now is when Bob enters the picture and the wretched excess gets weird. Along with several other bright young executives on the rise in the GGF hierarchy, Bob was given the honor of spending time prior to the golf-o-rama weekend tending to a myriad of details, making certain that absolutely nothing unpleasant would intrude into the consciousness of the VIP guests. Among Bob's duties was product-advance. This involves obtaining a list of all products manufactured or marketed by the company of each of the visiting CEOs. The appropriate brand names are then meticulously placed in the various suites of the executives—you don't want the head of Procter & Gamble, say, to open his bathroom medicine cabinet and suffer the indignity of finding Colgate toothpaste rather than his firm's Crest brand, do you? You certainly do not. Nor should the top man at Philip Morris, maker of Miller beer, be sickened by the sight of a Michelob in his cabaña's fridge. And you can imagine how traumatic it would be for the CEO of WestPoint Stevens textiles to freshen up when he arrives by splashing water on his face, then towel off before realizing, too tragically late, that he has a Fieldcrest towel in his hands.

Creating the perfect in-room product ambiance was the easy part for Bob. What about the resort's kitchen, the pro shop, the bars? Each one was its own field of land mines ready to destroy a CEO's fragile state of mind. The maker of Tylenol needs to be on the tee thinking "left arm straight, head down, smooth follow-through," not murmuring darkly, "Bayer aspirin, these goddamn goofballs at GGF are taunting me with Bayer goddamn aspirin in the gift shop."

From golf balls to cigarettes, from cereal to wine, the right brands had to be front and center, and the wrong brands had to disappear from the entire resort. How to make this happen? Al Capone once instructed: "You can get much further with a kind word and a gun than you can with a kind word alone." No, Bob didn't use a gun. That's not (usually) the corporate way. He did the job the old-fashioned way: with a kind word . . . and corporate cash. He was furnished a large sum of dollars by GlobalGigantica to spread bribes liberally among the kitchen manager, the golf pro, the bartenders, the director of procurement, and other key personnel to, as Bob expressed it, "cleanse the commercial landscape."

It would be one thing if Bob's story was about one wild and wacky weekend—a special splurge for very self-important people—but he and others can confirm that such white-glove treatment is no longer exceptional, that it is a fair reflection of the deference now accorded the executives who, despite our democratic pretensions, have emerged atop America's economic, social, and political structure. When it comes to making decisions that matter, it's not public officials who are the arbiters but these CEOs and their financiers. Let's admit it, we have a royalty! It's not an inherited royalty—à la the queens and other poobahs of the world—but it's nonetheless authoritarian and antidemocratic, being self-selected from inside maybe a thousand private firms by self-perpetuating boards of directors. Top executives are like sultans, each one living a protected and pampered life while exercising practically unchecked power over people and communities. At the same time, each one is collecting millions of dollars every year in pay and perks—part of the tribute that comes to them as a result of their global raids on workers, consumers, the environment, their competitors, and our government treasuries. They rule the world, yet they are not in the world. Their positions and their fortunes isolate them from the rest of us and from ever having to come face-to-face with the consequences of what they do to us by corporate fiat.

MILLIONAIRES, SCHMILLIONAIRES. I'm talking here about power wealth, not mere millionaires. Four million Americans have attained millionaire status, but this does not put most of them in the neighborhoods of the power elites (I mean, one Silicon Valley zip code—94062, Woodside, California—is reported to have 250,000 millionaires tucked into it. How common. Silicon trash, I say). Instead, I'm talking about the top partners at Goldman Sachs and other Wall Street brokerages who're knocking down $25–$50 million a year each; I'm talking about annual paychecks of more than $50 million being hauled home by the likes of Charles Heimbold at Bristol-Myers Squibb, Sanford Weill at Citigroup, M. Douglas Ivester at Coca-Cola, Reuben Mark at Colgate-Palmolive, and Jack Welch at General Electric; I'm talking about head Mouseketeer Michael Eisner at Disney taking $287,000 in 1998—*an hour* (total pay of $575,292,100); I'm talking about the $625 million it took in 1999 to rank number 400 on the *Forbes* magazine list of the 400 richest Americans; I'm talking about the 268 Americans who are *billionaires;* I'm talking about J. Paul Getty, who said, "If you can count your money, you don't have a billion dollars."

By the way, how much is a billion bucks? Think of it in terms of time:

- A billion *seconds* ago, it was 1969.
- A billion *minutes* ago, Jesus was walking in Galilee.
- A billion *hours* ago, no one walked upright on earth.

How far away from terra firma does such income and wealth put you? Ask John K. Castle: "One of the things about my lifestyle is that I don't want to know what anything costs. Once you're well-to-do," he told the *Wall Street Journal,* "price doesn't really make any difference."

In the 1980s, Castle was president and CEO of Donaldson, Lufkin & Jenrette Inc., the Wall Street investment bank that financed many of the corporate takeover schemes back then that resulted in thousands of people losing their jobs. Lost jobs were just collateral damage, though—the *Journal* reports that Castle kept the original drawing of a *New Yorker* cartoon on his wall that declared: "Money is life's report card." Give John an A+, for he has amassed a personal fortune that is circumspectly described as "well in excess of $100 million." He now spends wads of money on adventurous travel, Thoroughbred horses, and houses, among other fancies. In 1995, he bought his fourth house—the 13,000-square-foot Florida oceanfront home in Palm Beach that had belonged to the Kennedy family and had served as JFK's winter White House. The *Journal* says that Castle now delights in letting visiting CEOs plop down on the assassinated president's personal bed and in occasionally sending out letters written on stationery printed with his name and the words "Winter White House."

What is it about houses? There seems to be a wealth gene that involuntarily causes the recipients (of the gene and of the wealth) to pursue a "mine is bigger than yours" building program. Anyone who has traveled to Newport, Rhode Island, and cruised by the "summer cottages" built by the Vanderbilts,

Astors, Kings, Oelrichs, and other Robber Barons of a century ago have seen this historic gene in action—the "cottages" are massive, ornate, and, some would say, grotesque mansions—examples of taste being trumped by wealth, in spades.

Some things never change. Today, a favored expression of edifice-erectile envy by your modern barons is the infamous "teardown"—spend millions to buy a place, knock the old mansion down, then spend millions more to construct something bigger and/or elaborately ugly in its place. Steven Wallace is exemplary here. He sold his Pacific Brokerage Services to Mellon Bank in 1997, then got the edifice-erectile itch and bought Jimmy Stewart's old 6,300-square-foot Italian-style villa in Beverly Hills for $5.6 million. A couple of months later, Jimmy's house was gone, nothing left but a hole in the ground. Rosemary Clooney, who lives just up the street, was out of town when Wallace's hired bulldozers did the destructive deed, but she says she was saddened by the loss of her old movie friend's 1928 house: "If only we'd known," she said to the *New York Times,* "we'd have taken a brick or something." No time for sentimentality, though, for Mr. Wallace said Stewart's house had cracks in it and "was just a dump. How he could have lived there I don't know." No problem—Jimmy's dead, the house is gone, and Wallace has built a new 12,800-square-foot structure with a three-car garage. It's "kind of an Italian villa," he says, noting that it's new but built to look old. Plus, he hired Jimmy Stewart's maid as his own. Ah, tradition.

A man's home might be his castle, but even castles have problems. The difference between the wealthy and us is that they don't have to deal with these problems personally—they hire people to do that. Barry Gesser, a Wall Street hedge-fund manager (don't ask) found the house he wanted in the posh town of Bedford, New York, but he wanted it renovated and decorated so it would be loaded with personality and cause visitors to go "wow." Problem was, he apparently isn't loaded with personality himself: "We Wall Streeters want the best," Barry told the *New York Times*. "We want to buy the right stuff, but we don't necessarily know what it is. I figured if anyone knows what the right stuff is, they do," he said of the two pricey Manhattan decorators he hired to "do" his new ten-bedroom manse, which came with a pool house, stables, tennis courts, and not one three-car garage but two. His personality outfitters assembled a team of 170 people who saw to every detail—the monogramming of mint julep cups for Gesser, choosing the right clothes hangers, stocking his paneled library with books they selected for him, bringing in peacocks to strut about the terraced lawns, registering him as a member of the local historical society, and buying picture frames and knickknacks to add the homey touch. The only thing they asked of Barry was for personal photos to go in the frames. The house was done, the guests were arriving for the Fourth of July housewarming party he was throwing—and still he had not furnished the photos. So, the *Times* reports, one of the decorators put various snapshots of his Chihuahua, Pancho, into the frames. About a year later, Barry bought a multimillion-dollar town house on Manhattan's Upper East Side, and he asked the same decorators to "do" it for him. They met to discuss arrangements with Gesser at the Bedford house and noticed that Pancho was still there in the picture frames, providing loads of personality.

Now here's a problem all homeowners can identify with: a leaky roof. Aaron Spelling, the television mogul, however, doesn't simply have a roof over his Holmby Hills manor in Los Angeles. He has a "roof system." He and his wife, Candy, bought and bulldozed Bing Crosby's estate to build their 56,500-square-foot "house," which is approximately the size of the U.S. Capitol. Just the roof cost $5 million. And it leaks. So the Spellings' lawyers are suing everyone in sight. This is not Aaron's only complaint about the craftsmanship on a home that includes a bowling alley, a personal doll museum, and a gift-wrapping room. He previously protested that the bowling balls provided for them were too heavy.

The award for "Whiniest Executive with a Huge House," however, goes to my fellow Austinite, Michael Dell. He's the namesake of Dell Computer Corporation, and his personal fortune is a few hundred million above $16 billion. He and his wife, Susan, had an earthmoving firm scrape off the top of one of Austin's scenic hills west of town so they could have a relatively flat surface of sixty acres on which to build a sprawling, 33,000-square-foot edifice. The thing is three stories of concrete-granite-limestone-and-steel construction, with eight full bathrooms, thirteen half-baths, a conference room, a kitchen big enough to hold Paul Prudhomme *and* Emeril Lagasse, an exercise room, an indoor pool, an outdoor pool, cabañas, a three-story spiral staircase, separate quarters for domestic help, and a five-level terraced lawn. I've not been inside, but I can report that the outside looks like a combination conference center and a strip shopping mall, though without the charm. As the Yiddish proverb puts it: "If you want to know what God thinks of money, look at the people he gives it to."

The ugliest part, however, was not the house, but Dell's little tax tantrum. The billionaire computer tycoon built the place to show his billions as ostentatiously as possible, but then he tried to weasel out of paying his full and fair share of local property taxes, which fund everything from our schools to the county roads going out and up to his Xanadu. Of course, the Dells have their children in private schools, but it has always struck me as curious that computer barons like him (Bill Gates is another who has tried to duck the tax bill on his Taj Mahal outside Seattle) moan so loudly about the American education system's failure to turn out enough graduates with the skills to fill the cubicles in their high-techie empires, yet they are the first to unleash the sharp-fanged hounds from their legal and lobbying departments to avoid paying their share of the cost. If hypocrites could fly, they'd be jumbo jets.

The Dells' house is the most expensive in Texas, and I'm counting Ross Perot's! Michael and Susan didn't skimp on

architects, landscaping, interior decorators, furnishing, or anything else to build their palace—they only got cost conscious
when their tax bill arrived. The initial estimate by the county
tax appraiser was that the thing on the hill was worth about
$22 million, which would mean (based on the flat-tax rate that
everyone in Austin pays) that the Dells owed some $600,000 in
school, county, and city property taxes. For you and me, that's
a lot of money, but for this thirty-three-year-old who paid himself $1.4 *billion* in 1998 (the largest one-year paycheck ever
recorded for a CEO, according to compensation expert Graef
Crystal) and who sits on a burgeoning net worth of $16 bil-
lion, it was pocket change (the equivalent of 42 cents for a
family whose net worth is $30,000—the national median).

But he squawked like a little red rooster, siccing his lawyers,
accountants, appraisers, and other hirelings on the local
appraisal board, asserting that his showcase estate was really
worth only around $6 million. Since there are no houses locally
or even in the state to compare his "very unique property" to,
the county had to hire Vickie Gill from California, who is an
acclaimed expert known as "the appraiser of the rich and
famous." (She had assessed Aaron Spelling's leaky-roof temple,
O.J.'s Brentwood estate, and Donnie Trump's Palm Beach digs,
among others, and she once appraised the chateau of an executive whose self-esteem and extravagance were such that he had
a beveled glass skylight installed in the shower to create the
illusion of a crown on the owner's head when the sun beamed
in.) With the Dells, though, Ms. Gill really had her work cut
out, since it took a year of negotiations by Dell's nitpicking and
stalling legal team before she was allowed to step on the property. Even then, she and a videographer were given only three
hours to scamper through the place, as opposed to the twenty-
four hours it normally takes to do such a large job. Still, with
the videos, she was able to make her calculations and present
her expert opinion: $15 million. No way, wailed Dell, and his
lawyers resumed snapping and snarling at everyone who was

vexing their deep-pocketed client. At long last and at great expense to us taxpayers, the opera ended when the county's own hard-pressed appraiser agreed to come down to $12 million. Since Dell is also entitled to a $2.4 million "homestead exemption" on his billionaire's bungalow, he actually ended up with a taxable value of $9.6 million.

This was not Michael Dell's first petulant brush with the real world. In 1993, he stamped his little feet and demanded that the city of Austin provide more than $100 million worth of tax breaks and other special benefits to his company or he would move his sales, service, and support operations elsewhere. He was acting like a spoiled brat, and, to their credit, the local council members didn't surrender to his highway robbery. This put him in such a snit that he moved just across the county line to the town of Round Rock, where he got everything but the rock for which the place is named: $50 million to construct buildings, twenty years of property tax abatements, waiver of city permit fees, and a kickback of half of the sales taxes the company would owe the town. His public petulance and demand for tribute was such an embarrassment that Lee Walker, the former president of Dell Computer Corporation, felt compelled to express his disgust in an op-ed piece: "Our community has nurtured and supported Dell from its infancy, and we deserve better than to be regarded as just another cost center to be managed. We need corporations that are committed to staying in Austin and that regard paying their full burden to the common good as a necessary and desirable responsibility. We need corporations that deeply believe that paying one penny less for our schools, police, and fire protection is a false saving. We need corporations that will lead us by example, not tell us through their actions that might makes right."

THE MONEY POWER. Mark Twain once observed: "Make enough money and the whole world will conspire to call you a gentleman." America's corporate barons—no less than the Robber Barons of a century ago, and no less than the royal barons of the Middle Ages who lived in splendor off the labor of serfs—are obsequiously referred to and deferred to in gentlemanly terms by politicians of both political parties, the media (which is its own barony), the leaders of academia hustling for spare corporate change, the clergy with its always needy building fund, civic and charitable organizations seeking favor, and practically every other part of the social order—save the people themselves.

There's a local gentleman's club (i.e., a titty bar with airs) called the Show Palace. It regularly runs a newspaper ad that highlights its "Gourmet Kitchen," its limousine service to and fro, and, demurely, its "Exotic Entertainers." Occasionally, though, the ad will blow the club's sophisticated cover by including a special promo for such upcoming events as: "Wed. May 5th OIL WRESTLING MANIA!!!" In similar fashion, the country's establishment institutions can conspire to call corporate and financial CEOs "gentlemen," but polls and experience show that ordinary people see these barons for what they are—aristocratic authoritarians who routinely run roughshod over anyone who gets in their way.

This is not to say that, personally, CEOs are all a bunch of heartless bastards, but they have willingly clambered atop a corporate system that flatly rejects any suggestion that its executives have any responsibility whatsoever to anyone except major corporate shareholders—an elite group that includes the CEOs. The system unapologetically insists that the sole goal of those at the top is to increase the price of stocks, no matter who else gets hurt. Hearts be damned. The operating corporate ethic is that maybe might doesn't make right, but if you're mighty enough you sure as hell can beat right to a pulp, and make a pretty penny for yourself while you're doing it. I'm sure that most of these CEOs (I know a few) are sweet to their families, love puppies, and have a gentle inner child within them—but that's not who goes to the office.

Not only are these people enriching themselves with absurd levels of loot by being as ruthless as they wanna be or gotta be, but they also operate in a rarefied atmosphere that seals them from having to be aware of, much less accountable for, the havoc they wreak on others. Corporate headquarters is like a castle of old—there's a moat of carefully crafted laws that encircles the HQ, separating the top executive's actions from any legal responsibility for the consequences; there's always a gaggle of staff and servants saying "yessir" and ready to hop to every need of the chief, including handling personal chores like buying gifts for the children's birthdays and anything that requires standing in line—CEOs don't do lines; there's a hand-selected coterie of counselors called the board of directors that gathers ceremonially from time to time to authorize whatever plunder the CEO has in mind; there are palace guards everywhere, both electronic and human, to keep the masses from getting close and to fend off any aggression (in these times of global unrest and downsizing, the Pinkertons and other agents are increasingly being hired by such firms as AT&T, General Motors, The Limited, and UPS to provide "executive protection," which can top $1,000 a day in expenses); there are the golden chariots, including the dark-tinted chauffeured limousines and the fully appointed company jets and helicopters, which let the executive go anywhere without hassle, either zipping through or flying over neighborhoods and communities where depression, impoverishment, anger, or other unpleasantness reside; and there are skilled attendants in the royal court to powder and puff the image of the CEO whenever a decision goes awry and creates a public fuss—it was only after Microsoft's bullying business practices landed the company in a widely publicized antitrust trial, for example, that Bill Gates suddenly started appearing in fuzzy, self-deprecating, regular-Joe ads about his golf game and that he just as suddenly became both a celebrity philanthropist and a million-dollar contributor to Washington politicians.

Isolated by their phenomenal wealth and power, the barons issue decrees from on high that enhance their own wealth and power, without ever having to see the fallout. From the seventy-fifth floor of a Manhattan skyscraper comes some edict like "The executive committee approves the FC–7.g site for the new repository for manufacturing parings and production remnants." Translation: An unsuspecting, poor neighborhood in East St. Louis is about to get a cancer-causing toxic-waste dump as a neighbor. From the corporate campus of a *Fortune* 500 firm comes an obscure notice to shareholders that "the board of directors has authorized a fourth-quarter charge of $800 million against earnings." Translation: 4,100 employees will receive pink slips in December—Happy Holidays. Of course, the CEO, the executive committee, and the board of directors will never go to East St. Louis and will never see the faces or the families of the 4,100 terminated people, nor will those people ever get to confront the ones who did this to them or discover how much money the CEO reaped personally from the decision.

Last year, Burlington Industries announced it was closing its textile plants in Mooresville, Forest City, Oxford, Cramerton, and Statesville, North Carolina, as well as plants in Bishopville, South Carolina, and Hillsville, Virginia. In one blow—BAM!—2,900 jobs were gone. These seven are tiny towns, with populations like 2,008 (Hillsville), 7,475 (Forest City) and 3,560 (Bishopville). To lose a plant employing some 400 people at maybe $9–10 an hour is like a nuclear bomb going off in the very heart of these small communities. Whole families will have to pick up and move, the others will be lucky to get $6-an-hour jobs, the corner grocery will close, the church collections will drop. Did Burlington's executive committee decide it didn't need this amount of manufacturing capacity? No, it decided it didn't need it in the U.S. of A.— while shutting these seven plants, Burlington was spending

$300 million to build seven low-wage plants in Mexico, all of which are to make clothing for sale in the United States. A Wall Street analyst was delighted with the executive decision, commenting that the job slashing here at home should put Burlington "in good shape." Tell that to the good people of Mooresville, Forest City, Oxford, Cramerton, Statesville, Bishopville, and Hillsville. Meanwhile, Burlington's CEO, George W. Henderson III, was paid more than $3 million last year, plus being given stock options in Burlington worth at least $1.6 million. No matter how the employees, the communities, or even the company fare, George truly is "in good shape."

Being CEO means never having to say I'm sorry, even when you screw up. Jerry McMorris is a multimillionaire trucking magnate in Denver, as well as part owner and chairman of the Colorado Rockies baseball team. One of his trucking companies, NationsWay Transport Service Inc., was a successful regional firm with some 6,500 employees until Jerry began making what some say were strategic business mistakes around 1993, about the time he got involved in the Rockies. For the past few years, while McMorris became a peer of Denver's downtown establishment, NationsWay drivers and other workers have been suffering through a series of downsizings, delayed payment of wages, deteriorating working conditions, and a continuing squabble with the CEO over money he owed their pension plan. The final blade fell on May 20, 1999, when the remaining 3,000 workers were issued letters coldly stating: "Employment is terminated today." McMorris had filed for bankruptcy protection that day, owing the pension fund $4 million.

"The guy just let everybody down. He let things go," said Mike Martin, a driver who'd been with NationsWay for fourteen years. "He'd never admit it, but in the last six years, he's made some damn poor management decisions," twelve-year veteran Rick Smidt told the *Denver Post*. "Jerry McMorris does not know the people he has hurt," said Bob Vigil, who had driven for the company for twenty-two years. Even company supervisors were stunned: "I have no plans at the moment. I didn't anticipate this, and I'm totally unprepared for the future," one said.

For Jerry, however, things were not nearly so bleak. "I have not personally guaranteed anything or cross-collateralized anything," he told a press conference, explaining that he and his legal team had taken care to build corporate firewalls between NationsWay and his personal fortune, as well as between the failed company and his other businesses. So he screws up, costs thousands of people their jobs (and maybe their pensions), yet he's off the hook, still holding two other trucking companies, ranches and farms covering 53,000 acres, and the baseball team. "I plan on being here at the Rockies full-time as early as next week," McMorris told the media when he announced the demise of NationsWay.

It is certainly true that such aloofness, arrogance, and abuse by the economic elites is not new in the relatively brief trial of American democracy. "The money power preys upon the nation," said a weary Abraham Lincoln, who had experienced the likes of J. P. Morgan, a banker's son who bought 5,000 defective rifles for $3.50 each from a U.S. Army arsenal, resold them to a Union general in the field for $22 each, and skipped away to the bank with his profit while the rifles exploded in the hands of soldiers who fired them. (Historian Howard Zinn notes that Morgan himself had bought his way out of military service in the Civil War by paying $300 for a substitute, as had such other Robber Barons-to-be as John D. Rockefeller, Andrew Carnegie, and James Mellon—indeed, Mellon's father wrote a letter to him stating the elitist case frankly: "A man may be a patriot without risking his own life or sacrificing his health. There are plenty of lives less valuable.") Lincoln added that the money power "is more despotic than monarchy, more insolent than aristocracy, more selfish than bureaucracy. It denounces, as public enemies, all who question its methods or throw light upon its abuses."

The difference between Lincoln's day and ours is that, back then, there were national politicians willing to question the money powers rather than suck up to them.

WHEN TOO MUCH IS NOT ENOUGH

Ted Turner—the media mogul, sports owner, philanthropist, and famous husband—was being interviewed in 1998 by the *New York Times* about his underwriting of the Goodwill Games. This quadrennial event, which is sort of an Olympics for the world's professional track-and-field stars, had bled a $100-million river of red ink in the dozen years Turner had been financing it, and the *Times* reporter wanted to know if this loss bothered him. In answer, Turner jumped up from his chair, darted over to his computer, and checked the price on the 60 million shares of Time Warner stock he owns. "Ha!" he exclaimed, turning back to the reporter, eyes twinkling. On that one day, he made $120 million on his stock.

This is impossible to fathom for most of us. Let's say you work from the time you're twenty years old until retiring at sixty-five and that you made $30,000 in each of those years, which is what the typical American earns. In your lifetime of work, then, you would bring in roughly $1.3 million—about a hundred times less than Ted landed in *one day* without lifting a finger.

How to spend such money? Of course, you can't. If you had a billion dollars, and spent $100,000 a day, every single day of the year, it would take you twenty-eight years to deplete your fund. Ted has $8 billion. Still, those with power wealth do buy things, just like the rest of us, sort of:

UNDIES. Eddie Arcaro, the champion jockey who hung out with a lot of rich people and made some bucks himself, has observed that "once a guy starts wearing silk pajamas, it's hard to get up early." Well, who says you've got to get up—you're rich! But no matter how rich you are, there are certain basics you've got to have, like underwear. Silk is nice, but would it be enough? No. For the truly rich, mere silk is as plebeian as popping into Kmart to pick up a couple of packets of Jockey undies on sale. For your undergarments, you want something much more distinctive, like the $3 million bra offered by Victoria's Secret. This extraspecial Miracle bra has been available the past couple of years during the holiday season, and the miracle is that "some" have been sold (such sales info is one of Victoria's secrets, we're told). Apparently, the attraction is that this item of intimate luxury is somehow or other bedecked with rubies and diamonds set in platinum. If you have to ask how to wash the thing, you can't afford it.

CARRYOUT. Sheesh, you can't eat at Lespinasse or some other four-star restaurant *every* night, and sometimes you get tired of the concoctions of your home chef—what you really want is a yummy pizza or Chinese carryout from your favorite joint. If you've felt this way before, then you know why Steve Wynn, the billionaire baron of gambling casinos, has been known to send his Gulfstream jet from his Sun Valley chateau back to Las Vegas to pick up some Chinese food for him. The thousand-mile round-trip sets Steve back more than $5,000. But when you get the hungries, you can't let a few bucks get in the way. Know what I mean?

PETS. What kind of human being would you be to pamper yourself, yet let your pooch live like a common dog? It just won't do, so you buy the Gucci. The same purveyor of luxury apparel that sells $300 loafers also makes the ultimate in pillowed comfort for the privileged canine: a doggie bed that's twenty-four by sixteen inches, made of Lucite with a stainless-steel frame. The bed and mattress go for $1,490. Well, it *is* a

Gucci. But you won't want to stop there. Gucci also offers a matching set of stainless-steel food and water bowls with their own Plexiglas tray that attaches right onto the bed frame—$1,100 for the set, not including Perrier water. To complete the package, go ahead and get the rabbit-fur pillow for only $395. The total tab to bed down Fido in Gucci style: $2,985.

SPORTS. The thing is not merely to engage in a suitable sport (yachting, polo, golfing, horse racing, mountain climbing, competitive ballooning), but to make a power statement with your sport of choice. Any fool with enough money and the proper corporate ties, for example, can join an exclusive golf club, but Wayne Huizenga raised the bar a notch for his fellow billionaire golfing buddies. The CEO of AutoNation bought his own country club in exclusive Palm City, Florida, registering him and his wife, Marti, as the sole members. It's a 2,000-acre spread with an eighteen-hole golf course, a 55,000-square-foot clubhouse, three helicopter pads, two guest houses, and sixty-eight yacht slips. Still, nothing says wealth like polo, and Mickey Tarnopol not only plays, he also bought Team Revlon, a pro polo team that operates out of the tony Hamptons on far-out Long Island. Tarnopol, the vice chairman of the Wall Street investment house Bear Stearns, foots the bill of some $2 million a year for fielding the professional team, and he also insists on playing, even though he rates only a "1" on the sports skill-rating scale of 0 (truly bad) to 10 (excellent). "It's in my blood," Tarnopol told the *Wall Street Journal*. At least he hasn't tried to own the very name "polo." Leave that to Ralph Lauren, the billionaire marketer of upscale clothing and other stuff bearing the Polo logo, which features a little polo man and horse. Lauren himself doesn't have any involvement with the sport, but nonetheless his stable of corporate lawyers have gone after *Polo,* the official magazine of the U.S. Polo Association. They claim that the magazine is violating Polo Ralph Lauren Inc.'s. trade-mark on the word. The editors fired back with their own lawyers and this riposte: "Who is the interloper here? Ours is the game of polo, but his seems to be monopoly. Get a grip, Mr. Lauren, not a stranglehold. If you decided to call yourself Football Ralph Lauren, does that mean you can keep others from using the word football? Let's get real. Just because Mr. Lauren chose to change his name from Ralph Lifshitz does not mean that we are willing and able to give up ours." The case still is in the hands of lawyers, which is the main thing wealthy CEOs spend their money on.

BATHROOMS. Ask your regular working family living with their kids in tight quarters what they'd most like to have, and chances are they'll snap back with "another bathroom." The same with your corporate elites, though it's not the number of bathrooms that concerns them (they have at least a couple per person), but the self-indulgent opulence therein. And please don't call theirs a bathroom. It's a "clean suite," according to *New York Times* "House & Home" reporters. You can have your modernistic, white-tiled, two-room bathing sanctuary, featuring a spacious sitting room with daybed and chair in one part and, in the other part, an elegant cleaning complex with silver-plated appointments, a two-sink "prep station," and a shower large enough to wash your SUV. Or, if you love the luxury of a good tub soak, go for the Romanesque bath suite, including a tub ensconced within a two-step limestone-and-mosaic platform and surrounded by walnut bookcases holding volumes conveniently enveloped in plastic for your watery reading pleasure.

AIR TRAVEL. Not first class, chum, but *your* class. CEOs don't stand in line (even though first-class ticket holders now get to board before children, people with infants, and people with disabilities) and they don't wait on someone else's schedule—they have their own planes. Nathan Myhrvold, the billionaire CTO (chief technology officer) at Microsoft, loved the high-flying world of corporate jets so much that he bought his own jet, then penned an almost orgasmic article in *Vanity Fair* about how everyone should buy one. Titled "My First Gulfstream," Myhrvold tells us how he paid $10 million for a used Gulfstream III, then had it custom redesigned: Italian faucets for the lavatory; $25,000 for a hand-woven carpet by the top carpet weaver in the world; halogen reading lights for $15,000; two flat-screen TV sets costing $36,000; $100,000 for a digital telephone and $20,000 more for a fax machine adapter; $80,000 for a sound-absorbing floor pad. Nathan gushed about the work done by Lee, his interior designer: "In the end, every stitch of fabric in the plane was custom-woven. The plates in the galley were custom-designed and painted in Austria to match the stripe Lee did for the exterior. Much of the leather was custom-dyed, and Lee traveled to the sawmill to select the logs that would be turned into veneer." Total tab for the interior re-do was $2 million. Then there's operational costs—half a million a year to hire the crew and mechanic, rent a hangar, pay insurance, etc., and that's without flying anywhere! At $2,500 an hour to put the Gulfstream III in the air, Myhrvold's travel is an extravagance, but he points out that "in bulk, jet fuel . . . is actually cheaper than Diet Coke." He says it costs him $1.5 million a year in fuel and operating costs, but it's worth it: "A trip across the country is now no more daunting than hopping in the car for a drive. I can attend an event in Santa Barbara, a party in Chicago, and a meeting in Manhattan in as many days without breaking a sweat. It's no longer a big deal to pop down the coast to have dinner with somebody. . . . My view of geography has been fundamentally transformed."

TOYS. It's your boy's tenth birthday. How about getting him that toy car you saw advertised? Not the one that scoots around on command of a handheld radio transmitter. That's fun, but he can't get in it and ride it, like he can with the Range Rover for kids. I'm talking about the real thing—a quarter-sized Range Rover that'll do 20 mph. It has a five-horsepower gasoline motor, leather upholstery, and an AM-FM radio. At $18,500, it costs more than a Ford Taurus.

VACATIONS. The rich are not merely different from you and me, they're weird. You would assume that they vacation at posh hideaway resorts where they are pampered with every luxury, and they certainly do go to such places. But they also go to such places as the Meridian Club in the Caribbean. The *Wall Street Journal* reports that the club is on a private island and caters to the hoity-toity set. Yet, its rooms have no television or radio, no telephone, no air-conditioning, and not much of anything. It's "almost like a motel room," says one guest who returns to the Meridian Club every year. Yes, but you can get a Motel Six for under $50 a night—the Meridian charges $675 a night! You can get room service, says a club spokesman, "but it's just a waiter with a tray. There's no silver dome." Such places are called "downscale deluxe" by the upscale hospitality trade, and they've become very trendy. Nonamenities in these less-is-more resorts include no golf, no tennis, no drinks at poolside, no fax, no e-mail, no newspaper, no bedtime chocolates, and, if there is a TV, *no remote control*. Primitive. One guest at an upstate New York resort paid $1,200 for a weekend stay and got a room she described as being decorated in the Bates Motel motif right out of *Psycho*.

SOUP. Proving that "excess" now must be redefined when dealing with the consumption patterns of those at the top, Lespinasse, one of New York City's swankiest restaurants, began about a year ago to charge $35, not for an entrée, but for a bowl of soup. "Thirty-five dollars?" responded another upscale restaurateur when queried about it by the *New York Times*. "You sure that's for one person? Maybe it's for six." No, it's one bowl for one person, literally moving luxury spending from soup to nuts.

"America now has the strongest economy in the history of the United States," beamed Al Gore when he launched his presidential drive. Bill Bradley, George Bush, John McCain, and the rest of the Election 2000 menagerie pretty much concede the point, as though it was true. Like the media, politicians swallow whole the monthly statistics about consumer spending reaching ever higher heights, never questioning what's inside the numbers, like a $5,000 Chinese carryout and a $3 million bra, and never publicly engaging the reality that most people's "unbridled consumption" is a struggle to meet the basics—food, rent, utilities, clothing, and transportation—and that a growing portion of their spending is being put on already strained credit. Nor do the political and media sparklies ask the obvious questions of how an economy can be strong when it is destroying the mass-production jobs of the middle class and pretending that selling foreign-made $3,000 dog beds and $18,500 toy Range Rovers is a positive contribution to our gross domestic product. And we didn't hear the candidates of either party challenge the fact that we ordinary taxpayers are subsidizing the multiple homes of the corporate barons (with their clean suites), their corporate jets fueled by Diet Coke, and their power lunches (that start with $35 bowls of soup).

GLOBALIZATION
IS GLOBALONEY

"Alice in Wonderland" almost killed me.

I was but a small boy when my mother took my brother Jerry and me to the Rialto theater to see the animated film of this great story, and I was quite taken by the many fantastical scenes, such as the fading Cheshire Cat with nothing left but the grin, and the regal blue caterpillar that smoked from the long flexible tube of a hookah, blowing smoke rings and saying to Alice in theatrically elongated phrasing: "Whoooo are yoooou?" I thought that caterpillar was hilarious, and I was still mimicking the "Whooo are yoooou?" routine when, after the movie and supper, Jerry and I were dispatched to take our bath and get ready for bed.

I was first in the tub, and, to my delight, I spotted my daddy's electric razor cord. He kept it plugged into a socket on the light fixture above the sink, letting it dangle off to the side by the tub. It was handy for him, and I never thought a thing about it until that silly night, when it dawned on me how much it resembled the smoking tube of the caterpillar's water pipe. I quickly had it in my hand, lying back and taking drags on it like the caterpillar did, and saying "Whoooo are yoooou?" Next thing I know my "smoking tube" had latched hold of my tongue like a rattlesnake locking on a horse's leg. It was shooting electricity through my scrawny body, and I was screaming,

thrashing about, ducking my head under water a time or two
(which was real helpful), going every which way at once trying
to get loose, but it stayed stuck. Luckily, I ricocheted off the
wall at the back end of the tub and shot straight out onto the
bathroom floor, knocking poor, horrified Jerry down and crack-
ing his head on the toilet. With this, the cord popped loose
from my electrified tongue and swung back to its usual place,
innocently dangling there as though nothing had happened.

There's another Alice-in-Wonderland adventure taking
place today, and it is delivering a bigger shock to the hard-
working people of the world than that razor cord did to me.
"Globalization" is the moniker attached to it by its political,
corporate, and financial architects, and, Oh, Golly, what a
fantabulous concept or process or thing or whatever it is!
Remember the late-night television ad touting Veg-O-Matic
that could slice, dice, chop, peel, grate, puree, drive you to
work, and pretty much do anything you needed done? Well, it
was as nothing compared to the widely advertised glories of
globalization, which we're told again and again promise prosperity to all, has "democratizing action" built right in, cleans
whiter than white, contains no saturated fat, has a thirty-two-
valve V8 with a maximum torque of 290 ft./lbs., and is more
thrilling than a trip to Disney World.

For some, even the term "globalization" is inadequate to
express the fullness of the blessings they believe to be inherent in this economic/technological/cultural phenomenon.
Author Daniel Yergin, who seems caught up in the fever of the
phenomenon, wrote in *Newsweek* in 1999 of his "gnawing dis-
satisfaction with the word" and of his struggle to conceive
something more apt. He explained that he was "trying to con-
vey something else, something larger than business and economics, though encompassing both: something pointed more
towards the new century. Not a process, but the results of a
process—a place, a condition, the situation that comes after-
wards." Uh-huh. Whatever that means, he says he suddenly

found the word he was seeking: globality. Rhymes with banality. "Globality popped into my head in the middle of the night," Yergin explained excitedly. Probably the work of that gorgonzola-and-sardine sandwich he had before retiring for the evening. "But what," Yergin finally asks, "is globality?" He answers breathlessly: "It is the 24-hour interconnected, hyperactive world, in which sleep deprivation becomes endemic as one pounds out e-mails in time that should belong to deep sleep and alpha waves. It is the world symbolized by Amazon.com, which sold its first book less than four years ago and now has 6.2 million customers. It is a world where governments, as the finance minister of one of the world's leading economies put it, have less leverage over their own economies. And where companies really do operate on a global basis—increasingly, as Hewlett Packard CEO Lewis Platt put it, in 'a 7-day, 24-hour work week where things are changing very rapidly.'" Whew. He should save some of that breath for breathing.

Of course, *globality* is not in the dictionary. There is *glob, globalize, globate, globigerina ooze, globoid,* and *globuliferous.* But Bill Gates likes Yergin's confection so much he wants it for Microsoft's computerized dictionary. Now *that's* globality—manufacture a word one day, and Bill Gates has it on your spell check the next. Is this a great globe we live on, or what?

THE HOLY HYPE. With all due respect to Mr. Yergin, I'll stick for now with the old-fashioned "globalization" (which itself was coined only about a decade ago). However, to imbue the term with the awe that its devotees expect it to hold for us heathens who are the objects of their missionary zeal, it should always be written and pronounced as though God was speaking, as in "GLOBALIZATION!" Why not, since it is offered as a new utopian theocracy, with FREE TRADE as its inviolate precept? Reduced to its core, the holy dogma of globalization is as simple-minded as Ronald Reagan's old

Laffer-curve concept of trickle-down economics, only writ worldwide: Just get the world's governments the hell out of the way so the Great Stallions of Global Commerce can be unleashed, then, By Gipper, through their strength and cunning, these beasts will naturally generate wealth here, there, and everywhere—wealth that will ripple and trickle, eventually lifting all boats by their bootstraps, just as Adam Smith predicted when he wrote the Horatio Alger series, starring Mickey Rooney and Dolly Parton. Sillier yet are the actual elements of the globalization agenda, which include these basic demands:

- Throw open the borders of all nations so that any corporation can control the market in any country for everything from auto sales to grocery shopping, from air travel to banking.
- Rewrite the rules of investments so that any corporation or speculator group can own the factories, farms, mines, banks, hospitals, and other essential resources of any and all countries.
- Delink trade and investment policies from any principled concerns over such matters as human rights, working conditions, impoverishment, ecological destruction, and totalitarian repression, having faith that "free trade" (the unrestrained movement of corporate power and money) must come first, and all else will follow.
- Do not allow any national, regional, state, or local government to impose any restrictions on any corporation's exercise of free trade, specifically including any attempt by governments to protect their workers, farmers, or environment from the ravages of free traders.
- Establish supreme tribunals through NAFTA, the World Trade Organization, and other supranational trade entities to protect the rights of corporations and speculators against infringements by individuals, groups, or governments.

You don't have to be the sharpest knife in the drawer to realize that this is insane. A reader could be excused for thinking, "This time, Hightower, you most certainly are pulling my leg, for no people would freely submit to such a preposterous grab for power, allowing the narrowest and minchiest segment of world society (corporate CEOs and global speculators) to reign supreme over all other interests." Indeed, we did not freely submit to this new global sovereignty, for it never has been submitted to us—either as a demand from a conquering force or as a proposition for democratic debate and vote. Yet, there it is. In the pages to come are stories about how much of the dogma of globalization is already in place and having the most absurd consequences.

Meanwhile come the media, academic, and political apologists for this stealth coup, rationalizing it as both a secular blessing and the preordained march of history. Thomas Friedman, for example, the *New York Times* columnist who can't seem to stop his tail from wagging with delight whenever he gets within butt-sniffing distance of a member of the global elite, hails globalization as a "golden straightjacket" that prevents governments from interfering with business schemes, thus, he says, allowing people in even the most impoverished lands to park a Lexus in their garages. Never mind that most families in those lands make the equivalent of maybe $350 a year and *live* in places smaller than it would take to park a Lexus, Friedman constantly pounds out columns and books extolling what he calls the "globalution" of consumerism made possible by the "Electronic Herd" of speculators roaming the world and dumping cash on low-wage, high-return investments in any country with a welcome mat for unbridled greed.

In 1999, Friedman's *Times* colleague, Paul Lewis, brought the dialectic of history to the rationalization process, citing assorted academicians who maintain that global corporate rule is the next big step in the natural order of things: "Once nation-states exercised absolute sovereignty over a clearly defined territory, 'bundling together,'" he wrote, noting that "no higher authority existed than the ruler of such a state, be it a king or a parliament. But no longer. Today, nation-states are being 'unbundled.'" With great enthusiasm, Lewis cited multinational corporations, global markets, and cyberspace as the great "unbundlers," adding that "increasingly nation-states are surrendering sovereignty by joining together in international organizations."

Oh? When did *you* vote to surrender your country's sovereignty to the WTO or any other international organization? Did either Bill Clinton or George Bush put this proposition to you in the '92 election? Did Clinton or Dole discuss it with you in '96? Did you hear Al Gore or George W. Bush put it on the Election 2000 agenda? In this past decade of surrendering sovereignty, did your member of Congress ever come talk to you about undoing what Jefferson-Adams-Washington-Madison-and-the-boys put together 200-odd years ago?

Lewis even lifts the march of globalization to the religious level, stating that while Christianity was the unifying belief for the Crusaders of the Middle Ages, "Free markets seem to be now," asserting, "Free markets are an almost universally accepted ideology." Gosh, Paul, you might want to check that with the masses of folks in Thailand, Indonesia, Malaysia, South Korea, Russia, Mexico, Brazil, and other nations where turbocharged free-market speculators sucked the lifeblood out of their economies, then unleashed the autocrats of the IMF to impose draconian economic rules that put the burden of recovery on the backs of the very people who were left impoverished, while the speculators were bailed out with billions from the world's taxpayers. He might also want to check with some folks here at home, where six out of ten people say that the free-trade policies of the last decade have been bad for America—an opinion not based on trade theory but on the attention-riveting experience of losing hundreds of thousands of jobs, factories, whole industries, and even communities to the new Global Crusaders who are in holy pursuit of ever cheaper labor. God save any and all who are in their path.

Averting his eyes from such collateral damage, Lewis presses on, referring approvingly to the present period, in which the musty old concept of national sovereignty is being dumped on the ash heap of history. He calls the new century "neomedievalist," which he explains is a throwback to the Middle Ages "when the boundaries of kingdoms were often vague and subject to the fortunes of war and dynastic marriages." In today's delightfully retro medievalism, the "kingdoms" are corporate; the "wars" pit CEOs and shareholders against the world's workers, farmers, environment, and governments; the "boundaries" are whatever the various Star Chambers established by the WTO and NAFTA say they are; and the "dynastic marriages" are the global mergers consolidating corporate power into even fewer hands.

THE WIZARDS OF WASHINGTON

American humorist Don Marquis said, "An idea isn't responsible for the people who believe in it." So we mustn't blame poor little globalization for being puffed up so grandiosely by extollers like Friedman and Lewis when it's really not much of an idea at all—it's more of a rationalization, giving pseudo-intellectual and political cover to money and power as they stomp their way around the world. And the notion that "globalization" and "free trade" comprise an overarching belief system for the reordering of the world, après the nation-state, gives new depth to the term "shallow." These two vacuous concepts embody no framework for a civil society—no Bill of Rights, no social contract, no ethos of fairness and justice, no religious and/or moral conscience, no nothing beyond the schoolyard bully saying, "Gimme your lunch money, you Twinkie, or I'm gonna pulp your face into guacamole."

Yet the dynastic duo of globalization and free trade is being religiously pushed from the highest pulpits of the land, as though they were inscribed on the stone tablets that Moses brought down from the mountain. From the bully pulpit of the Clinton presidency, from Bush's before him, and from the new incumbent of 2001 comes a steady stream of hosannas for the process and for the manna they say is being showered on us from Free Trade Heaven. Clinton was some combination of Elmer Gantry, the Music Man, and the Flimflam Man in trying to sell the concept. So desperate was he to legitimize his shameless fronting for Wall Street's global designs that he began a 1999 formal foreign policy address "with a little history," quoting from a previous president who was similarly enraptured by the glitter of world trade. It was William McKinley! A Democratic president has to be mighty hungry for political company to dig up the bones of Ol' Bill McKinley, a notorious Republican whore of the Robber Barons, a rank imperialist, and a man described by Teddy Roosevelt as having "no more backbone than a chocolate éclair."

Clinton did a great deal more than talk, however—the candidate of '92 who railed against George Bush's corporate vision of "a New World Order" and against Bush's coddling of "the Butchers of Beijing," quickly hired on in '93 as Wall Street's coddler-in-chief and the general contractor for building the vision: He teamed up with congressional Republicans to ram NAFTA and the WTO into law and to gain privileged trade status for those same Butchers of Beijing; he has signed off on more than 270 separate trade deals; he engineered multibillion-dollar bailouts of speculators whose global gambles went sour in Asia, Latin America, and Russia; he used hundreds of millions of our tax dollars to underwrite the movement of U.S. factories and technology out of country; he extended NAFTA to Africa and to the Caribbean, and he dispatched cabinet members to join planeloads of corporate exec-

utives on trade missions throughout Asia so they could cut
deals that shipped still more of America's manufacturing jobs
into low-wage hellholes there.

All of this has been done without the approval of the American people, who consistently have opposed these "free trade"
schemes for being the Wall Street scams they are. Occasionally, Clinton tried to gain public support by putting a little PR
gloss on his overall globalization scam, but these staged events
never seemed to get beyond their hokeyness to connect with
ordinary folks, and sometimes the hype backfired on the
hypers. In September of '98, he put the national spotlight on a
policy-wonk forum convened by the New York University
School of Law, ponderously titled "Strengthening Democracy
in the Global Economy: An Opening Dialogue." The dialogue,
rather pathetically, was between the globalization establishment and the globalization establishment—Bill *and* Hillary
were there, England's Clinton clone Tony Blair was perkily
present, Wall Street execs were prominently arrayed, media
barons were there both to cover the confab *and* to participate,
supportive professors were invited to puff their pipes and puff
up the academic aura of the proceedings, and some 300 other
members of the palace court were allowed inside. Not present
were the people who actually are fighting for democracy in
the antidemocratic global economy that this crowd has done
so much to build. Nonetheless, the show went on, with some
thirty television cameras and all the right newspapers covering
it as though something real were happening.

Luckily, the iconoclastic Lewis Lapham, editor of *Harper's*
magazine, wandered into this gathering of soft-headed and
soft-handed establishmentarians and was there when the one
discordant note of the day was hit. It went unreported, except
later in Lapham's own column. Until the "incident," Lewis
wrote, the proceedings were going according to script. He
observed that the panelists were expert at the decorous, som-
nolent mouthing of all the approved conventional wisdoms of

the moment, including the self-reassuring line that the recent untidiness in Asia, where the work of the global schemers in this very room had come spectacularly unglued, was not their fault or the fault of the scheme itself. No, no, no—it was the crude implementation of the scheme by Asia's own governmental leaders and bankers, don't you see—the problem was too much Cronyism, a lack of computerized data for sufficient market oversight, a problem with transparency, and so on . . . and on, and on. Lapham likened the tone of the dialogue to "the murmur of contented bees."

But then Laura Tyson spoke up unexpectedly and out of turn. The former head of Clinton's Council of Economic Advisors, she has now retreated to the security of academia, where she apparently has reclaimed her own voice. As Lapham describes the unusual moment, she "interrupted the discussion to observe that the heavy capital flows that had drowned the Asian economies didn't come from Asia. They came from Europe and the United States, from fully developed industrial countries well equipped with sufficient data and the instruments of democratic oversight. What we are talking about here, she said, is greed . . . stupidity, cowardice, and greed . . . about investors in London and Paris and New York seizing the prey of easy profits and then, when the luck went bad, seeking to transfer their markers to a government . . . about privatizing the gains, socializing the losses."

Wow! Wonder why that outburst didn't make the nightly news? Could it be because General Electric (which owns NBC), Westinghouse (which owns CBS), Disney (which owns ABC), NewsCorporation (which owns Fox), and Time Warner (which owns CNN) are all heavily into globalization schemes of their own and don't need any public questioning of the underlying correctness of the concept that their news networks have pushed as an absolute truth—especially criticism from an insider? Some questions answer themselves. Not only did the only newsworthy comment of the day fail to get a single second of airtime, it also failed to get a single response at this so-called dialogue. Lewis Lapham completes the story: "The distinguished company didn't pursue Ms. Tyson's line of argument. A gentleman associated with Goldman Sachs coughed discreetly into his microphone, Hillary Clinton smiled at a television camera, two media hierarchs adjusted their ties, and the murmuring resumed."

Last year, Clinton made one more try to sell globalization to the heathen masses. With his effort to win congressional approval for China's entry into the World Trade Organization coming a cropper, the president decided to go to the countryside. Well, he wasn't about to go out there *personally,* but he did dispatch Commerce Secretary William Daley to carry the message of globalization's glories into the hinterlands. The pitiable secretary was teamed up with CEOs from such job-killing outfits as Boeing, AT&T, Merck, and Tenneco to launch a "National Trade Education Tour," which would travel by luxury motor coach on five different jaunts in and around Boston, Chicago, Louisville, the Carolinas, and Los Angeles, stopping at factories, schools, and cafés to talk with the "common folks of America" about joining in a "national consensus" for Clinton's trade policy. It was as absurd as a pack of coyotes going out to invite a flock of lambs to join them for supper.

The tour turned into a PR disaster, which could have been predicted, given the message and the corporate contingent he was hauling around. On all five trips, feisty groups of local protesters, led by the Citizens Trade Campaign, dogged Daley's deluxe bus in a yellow van with a huge sign warning: "Free Trade Fat Cats On Board." The receptions inside the scheduled events, which were supposed to be orchestrated for positive media coverage, were not much warmer. At Al Mac's Diner in Fall River, Massachusetts, the secretary and his traveling troupe of CEOs were cornered by clothing and textile workers from local mills, asking more hard questions than the big shots could answer. Also, in an example of sadistic scheduling, Daley and group found themselves in Racine, Wisconsin, for a tour of the Case tractor plant. The plan was to highlight happy workers making tractors for export in the global economy. However, it turns out that Case had recently been bought by New Holland, a Dutch equipment maker, which in turn is owned by Fiat, the Italian auto giant. The Case factory workers' sentiments about globalization were a lot less bullish than the official entourage had hoped for, since the new foreign owners were talking of streamlining and outsourcing work—code words for downsizing. Would jobs be lost at this plant, the Case president was asked during Daley's stop. "There's always that possibility," he replied.

If the gods on high have ordained corporations and their financiers to assume global sovereignty, why does this sovereign need so many legislative fixes, subsidies, PR campaigns, and other heavy lifting from its earthly adherents to get to the throne? Maybe it's not such a natural and inevitable ascendancy after all, contrary to what the dogmatists tell us. Clinton Democrats are hardly alone in trying to engineer the "inevitability" of globalization—the congressional Republican leadership has been equally engaged in the heaving and ho-ing. One rarely gets to pull back the Wizard's curtain for a peek at the real force propelling the march of globalization, but the curtain did part slightly in the spring of 1998, thanks to an internal tussle between the House GOP leadership and corporate lobbyists. This little reported contretemps came in the waning days of the Age of Newt, when Newt Gingrich still was House speaker. He had fallen into a snit because he felt big-business lobbyists were slighting him and his party on campaign donations (lobbyists were giving much more to the GOP than to the Dems, but not *enough* more to satisfy the Napoleon of Marietta). Gingrich, whose daily output of ego could inflate the Goodyear blimp, was good at snits. His tactic in this case was not subtle—he halted any movement of the globalist's congressional agenda, which included getting Congress to put $18 billion more of your and my money into the IMF for more bailouts of their failed speculations around the world, plus getting approval of a special legislative procedure called "fast track" that would allow more trade scams like NAFTA to be railroaded into law.

It didn't take long for the speaker's ploy to work. "The Business Round Table had a meeting with Newt yesterday," one of his top lieutenants told *Roll Call,* a Capitol Hill newspaper, "and he told them that fast track and the IMF would all be taken care of." Likewise, Myron Brilliant (I promise I do not make these names up) of the U.S. Chamber of Commerce and also head of the "Ad Hoc Coalition for IMF Replenishment" (neither do I make up the preposterous names of their groups) said after the meeting with Newt that he was "cautiously optimistic" that the IMF money would move. To seal the deal, Newt cleverly announced it publicly a couple of days later at a Republican congressional fundraising dinner packed with corporate executives and lobbyists. "There was a huge roar in the room when he mentioned fast track," said an attendee, adding that "members who didn't favor fast track were surrounded by members of the business community who support them and were cheering and looking at them." It turned out to be the biggest fundraiser the congressional Republicans had ever had. And Mr. Brilliant did get his $18 billion in bailout funds. Thus are sovereigns hoisted to their thrones—not by gods, but by the most mundane collusion of money and politics.

Particularly insidious and insulting to the larger public is the way that the corporate executives, their lobbyists, their politicians, and their other apologists frame the issue of globalization as one that pits those with the daring and compassion to be engaged in an interconnected world against the rest of us who are mouth-breathing, knuckle-dragging, xenophobic, isolationist cretins who would rather drink the blood of foreigners than have "foreign relations" with them. Bill Clinton is especially given to this rhetorical thrust and parry, picturing himself as Sir William of the Global Village with lance drawn against the infidel hordes of stony isolationism. In San Francisco last year before a selected audience, Sir William spaketh: "Some of the folks outside who were protesting when I drove up were saying by their signs that they believe globalization is inherently bad and there's no way in the wide world to put a human face on the global economy."

Horsedooties. I know some of the people and groups that were protesting outside (which is where ordinary folks have been relegated by this administration) against the sheer elitism and human destructiveness of his brand of globalism—a brand that has the money powers of our country making backroom financial and business arrangements with the totalitarian thugs who rule China, the forty families of Mexico, the corporate oligarchy of South Korea, and the thieving entrepreneurial mafia of Russia, among others. He wants us to salute that? I know Medea Benjamin at Global Exchange, Charlie Kernagan at the National Labor Committee, Harry Wu at Laogai Research Foundation, Randall Robinson at TransAfrica, and so many other true American internationalists who know more and care more about the "human face" of the global economy than an aloof, pampered, cynical, and glib Bill Clinton can ever imagine. What an ass! These are people on the front lines where his globalism is not a market theory but a brutish reality. They are working directly with the human faces trapped in the global sweatshops of Nike, Disney, the Gap, and so many other brand names, while Clinton hobnobs in luxury with the global rulers and corporatists who literally are smashing those faces he uses so freely as rhetorical props. *This*, not Monica Lewinsky's face, is why I find Clinton such a despicable president and such a pitiful excuse for a Democrat.

In *The Wizard of Oz*, when Dorothy, the Lion, the Tin Man, and the Scarecrow learn that the Wizard is just a little man who has been bamboozling everyone, Dorothy angrily says to him: "I think you are a very bad man." Shamefaced, he replies, "Oh, no, I am really a very good man, but I will admit that I am a very bad Wizard." Clinton certainly is a very bad Wizard, but he's not at all a good man, either.

PERCOLATE UP, NOT TRICKLE DOWN. We progressive critics of free-trade follies damn sure won't take a back-seat to any Washington official or Wall Street CEO over who cares more about being engaged with the peoples of the world. Let me say it as plainly and proudly as I can: *I am an internationalist!* There, I feel better. All true progressives are. Our internationalism, however, is tied not to the dictatorial thugs and moneyed elites but to the people themselves. I believe it is un-American for our government to support Wall Street's endless pursuit of the cheapest wage possible—rather, America should be a global force for the same democratic values we espouse at home: economic fairness, social justice, and equal opportunity for all. Specifically, American policy should be to raise standards the world over for workers, farmers, Momma Earth, and all others being overrun by the forces of greed. Clinton himself keeps lecturing us that we are all one people on this great globe and that our interests are totally interlocked. Absolutely true. But here's what separates bullshit from bingo: The chief global interest of people everywhere is to keep the greedheads of globaloney from stealing our labor, stifling our middle-class aspirations, and subverting our sovereignty as free peoples. On these counts, Clinton and pals are bullshit.

I bring some internationalist bona fides to this table, for I have personally been involved in building trade relationships, though mine have been developed through a much different approach than that of Wall Street and Washington. As commissioner of agriculture in the 1980s, one of my goals was to help Texas farmers and small food processors break through the middleman marketing blockades that separate them from consumers in Texas, as well as from consumers across the country and around the world. It's not generally known (for it's not much reported by the media), but food producers mostly are kept a far distance from us consumers by a corporatized, conglomerated, and increasingly anticompetitive structure of shippers, traders, processors, packers, and wholesalers. Only a few companies dominate each of these middle sectors—three grain shippers (ADM, Cargill, and Continental), for example, control 80 percent of all the grain shipped in the world, and two of them are merging. This monopolistic structure puts both farmers and consumers at its mercy, which is not terribly tender, so farmers are paid barely a breakeven price for their crops (and that's in the *good* years), while food prices keep going up for us. Farmers today get only 20 cents of the food dollar that you and I spend, a nickel less than just a decade ago.

Small food businesses face a similar middleman structure that separates their amazing new peach salsa, their phenomenal corn cake mix, their mouthwatering crawfish étouffé, their superb merlot-grenache wine, and all their other innovative delectables from the supermarket shelves. Some prisons have fewer walls, razor wire barriers, and armed guards than food wholesalers and retailers use to keep upstart food makers off the shelves.

Susan DeMarco, who is brighter and filled with more spark than a bolt of lightning, agreed to be our assistant commissioner for marketing at the ag department and to figure out how to get these family farmers and homegrown processing businesses as directly as possible to consumers at all levels— local, statewide, nationally, and internationally. Every step closer would narrow the middleman gap and put more money in the pockets of the producers. She quickly assembled a unique and talented staff that combined grassroots organizers, experienced marketers, and creative promoters to go forth and do what had to be done. (The Bible teaches that Jacob died leaning on his staff, and I was equally vulnerable, but I had a happier outcome, for the staff I leaned on saved my political butt with the great work it did.) Within a short time, good things were happening:

- Small farmers were being organized into co-ops and were selling top-quality produce directly to Kroger, Safeway, and other supermarkets. (I literally rode into Houston sitting atop a truckload of watermelons, delivering the first of many loads to Kroger from a co-op of black farmers around Hempstead.)
- Wheat farmers were organized into an association to build their own flour mill in the tiny Panhandle town of Dawn, gaining not only a premium-priced, locally controlled market for their grain but also the value-added profit from the packaged flour they made—just one of some 300 locally owned processing facilities we helped folks develop across Texas during our eight years in office.
- More than a hundred farmers' markets were eventually organized in both big cities and small towns, helping even large farmers get an additional source of cash income by selling directly to consumers in these wildly popular and festive markets.
- A "Taste of Texas" program was launched by DeMarco and team, which not only gave small processors an identifying logo that was a marketing plus inside the state, but the program also held annual food shows around the country, allowing hundreds of our small companies a chance to connect with brokers who could put their products on the shelves in New York City, Boston, Chicago, San Francisco, and other places where we put on our high-stepping, good-tasting extravaganzas. The shows featured the companies' wonderful foods prepared on the spot by such renowned Texas chefs as Dean Fearing, Robert del Grande, and Stephen Pyles, as well as Texas beer and wine, such rollicking Texas musicians as Cajun rocker Marcia Ball and the

outlandish Geezinslaw Brothers (I told the assembled brokers at our show in Tampa that if they did not agree to
enough deals with our food companies we would *leave* the
Geezinslaws in their city), and authentic Texas armadillo
races (Hey, it was show business)—all of which made a
good party . . . and produced millions of dollars in sales for
grassroots businesses. (In some cities, we persuaded supermarket buyers to create a section for various Texas foodstuffs on their ethnic aisles, so there would be Asian,
Middle Eastern . . . and Texan.)

This is the direct opposite of the Reagan-Bush-Clinton
trickle-down approach to economic development—it's *percolate up,* putting the tools of growth directly in the hands of
grassroots people rather than in the already powerful hands of
those at the top. DeMarco put the exact same principles and
skills to work in pursuing the international marketplace. Why
should farmers sell their grain, cotton, meats, and other commodities at cheap prices to a handful of giant exporting corporations when they could get a better price by selling directly
to the foreign buyers? Same with the small food processors,
who could bypass the international brokers and go directly to
buyers around the world—*if* there was an alternative system
to connect them to the buyers. As my friend Fred Harris, the
great populist crusader and former U.S. senator from Oklahoma, has noted: "The 'free' in 'free enterprise' is not an
adjective, it's a verb." At the Texas Department of Agriculture
we took that thought to heart, deciding that our agency could
help to free the incredible enterprise of Texas farmers and
small businesspeople from the monopolistic lock that a handful of international grain traders, cotton shippers, meatpackers, and processors had on the food export market.

While the Clintonites now serve the global plunderers, we
decided back in the eighties to try serving the grassroots enterprises. There is nothing terribly complicated about the con-

cept: Find the people who want to buy what we have to sell, connect them up, then get out of the way. With a sparse budget and a small but aggressive staff, DeMarco's international marketing division went to work to implement the concept: Regional specialists were hired for Asia, the Middle East, Africa, Latin America, and Europe—"specialist" meant they were from the region, spoke one or more of the languages there, and knew something about the market and knew some of the buyers; the department computerized a list of thousands of Texas producers with products for export, distributing this directory to buyers worldwide; the staff pioneered a computerized trade-lead network that could instantly link a buyer's order in, say, Taiwan with the Texans who had that particular product for sale, giving our producers a jump on making an offer; we hosted a regular stream of foreign buyers, offering translators, transportation to farms and food companies, and other services; trade seminars were held throughout the state, informing our food producers about the export possibilities and teaching them how to do it; and we sponsored Texas trade shows in foreign cities, taking our products and producers directly to the buyers.

It worked. A mom-and-pop honey operation in Beaumont found itself making sales in Saudi Arabia, independent operators on the Texas Gulf Coast began shipping frozen crab to Japan, cooperatives on the High Plains were making deals to send their high-protein wheat to German millers, a black family in southeast Texas went from the brink of bankruptcy to making a profit by exporting rice to Mexico, an El Paso maker of Tex-Mex specialties got its products on the shelves of supermarkets in England and Germany—just a few examples of the millions of dollars a year that were generated in new exports of commodities direct from Texas producers, bypassing the corporate-controlled export channels that siphon off all the profits from the actual producers.

Bill Clinton is not alone in believing in global trade deals,

either. We established two important ones during my tenure—
M-TEC, the Mexico-Texas Exchange Commission, which I
signed with Eduardo Pesquerira, the Mexican secretary of
agriculture in 1985, and TIE, the Texas Israel Exchange, which
I signed in 1986 with Abraham Katz Oz, the Israeli deputy-
minister of agriculture and a member of the Knesset, the
Israeli parliament. But, unlike the Wall Street/Washington
globalists, our approach to trade agreements was not to have
the elites of our country cut the deal with the elites of their
countries and pretend that somehow, someday, everybody is
going to benefit. The one rule of thumb that really counts in
any negotiation is this: If you're not at the table, you won't be
part of the deal. For the NAFTA and WTO negotiations, there
were no farmers, workers, environmentalists, human rights
advocates, or other popular interests at the table. Only the corporate and financial elites are the ones eating high on the
NAFTA and WTO hog, while the rest of us can't even get a
bag of pork rinds out of the deal. As Huey Long used to say in
his campaigns, which rallied the sharecroppers and other poor
folks in Louisiana, "If you want some ham, by God, you've got
to go into the smokehouse," since that's where the ham is.
When I ran for ag commish in 1982, I was dubbed "Whole
Hog" Hightower because I cited that Huey Long proposition in
all of my tub-thumping speeches across the state and
promised that, if elected, we were going to "kick open the
door of the smokehouse and bring the people inside."

Having been elected, that's what we did. In both M-TEC
and TIE, the role of us government muckety-mucks was simply to be a catalyst for bringing plain old dirt farmers, small
processors, grocers, and other folks from the state of Texas
together with their counterparts in Mexico and Israel. Ours
was the Big Table approach to international deal making,
essentially constructing a "table" that anyone could come to if
they wanted to deal. With M-TEC, for example, the Mexican
and Texan ag departments sponsored annual meetings at bor-

der cities where buyers and sellers of foodstuffs from both sides could gather and break into sessions dealing with their particular commodity or interest. There were also sessions on transportation, financing, bureaucratic problems, and anything else the participants wanted to add.

One final tale of my internationalist adventures came as the result of a dust-up between the United States and the European Union over hormone-free beef, in which I found myself siding with the Europeans (and common sense) against the Bush administration, which was fronting for America's corporate cattle feeders and beef packers. The EU was (and still is) rejecting U.S. beef that contained antibiotics and sex hormones, wanting an additive-free product. The additives are present because of the industrialized factory methods employed by today's huge feedlot operators—the hormones cause the cattle to add weight in an unnatural hurry, and the antibiotics are necessary because the animals are so jammed up against each other and unable to move about in these meat factories that disease is constant. At the behest of the feeders and packers, the Bushies worked themselves into a high outrage, barking that the EU was a bunch of sissies for worrying about a few hormones and antibiotics in their steaks and that their health concerns were just an anti–free trade ruse to keep our tender beef out of their markets. The Bush administration shouted across the Atlantic at our European customers: "Eat our hormones and shut up!" "No," said the EU, and there we were about to tumble into a truly dumb trade war over beef additives.

"Ahem," I said from Texas. "If the Europeans sincerely are not attempting to ban our beef exports, but only want to avoid the additives, then why not sell the customers what they want?" I pointed out that the farmers and ranchers of Texas have beaucoup cattle roaming the range without one iota of hormones or antibiotics in them, and that we had many small feedlot operators and meatpackers who would be delighted to sell and ship additive-free beef to them. Oh, what a hullabaloo came my way—you would have thought I had pissed on the Oval Office rug! President Bush himself whined about my "interference," and the U.S. Secretary of Agriculture fumed darkly that I was consorting with the enemy and possibly violating the Logan Act of 1800, which can get a citizen thrown in the federal pokey for engaging in unauthorized diplomacy with a foreign government. "If offering to sell Texas beef violates the Logan Act," I retorted, "then haul me to the dungeon, for I am guilty!" They looked like the fools they were and had to back off, and we did sell shipments of hormone-free beef to European buyers.

The real issue of globalization is not whether one believes in connecting to an interdependent world (of course we must), but whether that connection is going to be of, by, and for the few . . . or the many. True internationalization can and should build new channels around the present corporate blockages, giving workers, environmentalists, farmers, consumers, and others power and opportunities outside the grip of the global financial elites. But Ol' Bill just kept plodding ahead like a mule with blinders, doing what he learned to do in Arkansas, which is to pull the load for the Tysons and other moneyed powers. It's as absurd as it is antidemocratic (and anti-Democratic)— these guys already have power; they don't need a president's help! Yet, he kept pursuing a perverse policy of globalism (tightly embraced by the Republican hierarchy as well, but you would expect that) based on the elites getting an even tighter grip on the reins. In the 2000 election, neither Gore nor Bush carried the internationalist flag. Instead, both plodded blindly ahead, like Bill, pulling the wagon for corporate managed trade.

In 1999, an event took place that indicates just how selfishly the governmental and financial elites guard their exclusionary control of their globalization process. President Clinton, German chancellor Gerhard Schröder, and other Mr.

Bigs sat down behind closed doors in Bonn for the semiannual U.S.-EU Trade Summit. They weren't alone, however, in mapping their latest schemes. Sitting with them were members of the TransAtlantic Business Dialogue, a group of corporate executives organized in 1995 at the request of the government leaders, specifically to work with them in framing public policies. The TABD group has been inside every summit since.

Finally recognizing that this formal relationship with the corporate interests put a bit of stink on them, the U.S. and European leaders agreed in 1998 that a TransAtlantic *Consumer* Dialogue and TransAtlantic *Environment* Dialogue should also be set up, loudly proclaiming that the trade agenda "should be shaped and driven . . . with the full participation of people from all walks of life." Clinton himself spoke in June of '99 about getting more openness and balance into the process. (Why do I have a sense of being suckered every time Clinton talks of inclusiveness, like Charlie Brown being enticed once more by Lucy to trust her to hold the football for him to kick, only to have her yank it away at the last moment as poor Charlie Brown kicks mightily at nothing but air and—kersplat!—falls on his back?) Sure enough, the TACD and TAED were formed, but just days before the trade policy discussions were to convene in Bonn, the requests by consumer and environmental leaders to attend and participate were summarily rejected. They could form a group, but it couldn't sit at the table! Yet, as always, the corporate "Dialogue" group was invited to take its usual seat adjacent to the governmental leaders. Public Citizen president Joan Claybrook, who had agreed to join the TACD, even though she was wary that it would turn out to be "diversionary busy work," said of this rebuff, "It's hard to imagine what could be more hypocritical than President Clinton calling for a more open, balanced trade policy one week and the next week locking out consumer and environmental representatives from a trade summit where he will meet with industry."

Years ago, whenever company came to visit my parents, we kiddos would not get to eat at the dining table with them but would be put out on the back porch at a folding card table and eat only after the big people had gotten their fill of the fried chicken, fresh green beans, yams, pie, and whatever else was being served. That's where I learned to appreciate chicken necks, and if even the neck was gone, we'd get a baloney sandwich. Today, the larger public is being treated like children by the governmental and corporate big shots—we're told to sit out on the back porch while they sit at the policy table and decide who gets what from the global economy. They promise that "everyone" will eventually get a seven-course dinner, but ours turns out to be a six-pack and that baloney sandwich.

Election 2000 offered more of the same. George W. Bush's policy advisers represented a rehash of his daddy's "New World Order" wizards. Al Gore's advisers were an extension of Clinton's same old same old. Both had gone to the inner sanctums of the global corporate leaders where they gave the secret handshake, pledged their fealty to GLOBALIZATION!, promised to push for even more of it, then accepted millions in campaign funds to seal the deal. Both were already on record for the full platter of globalization goodies currently being requested by the corporate leaders—extension of NAFTA everywhere, putting in the rules of the World Trade Organization's new protections for global investors, membership for China in the WTO, continued subsidies for foreign factory-building by U.S. firms, etc. etc. etc. Far from questioning any of this, these two engaged in a one-upmanship contest, trying to outdo each other on who could pledge the most to their corporate benefactors.

One measure of just how short a leash they were on was taken in May of 1999 when young Shrub momentarily got ever so slightly off script and seemed to be criticizing the global agenda in China. It was a scream to watch him almost bodily yank himself back in line! The matter at hand was the issuance of the "Cox Report," the voluminous congressional denunciation of the Clinton administration for allowing China to steal our nuclear secrets and for letting some high-tech firms give away our missile technology to the Chinese. Bush, who was getting roundly ridiculed at the time for being ignorant, evasive, or both on foreign policy issues, had been prepped by his staff so he could show his smarts and demonstrate his decisiveness on this one. Like an alley cat pouncing on a small rodent, he leapt as soon as the Cox Report was released, declaring to the assembled media; "Today's report . . . shines a glaring light on the current administration's failed policies toward China."

Spontaneously and simultaneously, shrieks of horror emanated from within America's executive suites as CEOs from Wall Street to the Silicon Valley bolted upright at this bit of unintended heresy and shouted in unison at Bush: "Good-God-A-Mighty, Junior, those are *our* policies toward China you're talking about! Are you dumber than a sack of sand or have you simply gone insane?!" A chastened Shrub was very quickly issuing clarifications to explain that oh, my, no, not in any way did I mean to even hint that there should be any kind of *economic* sanctions against the Chinese, and most certainly these thieving thugs deserve full membership in the WTO PDQ, and let me reiterate my long-standing position that we must never let a country's cultural quirkiness (slave labor, forced abortions, totalitarian repression, and so forth) get in the way of our companies' being able to manufacture their products there, and everyone knows that free trade is about freedom, and, besides, I was only talking about that spy thing, certainly not about global trade policies, and it's really upsetting to me that the media misconstrued my words, and you can bet I won't be using those words again.

So much for the chance that any profiles in courage would

emerge from our millennial presidential election, and the absurdities of trickle-down globalization will continue to pile up.

TOM DELAY DOES SAIPAN

Every time I see Tom DeLay, I can't help thinking: a hundred thousand sperm and *you* were the fastest?

This most unctuous member of Congress comes to you from the Houston area, where he previously was a bug exterminator servicing the finer homes in the ritzy River Oaks section. Now he is the number-three-ranking Republican in the House (the majority whip), though it's widely conceded that he is the real power behind the paper throne of Speaker Dennis Hastert, who is even more widely conceded to be an affable nincompoop who pretty much does what Tom says. A lot of people on Capitol Hill do what Tom says, which seems amazing at first because he says so many wacko things that one assumes he must have done way too much fumigating without wearing a mask in his earlier profession. For example, DeLay told a Hispanic Republican organization that he related well to U.S. Hispanics because, as a boy, he and his mother were flying from Venezuela to the USA, with a brief stopover in commie Cuba. While there, Tom vividly remembers, he and his mom had to walk from the plane to the terminal past "these really smelly, ugly soldiers." Apparently this single sniff of Castro's rebel (and decidedly Hispanic) soldiers has stuck with DeLay all these years, for in his talk to the Hispanic Republicans he set his jaw firmly, dropped to his sincerest tone of voice, and delivered the punchline to this tale of a boy's brush with Latin communism: "The fight for freedom in Cuba is sort of personal for me."

If coherence were money, Tom couldn't make change for a nickel, but this has never been a burden in Washington, where a position of real power can magically turn ugly men handsome, and make idiots seem suddenly sagacious. DeLay has that kind of power, including the power to create or kill legislation. Checking around, I've found that his various actions and habits have made him a man of many nicknames on the Hill: "The Exterminator," for obvious reasons (though the unkind reduce this to the less flattering "Bug Man"); "The Hammer," which is derived from the Mafia-like whammy he puts on corporate lobbyists when he feels they are not paying enough in campaign contributions to the GOP for the legislative favors they are getting; "Tom the Strange," again for obvious reasons; and, most interestingly, "The Man from Saipan."

To understand this last one, you have to look some 8,500 miles west of Washington to the Northern Mariana Islands—a balmy and beautiful place that has become an unlikely but important outpost in the new global economy. Unlikely because this fourteen-island archipelago in the Pacific is tiny, quite remote, and has little population and no industrial resources. The islands have only 70,000 residents, most of whom live on Saipan, the largest island—thirteen miles long and six miles across at its widest point. The economy seems naturally geared to the tourists who come here, mostly from Japan. They come for the warm clime (the sun shines *every* day, and daytime temperatures rarely go above eighty degrees or below seventy) and to enjoy the lolling pace, glorious beaches, lazy palms, luxury resorts, snorkeling, championship golf courses, and other pleasures. If Americans know of the islands at all, it's because Saipan was the scene of a ferocious, monthlong battle against the Japanese during World War II. How many of us are even aware that Saipan and the other islands are now formally a part of the United States, having become a U.S. commonwealth in 1976?

WELCOME TO THE USA. There are a few Americans, however, who know all about Saipan, though they would just as soon keep their knowledge under wraps. This group includes such prominent citizens as Abercrombie & Fitch, Brooks Brothers, Gap (including its subsidiaries Banana Republic and Old Navy), JCPenney, Levi Strauss, Talbot's, and Target. These and other clothiers have been importing a billion dollars' worth of garments from Saipan to the U.S. mainland every year. The reason they would rather you not know about this is because they are getting their boatloads of goods by participating in a pernicious, tightly organized Saipan sweatshop system that ruthlessly exploits thousands of the world's poorest, most desperate workers who are brought to the island as indentured servants.

The system works according to the natural law of greed: (1) The brand-name clothing companies, practicing the most basic tenet of globalization, have long been abandoning their U.S. factories and scouring the globe for the cheapest manufacturing labor they can find; (2) knowing this, entrepreneurs from China, Taiwan, and South Korea smelled a chance to make a bundle and began building huge sewing factories on the island of Saipan in the 1980s, getting contracts with the companies by promising to produce clothing *very* cheaply; (3) to fill the sewing benches of these factories, the owners hire "recruiters" who travel the backroads of China, Bangladesh, the Philippines, Thailand, Sri Lanka, and other impoverished lands in Asia to entice the uneducated (mostly girls and very young women), desperate to make life better for themselves and their families, to become "guest workers" in beautiful Saipan, USA, promising wages as high as $1,000 a month, which is a fortune to people whose incomes average $250–$350 a year; and, (4) the "guest workers" sign an indenture (a work contract) that commits them to up to three years on the job, they pay a fee of $2,000 to $7,000 to the recruiters (usually borrowing from their extended families or from usurious money lenders) for having brought this amazing opportunity to them, then they pack up and leave their loved ones for a great and prosperous adventure in what many are told is "America."

More than 40,000 of these foreign "guest workers" are in

Saipan, which makes them more than half the population of the islands. When they disembark to begin their American adventure, they quickly discover it is going to be a nightmare of peonage:

- Passports are seized, which makes each of them a "global prisoner," unable to go back home or anywhere else without getting their passports back, which they do only if they complete their contracted term and cause no trouble.
- Many must sign what are called "shadow contracts" waiving basic human rights—including freedom of speech, the right to practice their own religion, the right to date or marry, the right to seek a raise, or the right to look for another job.
- They spend their days sitting on hard benches and sewing at a grueling pace for twelve to sixteen hours a day, often seven days a week, technically being paid $3 an hour, but many hours of "off-the-clock" work without pay is expected, and there are weeks when some workers are denied any pay because a supervisor arbitrarily rules that they were not "efficient."
- They are screamed at, groped, harassed, and beaten by factory supervisors—Robert Collier of the *San Francisco Chronicle,* who traveled to Saipan and interviewed workers away from their factories, reports on one woman from northern China: "She was forced to work long hours of unpaid overtime to meet production quotas. Her supervisor yelled constantly and beat the workers 'whenever he felt like it,' she said. He also forced her and others to 'lend' him money that was never repaid."
- The factories literally are sweatshops, usually having no air-conditioning, no fans, poor ventilation, air that is filthy with cotton and synthetic fibers, heat so intense that workers faint, and no water available to the workers, plus such dangerous conditions as fire exits chained shut and safety

shields (to protect workers' hands) removed from the sewing machines to speed up production.

- Factory housing compounds are more a prison than a home, with the barracks being locked down at night, surrounded by inward-pointing wire fences that are topped with razor wire and watched constantly by company guards who prevent workers from leaving without permission, which not only controls their movements but also prevents them from being visible to tourists and the local residents.

- Living conditions are abominable—as Collier described one place he saw on his trip, "In the company dormitory where 120 workers lived, eight to a room, conditions were primitive: Food was unsanitary and there were a total of three working toilets and five showers." Each worker is charged about $100 a month for the bug-infested food, and another $100 for their crowded rooms, which usually come with bare concrete floors and a bed made of plywood and a thin pallet.

Why do they stay, you ask? Aside from that nasty little passport problem, they or their families have gone deeply into debt to get them here, so they are stuck in a grotesque catch-22, having to stay until they earn enough to repay what they had borrowed to pay the recruiters who sent them on their American adventure. Some become so desperate that they attempt to sell one of their kidneys or other organs to pay off the debt.

But wait a minute, this is the USA, right? It's a territory like Puerto Rico and Guam, which have to comply with U.S. labor and immigration laws—so why not Saipan? Two words: "loophole" and "screw-you." First, the loophole. Under the "Covenant" that made the Northern Marianas a U.S. commonwealth in 1976, the islands were allowed a ten-year exemption from our minimum-wage and immigration laws—sort of a "breather" period during which they could attract some business investments, with the understanding that Congress would then bring them up to snuff with everyone else. By 1986, however, the Saipan sweatshop operators were already moving in, and lobbyists for them and the clothing companies were able to stall any congressional action. There was no great push in Congress to do it anyway, since few members had ever heard of this place and shipments of apparel from there were small. This ho-hum attitude allowed the operators time to build their exploitative system through an unregulated flow of immigrants and a subminimum wage.

Second is the screw-you factor. Even the federal and local laws that do apply are routinely ignored by the factory owners and unenforced by the authorities. Violations of federal safety and health standards, for example, are rampant in the island's garment industry, and the abuse of the immigrant workers has been so extreme that both the Reagan and Bush administrations were compelled to complain to the commonwealth's governor—yet nothing changes. The scandalous Saipan system has thumbed its nose at the feds, saying in essence that "we're-8,500-miles-away-and-we-know-that-you-don't-have-the-gumption-to-go-against-us-and-the-clothing-companies-so-screw-you." As for the extremely minimal local laws, Representative George Miller (who has been to Saipan, issued two landmark reports on labor and human rights abuses there, has sponsored legislation to stop the abuses, and generally has been a steadfast champion for reform) politely refers to enforcement as "episodic at best."

As for the Gap, Ralph Lauren, Donna Karan, Tommy Hilfiger, and the other labels that profit from the exploitation, they claim to know nothing, *absolutely nothing*, about what goes on, and if anything does go on please understand that they find such goings on to be *absolutely deplorable*, not to mention being against their "corporate code of conduct," which is *absolutely firm* on the matter of opposing such gross exploitation, but you've got to understand that some of these foreign factory owners can be *absolutely unscrupulous,* so what's a company to do?

Hold it right there, You-Who-Speak-With-Forked-Tongue. Even P. T. Barnum couldn't sell that line to a roomful of suckers. What do you mean you don't know what goes on in the factories? You regularly send your quality-control inspectors inside, and your buyers routinely are in the Saipan garment district to review production quality and discuss orders with the owners and managers. As for putting a "code of conduct" poster on the factory wall, that's about as effective as putting a "Please do not use profanity" poster at the entrance to a Marilyn Manson concert.

Carmencita Abad says such corporate innocence is an insulting sham, and she should know. She left her home in the Philippines in 1992 to come to a Saipan factory, where she spent more than six years in a factory making clothes for companies like the Gap. Now she's a plaintiff in a historic class-action suit against eighteen of those companies, alleging a racketeering conspiracy among them to profit from the use and abuse of indentured labor: "This abuse occurs while U.S. retailers watch," she says. "I have seen many times the Gap inspector come into the factory, look at the garment and fabric, then turn and walk out the door. In my factory, the Gap code of conduct is posted over the water fountain. But the code is written in English, a language the . . . workers can't speak or read. Some U.S. retailers have offices on the island where their fabric inspectors work. Where are the people inspectors?"

Some companies go further than plastering codes of conduct around, claiming that they only contract with Saipan factories that have "good working conditions." But a human-rights watchdog group called Global Survival Network, which sends its own investigators into labor-trafficking areas like the Northern Marianas, looked into one such claim by a U.S. brand-name apparel firm and found its garments being made in at least two substandard factories "where workers endure appalling working conditions." The investigator also checked the barracks of workers making clothes for this firm and found less-than-charming accommodations, including one where "fourteen women shared a single room with one toilet."

Why do these corporations play such games, pretending that nothing is amiss here, and even if there is it's not of their doing? Because they desperately want the Saipan Sweatshop System to continue, since it's a bonanza for their bottom lines. Here they not only get the indentured labor savings in the making of their shirts, blouses, pants, and whatnot, but remember, Saipan is the USA. They can ship these items straight to a store near you without paying a penny in tariff or having to worry about any quotas! It's as though the clothes were made in Massachusetts rather than the Marianas—open up the ports and let the goods roll in, duty free! With a billion dollars a year *wholesale* arriving on our docks from Saipan, the brand-name companies save $200 million they otherwise would owe in tariffs.

There's another Saipan subsidy built in, too. All other U.S. territories and commonwealths must ship their products to the United States on U.S. ships rather than on the notorious cheap-labor boats flying certain foreign flags. Once again, however, the Northern Mariana Islands were given a temporary exemption when they gained commonwealth status— another loophole that Congress has not gotten around to plugging. So the apparel marketers get another special financial break by shipping from Saipan USA to mainland USA aboard foreign ships.

Let's tally the apparel subsidies available solely from this tiny island. One: You get your goods made dirt cheap for you by practically enslaved labor. Two: You can transport the goods at rock-bottom price some 5,500 miles to our West Coast ports on substandard ships using crews that themselves are wage slaves. Three: You get to unload without even nodding to Mr. Customs—Welcome to America, land of the free! And, just to put a pretty bow on the package, your whole load gets to have a "Made in the USA" label attached to it! After all, Saipan is America, too—even if its sweatshop system is decidedly un-American.

Factoid: In the 1990s, while Saipan's sweatshops were swelling with some 40,000 "guest workers" from the most impoverished regions of Asia, some 66,000 mainland Americans lost their jobs making the very products now made in Saipan.

TOM, DICK, JACK, AND WILLIE. This brings us full circle to "The Man from Saipan." In a refreshing respite from the dreary Washington winter, Representative Tom DeLay journeyed to the sun-splashed commonwealth of the Northern Mariana Islands in January 1998 for a week of "fact-finding." To help him search for facts, he brought his wife, Christine, his daughter, Dani, his chief of staff, his general counsel, and his PR man. Tom and team looked diligently for facts on the beaches, in their luxury resort, on the golf courses, in the CNMI governor's office, and in the executive offices of the owners of Saipan's garment factories. I'm sure he would have loved to have cocktails with Carmencita Abad, but the whip is a mighty busy guy, and you just can't see everybody.

His fact-finding mission was one of dozens that members of Congress (mostly Republicans) and their staffs have taken to the islands, usually in the prime fact-finding months of December, January, and February—all paid for by the government of the Northern Marianas. The price of these trips does not have to be publicly itemized or disclosed by the CNMI nor by the congressional offices, because the islands are considered to be the USA, so a congressional trip there is treated no differently from, say, a trip to Maryland. However, *Roll Call* newspaper estimates the total travel tab at more than half a million bucks for a dozen lawmakers and about ninety staffers. Every GOP leadership office has had staff members hosted on the islands as part of what Jack Abramoff describes as "an aggressive campaign to educate members." Abramoff is chief lobbyist for the Washington firm of Preston Gates Ellis, and *Roll Call* reports that he has hauled in more than $5 million in fees from the Northern Marianas' government for being its point man in the Nation's Capital. The upshot of his work is to preserve the status quo for Saipan's sweatshop system—no change in the wage and immigration loopholes, no change in the shipping loophole, no change in the island's free-tariff and quota status, and no change in the Made-in-the-USA privilege. Jack is a good choice for the government (which is nothing but a front for the powerful sweatshop owners, who account for a fourth of the commonwealth's total operating budget and are the backroom puppeteers of local politics), because Jack is connected.

He's especially tight with Tom. Abramoff and his wife, Pam, have given $28,000 to DeLay's assorted political committees. Also, to help coordinate business between the lobbyist and the lawmaker, DeLay's former top assistant has moved to Abramoff's lobbying firm, where he, too, lobbies to keep the sweatshop system intact.

Enter Dick Armey, the House majority leader. Five of his top aides have done the Saipan run, and he also has been the beneficiary of funding largesse from Abramoff. In turn, Dick has joined Tom in helping Jack and his faraway clients prevent any intrusion into the "Saipan way" of doing business. In June 1997, the two powerful lawmakers wrote to Froilan Tenorio, then the commonwealth's governor, to assure him and the island's garment moguls that they would be like two snarling Dobermans guarding against any Washington attempt to mess with their arrangement. As reported by the Global Survival Network, Dick and Tom wrote: "It has come to our attention that President Clinton recently advised you by letter of his belief that certain federal immigration, naturalization, and minimum wage laws should be applied to the Commonwealth. We are surprised by the President's position. . . . We want our fellow Americans living in the Commonwealth to rest assured that any legislation that would negatively alter the Covenant or in any other way harm the economic, social or political well-being of the CNMI is counter to the principles of the Republican Party, and this congress has no intention of voting such legislation. We commend you on the achievements you have made in the causes of freedom and encourage you to continue on your path to bring prosperity, liberty, and justice to the Commonwealth of the Northern Mariana Islands."

You can imagine, then, that when DeLay and his entourage arrived in Saipan for their January '98 visit, they were met with hallelujahs and cries of jubilation. DeLay was feted at a special New Year's party that was jointly hosted by Governor Tenorio and Mr. Willie Tan, a Hong Kong tycoon whose Tan Holdings Corporation is the biggest garment maker on the island (and one accused of stomping on more labor laws than the Pinkertons).

Tan and Tom were already buds, since Mr. Tan maintains his own lobbyist in Washington and had visited the whip before. Being in Tan's own domain and getting such an effusive reception, an ebullient DeLay overflowed with praise for their sweatshop system. In a speech first reported by *Salon,* the on-line magazine, DeLay said, "When [Willie Tan] came to my office at the Capitol, he told me about the conservative policies that the CNMI have implemented. . . . When I played golf with [Tan's Washington lobbyist] and the Speaker in Houston, they told me about the attempts of the Clinton Administration to kill prosperity on the islands. And when one of my closest and dearest friends, Jack Abramoff, your most able representative in Washington, DC, invited me to the islands, I wanted to see firsthand the free market success in the CNMI and the progress and reform you have made. Even though I have only been here for 24 hours, I have witnessed the economic success of the CNMI, and I have witnessed the friendship and good will of its people." Building to a crescendo, DeLay once again lambasted Democrats, promised to be resolute in his defense of the island's system, and closed with this: "Stand firm. Resist evil. Remember that all truth and blessings emanate from our creator. God bless you and the people of the Northern Marianas."

Goodness. Rhetoric like that should be bottled. Then put on a rocket and shot so deeply into darkest space that it'll never come back to harm anyone again!

Steven Galster, the director of Global Survival Network, conducted an undercover investigation that produced an unusually candid snapshot of how money power and political power collude. Posing as a garment buyer from New York, he arranged a meeting in Saipan with Willie Tan to discuss doing business together, but first he told Tan that he needed to know whether buyers like him could count on the sweatshop system continuing. Here are excerpts from their discussion, which Galster videotaped with a hidden camera:

GALSTER: I'm hearing about issues with wages and federal regulation. . . . What do you forecast in terms of Congress? Is that going to change?

TAN: I have a real good friend of Tom DeLay, the majority whip. And Tom tell me, say, Willie, as long as we are in power, they can't even see the light at the end of the tunnel, they don't even see the light. . . . Now, it look like George Bush son will become the next president. . . . Quite possibly. If we are Republican, we have no more problem again. . . .

GALSTER: So you think as long as the Republicans are in control there won't be a problem?

TAN: We have no problem. . . .

GALSTER: Yeah, well . . .

TAN: I'll be in DC next Friday. . . . I go to visit Tom, you know, some of my friends who are always helping me, they looking at schedule me to visit him.

GALSTER: That's another important thing for us to know, that political backing and stability . . .

TAN: Don't worry. . . . Because Tom DeLay will never let it go.

GALSTER: You're sure?

TAN: Sure. You know what Tom told me? He said, Willie . . . as majority whip, I make the schedule of the Congress. And I'm not going to put it on the schedule. They got to go through all committee before it come to me. Even if it come to me, I'm not going to schedule it. . . . So Tom told me, forget it, Willie, not a chance.

GALSTER: And you're sure his loyalties aren't going to change?

TAN: We very close friend.

Mr. Tan went on to offer a testimonial to DeLay's friendship and power, referring to the effort by George Miller to move his reform bill, called the "US-CNMI Human Dignity Act," which is graced with more than eighty cosponsors. Miller has been turning up the heat on Don Young, the Republican chairman of the committee that has jurisdiction over U.S. territories, demanding that the committee at least hold a hearing on his bill. He's not asking that Young approve of the bill, but that he just have a simple public airing of the Saipan situation. Willie Tan told Galster that his friend DeLay showed real leadership on this dangerous threat to debate a public policy issue:

TAN: And you know what he did, he call those guys. He call up the guy who is in charge of the committee, his name is Don Young from Alaska.

GALSTER: Yeah, I know who he is.

TAN: And he said, Don, nothing wrong with CNMI. He say, you gotta go there. . . . Tom explain to them. So, Don Young backed off.

Don also took Tom's advice to "go there." In February of '99, Chairman Young also took the winter trip to the Northern

Marianas, declaring as he started, like some Marco Polo going west, "For too long, the people and issues of the U.S.-affiliated islands in the South Pacific have either been ignored or given little attention. This oversight trip will provide important insight into a number of the vital issues that will be addressed by [my] committee this session." Like DeLay before him, Young holed up in a luxury resort and met with the governor and the executives, never quite finding time to conduct unannounced inspections of the factories or barracks where the "guest workers" are so discreetly tucked away. He did meet for fifteen minutes with some Bangladeshis who were conveniently made available to tell him they had zero complaints about the Saipan system. An hourlong meeting with less controlled workers had been set up, but Young walked out as this session started. Perhaps he had a tee time he couldn't miss.

Whatever, when Young got back to Washington, he reneged on his Marco Polo speech, not only refusing to hold any hearings on Representative Miller's bill or address "the vital issues" of the islands but also sending a three-page letter to GOP senator Spencer Abraham of Michigan, who is sponsor of his own Saipan reform bill. The essence of Young's message: I've been over there . . . no problem . . . stay out of it. So far, everyone in the GOP has, and the system rolls on.

Meanwhile, "The Man from Saipan" has come away from all of this with a global lesson for us. He says that we should import the Saipan system to our shores! Do away with the minimum wage, Tom urges, let corporations here at home send recruiters into Mexico to find impoverished people who, he believes, would gladly sign an indenture for the chance to come to the USA, and have these "guest workers" labor in our factories, building a "free market success," Saipan style. Stand firm. Resist evil.

There is a ray of light in this dark story, however, for the companies involved in the Saipan scam are not all standing as firm as Tom would like. Under pressure from consumers, four retailers broke ranks and settled the claims against them brought by Carmencita Abad and others in the class-action racketeering lawsuit. J. Crew, Cutter & Buck, Gymboree, and Nordstrom have agreed to set up a $1.25 million fund to finance an independent monitoring program of their contractors in the Northern Marianas. Verité, a highly regarded human rights group based in Massachusetts, will monitor compliance with strict new employment standards that include elimination of "recruitment" fees, payment of overtime, obeying U.S. labor laws, providing safe food and water, and guaranteeing basic civil rights. Verité will establish an ombudsman's office on Saipan to oversee the conduct of contractors, and it is authorized by the four retailers to make unannounced visits to the factories and dormitories, to investigate worker complaints, and to terminate contracts with factory owners who continue the abuse.

The Gap and others, sadly, have remained arrogantly recalcitrant, but as more and more Americans learn of the Saipan stain, these brands will have to come clean, too. When fighting for justice, think of the common mushroom—it seems so soft, so momentary, even fragile, yet it has the power and perseverance when growing to push through three inches of asphalt to get to where it wants to be. Now think of Tom DeLay's head. Three inches of asphalt. We can do it.

FREE TRADE GOES BANANAS

Alferd Packer had a bad winter back in 1873–74, but not as bad as the five other men who had joined him on a gold-digging expedition. Leaving their homes in Hinsdale County, Colorado, the prospectors set out to seek their fortunes in the Uncompahgre Mountains but got trapped by a blizzard and were forced to endure two months of bitter winter without adequate supplies. Finally, Packer made his way out, arriving at an army post to tell of cold so terrible and hunger so prolonged that only he had survived. The army officer in charge, however, noted that Packer seemed uncommonly healthy for a starving man. Even well fed. Alferd quickly found himself arrested on suspicion of murder and—gulp!—cannibalism. He never confessed, but back in Hinsdale County, Judge M. B. Gerry found him guilty and, when sentencing him, added a political dimension to Packer's repugnant deed: "There was only sevin Dimmycrats in Hinsdale and you, you voracious, man-eatin' sonuvabitch, you et five of 'em. I sentence you to hang until you are dead, dead, dead!"

Absurdist "free-trade" policies have become the Alferd Packer of the Dimmycrats 126 years later. In an act of stunning betrayal, national Democratic leaders have embraced the cannibals, advancing a policy of unbridled corporate globalism that is devouring the majority constituencies of the party, including working families, family farmers, and environmentalists. As a result, the expansion and protection of profits for global executives and speculators have been given primacy above everyone else and every other value and goal in the world—including the shared value of democracy itself. Oh, sure, Washington and Wall Street alike *talk* about how free trade and democracy go hand in hand, but most often you'll find them gladly *walking* hand in hand with even the most vicious of the world's despots, providing capital, political support, and legitimacy for their ruthless snuffing out of the faintest spark of democracy in their homelands. The major media outlets join the cheering for trade *über alles*—a 1998 *New York Times* piece, attempting to provide cover for the embarrassing fact that globalism and despotism seem to be such frequent buddies, bore the title: "Finding Reasons for Optimism About Authoritarian Regimes." I can hardly wait for the follow-up: "Thinking Positively About Child Labor."

The American government has a long history of being on the wrong side of democratic struggles, so today's two-party collusion with corporate profiteers to stomp on democracy's flickering flame around the world is not surprising, though it continues to be appalling. What is surprising—and what I think the American people are going to find appalling to the point of rebellion—is this little known fact: *Our own democracy is being subverted*. The corporate powers and their politicians have quietly been putting new governing structures and rules in place that effectively cancel democratic autonomy in the USA and elsewhere. This subversion has been going on without the knowledge of "We the People," much less with our participation and consent.

These global governing structures and rules are so undemocratic that they are autocratic. They put the world's corporate interests above our national interest and supersede your local, state, and national authority to make your own rules on everything from environmental policy to wages. The new structures and rules exist solely to protect corporate and investor interests, and whenever one of your laws is in conflict with theirs—theirs prevails. It is every bit as awful as it sounds—nothing less than the undermining of the people's right to self-government. Believe it or not, Washington has already agreed to this, and more of it is to come. The corporate assault on our sovereignty has been officially sanctioned by a little-known provision buried deep inside the North American Free Trade Agreement, which was rammed through Congress by hook and crook in 1993, and by the WTO (World Trade Organization), which was okayed by a special lame-duck session of Congress in December of 1994. The passage of both of these massive and momentous bills was accomplished on a rush-rush basis, with the razzmatazz of the media, the lobbyists, and the two-party PR machine going full-tilt, promising *Jobs *Growth *Prosperity *Democracy *Ice Cream *Hugs *Free Beer, and *A Partridge in a Pear Tree for everyone. Alas, few members of Congress ever read either of the bills, much less comprehended them, and many would be as aghast as you are to learn what they hath wrought. From the Caribbean to Massachusetts, Canada to Mississippi, people of the world are being rudely awakened to the fact that someone, somewhere, has subjected them to the selfish rule of an awesomely powerful global regime.

BANANAS. In the fall of 1995, the most amazing exchange took place between Bill Clinton and comedian Paula Poundstone—amazing because it was hilarious, totally unexpected, unintentionally embarrassing, and, of all things, broadcast live on television. The show was at Ford's Theatre, where Lincoln had been assassinated, and the occasion was a gala benefit that drew a live audience of Washington big shots and major political donors. Clinton was in the front row, and Poundstone was onstage doing an impromptu bit in which she was asking the president how it was determined whether someone got to sit with him or was relegated to the back row:

POUNDSTONE: What determines who gets which seat? Do you do the whole seating chart? (Laughter) Do you know who that is behind your head . . . ? Who is that?

GALA HOSTESS SEATED NEXT TO CLINTON: Carl Lindner.

POUNDSTONE: Carl Lindner. I'm sorry, I'm not familiar. All right, what made you give him that seat? (Laughter) All right now, tell us who it is.

HOSTESS: A whole lot of money! (Laughter)

POUNDSTONE: A whole lot of money! (Applause and laughter) Carl, I'm sure it was much deeper than that, sir. It was money and love, little buddy, don't you worry. (Laughter) What's Carl's role in the community? Carl, why do you have so much money? (Laughter) Is that rude to ask? (Applause) Sir, what do you do for a living? I should know, but since I don't, would you tell me? Mr. President, do you know who Carl Lindner is? (Laughter)

CLINTON: (Nods yes)

POUNDSTONE: Would you mind telling me?

CLINTON: It's a secret.

POUNDSTONE: It's a secret!! (Laughter)

CLINTON: He's in bananas, sort of like you are.

POUNDSTONE: He's in bananas! Is that true, sir? He's what? He's the Chiquita banana guy! Gee, sir, without the fruit on your head, sir, I didn't recognize you. (Laughter and applause) Is that true? Why does the President know the banana guy?

Bang! Lincoln was not the only president who got shot in Ford's Theatre! Unbeknownst to her, Poundstone's joking question was right on target, and Clinton was dying on the inside even as he laughed outwardly. Why *does* he know the banana guy? Because Clinton and this right-wing Republican businessman from Cincinnati have been engaged in a long-running globalist power play against Europe. Clinton and Lindner are unlikely political partners in a deadly serious effort to force the European people to buy more of Carl's bananas, which he produces on plantations in Central America, rather than their buying their bananas from small farmers in the Caribbean. Say what? I know this is hard to believe. In fact, it is so bone-deep stupid that even I can't believe it as I write it, yet there it is in all of its majesty: The President of the United States of America has been taking his time (lots of time) and the time of his cabinet and staff (lots and lots of time), using the full authority, power, and prestige of the U.S. government to tell the sovereign nations of Europe which bananas they can allow inside their own borders. This is how ridiculous U.S. policy, U.S. politics, and the whole globalization process have become, turning the world's most powerful nation into a shabby huckster for one particular banana baron.

How did it come to this? Let's start with the European Union, whose fifteen member nations buy about $5 billion a year worth of bananas from all around the world. In 1993, the EU decided in its wisdom that it would set aside a small part of these imports for its banana-producing former colonies, especially the tiny Caribbean nations of the Windward Islands, including Saint Vincent, Saint Lucia, and the Grenadines. These countries are largely populated by descendants of Africans who were enslaved and taken there by the Europeans, so part of the EU's Caribbean banana policy reflects this history and a sense of obligation to be economically involved with them. In other words, guilt. On the other hand, many Europeans simply prefer the Caribbean fruit, which is slightly smaller than others, but tastier. Whatever their reasons, it strikes me that Europeans ought to be able to decide for themselves where they'll buy bananas. But then, I'm old-fashioned like that.

Enter "Crazy Carl," the Cincinnati Chiquita man. Lindner, a corporate buyout artist who has amassed an $830 million personal fortune through ownership of various businesses, made a hostile raid on United Brands Inc. in 1984, grabbing it and its premier brand, Chiquita bananas. This takeover literally makes him the globe's Top Banana, giving him control of 26 percent of the world's market (the Big Three—Chiquita, Dole, and Del Monte control two-thirds of all banana sales on earth). He's the biggest banana peddler in Europe, too, but the bigger the hog, the hoggier he gets, and Lindner wanted it all.

The *Wall Street Journal* reports that Lindner is fond of handing out cards proclaiming: "Only in America! Gee, am I lucky!" His homilies on America's free-enterprise mystique aside, Lindner doesn't count on luck or free enterprise for his fortune; he counts on pure political pull with his friends in high government places. When the EU announced its 1993 plan to award *less than 10 percent* of its market to the tiny Caribbean nations, Lindner didn't say, in true Adam Smith fashion, I'll become more efficient and earn more of the 90 percent-plus of the market not designated for former colonies. No, instead he went running to Washington, demanding that our government do something to squeeze out these small competitors.

He has plenty of swat in our Nation's Capital, since he and

his company have stuffed more than $5 million into the campaign coffers of both parties this decade, the bulk of it to Republicans. Being such a longtime GOP fat cat, Carl naturally turned first to his retainers in that party. Former Senate majority leader Bob Dole was an early stalwart for Mr. Banana, having taken more than $150,000 in contributions from him since the Chiquita purchase, and having taken many rides on Lindner's fleet of corporate jets when he was running for the Republican presidential nomination in 1996. It had been puzzling to Capitol observers when, from somewhere out of right field, Dole up and announced in 1995 that his "top priority" in the congressional session was going to be getting a grip on the banana issue. Whoa, Bob, get a grip on yourself, thought many. But Dole was not alone among GOP leaders standing tall on this crucial matter of such concern to every American—Newt Gingrich, Trent Lott, and others joined Lindner's banana bunch, introducing legislation, holding up executive-branch appointments, writing official letters, making speeches, and generally beseeching and screeching, demanding that Europe get those little Caribbean Davids off the back of their favorite Cincinnati Goliath. But Europe didn't budge.

Then, a new sledgehammer fell into Lindner's hands. Congress approved U.S. membership in the World Trade Organization in the fall of 1994, and this obscure entity soon opened for business in Geneva, giving Lindner and his ilk just the tool they had been wanting for busting up the sovereignty of nations. Under the corporate-skewed rules of the WTO, any governmental action deemed to interfere in any way with a global corporation's sacred right to make and sell stuff wherever it wants, even when this does damage to others, is illegal. Deemed by whom? By a special international tribunal of global trade bureaucrats, whose sole criterion for judging a case is whether the governmental action gets in the way of a corporation's profit making, regardless of whether the government was doing something right for the larger community—like protecting the environment, preventing worker exploitation, promoting the growth of small business . . . or providing a market lifeline for former colonies.

These WTO tribunals are Star Chambers. They meet in secret (usually in Geneva), they are presided over by "judges" who come from the corporate trade world and are in no way democratically chosen, they do not have to publish the reasons for their decisions, and there is no appeal of their rulings.

In short, they are an autocratic world court with a built-in corporate bias. "Purrrrfect," thought Lindner, "tailor-made for the likes of me." Carl's only problem was that he couldn't take his Chiquita case directly to the WTO—only governments can bring the cases, which in this case meant the White House. Hence, Republican Lindner's sudden fascination with Democrat Clinton, and vice versa. Necessity is also the mother of corruption.

The banana guy quickly moved onto Clinton's A-list—he had coffee in the White House, became one of the infamous "Lincoln Bedroom 938," and was one of Clinton's ten biggest contributors for his '96 reelection campaign. All the while, Lindner was pushing the administration to file a formal restraint-of-trade case against the EU on behalf of Chiquita. As *Time* magazine's Michael Weisskoff has reported, Lindner had been all over Mickey Kantor, a longtime Clinton confidant who was the U.S. trade representative. Weisskoff notes that "though hundreds of companies ask Washington to investigate unfair trade practices, the [trade rep] accepts only about fourteen cases a year. Even fewer are taken to Geneva for resolution by the World Trade Organization. And only rarely do such cases make the cut when hardly any U.S. jobs are at stake; Chiquita employs most of its 45,000 workers in Honduras and Guatemala. And yet Kantor took the case."

Despite the fact that the U.S. produces no bananas for export and had no national interest at stake, Kantor decided on April 11, 1996, to go to bat for Chiquita, filing a formal case with the

WTO. *The very next day,* April 12, Lindner and his top executives began funneling more than $500,000 to Democratic Party committees in about two dozen states that were key battlegrounds for that year's presidential election. Lindner had been instructed by the Clinton campaign to send the money directly to these states, which have far looser public disclosure requirements than does the Democratic National Committee. Concerned citizen that he is, Lindner continued to shove money at the Democrats while his case moved through the WTO process, contributing $260,000 in 1998 (though he also continued to favor the GOP, putting $660,000 into its coffers in '98).

The WTO being what it is, Lindner won his case, which speaks volumes about the insanity of this organization's rules and the double insanity of our agreeing to let such a narrow interest reign supreme. It certainly was true that the Europeans were giving a small preference to bananas from one region of the world, but . . . "NO BUTS ABOUT IT, BUCKO, THAT'S ALL WE HAVE TO KNOW," shouted the WTO tribunal, bringing down the hammer and declaring Chiquita the winner.

Some victory. Families in Europe will no longer get the product they prefer, and they can anticipate steadily rising banana prices as Chiquita locks up more of their market. In addition, when some guy named Lindner from some place called Cincinnati can go to something called the WTO and take away their right to decide which bananas they'll eat, Europeans have to admit that they no longer are a self-governing people.

But their dismay can't begin to compare to that of the islanders, who feel blindsided by their huge neighbor to the north, with whom they have been very friendly over the years. "Everyone is cursing the United States," Moses Eugene of Saint Lucia told the Associated Press shortly after the WTO ruling for Lindner. "When someone from down the street wants to buy your stuff and your neighbor interferes, it's not right." The entire economies of these Caribbean nations face devastation, for bananas are to them what cars are to Detroit. More than half of their export earnings come from sales of bananas, and nearly 20 percent of their total economic output is tied to the fruit. Well, you might ask, why don't they just switch to another crop? Because, one, why should they be forced to do that? And, two, they can't, at least not satisfactorily.

No other crop is nearly as suitable to these islands as bananas. The hilly terrain prohibits having fields for row cropping, but the banana plant can cling to a hillside and produce an enormous amount of fruit in a small space, plus the plants are naturally resilient, capable of withstanding the frequent battering of hurricanes that would destroy other crops. Also, bananas are ideal for the islands' small-farm economy and culture, since a family can make a living on the average farm of less than four acres—some 24,000 independent farm families produce the fruit here. Contrast that to Lindner's massive banana plantations in Central America, where he and a handful of other barons own the land, while the people are reduced to propertyless laborers who are paid poorly and exposed to a toxic soup of chemicals in the fields, in their homes, and in their water. Chiquita alone has 38,000 banana workers on its plantations, and the company is aggressively antiunion, holding down its production costs by forcing powerless working families and the environment to pay the price. Yet, in the wondrous world of globalization, the Chiquita way gets rewarded and the Caribbean way gets punished.

In an article for *AlterNet,* David Morris tells us about Winston Graham, a banana farmer from the Windward Islands, who says, "We are told that the world has changed, that because of the WTO there must be a free market in bananas. But the market should not be so free that it can destroy people's lives."

FUNERALS, GASOLINE, TEA PARTIES, AND BLUE GOLD

It's common today for editorialists to call for gentility in political campaigns and to bemoan any personal criticism of an opponent, even if the so-and-so has the brain of a tapeworm and the ethics of an HMO executive. The result is to cleanse politics of its rhetorical spiciness, of the hot sauce and garlic that can give campaigns both pungency and truthfulness. I'm not defending the cowardly, negative attack ads on television, where candidates hire professional savagers to distort and lie about their opponents, but I'm referring to the insistence that candidates themselves must be oblique in referring to one another's political and personal failings. The result is a Bland-a-thon, a Bore-off, and a needless sanitizing of America's rambunctious and rowdy political tradition. I much prefer both the color and clarity of a good verbal shot, such as this one that Sam Houston fired at David Burnet in the 1842 campaign for president of the Republic of Texas: "You prate about the faults of other men, while the blot of foul, unmitigated treason rests upon you—you political wrangler and canting hypocrite, whom the waters of Jordan could never cleanse from your political and moral leprosy."

Even if the bland Al Gore or the beige Shrub Bush actually gave enough of a damn about some issue to work themselves into a genuine froth, their scripters and scrubbers would nix it instantly, instead arranging a carefully staged media event at which the candidate would be allowed to read a precisely worded statement that had been vetted through their top contributors and run through a focus group. You won't hear it from their lips, but one issue that cries out for the Sam Houston touch is the blot of foul, unmitigated treason that rests upon those members of Congress and those within the Clinton administration who knowingly saddled us with provisions in NAFTA and the World Trade Organization that strip us of our democratic right to self-government. (I have to use the adverb "knowingly" because, sadly, most lawmakers who voted for these two sovereignty-busters had not read or understood the legislation they were voting on—if malfeasance won't get you, ignorance will.)

Knowing that our leaders have lied to us again and again, including in contemptible ways that sank us into wars costing the lives of tens of thousands of trusting young people sent to do their patriotic duty, I should not be shocked and amazed that they would so crassly sell out our very sovereignty at the request of their corporate contributors. But I am. More and more Americans are being shocked, too, as they discover, case by case, what has been done to them.

FUNERALS. Michael S. Allred of Jackson, Mississippi, was more than shocked to learn about the arcane and obscure "investor rights" provisions that lurk in Chapter 11 of NAFTA—he was dismayed, discombobulated, disheartened, flabbergasted, flummoxed . . . and ultimately furious. "It is a Gotcha that I certainly never thought was in there," he said in an interview on my *Chat & Chew* radio show.

Mike Allred is not a fellow who is easily stunned by any-thing in politics, nor is he a knee-jerk anticorporate lefty. He is a Goldwater Republican and an attorney who makes his living by representing businesses. When I say he's a Republican, I don't mean he has a casual affiliation with the party—he has been state chair of the Mississippi Young Republicans, a field rep for the state party, chair of Young Mississippians for Nixon, and general counsel of the state party for more than twenty years, and he remains today a legal adviser to the Republican National Committee. He counts Senator Trent Lott, Senator Thad Cochran, and former RNC chairman Haley Barbour as good personal friends. "You don't get any more true-blue Republican than me," he's pleased to say. But what, Allred wonders now, could Trent, Thad, and Haley have been smoking when they teamed with President Clinton to shove NAFTA through the Congress, Chapter 11 and all?

He became entangled in Chapter 11 after Jeremiah O'Keefe, a Biloxi, Mississippi, funeral parlor owner, asked him to handle his case against the Loewen Group, a massive funeral home conglomerate based in Canada. The business of burying people (or of providing "bereavement services," as the industry prefers to put it) has long been in the hands of local families like O'Keefe's. But, before you could say "ashes to ashes," a few very large corporate operators have swept into markets all across the country and locked them up, either by buying out the locals or muscling them aside. O'Keefe claimed that Loewen was muscling him, using various unlawful anticompetitive maneuvers in a strategy designed to drive him out of business, monopolize the market in the Biloxi area, then jack up the price on funeral services for the local people.

In 1995, a Mississippi jury not only agreed with Allred's arguments that Loewen was doing all of the above, but the jury was outraged by the conglomerate's unscrupulous behavior. "If there ever was an indefensible case," said juror Robert Bruce, "I believe this was it." O'Keefe was awarded $100 million in damages by the jurors, and they assessed another $160 million against Loewen in punitive damages, which are meant both as punishment and deterrent (just as jail time is for people), trying to prevent the corporation from doing it again. Loewen's lawyers, however, got the judge to force the jury to reconsider the punishment level, figuring that a new round of arguments in the courtroom would convince them that $160 million was too much. Arguments were held, the jury withdrew for deliberations—and this time they came back with $400 million in punitive damages.

Loewen next tried a couple of legal end runs to avoid the judgment, but they were unsuccessful, so it finally agreed in 1996 not to appeal the decision in return for a settlement that paid Mr. O'Keefe $175 million. And that would have been that. Except for NAFTA.

One can imagine some Loewen lawyer reading through NAFTA one night (yes, corporate lawyers often pass their time like this, hoping to come upon some morsel of legal avoidance, much like a hog rooting for acorns) and stumbling on Chapter 11. "Holy Saint Shyster," you can hear the lawyer shriek with delight! What this thing does is to give corporations like Loewen rights that you and I don't have, and rights that no corporation has ever had until this infamous trade agreement between Canada, the USA, and Mexico was passed into law. I'm going to be merciful here and skip the legalese, but what it comes down to is that, in 1998, Loewen suddenly sued the U.S. government for money, claiming that the Mississippi court system *expropriated* the assets of its investors and harmed their *future* profits. Was the company guilty, was it a thug, was it a complete asshole in its business dealings? Not an issue, assert the Loewen lawyers—the workings of Mississippi's legal procedures took money from us in violation of our international investor rights under NAFTA.

This is getting Kafkaesque. Bear in mind that these are the same legal procedures that U.S. citizens and corporations abide by in Mississippi, and that Mississippi, as Allred says, "follows the federal rules of civil procedure, so if there's anything wrong with our procedures they're wrong with every court in America." In other words, NAFTA has bestowed a legal right on foreign corporations that allows them to avoid the punishment our state courts impose on them when they do wrong, allowing them to demand that our national government pay for any fines and financial losses the corporation incurred as a result of the guilty verdict. In this case, Loewen is demanding $725 million from us taxpayers! (This might be a good time for you to pause, look up from your reading, take a deep breath, shake your head a time or two, and maybe pinch yourself, just so you know that what you just read is, indeed, what you just read.) What Loewen is claiming is so breathtakingly absurd that it needs restating: A foreign corporation can come to your state, attempt to monopolize your market illegally, get caught and convicted, agree to a cash settlement — then, citing NAFTA, claim that the state court has "expropriated" its investors' funds and that therefore American taxpayers must pay the cost of the settlement plus other financial setbacks it claims the court verdict caused. Shouldn't they have to wear clown suits when they make such claims?

Now, Kafka meets Orwell. NAFTA also allows the foreign corporation to bypass the legal system of the country it is suing. That's right: *The Loewen case is not subject to U.S. courts*. Instead, the case goes before one of two special "corporate courts" (international trade tribunals) designated by NAFTA. Loewen has chosen the International Center for Settlement of Investment Disputes as its legal forum. ICSID is an arm of the World Bank, which is one of the most elitist, corporate-friendly, antidemocratic institutions in the whole wide world. Going there is like a racketeering mafioso saying, "Instead of letting a federal jury judge me, what say I just keep it in the family by letting my Godfather decide the case?"

And what a setup these tribunals are. For starters, the good people of Mississippi, whose judicial fairness and integrity are under attack by Loewen, are not even allowed to participate in the ICSID proceedings. The Loewen case is being heard and ruled upon by three trade arbiters — *one of which is chosen by Loewen itself*! Allred points out that this tribunal "is a court of Star Chamber in the sense that it is not responsive to any people, any nation, any government, any electorate, and it does not have any organic law, such as our Constitution, that limits the breadth of its powers. It meets in secret, does not allow you to confront witnesses or cross-examine, and does not have to publish its proceedings or findings. . . . We understand [in U.S. courts] that anything that is vague and allows a judge to be a tyrant is unconstitutional. [The tribunal] has an informal procedure that consists of whatever they want it to be." ICSID literally can say, on behalf of Loewen, "Off with their heads," forcing the heads of our national government to pay $725 million to the Canadian corporation. There is no appeal.

Adding to the totalitarian absurdity is the fact that these Chapter 11 NAFTA cases can be filed, adjudicated by a tribunal, and paid out without you and me ever knowing they happened. There is no requirement that either the corporation bringing the claim or the government charged with the "investor-rights" violation has to make the case public. Indeed, the Loewen case only came to light because of the diligence of the watchdog group Public Citizen, which came across a tiny reference to it in a securities filing the company had made elsewhere. This raises questions about how many other cases have been filed—and the Department of Justice isn't talking.

Joan Claybrook, president of Public Citizen, says that a victory for Loewen "would completely undermine the American civil justice system." But even if Loewen loses on the merits of this particular case, the NAFTA Gotcha is still operative and available for other corporations to use. Loewen's lead attorney, James Wilderotter (no snickering, please, that's his real name), says we should just get used to it: "NAFTA is part of the American legal system, and the right to bring the action we have brought is clearly found within NAFTA." Slavery was once part of America's legal system, too, Mr. Wilderotter, but that didn't make it right, and a bloody war was fought to abolish it. I don't think that NAFTA's usurpation of our right to self-government will last long, once people see more foreign corporations using this special "right" to bring such actions against us. Our leaders in Washington might be bamboozled (or bought) by those global elites who are trying to force such an antidemocratic crown of thorns down on America's brow, but the people will not accept it.

Mike Allred says he is a libertarian Republican who supports the idea of free trade, but the kind of globalization games embodied in NAFTA are not at all what he has in mind: "I am extremely concerned for my country. I am concerned that the world seems to be more and more and more governed over by supranational corporations that are answerable to no one, and I am concerned that, in this specific instance, [Loewen] can supersede the Constitution that our fighting men fought and died for, letting a foreign corporation deprive the American people of their rights. . . . It is a surrender of the sovereignty of the United States."

GASOLINE. We are not alone in our concern. Canadian sovereignty already has succumbed to Chapter 11 in a case brought by Ethyl Corporation, based in Virginia. Ethyl is the sole producer of MMT, a gasoline additive used to enhance octane. MMT's primary ingredient is manganese, which is known to be toxic to the human nervous system, so here in America, the EPA is working to ban the additive from our gasoline.

Equally concerned about the health of its citizens, Canadian officials banned imports of MMT in 1997. But here came that Orwellian twist from NAFTA again—while Ethyl had no legal grounds to stop the MMT ban in its home country, it is a *foreign* corporation in Canada, so it was eligible to use Chapter 11 there. It claimed that the Canadian ban was an "expropriation" of its investors' profits, and an expropriation of the "good reputation" of the corporation. Pay us $251 million, demanded Ethyl! (I wonder if it used cutout letters from magazines to spell out this demand, as robbers sometimes do?)

In 1998, the Canadian government meekly submitted to the robbery. Fearing that it would lose the case in the NAFTA tribunal, officials settled by revoking their ban, paying $13 million to Ethyl, and even apologizing for implying that MMT is nasty stuff, even though they know it is. What we have here is a case of the presumed "rights" of corporate investors being given a morally superior legal status to the public's right not to be harmed by a corporation's industrial toxins. The term "absurd" seems completely inadequate here, so you choose: □ asinine □ barmy □ empty-headed □ farcical □ grotesque □ harebrained □ icky □ kooky □ moronic □ perverse □ poppy-cockish □ so stupid it makes my stomach hurt □ wacky to the max.

Californians, too, are learning about the new corporatocracy that has been sanctioned by trade schemes like NAFTA. Alarmed by the health risks of another gasoline additive (methyl teriaty butyl ether) that is leaking into the state's lakes, wells, and groundwater, Governor Gray Davis stepped forward in March 1999 and ordered a phase-out of MTBE, to be completed by 2002. Fine, California is a big boy, right, so it can do what it wants? Not so fast. Methanex Inc., a Canadian corporation that manufactures an ingredient used in the banned additive, has since trumped the governor's announcement by saying it will sue the United States under Old Mister Chapter 11. Its claim is that there was an eighteen-month "period of MTBE uncertainty" during which the ban was being discussed publicly in the California legislature and in the media, and that this very discussion caused Methanex's stock prices to drop, which is an "expropriation" of money from its shareholders.

I don't know about you, but I'm getting slaphappy from all these creative uses of NAFTA! Now we supposedly sovereign peoples cannot even talk about the possibility of regulating some killer of a product because some company somewhere might take a dipsy-doodle in its stock, which is a NAFTA no-no. Methanex Inc. says the California ban must be lifted and that American taxpayers owe the company $970 million for California's "expropriation" of its stock value and its market share. This nonsense would be hooted out of a U.S. court, but once again the case won't go to our judicial system but into the nether world of another NAFTA tribunal.

TEA PARTIES. Should you, through your local and state government, be allowed to apply moral and political principles when your tax dollars are used to buy computers, uniforms, gasoline, office furniture, trucks, and other goods? Should you, say, be able to decide through your local democratic process that your city hall should give a preference to Made-in-the-USA products, or refuse to buy products that contribute to rain-forest destruction, or say no to purchases from corporations that are involved in sweatshop labor or are doing business with horrendous human-rights violators in China, Nigeria, Burma, and elsewhere? Can you believe I'm even asking these questions? OF COURSE YOU SHOULD BE ABLE TO TAKE A PRINCIPLED STAND WITH HOW YOUR LOCAL GOVERNING BODIES SPEND YOUR TAX DOLLARS. SHEESH, THIS IS AMERICA—IT'S YOUR MONEY AND YOUR SOVEREIGN RIGHT AS A SELF-GOVERNING PEOPLE! Both as individual citizens and as a democratic electorate, we have the right to boycott brands based on our principles. The use of such direct economic action by local folks has been a noble part of the American experiment from the Boston Tea Party of 1773 to the boycott movement against South African apartheid some 200 years later.

If the corporate globalists get their way, however, Tea-Party democracy in America will formally come to an end. "Stand on principle?" they gasp. "How naive. Stand on *principal* maybe, but principle, forget it. There are bucks to be made, boy, now get out of the way." They are out to slap down such local initiatives, and their first target is the fast-spreading grassroots movement to apply state and local sanctions against the bloody thugs who rule Burma. If there is a single poster boy for global horror, it is not Slobodan Milosevic but the SLORC of Burma. Not since Vlad the Impaler has a ruthless regime been more aptly named—just to say "SLORC" (the State Law and Order Restoration Council) conjures the image of some mutant creature from a 1950s horror flick, but these guys are all too real, and their military dictatorship gives brutality a bad name. During the past decade, the junta has crushed democracy and ruled by terror—routinely raping, torturing, enslaving, and killing the people of Burma. Sadly, its rule has been propped up by hard currency delivered to these thugs by brand-name corporations that have been all too eager to do business with them—producing oil, computers, clothing, and millions of dollars' worth of other goods. As Thomas Jefferson put it, "The selfish spirit of commerce knows no country, and feels no passion or principle but that of gain."

Like Sam Adams and his rowdy boys of 1773, however, groups of Americans have rebelled against these SLORC-made corporate goods and have organized across the country to "throw them overboard." Starting, appropriately enough, in the state of Massachusetts and spreading to more than twenty cities (including Boulder, Chapel Hill, Los Angeles, Madison, Oakland, and Portland), sanctions have been passed that are more than mere resolutions of conscience—these have teeth. These autonomous governments have decided that they will not purchase any products from corporations that do business with the Burmese junta. Some may think, so what if a few cities get uppity? But, as the motto of the Free Burma Coalition puts it, "When spiders unite, they can tie down a lion." If even one city puts its money where its mouth is, it makes a noise that the largest corporations notice. But when a state and a couple of dozen cities speak as one, billions of dollars in purchasing power are represented, and this startles the whole corporate world.

One important person who has heard the roar from the United States and been greatly pleased by it is Aung San Suu Kyi. She is leader of the Burmese Democracy Movement, a winner of the Nobel Peace Prize, and a prisoner of the SLORC. She has praised the "selective purchasing laws" in the United States as an effective way to defund the thugs and give her movement a chance to restore democracy.

There is no doubt that the laws have been effective—Apple Computer, ARCO, Disney, Hewlett-Packard, J. Crew, Kodak, Motorola, and Pepsi are just a few of the corporations that have withdrawn from Burma since 1996, after Massachusetts and others took action. The laws have been so effective that, beginning in 1997, the global corporate powers launched a massive counterattack, claiming that these laws "interfere" with the global marketplace and, ironically, that they just don't work! Logic aside, they are using the World Trade Organization, the Clinton administration, the federal judiciary, and tons of corporate cash in a coordinated campaign to stomp on your and my right to decide how we spend our local and state tax dollars.

They have zeroed in on the Massachusetts law, presuming that if they kill it, all others will die, too. State representative Byron Rushing might not be a direct descendant of Samuel Adams, but he definitely is an heir to his rebellious spirit. Working with Boston-area businessman and Burma activist Simon Billenness, Representative Rushing sponsored the state's selective purchasing act and got it enacted. These two citizens, backed by thousands of supporters, have stood up to an incredible barrage of political and legal artillery hurled at them during the past two years.

First came Japan, wailing on behalf of Toyota, Mitsubishi, and twenty-eight other Japanese corporations consorting with SLORC that Byron's law was denying them their sacred global right to do business in Burma *and* with the state of Massachusetts, human rights and democracy be damned. The European Union joined in Japan's assault, complaining to Washington that this rogue state was violating a holy global commandment called the "Agreement on Government Procurement," found inscribed in tiny print upon the stone tablets creating the World Trade Organization. In January 1997, six months after Representative Rushing's law took effect, the Europeans sent a "démarche" (a formal diplomatic statement, often delivered by a stuffy guy in striped pants, morning coat, and silk top hat) to our state department, demanding repeal of the Massachusetts law or they would go to the WTO and file an AGP complaint ASAP. Rushing, Billenness, and group rallied the entire congressional delegation of the state to fire back at the EU with this formal statement: "We do not believe it is appropriate for the European Union to involve itself in the internal affairs of Massachusetts. If the EU chooses to place dollars ahead of human rights, it has that sovereign right, but the EU should not attempt to intimidate Massachusetts into changing the standards it has established for doing business with the state government." All right, Ye Sons of Liberty—take that, King George!

Alas, under the rules of the WTO, Massachusetts has no legal standing to defend itself there and had to count on the Clinton administration to protect its interest, which is like hiring Willie Sutton to guard the bank. This is the president, after all, who had pushed, prodded, and prostituted to get the WTO, including its procurement provision, enacted. His undersecretary of state, Stuart Eizenstat, was openly strategizing with the corporate interests to kill the Massachusetts law, and had testified before Congress in 1997 that "efforts by state and local officials around the United States . . . to impose various economic sanctions are inappropriate and counterproductive." Likewise, Commerce Secretary Bill Daley was hard at work trying to undermine the sovereign people of Massachusetts, telling a group called the European Institute in March of '97 that the Clinton team has "the same concerns on this" as the EU does, and assuring the assembled proponents of corporate sovereignty that he and other top officials were working with U.S. companies to put the squeeze on Representative Rushing and other Massachusetts stalwarts: "We've encouraged the business community to make their views known. Local legislators will respond better to local companies."

The business community did more than besiege Rushing with their executives and lobbyists; they filed suit in federal court to kill his law. The National Foreign Trade Council, a corporate lobbying outfit in Washington with some 600 members, is the complainant in the lawsuit. It has refused to release its membership list, but Simon Billenness and his New England Burma

Roundtable rooted some of them out. NFTC's board of directors includes such "local companies" as Allied Signal, Amoco, ARCO, AT&T, BankAmerica, Boeing, Boise Cascade, Caterpillar, Chase Manhattan, Chevron, Chrysler, Citibank, Colgate-Palmolive, Du Pont, Duracell, Ernst & Young, GE, GM, IBM, ITT, Johnson & Johnson, Kodak, Mobil Oil, Monsanto, PepsiCo, Pfizer, Procter & Gamble, Rockwell, Texaco, United Technologies, and Westinghouse.

The Trade Council's legal strategy cleverly shifts the focus from the global corporate interests by pretending that the issue is one of U.S. federal power versus state authority. The claim is simply that the people of Massachusetts are meddling in foreign policy with their Burma law, and foreign policy is the sole prerogative of Washington. Lest anyone doubt, however, that this is about globalism, the European Union took the most unusual step of filing a brief in federal court in support of the NFTC. Also, in solidarity with the U.S. corporate powers bringing the suit, the EU retained the politically connected law firm of Hogan & Hartson (where Clinton's national security adviser Sandy Berger held forth prior to moving to the White House) to represent its interests in the case and, pointedly, to be present during the trial. "We're not trying to intervene in a domestic constitutional issue," an EU official explained to the *Journal of Commerce* as the EU intervened in a domestic constitutional issue. "All we're interested in is the foreign policy powers argument." Hello, Mr. EU-man: The foreign policy powers argument *is* a domestic constitutional issue. Now, go home.

AWOL in this legal battle was the president, who could have had his Justice Department filing briefs and working with the outgunned state attorneys, raising the issue from one of legal technicalities to one of common sense and principle. Clearly, the Massachusetts legislature was not making foreign policy—it has no military force to send to Burma, nor can it tell Toyota or Texaco not to do business there. But it most certainly has the sovereign right to spend its own tax dollars on whom it chooses. But Clinton stayed low, choosing sides by his inaction on the case.

Unfortunately, with the EU and the NFTC locking arms and feeding their herd of silk-suited, Gucci-clad lawyers a steady stream of $1,000 bills, they prevailed with the judge, who sided with the powerful and against the people. He ruled that cities and states cannot use their purchasing power to reflect the local citizenry's moral principles on foreign policy issues. As Byron Rushing said after the verdict, "If a ruling like this had been made ten years ago, Nelson Mandela might still be in jail today." This fight, however, is not ultimately about foreign policy powers or state purchasing preferences, says Rushing: "It's a decision about whether, in a globalized economy, corporations have any accountability at all." He adds that the global corporation "doesn't want popular grassroots democratic actions to affect any of the business they do anytime, anywhere. . . . This is the tyranny of corporate America at work."

But Rushing, Billenness, and all the rest were not about to back down, and the fight goes on. The Massachusetts attorney general appealed the case to the U.S. Supreme Court, which basically dodged the issue in a ruling last year. Noting that the federal government has imposed an investment ban of its own against the outlandishly bloody junta repressing the people of Burma, the Supremes simply decided that this federal action supersedes the Massachusetts sanctions. The court took care to say that it was not ruling either for or against the right of state and local governments to use their spending powers to express their moral sensibilities.

BLUE GOLD. Should we invade Canada? I mean with armed forces! Sure, they're nice people, and they're ever so peaceable. (It's going to be hard, I have to admit, to work up much xenophobic hatred in America toward a country that thinks "jeepers" is an expletive, that has "Be Polite" in its national constitution, and that merrily flies a flag with a

friendly maple leaf on it.) But Canadians have something we
need, and I don't mean hockey players. "Blue Gold," it's been
dubbed by a Canadian newspaper, but it's far more valuable
than that implies, since the world can actually do without
gold.

Water. That's what Canada has that parts of our country
and much of the world might literally kill for.

Hell, you say, water's everywhere, 70 percent of the earth
is covered in the stuff. Yes, but as Canada's Maude Barlow
points out to anyone who'll listen, less than one-half of 1 percent of all the water on the globe is *fresh* water available for us
to drink. An author and agitator for common sense, Ms. Barlow heads the Council of Canadians and is founding chair of
Action Canada Network, two grassroots groups working for
progressive politics and policies. "Worldwide, the consumption
of water is doubling every twenty years," she writes in a stunning report entitled "Blue Gold: The Global Water Crisis." Barlow calculates that in a very short while, *most* of the world's
people will face shortages or absolute scarcity. This is not a
matter of your having to see more news stories of wretched
African children dying in horrible droughts, but of imminent
water crises in America (the Southwest, Florida, and California especially), in southern Europe, in India, in England, in
China ("the first country in the world that will have to literally
restructure its economy to respond to water scarcity," predicts
Barlow), and in other nations not usually thought of as facing
massive water shortages.

Canada, on the other hand, has a blessing of *agua fresca*.
W. C. Fields, who once complained of being stranded in the
desert for three days with nothing but water to drink, would
have gotten the heebie-jeebies in Canada, for there is water
everywhere. Some 20 percent of the world's entire supply of
fresh water is in the winding rivers and countless lakes
splashed all across the vast land (more lake than land in many
regions). This is not a reality that has dawned on Canadians

alone. Others are casting their eyes northward, thinking, "There's gold in them thar hills." But it's not countries making invasion plans—it's corporations.

To get their hands on the gold, the corporate grubbers first have to change the way the world's supply of drinking water is managed. Instead of letting countries treat it as a *resource* to be held in common and allocated by the public for the general good, they want it to be considered as just another *commodity* to be held and traded by private investors strictly for their own profit. Like oil or pork bellies . . . only this is your drinking water they want to privatize and commodify. Will it surprise you to learn that those bratty globalization twins, NAFTA and the WTO, contain provisions that advance the commodity concept? Thought not. Both incorporate the bald assertion that "water, including . . . ordinary natural water of all kinds (other than sea water)" are "goods" that are subject to the new rules of global trade.

We're talking here about much more than bottled water—Perrier, Evian, Yellow Snow #5, and your other favorite boutique brands. We're talking about *bulk* sales, including whole lakes and aquifers being bought and mined, the flow of rivers being siphoned off, the Great Lakes themselves being put on the market. Maude Barlow and others report that corporations worldwide are already organized to do the deed, using supertankers, pipelines, canals, the rerouting of rivers, and every other mammoth scheme known to humankind to shift the product from water-rich nations to those markets willing to pay top dollar for it:

- Nordic Water Company now totes H_2O from Norway to thirsty European countries by tugging it across the sea in giant, floating plastic bags, like some surreal scene from the Beatles *Yellow Submarine* movie.
- The aptly named Global Water Corporation, a Canadian firm, has cut a deal with the town of Sitka, Alaska, to take

eighteen billion gallons of water per year from nearby Blue
Lake and haul it to China, and it is joining with a Houston
maritime outfit to ship more Alaskan water aboard bulk
tankers to Singapore—"Water has moved from being an
endless commodity that may be taken for granted to a
rationed necessity that may be taken by force," GWC says
in a chilling statement.

- The GRAND Canal (Great Recycling And Northern Development Canal) is an engineer's wet dream, involving the
  building of a dike across the huge James Bay (get out your
  atlas, kiddies!) to capture the water of the twenty rivers
  that flow into it, converting the bay into a giant freshwater
  reservoir, then building a network of canals, dams, and
  locks to move the water four hundred miles south to Geor-
  gian Bay, where it would be "flushed through" the Great
  Lakes into pipelines that would take it to America's Sunbelt
  for the watering of lawns, sprinkling of golf courses, and
  other essential needs.

- McCurdy Enterprises of Gander, Newfoundland, plans to
  "harvest" (you've gotta love their PR firms) some thirteen
  billion gallons of water a year from one of that province's
  lakes, pipe it to the coast, pump it into old oil tankers (well
  scrubbed, I'm sure), and ship it to the Middle East for a
  hefty profit.

- Monsanto sees a multibillion-dollar business opportunity in
  the emerging water crisis, with one executive saying
  bluntly: "Since water is as central to food production as
  seed is, and without water life is not possible, Monsanto is
  now trying to establish its control over water. . . . Monsanto
  [has launched] a new water business, starting with India
  and Mexico, since both these countries are facing water
  shortages."

"Canada," barked editor Terrence Corcoran of the *Financial
Post* in a 1999 editorial, "is a future OPEC of water," urging

that the country begin trading in this rich commodity pronto. Likewise, Dennis Mills, a member of Canada's parliament from the governing Liberal Party (which actually is an arm of the country's financial and corporate elites, à la the Democrats in Washington), is a "Blue Gold" booster and is pushing for assorted water projects and trading schemes, declaring with gusto, "Fortunes are made by those who control the flow of water." Thanks to citizen groups like the two Maude Barlow heads, however, the Great Canadian Water Sale-a-Thon has yet to surge forth, for they have alerted the citizenry and generated a national debate on the wisdom of shouting "y'all come" to every global greedhead with a big bucket. Their vigilance has produced a temporary moratorium across the country on bulk sales. This might be a good place for me to add that Maude, and Canadians generally, certainly are not saying "It's our water and the rest of the world can go suck eggs" (remember, these are *extremely* nice people). To the contrary, they are the ones pushing for a public policy of sharing their bounty to meet the global water crisis, allocating water particularly to help those people in need.

But the pressure is intense to simply turn the water loose and let "the market" decide who needs it. And that little nasty, Chapter 11, is being wielded to break the dam and turn the water loose. Sun Belt Water Inc., based in Santa Monica, California, has filed the first NAFTA water case. It had an agreement with a British Columbia company to take water from this far western province and ship it in huge tankers down the west coast to southern California. But such a public outcry ensued when the scheme became public that the provincial government stepped in to protect its water, nixing the shipment by enacting a moratorium on all water exports. Imagine if Sun Belt had quietly worked a deal to sink a siphon into Lake Tahoe and drain it into Los Angeles, and you'll get a sense of how the people of British Columbia felt about Sun Belt's raid.

"Screw the people" was the reaction of the California corporation. It sued Canada in 1998, claiming that its *future profits* were "expropriated" by British Columbia's export moratorium and that, under the infamous Chapter 11, the nice people of Canada owed it $468 million.

Money isn't enough, though. Sun Belt CEO Jack Lindsay also wants to slap the Canadians around a bit. He has expressed outrage at what he perceives as the stinginess of the Canadians: "California has 33 million people—more than the entire population of Canada. This is expected to double in the next 20 years, and they have been living in a permanent drought condition. In 20 years, the shortfall in California will be four million acre-feet of water [per year]—one percent of what spills into the Pacific Ocean from British Columbia—and they're saying 'Sorry, you can't have it'?" What a humanitarian. Jack just wants a few drops for the poor parched people of California. Next thing you know, he'll have Sally Struthers doing heart-rending ads on the BC telly, pleading in a quavering voice for the people of this watery province to "save the thirsty children of Beverly Hills."

What a crock. For the privateers and commodifiers like Lindsay, bulk water deals have nothing to do with global need and everything to do with global greed. As Barlow tells us, they'll deliver the water to whoever will pay the most to get it—like the water-gobbling high-tech companies of Silicon Valley and the sprawling agribusiness corporations that suck up irrigation water like insatiable sponges. Then there is Lindsay's snide comment that, after all, much of the province's water just "spills into the Pacific Ocean." This is a common refrain from the water corporatizers, who claim that if water isn't being used commercially it is being "wasted"—or, as one forest company exec says, if it's unused it's just part of the "decadent wilderness." Never mind that water running to the sea is an essential part of the ecological cycle, delivering nutrients, sustaining the whole fishing economy, replenishing wetlands, and doing much more useful chores than fattening the wallet of a would-be water baron.

Jack just keeps yakking, though, apparently confusing verbosity with profundity. Why is water any different from any other commodity, he wonders: "Canada chops down its trees so we can build houses in California. . . . But I'm watching this debate [over water exports] where Canada is saying this is hockey, this is apple pie." No, Mr. Lindsay, not apple pie, it's water—the essential of life, the unifying essence of the ecosystem, the invaluable resource that belongs to the whole public.

Also, Lindsay and his California corporation are not just "watching" the debate, they are doing all they can to decide its outcome. While they can't claim to be "naturalized" citizens of Canada, thereby legitimate participants in the debate, they do claim some sort of mutant "NAFTA-ized" citizenship in the country: "Because of NAFTA," Lindsay told the *Montreal Gazette* last year, "we are stakeholders in the national water policy of Canada." Sun Belt Water Inc., Ms. Barlow reports, "is openly courting BC coastal communities to consider water exports and is urging local politicians to lobby the provincial government to reverse its ban on exports."

Dealing with NAFTA is trickier than playing hockey in hell, and, for the Canadians, there is another nasty trick in the trade agreement that makes them vulnerable to an all-out corporate raid. Sun Belt and the other water hustlers only need *one* export deal in any one province to break the dam for *all* of Canada's water. This is because the devils who set up the NAFTA game rigged it with a provision called "proportionality," which means that if one company gets a deal, the country has to treat every other company the same. So when one company exports even a trickle of water out of Canada, that opens the tap for all other export deals, and the tap cannot be turned off—even if it is later proven that the massive outflow is doing horrible damage to the environment, to other businesses (fishing, tourism, etc.), or to the country as a whole. Tough luck—

you made your deal with the devil, even though the vast majority of legislators (much less the people) really didn't have a clue what was in the deal. That's the way the devil plays.

This is why Sun Belt Water Inc. is squeezing so hard in British Columbia. Canada's national government, rather than imposing its own ban on water exports, took the kind of half-assed approach our national politicians would take—they asked each of the ten provinces of Canada to implement their own voluntary moratoriums. This makes the politicians look like they've done something, when in fact all they've done is to create betting pools in offices across the country on which province will be the first to crack. If (or when) one province allows an export deal, all the other provincial moratoriums are immediately null and void—and the "Blue Gold Rush" is on.

YOU SASS

Ralph Lauren, the multibillionaire fashion baron known for his preppy "Polo" line of clothes and other goods, made a news splash in 1998 when he engaged in a bit of "conspicuous philanthropy." He wrote a $10 million company check to the Smithsonian Institution to go toward the restoration of The Star-Spangled Banner, the badly deteriorating 187-year-old flag that had inspired Francis Scott Key to write our national anthem, which, let's admit, is unsingable (but it's the thought that counts). Lauren Inc.'s donation produced what is known in public relations lingo as an Op-op—the optimum photo op. Held just after July 4th, it included the President of the United States, the First Lady, a brand-name CEO, the massive and historic flag itself, *and* a really big check—all of our national symbols arrayed for this one media moment. The only thing missing was a football.

The star-spangled ceremony was a promotional coup for Lauren's company, well worth the ten mil, for he received saturation media coverage as he wrapped himself in Old Glory, and he was given both a product endorsement and testimonial to his character by the First Couple. President Clinton: "You know, most of us have—well, maybe not most of us, but a lot us, including Hillary and me—have these great Polo sweaters with the American flag on it." Next the First Lady: "The phrase 'Ralph Lauren' has become an adjective for a certain kind of style. Now it will be a symbol of another aspect of the American way: good citizenship." Then Ralph stepped forward to add just the right touch of billionaire humility, saying that he was giving the money because "I am a product of the American dream, and the flag is its symbol." Nice.

But half a globe away one could get a totally different view of the Polo label and of Mr. Lauren's character. In Shenzhen, China, some 350 young women, eighteen to twenty-five years old, work at the Iris Fashion factory, making the clothing that has made Ralph Lauren so much money that he can live the American dream and still give away $10 million. The factory is a sweatshop. "I begin work daily at 7 A.M. six days a week," says a twenty-year-old who sews collars onto shirts for Lauren. "On a normal day, work ends around 9 P.M. If we are under pressure for a rush delivery, we work until midnight. Right now I average eighty hours per week. . . . I'm paid on a piece-rate basis, two cents per collar."

Every four minutes (*Oh, say can you see*) she has to complete a collar (*By the dawn's early light*), which she does for more than fourteen hours a day (*What so proudly we hailed*), six days a week (*At the twilight's last gleaming*) for an average of 29 cents an hour (*Oh, say, does that star-spangled banner yet wave*), which is a poverty wage even by China's standards (*O'er the land of the free*), and she lives jammed with her co-workers six to a room in a prisonlike factory dorm (*And the home of the brave!*).

Hers is but one of hundreds of thousands of real-life stories that are behind the labels of so many of the goods now sold in

American stores—goods that make philanthropists of the Ralph Laurens of the world, even while they bring the stench of rank exploitation to the Star-Spangled Banner itself. Cynics say the public doesn't give a damn, and the global manufacturers sure do all they can to keep the curtain pulled, hoping to keep the public in the dark about their manufacturing methods. Phil Knight, the Baron of Beaverton, Oregon, who has built his Nike empire and a personal fortune on the backs of sweatshop workers throughout Asia, is dismissive of those who raise sweatshop concerns: "This isn't an issue that should even be on the political agenda. It's just a sound bite of globalization." Now there's a guy who loses IQ every time he opens his mouth.

Cynics who think people don't care haven't met Tico Almeida or Eric Brakken, and if Nike's knight thinks he can keep this issue off the political agenda, he has not met Suzanne Clark or Joe Sexauer. These are but a few of the savvy and determined nineteen- and twenty-year-olds who are raising righteous hell about the immorality of the global sweatshop system and are taking matters into their own hands on college campuses all across America. The establishment media are only beginning to notice, but student activism today is not an oxymoron—it's back in a big way. From an insurgency that sprang up on five campuses in the fall of 1997, the movement (yes, it's already advanced to this lofty status) has spread in barely two years to more than 200 campuses, from liberal Harvard to conservative Claremont College in Southern California, from rural Cornell to NYU in downtown Manhattan, from Ann Arbor to Tucson. In the summer of '98, the students created a national umbrella organization so they could work together, naming it United Students Against Sweatshops. USAS is the acronym, but you have to say it the way the students do to get the energy and attitude they're bringing to the cause: "You-sass" is how they say it.

Sass indeed. These kids are smack in the face of their university presidents, are stripping bare the wussiness of the Clinton administration (not a pretty sight) on this basic issue of social justice, are rejecting outright the corporate shuck and jive intended to keep the exploitation going, and, most importantly, *are winning*! Well, they haven't won yet, but, my God, what strides they are making on an issue that few of the political cognoscenti, including the liberals, would have predicted (or wanted) to become "The Cause." How did this happen? Why *this issue*?

Because, first, students today are no different from those of us who rose up in the sixties against the outrage of denying civil rights to black people or against the insanity of the Vietnam War—these are people who have not had their ideals bought off or kicked out of them, and they are unafraid to Question Authority, as the bumper sticker keeps urging. Second, there has been a recent organized effort by unions (especially UNITE, the garment workers union) to expose the ugly truth of sweatshop labor to students, just as CORE, SCLC, and other civil rights groups did on campuses in the sixties, rallying a generation to act on conscience and join in the struggle to assure basic liberties for African Americans. Third, students take the sweatshop issue personally, and they can do something about it right where they are. Their focus is on the $2.5 billion a year that American universities pocket on licensing fees for the sales of sweatshirts, windbreakers, caps, Frisbees, stuffed animals, and other "stuff" that is sold bearing the logo of the Wildcats, Blue Devils, Badgers, Tigers, Tarantulas, Mud-Bugs, and other critters that are the mascots of the schools. University administrators license Nike, Reebok, Sara Lee, and other companies to sell these school-branded products, then the companies go shopping around the globe for subcontractors who will produce the goodies for next to nothing.

It doesn't take a very bright bulb to see the light here—the cheapest goods are sweatshop goods, and the university is profiting from the exploitation, paid for by student dollars.

This reality has struck a nerve with students who don't really want to put on a sweater made by someone as young as they are who is subjected to wage slavery and physical abuse as they stitch Bucky the Badger onto the sweater. "Free Bucky" became a slogan at the University of Wisconsin, where students have rebelled against their mascot being held captive by global sweatshop operators. Eric Brakken, a leader of the anti-sweatshop campaign on the Madison campus, says, "We're seeing a lot of people who've never been involved, because this is such a close issue for them."

So close that they have taken to the streets, protesting, marching, petitioning, and—déjà vu all over again—sitting in! University presidents who thirty-some-odd years ago were schooled on campuses where activists seized the offices of the presidents, now find their own offices occupied, though with some important differences. Like Dustbusters. Apparently, this is a much more polite, or at least a tidier, generation. While we were prone to shout the filthiest words in our vocabularies, write graffiti on the walls, cut phone lines, and generally trash an occupied office, the current crop of campus rebels literally have been known to bring Dustbusters and other cleaning equipment with them to clean up after themselves. They are very focused, very purposeful, and trash is not their objective.

Their objective is nothing less than to stop American universities from participating in the sweatshop system, and they are very clear and firm about what that requires:

1. A code of conduct that Nike and the rest must sign and abide by if they are to get any contracts from the university to sell products bearing the school name, logo, mascot, colors, etc.

2. A code that requires contractors to certify that their products are not made in sweatshops, which means at a minimum that there is no child labor or forced labor involved, that no sexual abuse or other violence is used against the

workers, that factory conditions are safe and healthy, that fundamental civil liberties are honored, that workers can exercise the right to form a union, *AND* (this turns out to be a mighty big "and") that wages are sufficient to cover a family's food, clothing, and shelter.

3. Agreement by contractors that any and all of their factories are open to unannounced inspections by *independent* monitors designated by the university.

4. Full disclosure by contractors of where their factories actually are, by specific addresses, including the location of all subcontracted work.

USAS leaders have learned the hard way that it's necessary to spell all of this out for university administrators, as though talking to small children—"No, dear, it's not enough to say the factory is in Asia, because, see, we want the nice inspectors to be able to go to the factory in person, and to go there means they need to know the town it's in and have the actual street address." Greased pigs are not as slippery as university officials get when asked to stand on principle against corporate power, so the students have had to learn the art of cornering them. One university president, desperately trying not to have to deal with the matter of decent wages, tried to slip by with this statement to students: "I think we can all agree that these people should be paid more than zero."

The officials, pressured by their corporate donors, were dallying with the activists, making soothing statements of principled concern while doing all they could to make the whole thing go away. "We cannot tolerate having the sweat and tears of abused and exploited workers mixed with the fabric of the products which bear our marks," said the Duke director of licensing, even as Duke's president was quietly trying to swing a deal for a code of conduct that would cover up the sweat and tears without doing anything to stop them. The first cover-up attempt came in November 1998, through something called the Collegiate Licensing Company, which is a middle-man broker between about 170 universities and hundreds of companies that make products for them. On the defensive as a result of the spreading campus protests, CLC produced its own code of conduct, which, not surprisingly, did not deal with sweatshop wages or require disclosure of factory locations. Grateful school officials were quick to cling to this thin reed: "Sometimes compromises are necessary," Duke president Nan Keohane lectured a group of students who were chanting "Principles, not politics" in protest of the CLC sham. The code was to be approved by February 1 of the next year, and she said she was planning to sign it. "I'd prefer to have a flawed code than no code at all," she told them, as though these were the two choices available to her.

No sale. The students regrouped during the holiday break, and on January 29, 1999, Tico Almeida and a hardy band of thirty other Blue Devil protesters walked into Nan's office and set up camp—the first ever sit-in over a code of conduct. Zapping a constant stream of e-mail updates to antisweatshop leaders across the country, the Duke action electrified the movement—all the more so when, after thirty-one hours, President Keohane agreed to require full disclosure of plant locations from any manufacturers their school dealt with.

A week later, Georgetown's no-sweat activists spent seventy-two hours in their president's office, also winning a commitment to full disclosure. In Madison, U. of Wisconsin students sat in for ninety-seven hours, with some three hundred students rallying outside the administration building, producing the first guarantee by a university that its products would be made only in factories that pay a living wage.

Reeling from this surge, the garment industry itself teamed with the always pliable Clinton administration to try to dodge the student demands. They have created a typically Clintonesque facade called the Fair Labor Association, which purports to be a "public-private partnership" to regulate the use of sweatshop labor. Nike and Liz Claiborne, two known sweat-shop exploiters, have seats on the FLA board. The association's rules have about as much bite as a Twinkie has nutrition. Rather than punish, the FLA seeks to reward, by allowing garment makers to sport a neat, "No Sweat" label on their goods if their shops aren't of the sweat variety. It surely would be no sweat for the corporations to get FLA approval, since they would get to designate which of their factories are to be inspected and when, they would hire the monitors, and the "investigative" reports would be made not to a public agency but to the companies themselves. Also, there would be no standards for wages and no disclosure of factory addresses. The FLA asked universities to join in this charade, and seventeen universities announced on March 15, 1999, that they would do so.

Stand back! Here came the students again:

- March 17, Joe Sexauer and other activists have a camp-out in the University of Michigan president's office for fifty-one hours, getting him to agree not to join the FLA and to require a living wage, full factory-location disclosure, *and* a women's rights provision from all of its product licensees.
- April 21, University of North Carolina students visit their president for seventy-two hours, televising their Chapel Hill sit-in live on the Internet and composing new lyrics to the old labor classic "Solidarity Forever":

> *We came to the chancellor*
> *with a list of our demands*
> *But when we left the room*
> *he was sitting on his hands*
> *Not gonna let him sell out Carolina to THE MAN*
> *For the sit-in makes us strong*
> *We need full disclosure*
> *and we need a living wage*

But chancellor you're not listening
and it's making us enraged
And we're gonna sit right here
until you sign the page
For the sit-in makes us strong.

Whether he gave in because of the singing or because of the principles being raised is not known for sure, but he did agree to a living wage, full disclosure, women's rights, and no FLA membership.

- April 22, an epic, ten-day sit-in begins at the University of Arizona, during which a recalcitrant president refuses to agree to some key demands and threatens repeatedly to bring in the police, but the students hang in there and, *226 hours* later, he relents, and the students walk away with the full package of agreements won elsewhere.

Another measure of the students' success is that various establishmentarian voices have been rushing out lately to say, tut-tut now, you kids might be well-meaning idealists, but you are way over your heads when meddling with the natural laws and realpolitik of globalization. A *Wall Street Journal* editorialist, drawing deeply on an ideological pipe that seems always fully packed with pomposity, tells us that "we would all do well to recognize that what looks like exploitation in Indiana looks an awful lot like opportunity in Indonesia"—clearly written by someone who's never had the opportunity to do sweatshop labor. *Newsweek* has also stepped forward, employing the tired old canard of "radical chic" to try tarnishing the students, then engaging in a sort of stream-of-consciousness wail that the students' ill-considered demands might actually succeed in raising the wages for sweatshop workers which would be horrible don't you see because this could force the factories to close causing the very people the naive students want to help to lose their jobs not to mention the possibility that elimination of sweatshops could ripple back to our shores in the form of higher prices for a Nike shoe or a Lord & Taylor blouse and the next thing you know you've got a consumer backlash on your hands and economic collapse and social chaos—and all of this because some students got to messing in something that's none of their business anyway.

Despite such tortured rationalizations from some of the media heavies, despite the government's weaseling on the issue, despite neither Gore nor Bush wanting to touch the issue, and despite the corporations and the universities doing their damnedest to squirm loose, the students have persevered and gained the upper hand. In only a couple of years, USAS activists have forced this issue into the open and put the debate on their terms, and they've also scored victory after victory, with fifty-seven universities so far having signed on the dotted line for the Worker's Rights Consortium, which is the code-with-teeth that USAS supports.

While their campus struggles continue, these students have also won a larger victory. By simply standing up and standing firm, they've shown us all that corporate globalization need not be accepted as a given, as a force that is either inevitable or too powerful to resist—in fact, it's a paper tiger, totally vulnerable to an organized and principled opposition. The students are in the forefront of a new politics based on the common needs of people worldwide rather than on the selfish whims of a few private interests. Making a better world means standing up to the bastards. As William Jennings Bryan put it, "Destiny is not a matter of chance, it is a matter of choice; it is not something to be waited for, it is a thing to be achieved."

PART THREE

THIS LAND
IS YOUR LAND

THIS LAND *IS* YOUR LAND

Woody Guthrie wrote "This Land" in 1940 while living in New York City, penning all six verses in one night while staying in a no-star hotel somewhere around Times Square. The song had been forming in his fertile mind for a long time as "he roamed and rambled" all around America, "walking that ribbon of highway." He wrote it not as a sweet sing-along glorifying the American landscape but as a proudly populist anthem for the hardscrabble people he traveled among. He had already written hundreds of songs that chronicled the lives and struggles of these workaday folks who are the strength of our great land, performing his songs for them on picket lines, in migrant camps, and at rallies, as well as performing on radio and at their dances. His music entertained, even as it encouraged people in their battles against the Pinkertons, politicians, and other authorities who fronted for the refined men with soft hands and hard eyes who ran things from afar.

When he wrote the words "*your* land," Woody was pointedly speaking to the steelworkers in Pittsburgh and dockworkers up and down the Pacific coast, the dust-bowl people (of whom he was one) who had lost their crops to drought and their farms to bankers, the workers who risked their lives to build the Grand Coulee and the itinerant harvesters who cut the wheat and stacked the hay, "trying to make about a dollar a day." Every schoolchild has sung "This Land's" gentle verses about the "endless skyway" and "diamond deserts," but the songbooks carefully excise Woody's verses that provoke ordinary citizens to rethink the established order, to realize their democratic strength, and to rebel against the structures of privilege that lock out the majority. Verses like:

> Was a big high wall there that tried to stop me
> A sign was painted said: "Private Property."
> But on the back side it didn't say nothing
> This side was made for you and me.©*

Woody knew that this land is our land only if we make it so, only if we have the stomach to confront the elites and challenge the insidious forces of autocracy that are continually at work to make it exclusively their land, in the sense that they control the economic and political decisions that rule us. The essence of democracy is self-government. Anything less is a fraud. Being connected to the Internet is not democracy, having a choice between Gore and Bush is not democracy, receiving 500 channels of digital television is not democracy, being awarded a slice of corporate-allocated prosperity is not democracy. Democracy is control. Whatever goals we strive for as a people—racial harmony, peace, economic fairness, privacy, clean water and air—all are dependent on our ability to control the decisions that affect these goals.

Pause for a moment to think of what an incredible treasure it is to have the right to govern ourselves. Precious few people in history have even had the possibility of asserting their common will over the will of the ruling powers, and the vast majority of earth's people today cannot even imagine such a right. But, in the Declaration of 1776, we have it in writing: ". . . governments are instituted among men, deriving their just powers from *the consent of the governed*." We're in charge! Not kings or feudal barons, congresses or presidents, and damned sure not corporations or World Trade Organizations.

Having it on paper, though, doesn't make it so. Indeed, when it was first written, it wasn't so for very many citizens at all. In the first presidential election, 1789, only 4 percent of the American people were allowed to vote. No women voted (they were chattel), no African Americans (they were slaves), no Native Americans (they were considered heathens), and no one who was without land (they were riffraff). A broader sense of self-rule came later, and only with great effort, pain, and suffering. From abolitionists to suffragists, from populists to Wobblies, from sit-down strikes to lunch-counter sit-ins, blood has flowed as generation after generation has battled the Powers That Be for a share of "Life, Liberty, and the Pursuit of Happiness." In the 224 years since Jefferson wrote of these "inalienable rights," thousands upon thousands of Americans have died in the ongoing struggle to democratize the Declaration, to extend the possibility of self-government to more citizens. What a debt we owe to those who have sacrificed so much to bring us this far, and what a gift this right to self-government is.

But will we hold on to it? Progress is never assured and democracy cannot be taken for granted, even in our country. As the previous chapters have spelled out, there has been a radical backsliding of democratic control in the past few years—a majority of Americans now find themselves effectively shut out of economic and political decision making, and even greater threats to our sovereignty loom in the ominous form of the WTO, NAFTA, and other antidemocratic creations of the global corporate powers. Democratic power is never given; it always has to be taken, then aggressively defended, and retaken when it slips from our hands, for the moneyed powers relentlessly press to gain supremacy and assert their private will over the majority. Today, our gift of democracy is endangered not by military might threatening a sudden, explosive coup but by the stealth of corporate lawyers and politicians, seizing a piece of self-government from us here, then another piece from over there, quietly installing an elitist regime issue by issue, law by law, place by place, with many citizens unaware that their people's authority is slipping away.

For the past couple of decades, this has been going on, greatly accelerating in the nineties, as corporate will has been enthroned, increasingly reigning supreme over every aspect of our lives—economics, politics, culture, and nature itself. We American people find ourselves, once again, at one of those "When in the course of human events" moments, when it is our time to face the reality that a despotic force is in our midst. In the name of all American rebels who have gone before, are we going to sit by, unwilling to confront the bully in front of us, which grows more powerful the longer we wait? You and I have the lofty responsibility to follow in the footsteps of those rebels, to oppose the corporate usurpers and fight for our nation's unique and hard-won right to self-government. Progress doesn't come by merely standing on guard but, as George Bernard Shaw said about a hundred years ago, "by attacking, and getting well-hammered yourself."

WHAT THE HELL IS A CORPORATION?

This ubiquitous critter called the corporation—we're stuck with it, right? We've just got to learn to live with it, don't we, kind of like we live with cockroaches? After all, a corporation has a natural right to do business, doesn't it? No, no, and no. First of all, a corporation is not a business. It's nothing but a piece of paper, a bit of legalism that does not create a business but instead creates a protective association for individuals who want to do business yet want special protections for themselves against other people, against the public at large . . . against the very workings of democracy.

You can make widgets, you can farm, you can sell hardware or groceries, you can operate a hotel, you can provide banking services, or be in any other business without being a corporation. Most of the businesses in the world are *unincorporated* enterprises—individuals, sole proprietorships, partnerships, co-ops, or other forms of operation. Taking on corporations is not antibusiness at all—we must have business, but that does not mean we have to have corporations.

Where did we get the corporate structure? From the jolly Brits, who devised a devilish scheme called "joint stock companies" during their colonial phase. Empire and all that, eh what? The corporate entity was (and is) a legal fiction, first invented by the crown to assist the barons, merchant traders, and bankers of the day in plundering the wealth of the Empire's colonies, including those in our fair land. It was a way to amass the large sums of capital they needed to plunder faraway places, collecting money from investors to finance the plundering, then distributing the booty back to those investors. The corporate construct is dangerous not only because it can agglomerate an absolutely domineering amount of financial power but also because it allows the owners of the corporation (the shareholders) to profit from its business activities, yet accept *no responsibility* for any harm done by their company's business activities. All gain, no pain. The corporation is a legal shield, granting its owners an extraordinary protective privilege that no other business owners are allowed. Oh, did my company spill eleven million gallons of oil into Prince William Sound (Exxon), did it kill 2,000 people in a chemical explosion in Bhopal, India (Union Carbide), did it defraud thousands of senior citizens who were persuaded to put money into bad securities (Prudential), did it dump cancer-causing PCBs into the Hudson River (General Electric)? So sorry, I'm sure, but that's none of my doing—the *corporation* did it. Yet, the corporation has no ass to be kicked, no scruff of the neck to be grabbed, no body to be tossed unceremoniously into the maximum security lockup, no conscience to make it contrite, and no soul that would allow the religious among us to believe that at least this wretched enterprise will be condemned to eternal hell.

To the built-in irresponsibility of the amorphous corporate entity, add the bottom-line imperative of the CEO and board of directors. Academicians, judges, and corporate executives themselves aver that the sole role of corporate management is to make as much money as possible for the shareholders (a group that prominently includes the managers). The managers have no responsibility—none—to workers, environment, consumers, community, flag, or anything else. To the contrary, the entire incentive is for management to cut corners, to short-change, to exploit. It is not a matter of a CEO's good intentions or bad—it is the bottom line, and it must be served. Put away all hope, ye who go in asking corporations to be "good," "responsible," "accountable." It is not in their self-interest or in their nature—you might as well expect a Rottweiler to meow.

As for corporations having natural rights, forget it. It's no longer taught in civics or history classes, and it's definitely not mentioned in today's politics or media, but corporations have no rights at all. Zero. Not even the right to exist. The state gives them the *privilege* to exist, but this existence can be narrowly defined and controlled by We the People. I realize this goes against the received wisdom, against the carefully nurtured assumption that corporations are somehow or other one of God's creatures with inherent powers that are larger and elevated above the powers of us common citizens. We can all be forgiven for assuming this, for that certainly is how it works in practice today. But it need not and should not work that way, nor was it meant to work that way when our country and most of our states were founded. Each corporation was and is the creature of the *citizenry,* allowed to exist only through receipt of a state charter. *We are the sovereign,* not them. They are supposed to serve us, not vice versa.

Back to the future: the American Revolution. Jane Anne Morris, a thinker, digger, strategist, and agitator on the issue of corporate dominance, writes: "The people who founded this nation didn't fight a war so they could have a couple of 'citizen representatives' sitting in on meetings of the British East India Company. They carried out a revolution in order to be free of oppression: corporate, governmental, or otherwise; and to replace it with democratic self-government." Adams, Jefferson, Paine, and the rest had not had a happy experience with the corporations of the crown and were unabashedly anticorporate at the founding, with Jefferson even speaking of the need "to crush in its birth the aristocracy of our moneyed corporations."

The citizens of early America knew what they were up against: raw economic power. They were rightly wary of the corporate structure itself, knowing that it allowed a few individuals in the society to stockpile a massive amount of money and power, then use this and the corporate shield to pursue their private gain to the harm of the common good. Eighteenth- and nineteenth-century Americans were prescient when it came to these entities—citizens expressed concern that corporations would use their money as bribes to pervert democratic elections and buy both legislators and judges; farmers worried that corporations would use their muscle to monopolize markets and control crop prices; and industrial and craft workers were concerned that corporations would, as historian Louis Hartz has written, turn them into "a commodity," treating them "as much an article of commerce as woolens, cotton or yarn." They knew that the unbridled corporation was antithetical to the democratic principles they espoused and a threat to the very system of self-government they had established. So they made damned sure the corporation was securely bridled.

Anyone so timid as to think that it is radical for citizens today even to consider "interfering" with the private will of corporations is not made of the same stout stuff as the citizens who created our states and our country. In America's first hundred years, applicants could get a corporate charter only by approval of their state legislature, usually requiring a two-thirds vote to win one. Few charters were awarded, and those few corporations that got them were limited in their function, in how much money they could aggregate, in how long they could exist, and in how they could function. Citizens took their hard-won sovereignty seriously, adamantly defending it against the possibility of corporate usurpation. State after state imposed strict terms on the issuance of a charter, leaving no doubt about who was in charge. This is our hidden history of proud and aggressive citizenship, and you're likely to be amazed if you look into how the people of your state have stood up to corporate power in the not-so-distant past. Jane Anne Morris dug into the records of her state of Wisconsin and found that from 1848 to as recently as 1953, the legislature had imposed such charter conditions as these:

- Corporations had to have a clearly stated reason for existing, and if they failed to fulfill that purpose or went beyond it, their charter could be revoked.
- The legislature could revoke the charter for any particular reason or, as the Wisconsin attorney general ruled in 1913, "for no reason at all."
- Corporate management and stockholders could be held liable for corporate acts.
- Directors of the corporation were required to come from among the stockholders.
- If a corporation's principal place of business was Wisconsin, it had to have its headquarters and its meetings there.
- Charters were granted for a specific period of time, like twenty years, rather than "in perpetuity."
- Corporations could not own other corporations.
- Corporations could own real estate only if it was necessary to carry out their specific purpose.
- Corporations were flatly prohibited from making any political contribution, direct or indirect, and it was a felony crime if they did so.

- All corporate records and documents were open to the legislature and to the attorney general.

From Maine to California, Wisconsin to Texas, all states had similar stipulations on their books—and they were enforced! Especially important were the revocation clauses, which allowed state legislatures or courts to yank the operating licenses of corporations that behaved badly. Imagine. The people were in charge, the general welfare was paramount over corporate profit, civic authority prevailed over CEO whim. Richard Grossman and Ward Morehouse, two thoughtful activists who codirect POCLAD (the Program on Corporations, Laws and Democracy), have published an excellent pamphlet worthy of Thomas Paine, entitled "Taking Care of Business: Citizenship and the Charter of Incorporation." It notes that the corporate charter was a sacrosanct oath: "The penalty for abuse or misuse of the charter was not a fine or a slap on the wrist, but revocation of the charter and dissolution of the corporation. Citizens believed it was society's inalienable right to abolish an evil." Charters were routinely revoked, including those of the most powerful—in 1894, the Central Labor Union of New York City cited a pattern of abuses against John D. Rockefeller's Standard Oil Trust of New York, asking the attorney general to request that the state supreme court revoke its charter. The AG did . . . and the court did.

After the Civil War, however, with the rise of the Robber Barons, a full-scale assault was begun by the moneyed interests against these inconvenient rules. Railroad baron Cornelius Vanderbilt issued the war cry of the antidemocratic elites when he thundered, "What do I care about the law? H'ain't I got the power?" For the next hundred years—stipulation by stipulation, state by state, bribe by bribe—the sovereign was steadily reduced to the subjugated. Corporate barons like Vanderbilt hauled sacks of money into state capitols to buy legislators and win charter changes favorable to them. The chief justice of Wisconsin's supreme court spoke as early as 1873 of "a new and dark power" that was looming, warning that "the enterprises of the country are aggregating vast corporate combinations of unexampled capital, marching, not for economical conquests only, but for political power. . . ." The Vanderbilts, Goulds, Rockefellers, and others had more money than hell has brimstone, and they used it to corrupt and dominate the same state legislatures that had been bulwarks of democratic resistance to the corporate empire builders. A Pennsylvania legislator is reported to have said, "Mr. Speaker, I move we adjourn, unless the Pennsylvania Railroad has some more business for us to transact."

Gradually, the bridle has been removed, resulting in what we have today—the runaway corporate autocracy that the founders predicted and feared. Shall we just accept it? Shall we timidly continue into another century with the status quo politics of the pathetic ClintonGoreLieberman Democrats, who demand again and again that the people must adjust to the private agenda of a handful of corporate executives and investors?

"This is an exciting time to be an American," a Californian wrote to me several months ago. "We are in a crisis. We are on the brink of the failure of our old democratic processes— swamped, subverted, perverted, and filibustered by the corporate feudal system and its totalitarian dominance of our lives. We have the opportunity and the duty to overcome all that," he wrote.

Bingo! In one succinct paragraph, this citizen has nailed it, and he is but one of a growing majority who know that "consent of the governed" is a mockery today, supplanted by a crude bribery system of corporate governance that is becoming as autocratic as anything imagined by King George III and his royally chartered British East India Company, Hudson's Bay Company, and the crown charters that ruled American colonies. Just a few examples: High-handed CEOs can, by fiat, off several thousand workers from the payroll, thereby jacking up the company's stock price and enriching themselves with tens of millions in stock gains, while the workers and their families are allowed no redress for their grievances; your bank, insurance company, credit-card firm, HMO, and other corporations can secretly collect the most intimate details of your private life, then use or sell this information in any way they see fit, without even informing you; imperious biotech corporations can mess dangerously with the very DNA of our food supply for no purpose except to enhance their profits, then force families to be the guinea pigs of their Frankenfood experiments, since there is no labeling of thousands of supermarket items (including baby food) already containing these genetically altered organisms; conniving corporations routinely extract millions from townspeople as the price of building a factory or sports stadium in their town, then can renege on any pledge of job creation and, on whim, pull up stakes and abandon the town altogether; haughty HMOs can make decisions that kill you, yet Congress protects them from legal liability and punishment for your death; "speech" has been perverted to mean money, authorizing corporations and their executives to buy control of the entire political process; a chemical company can callously pollute our air, water, and food, leading to thousands of deaths, birth defects, and other horrors, yet continue doing business and continue polluting, with no punishment beyond, perhaps, a fine, which it easily absorbs and, in some cases, can deduct from its income taxes as a "cost of doing business"; a handful of media giants have attained absolute control over the content of news and the range of ideas that are broadcast on the *public's* airwaves, arbitrarily shrinking the democratic debate; the democratic decisions of a city council, state legislature, or other sovereign government can be arrogantly annulled by corporate action through antidemocratic entities established by NAFTA and the WTO.

Who the hell are these people? Who elected them to run our world? Why are we putting up with this crap? As the bumper sticker puts it: LEMMINGS OF THE WORLD UNITE! YOU HAVE NOTHING TO LOSE BUT YOUR PLACE IN LINE!

We need to crank up a political fight that has some guts to it, some fire-breathing democratic passion in it, some of the revolutionary spirit of 1776 behind it. This is not a fight about regulations or really even about corporations—it's about control, sovereignty, self-government, *democracy*. Let's force the issue and put it as starkly as it is: Are corporations going to rule, or are we? From time to time, I hear veterans of the civil rights and antiwar battles of the sixties bemoan the lack of a "Big Battle" today, one that can unite a majority across traditional political lines, one that is about justice for all, is loaded with citizen outrage, has the spark of genuine passion within it, and is worthy of bloody heads. Well, here it is: The self-evident battle of our era is to defeat corporate autocracy and establish citizen rule over our government, our economy, and our environment.

WHEN YOU FIGHT THE DEVIL, FIGHT TO WIN

Practically every progressive struggle—campaign finance reform, rain forest destruction and global warming, sweatshops, family farms, fair trade, health care for all, unionization, military spending and arms sales, tax reform, alternative energy, healthy food, media access, hazardous waste dumps, redlining, alternative medicine, you name it—is being fought against one cluster of corporations or another. But it is not that corporation over there or this one over here that is the enemy, it is not one industry's contamination of our drinking water or another's perversion of the lawmaking process that is the problem—rather it is the corporation itself that must be addressed if we are to be a free people.

In his powerful pamphlet *Common Sense,* Thomas Paine touched the heart of the American Revolution when he wrote:

"Ye that dare oppose not only tyranny but the tyrant, stand forth." We can all object to consequences and seek remedial action, but will we finally face the tyrant itself? That is the question for progressives as we step into 2000. We can continue fighting the beast as we have been, through scattershot, uncoordinated efforts—a lawsuit here, an investigation there, some legislation, more regulations, prayer, and the always useful sacrificial goat. Occasionally, these approaches succeed. But, as Grossman and Morehouse have written, "Tactically, [this approach] means limiting ourselves to resisting harms one corporate site at a time, one corporate chemical or biotechnology product at a time; to correcting imperfections of the market; to working for yet more permitting and disclosure laws; to initiating procedural lawsuits and attempts to win compensation after corporate harm has been done; to battling regulatory and administrative agencies; to begging leaders of global corporations to please cause a little less harm."

In 1998, Britain's House of Lords dealt with the weighty matter of changing the official costume worn by the Lord Chancellor, that body's top official. The outfit included a long powdered wig, breeches, tights, buckled shoes, white gloves, and black stockings. The incumbent wanted very much not to look, as one reporter described him, like "the frog footman in 'Alice in Wonderland,'" so he proposed a switch to modern business attire. Traditionalists, however, opposed any change in the seventeenth-century garb. Lord Wattington put the case for tradition forcefully, summing up by declaring, "I can see no advantage to the Queen or the public if the Lord Chancellor removes his tights."

At the national level, inside the Beltway, too many of our progressive energies and resources are spent on fights that amount to removing the Lord Chancellor's tights. The piecemeal approach to fighting corporate abuses keeps us spread thin, separated from each other, on the defensive, riveted on the minutiae, and fighting on their terms (literally over the language of *their* laws and regulations, and in *their* courts and legislatures). More often than not, regulatory agencies are shams, working to sustain the business-as-usual tactics of corporations rather than to inhibit them, and the deck is stacked against the public interest anytime we find ourselves within these legalistic meat grinders. This is nothing new—historian Howard Zinn writes about the creation of the Interstate Commerce Commission in 1887, a "reform" pushed by President Grover Cleveland, ostensibly to regulate railroads. But railroad executives were told not to worry by Richard Olney, a railroad lawyer who was soon to be Cleveland's attorney general: "The Commission . . . is or can be made, of great use to the railroads. It satisfies the popular clamor for a government supervision of railroads, at the same time that its supervision is almost entirely nominal. . . . The part of wisdom is not to destroy the Commission, but to utilize it."

Piecemeal battles must certainly continue, for there is real and immediate corporate harm to be addressed for people and communities. But it's time for our strategic emphasis to shift to the offensive, raising what I believe to be the central political issue for the new century: *Who the hell is in charge here?*

It is an open question, despite the appearance that corporations have things pretty tightly locked down. Yes, they have the money, the media, the government, the two major parties, the police and military, and the deadening power of conventional wisdom. But so did King George III. We've been here before, we've done this, and we can do it again.

We've got a couple of things going for our side in this historic struggle. For one thing, our constitutional assertion of citizen control of corporations is still there, as is much of the language in the state codes that formally subjugates corporations to us. As Richard Grossman has found in his years of digging, "We still have the authority to *define* the corporations through their charters; we still have the authority to *amend* the charters; we still have the authority to *revoke* the charters—the language is still there. We still have the authority to *rewrite the state corporation codes* in order to *order* corporate executives to do what the sovereign people want to do." We have legal language and authority, a constitutional claim, a moral position firmly rooted in justice, and a powerful historic precedent that flows from the revolutionary patriots themselves.

We also have the common sense and revolutionary chutzpah of grassroots American agitators going for us. The commonsense side says: There are laws in our country that proclaim to human criminals "three strikes and you're out"— why not for corporations? Each year, hundreds of doctors, lawyers, accountants, and other professionals have their licenses to practice permanently revoked by the states—why not corporations? The Supreme Court has ruled that the corporation is a "person" under the law; people who murder are removed from society—why not corporations?

The chutzpah side says: Let's go get 'em. And they are! The national media have been practically mum about it, but there already is an important movement among the citizenry to begin reestablishing citizen control over charters. In Wayne, Pennsylvania, the locals passed a 1998 ordinance that prohibits any corporation from doing business there if it has a history of consistently violating laws to protect workers, consumers, the environment, and so forth. In Jay, Maine, a town of paperworkers, the people were fed up with the repeated pollution of their water and air by the recalcitrant International Paper Company, so they enacted the "Jay Environmental and Improvement Ordinance," which gives the town of Jay the authority to monitor and regulate pollution by IP's Androscoggin paper mill—the townspeople have their own full-time environmental administrator with full authority to fine and shut down the mill for violations. In 1998, the people of South Dakota just said "no" to corporate hog factories in their state, voting by a sixty-to-forty margin for a constitutional amendment to prohibit corporations from owning livestock. Also in 1998, New York attorney general Dennis Vacco, a Republican, showed that the Council for Tobacco Research had acted fraudulently and illegally in pretending to do objective research when in fact it was nothing but a lobbyist and a front for the tobacco industry, leading to a settlement in which the council surrendered its corporate charter. The state's current attorney general, Democrat Elliott Spitzer, is expanding Vacco's initiative, considering all corporate charters fair game: "When a corporation is convicted of repeated felonies that harm or endanger the lives of human beings or destroy the environment, the corporation should be put to death, its corporate existence ended, and its assets taken and sold at public auction." He has hired a highly regarded public-interest attorney to oversee this effort.

Meanwhile, in the small coastal town of Arcata, California, there has been a remarkable two-year effort to put the issue of corporate usurpation of democratic authority into the public debate again. It began with Paul Cienfuegos, Gary Houser, and a few others, who organized Democracy Unlimited of Humboldt County, which in 1998 launched a citizens' campaign to get on the ballot a local initiative called Measure F: Advisory Measure on Democracy and Corporations. After a few straightforward whereases about the sovereign power of people to govern themselves, the Measure resolved that "the people of Arcata support the amending of the California Constitution so as to clearly declare the authority of citizens over all corporations." The proposition then included a couple of practical steps that, very smartly, took a slow and minimalist approach toward advancing citizen sovereignty in Arcata, establishing a process for democratic discussion in town that could move people along, but not before they were ready to move. First was a simple provision that, if Measure F passed, the city council would sponsor two town hall meetings on this topic: "Can we have democracy when large corporations wield so much power and wealth under law?" Second was for the city government to create an official committee to develop policies and programs to assert democratic control over corporations doing business in Arcata.

The citizens' campaign hit the streets, and in just twenty-six days got the signatures needed to put the measure on the ballot. They gained key endorsements from Arcata mayor Jim Test and groups like the central labor council and students at Humboldt State University, and they delivered materials to the doors of nearly every household and business in this town of about 17,000 people. In the November 1998 election, their effort paid off: Measure F passed with nearly 60 percent of the vote. Since then, this town has been having what every town, city, neighborhood, and village green needs—a heart-to-heart airing out of the basic question of "Who's in charge?" Ralph Nader visited in 1999 in support of citizen control, likening Arcata's democracy dialogue to the ride of Paul Revere. On the other side, Kenneth Fisher, a *Forbes* magazine columnist and a financial speculator, gave a lecture entitled "Societal Ethics Are Always Unethical," bemoaning Measure F as an example of the "tyranny of democracy." Then came the town hall meetings in April and May of 1999, which produced a turnout of more than 600 people, far surpassing expectations. The opposition had been active, too, working hard to turn out a pro-corporatist crowd, led by a couple of very vocal officials with the Yakima Corporation, which is based in the area but manufactures at a Mexican border factory. The proceedings were structured so both sides made two presentations of eight minutes each—then the floor was open to the people. The freewheeling discussions went long past the set time, putting the lie to conventional wisdom that insists people are too busy, too satisfied, too uninformed, too unconcerned, too prosperous, too conservative, too short, too stupid, too whatever to get involved with something as "boring" as their own democracy. Overwhelmingly, participants favored

Measure F, and the town's people are now at work on developing the policies and programs for city hall that will put the well-being of the community above corporate whim on issues ranging from chain stores bankrupting local businesses to industry polluting the town's air and water.

Whatever the outcome at city hall, the effort already has accomplished something extraordinarily important: It has launched a citywide democratic conversation on a subject that hasn't been discussed in public for a century. Cienfuegos notes that thousands of local residents are now conversant with corporate rule and how it affects their lives. It's a conversation that has become common in the cafés, Laundromats, in line at the post office, and elsewhere—literally taking root in the culture of the community. The groundbreaking work in Arcata continues, and it is spreading to other California towns, and to places like Olympia, Washington.

The experts, of course, predict that these citizen uprisings won't succeed, but the experts have a long history of being spectacularly wrong. Christopher Cerf and Victor Navasky have documented this in wonderful detail in their fun book, *The Experts Speak,* which includes these glorious samples of missed predictions:

"Just so-so in center field."
> *—New York Daily News,* May 26, 1951,
> after the major-league debut of Willie Mays

"Displays no trace of imagination, good taste or ingenuity. I say it's a stinkeroo."
> *—New Yorker* film critic, 1939, reviewing *The Wizard of Oz*

"The singer will have to go."
> —The new manager of the
> Rolling Stones, 1963, referring to Mick Jagger

A great thing about the American people is that we are an optimistic, can-do bunch who will not be deterred by being told something cannot be achieved. Robert Benson is a good example of this spirited stubbornness: "I came to the conclusion some time ago that things happen when someone does the work, so the point is to just do the work." He's a professor at Loyola Law School in Los Angeles, and he has been a driving force (along with Ronnie Dugger, who cochairs the grassroots Alliance for Democracy organization) behind a national effort to revoke the charter of Unocal—the Union Oil Company of California. Benson has done a lot of work and made a lot happen by compiling a long rap sheet on this notorious and recidivist corporate reprobate.

Benson's dossier on Unocal includes a pattern and practice of polluting the locations where it operates (the company itself notes that it is named as a potentially responsible party in eighty-two Superfund or similar toxic sites in this country alone), the mistreatment of its employees (it has been cited for hundreds of workplace safety and health violations just in the past decade), and complicity in gross human-rights violations through its operations and working relationship with the repressive totalitarian regimes in Afghanistan and Burma (although pressure from this charter revocation effort and others has since forced Unocal to withdraw from Afghanistan). Prepared with the help of the National Lawyers Guild, the Unocal petition was not a political tract but a serious legal filing, alleging ten separate counts, citing twenty-four state and federal laws, forty-five cases, forty international laws, fourteen scholarly legal writings, and dozens of other relevant materials.

Unocal announced in 1996 that it "no longer considers itself as a U.S. company." But it is chartered in California, it operates here, and its major market is the good ol' USA, so a broad coalition of some 150 people and organizations (from the Feminist Majority Foundation to the Surfers Environmental Alliance, from pastors to professors, from the Green party to Greenpeace, from business to labor, from city council members to state legislators) have joined the effort, asking the California attorney general to use the statutory authority that has long lain ignored in his desk drawer—the authority "to procure a judgment [from state court] dissolving the corporation."

The very filing of the citizens' petition in September 1998 scared the constipation out of Dan Lungren, the Republican AG who was running for governor at the time. Benson reports that "Lungren's office went into a comical panic," calling the California Highway Patrol the night before the coalition was to hold a press conference at the attorney general's branch office in Los Angeles. He had the state police warn Benson, Dugger, and group not to appear because a permit was needed to have a press conference on state property. That was about as effective as calling "time-out" in a cattle stampede. Undeterred, the group held its press conference. Lungren's spokeswoman immediately responded that the AG had no authority to revoke charters. But—oops!—it was pointed out to her that section 803 of the code of civil procedure not only allows him to act but says he "must bring action" whenever he has "reason to believe" a corporation has violated the law. Well, she said, we'll need several months to study it, which conveniently would put the matter on the shelf until well past Lungren's election fight. But that couldn't have pleased Unocal executives, who would have wanted this dicey bit of legal unpleasantness bludgeoned to death with a sledgehammer on the spot. Sure enough, three business days later, Lungren suddenly dispatched a four-sentence letter to the coalition, the operative phrase of which was: "We decline to institute legal proceedings." He didn't bother offering an explanation. In response, the petitioners lambasted him far and wide for being "selectively soft" on crime.

But wait a minute, here came the Lone Stranger riding to the rescue! Bill Lockyer, a Democrat, was elected attorney general six weeks later to replace Lungren (who also had his gubernatorial ambitions thwarted by the voters). After taking office, Lockyer declared that he wanted to be known as a "Teddy Roosevelt" in taking on corporate criminals. So Benson and the coalition saddled up as Rough Riders and resubmitted their Unocal petition to "Teddy" Lockyer. However, the Democrat bested the Republican AG by rejecting the petition in only *three* sentences, including the exact same phrase used by the Republican: "We decline to institute legal proceedings." Again, no explanation. Benson called the AG's office and learned that the professional staff that normally analyzes such requests for action had never seen the coalition's filing against Unocal. Pressed by the coalition (which includes some prominent Democratic officeholders), Lockyer finally tried to explain his reasoning in an August letter that showed a breathtaking ignorance of the petition, of the issues raised, and, most shockingly, of his authority and responsibility under California law. The letter is three paragraphs of blah-blah-blah, punctuated by this courageous stand on policing corporate charters: "It's simply not my job." Who needs Republican enemies when we've got such Democratic "friends"?

The coalition continues to organize, using the Unocal petition to teach more citizens not only about this scofflaw company but more important about their own right to control all corporations. The legal process also continues, as does the political—public meetings are being held, with Lockyer invited, to educate the AG about his "job," and billboards bearing the new attorney general's mug appeared with the cutline: "Lockyer. Soft on Corporate Crime." Patronizing politicians like him make a mistake if they think they're getting away with anything or that this democracy movement will go away. Pols who misread the seriousness, preparedness, cleverness, and fighting spirit of people like Benson and Dugger remind me of General John Sedgwick, the Union commander whose last words at the battle of Spotsylvania Court House in 1864 were: "They couldn't hit an elephant at this dist—"

RUN RIGHT AT THE BASTARDS

When I first ran for political office in Texas, I was campaigning out near Abilene and came upon a fellow who bent my ear for a while, telling me a story about how he had really been furious with the local sheriff, who he felt was incompetent, crooked, or both. "I wrote letters to the editor about the guy, I called him up personally to protest his actions, I filed formal complaints," he told me. "But that was two years ago, and now I'm no longer mad at the sheriff. That's because I filed against the son of a bitch and beat him, so now I *am* the sheriff!"

Nothing gets the attention of the system quite like running against it. This is the most radical aspect of America's democratic experiment—not merely that you can vote for whatever choices the system throws up (literally throws up, it so often seems), but that we can generate our own choices! It's the difference between being a passive *consumer* of the process and being a *citizen,* a forceful participant in the democracy. When all is said and done, the gods don't give us candidates . . . we have to create them.

There's an unfortunate tendency among leaders of national progressive organizations and among progressive funders to focus on the quadrennial run for the White House or for control of Congress, ignoring the races for state rep, county commissioner, city council, and others at the ground level. This is where we should be—building a solid foundation for a genuine progressive political movement, framing the issues that can rally the workaday majority of people, developing political skills and talent, and steadily moving on up.

These are offices that can be won with people power, where we are less likely to be swamped by a tsunami of money power. Equally important to winning, we can put these offices to work for ordinary folks, siding with them against the corporate interests that are running roughshod over them, earning credibility with today's disenchanted voters, bringing them back into the process, and gaining the voter strength it takes to maintain the movement, lifting it ever higher. The key is to get back to the honest, painstaking, grunt-level work of party building, working continually in the communities, homes, churches, beauty parlors, saloons, and elsewhere to touch people, involve them, and demonstrate that we're there to stay, sticking with them for the long haul, not just for Election Day.

Happily, this is not a process we can only wish would happen—it's already under way. The Green party, the Labor party, the New party, the Reform party, and the Working Families party are among those offering serious progressive opportunities.

No group is doing it better than the New party. A coalition of labor, low-income advocates like ACORN, minorities, Democratic party dissidents, environmentalists, tax reformers, anticorporatists, seniors, gays and lesbians, and people simply fed up with business-as-usual politics, this grassroots political party has been winning offices from the Big Apple to Little Rock. In 1998, New party endorsees won thirty-two of the thirty-nine elections they entered, and for the past decade, the party has won two-thirds of the elections it has contested. More important than winning, however, it has been building the progressive foundation. To see it in practice, let me take you to Missoula, Montana.

When you think of hotbeds of progressive activism, the mind jerks to Berkeley, Greenwich Village, Ann Arbor, Cambridge, Madison . . . but Missoula? Situated along the Clark Fork River, this small city is home to the University of Montana, but it really can't be described as a college town—more like a working-class town with a university in it. It's certainly a picturesque and pleasant place, with a population of about 50,000 (and rapidly growing), and its downtown boasts agreeable touches of upscale urbanity, including cappuccino shops, restored buildings, and a good microbrewery. Just minutes away, though, are acres of trailer parks and low-income neighborhoods, home to Missoulians who think of coffee as a regular cup-a-joe rather than a two-dollar cappuccino. These are families who are employed at the nearby paper mill, casinos, and tourist businesses, working hard and poorly paid.

Out of this mix of modern American life way out in the Rockies has come some of the most vibrant, progressive politics in our country today, thanks to the Missoula New party (MNP), which has energized and mobilized people who had given up on a political process that has long been controlled by the business-as-usual Democrat-Republican power structure. What we have in Missoula is a snapshot of what can happen when progressives get their act together, get to organizing, and go head-on at that power structure. I'm not talking about protesting but about vying for political power—running for office and *winning*. In only eight years of existence, New party members in Missoula have gone from ground zero to being a power player, with its members now holding four of the twelve city council seats and two state legislative seats. How did they get there? Not luck, but potluck.

The MNP is known as the "Party that likes to Party." From its start, it has organized around the great American tradition of the neighborhood potluck—folks gathering in homes around good food and drink, talking about local matters and how things could be made better. Secky Fascione, about as feisty an organizer as you'd ever hope to meet, told me about the potluck she hosted early in 1993, when Dan Cantor was coming to town. Dan, then the national director of the New party, lives in New York City and was in Montana for a speech in Billings. A mutual friend had suggested that he should know the progressives working in Missoula, so he offered to stop by while he was in the state. "I guess people back east don't know it's a six-hour drive between Billings and Missoula," Secky shrugged, but Cantor came. "We told a couple of friends to come over and meet the guy and, to our surprise, about thirty-five folks showed up. That early crew was representative of much of the base of the New party today: the women's community, our low- and moderate-income organization, environmental activists, senior citizens, and a few of us progressive labor leaders."

What Cantor did that night was to offer a structural framework (the New party) for what these folks already were wanting to do—build an effective progressive movement—and to focus them on electoral politics. The Missoulians took it from there. They went door to door, neighborhood to neighborhood, talking with people long ignored by the existing political structure about the opportunity of having their own party, talking with them about the issues they could raise together. The issues were the need for living wages, affordable housing, stopping pollution, making growth work for people rather than vice versa, and other kitchen-table matters that neither established party was addressing. People signed up, more potlucks were organized in more homes, and more people got involved.

MNP also hit the ground running, literally. In their first year of existence, the group backed three unabashedly progressive candidates for city council, putting its burgeoning grassroots network behind them. The results were stunning, even to MNP members—all three of their candidates won sweeping victories in the September '93 Democratic primary, and two went on to win council seats in that year's general election (the third lost by only six votes). Among the brand-new New party activists who worked in this first electoral go-round was Ren Essene. "I was twenty-three, fresh out of college, and although having been involved with an unorganized group of college Democrats previously, was pretty disenchanted with politics, as was most of my generation. I thought of politics as entrenched and elite. I got involved with the New party but was cynical about what changes we could effect. Then we won! We had a voice, we were framing a different debate at the city level. We elected

candidates that gave voice to the everyday person concerns."
Ren later became cochair of MNP and now serves on the
national New party executive committee.

Here's a key to New party strategy: It's not concerned
merely with electing candidates but with implementing policy.
Jim "Flash" Fleischmann, chair of the election committee, tells
me that you don't get MNP backing by being smooth, winking
at the committee members, and promising to support "good
government." You have to promise to join the party if you're
not already a member, to acknowledge publicly your MNP
endorsement, to attend meetings where the rank and file can
get you by the short hairs, and to demonstrate on a regular
basis that you are pushing the policies that you pledged to
support. The people hold the politicians accountable for doing
what they said they were going to do. Outrageous.

Another key element of the MNP's success is that it doesn't
disappear between elections. Instead, it actually establishes a
relationship with voters (something the two major parties
reserve for platinum-level contributors). The monthly meetings are not sterile, *Robert's Rules of Order*–type affairs, but
lively, debate-filled, consensus-run sessions held in someone's
home with children running about, potluck dishes to savor,
and often some of that microbrew available to help lubricate
the little gray cells. As Ren says, "You've got to build FUN into
the Party, because you need to be able to keep coming back to
do the work. We have great cooks—being a community, we
socialize with each other and that keeps us together." This
sense of community extends to helping anyone who wants to
be better at doing the work of citizenship—training to be leaders in a campaign or even to run for office, learning more
about an issue, getting public-speaking lessons, and so forth.
It's more than politics, too—people active in MNP have
worked through other organizations to launch a day-care co-
op, a recycling program, and other community projects.

The party also is pragmatic rather than dogmatic—it agrees

to disagree on divisive issues within the party, focusing on the common issues that unite them, and it doesn't lose itself in meaningless ideological nattering about being "pure" as a third party, instead working happily with and even endorsing Democrats or other candidates willing to support the party's progressive policies. A good example of this is Peter Talbot. He wasn't involved in local politics until about a decade ago when Missoula's rampant growth became a concern to him. He went to the Democratic party in town, but found the leaders there an "uninspiring bunch of good ol' boys with few ideas." He heard of the New party that was just starting up, went to a meeting, and "found they were sharp and well-informed people who wanted to change things to be more responsive to regular folks." He's been a New party member ever since—but now he's also chairman of the Missoula Democratic party. The very presence of this new, grassroots, *successful* political player has altered the whole electoral landscape—the MNP's current four council members can often count on one or two other Democratic council members and occasionally on the Democratic mayor to stand with them.

Jim McGrath, an early New party member who is now on the city council (and who is so effective there that the chamber of commerce declared that its highest priority was to "take him out," yet he won reelection by a landslide) is particularly supportive of worrying less about structural purity than getting the job done: "Let's not forget what the real work is. For me, the real work is empowering the citizens (particularly those least powerful, such as low-income and minorities), creating the framework for people to have significant control over their lives and communities, and the ability to create a sustainable society."

Who are these people? "We've been vilified as coming from Moscow or—worse—New York City," says council member McGrath, who actually is a longtime Missoula resident. He and his wife, Julie, have two adopted sons who have Down's syndrome, she's a writer, and he's director of the Community Gardens program in town. Other MNP members who have run recently for council seats include a small businessman who raises llamas and takes people into the mountains on pack trips, a retired schoolteacher active on senior issues, a fellow who works for the Missoula Children's Theater, and a young mother who got into politics because of a proposal to close her child's neighborhood school. Not a lawyer, a lobbyist, a banker, or a millionaire among them.

Not that the party wins all of its elections—indeed, in '97 the old Democrat-Republican clique teamed up with the chamber-of-commerce crowd and a load of money from out-of-town developers to form a front group called Citizens for Common Sense Government, putting up a slate of candidates to wipe out these upstarts. A CCSG fundraiser was held, appropriately enough, at the Linda Vista Country Club, and an unprecedented amount of money suddenly flowed into Missoula politics. In the Ward 1 race, for example, New party candidate Dave Harmon was outspent two to one, with his CCSG opponent getting three-fourths of her war chest from developers, contractors, real estate brokers, bankers, and others determined to get a developer-friendly city hall. Harmon's money, by contrast, came from a logger, a few artists, teachers, some nurses, U. of M. professors, and a poet, among others, with his largest check being $150.

Harmon won anyway, but two New party incumbents on the council narrowly lost, cutting their margin from five seats to four. But the spirit of MNP members only rose—as Ren Essene says, "Having an opposition means you're doing something right. We're proud of bucking the system, and we won't back down from progressive stances." Is this bunch fun, or what?! Showing a maturity and confidence rooted in a solid base of support and good political organizing, MNP withstood the onslaught of money and has since redoubled its grassroots efforts. In its latest city election, the New party won three of the four seats it contested, losing the fourth by only fifty votes. It retains, with a couple of liberal Democrats, a working majority on the council. It also has won two seats in the state legislature, it supported a winner for county commissioner, it has put a living-wage ordinance on the agenda, and it has strong candidates for the next council election, with a chance to pick up additional seats. More important than the specific wins, however, is MNP's overall victory—it has changed politics for the good in Missoula, reframing the debate around people's issues, putting corporate power on the defensive, and energizing ordinary folks to take charge of their own destiny.

I've been to Missoula and met these people, just as I've met similar folks in Little Rock, Milwaukee, Seattle, Tucson, Minneapolis, Colorado Springs, Chicago, western Oklahoma, Durham, and elsewhere—ordinary Americans who are doing the extraordinary by fighting back against the established order, winning, and taking power themselves. Pessimists can say, "Yeah, yeah, Hightower, but these are localized victories, we need a national movement." Hello? Did the American Revolution begin in Philadelphia in 1776 with the approval of the Declaration of Independence, or had there been years of local rebellion that got the movement to that point? Did the populist movement, which completely altered American politics at the end of the nineteenth century, spring forth full-grown as a national movement, or did it begin in a farm kitchen near Lampasas, Texas, later spreading across the South, up the Plains, and into the upper Midwest? Did the civil rights movement begin with Martin Luther King Jr.'s 1963 speech at the Lincoln Memorial, or had it been built in hundreds of backwater southern churches by thousands of people who bled and died to get King to that majestic moment? The New party's strategic motto is: "Start local. Think long term." That's the ticket, and that's what thousands of good people all across our country are doing.

They are beautiful to behold. There's a sparkle in their

eyes, a bounce in their step, a sense of joy that they are doing political work that matters, organizing a new politics that cuts across the theoretical lines of right to left, realizing that the real political spectrum for Americans is top to bottom. Right to left is theory, and it divides us falsely. Top to bottom is experience; it's where people actually live and work—and the vast majority of people today know that they're no longer in shouting distance of the Wall Street–Washington, Republican-Democrat powers at the top. Here is the constituency for something big. As Jim McGrath of Missoula says, "We see a huge opportunity for a mass, democratic movement developing in America. With the continued decline for most Americans, and the lack of any coherent governmental response, the demand for a politics that imposes values (other than just profit) over the economy and pushes for real democratic reform will only grow."

People are ready for a politics that challenges the ongoing corporate grabfest. A recent series of focus-group sessions with middle-class folks (most of whom made in the range of $20,000–$60,000 a year) produced results that cannot be comforting to the Keepers of the Established Order:

- 68 percent of the people viewed corporate greed as an "equally important" or "more important" cause of working families' economic woes than big government—nearly half say corporations are the "more important" cause.
- 70 percent believe that such actions as massive downsizings, cutbacks on worker benefits, and sending U.S. jobs overseas are not motivated by the corporate need to be competitive and efficient, but by greed.
- 79 percent of Democrats in the groups, 67 percent of Republicans, and 74 percent of ticket splitters say the economic and human impacts of these corporate behaviors are serious enough to warrant purposeful government intervention.

I realize that this goes counter to the constant message from those on high who keep telling us that we Americans are a conservative people, but I find the regular folks of this country to be a gutsy bunch who, at their core, have an ingrained commitment to the ideal of democracy, a deep (and hard-earned) distrust of concentrations of economic and political power, and a fighting spirit that doesn't need much kindling to flare. People are not "conservative," certainly not in the corporate sense, nor are they "liberal," in the sense of believing that more social programs and nitpicking regulations are going to clean up the messes that are being made by global corporate greed. People are antiestablishment mavericks, and they know (as any mother or kindergarten teacher can tell you) that the better plan is not to keep trying to clean up the messes but to get control over the brutes that are making the messes.

If the progressive movement is going to matter, going to make any difference at all in twenty-first-century politics, it has to understand and act on the latent radicalism (à la 1776) and maverick spirit of the true majority. The term "maverick" even has revolutionary roots—a member of the Maverick family was one of the five "liberty boys" killed at the "Boston Massacre" in 1770. But the term as we use it today actually came from another member of this same family. Samuel Maverick was his name, a pioneer Texas rancher who had fought in the 1836 revolution against the Mexican authorities. A thoroughly independent sort, Sam refused to brand his cattle. So, out on the range, any unbranded calf or steer one came across was said to be a maverick.

Go into the coffee shops and bars where middle-class, workaday America hangs out, chat with cab drivers and grocery clerks, visit working-class churches and neighborhood block parties, talk with nurses, janitors, mechanics, clerks, and restaurant workers while they're on break, shoot the breeze with the regulars at the barber shops or in the feed-and-seed stores. Here's where you'll find the maverick majority for the progressive politics I'm talking about, a constituency willing to run right at corporate power. This is where the progressive future is—not in Washington, fidgeting with policy on the fringes of power, quibbling over which of the namby-pamby corporate suck-ups running for president will do the most for "the cause."

Hey, let's gut it up, decamp from Washington, put our resources into the countryside, slug the corporate bastards right in the snout, and get it on with a grassroots politics that gives regular folks a reason to be excited and to get involved. Why not start the new century and millennium with a political crusade that is worthy of all of our energies and capabilities, a fight that is big enough, important enough, and bold enough to rally the workaday majority? It's the fight to take our government back, take our economy back, take our environment back by taking our sovereignty back—taking back our constitutional right as a people to *be in charge* of our own destinies.

"I may not get there with you," said a prophetic Martin Luther King Jr. in a sermon on the eve of his assassination, but "I've seen the promised land." The land that Reverend King saw is the same land that Jim McGrath sees from Missoula, that Woody Guthrie sang about in his cross-country rambles, and that I see today as I travel. It's *our* land, an extraordinary land where ordinary people are the strength, a place with awesome *possibility* to implement the democratic ideals of the people themselves. Through the generations, Americans have taken historic stands to hold on to and advance those ideals. Now is our time, our chance, and our duty to make real the promise of democracy—if not for ourselves, then for our grandchildren.

This *is* an exciting time to be an American.

CONNECTIONS

"Agitator" is a word that the Powers That Be have tried to turn into a pejorative, as in "Those damn agitators have stirred people up." But being an agitator is what America is all about—if it was not for the agitators of circa 1776, we'd all be wearing white powdered wigs and still be singing "God Save the Queen." Agitation at the grassroots level is what it has always taken to produce progressive advances in our society. Think of it like this: the agitator is the center post in the washing machine that gets the dirt out.

The following is a list of some of the groups that not only are premier agitators themselves, but also connect up citizen agitators with solid information, with organizing assistance, with action steps . . . and with each other. There are many, many more groups than I list here, but these are ones from which I drew much of the information that's in this book. I pass the list along to assist readers who want more detail on particular issues I've raised here—and to urge you to connect up with them and other groups to agitate, agitate, agitate.

ACORN
Living Wage Resource Center
739 8th Street, SE
Washington, DC 20003
202-547-2500
www.acorn.org

Agribusiness Examiner
Corporate Agribusiness Research
    Project
P.O. Box 2201
Everett, WA 98203–0201
avkrebs@earthlink.net

Alliance for Democracy
681 Main Street, 2–16
Waltham, MA 02451
781-894-1179
http://afd.online.org

Campaign for America's Future
1101 14th Street, NW, Suite 600
Washington, DC 20005
202-955-5665
www.ourfuture.org

Center on Budget and Policy
  Priorities
820 First Street, NE, Suite 510
Washington, DC 20002
202-408-1080
www.cbpp.org

Center for Community Change
1000 Wisconsin Ave., NW
Washington, DC 20007
202-342-0519
www.communitychange.org

Center for Public Integrity
910 17th Street, NW, 7th Floor
Washington, DC 20006
202-466-1300
www.publicintegrity.org

Center for Responsive Politics
1320 19th Street, NW
Washington, DC 20036
202-857-0044
www.opensecrets.org

Ralph Nader
Center for Study of Responsive Law
P.O. Box 19405
Washington, DC 20036
202-387-8030
www.essential.org

Citizens for Tax Justice
1311 L Street, NW
Washington, DC 20005
202-626-3780
www.ctj.org

Committee for the Study of the
  American Electorate
421 New Jersey Avenue, SE
Washington, DC 20003
202-546-3221

Common Cause
1250 Connecticut Avenue, NW
Washington, DC 20036
202-833-1200
www.commoncause.org

Council of Canadians
502–151 Slater Street
Ottawa, ON, Canada K1P 5H3
613-233-2773
www.canadians.org

Economic Policy Institute
1660 L Street, NW, Suite 1200
Washington, DC 20036
202-775-8810
www.epinet.org

Environmental Defense
44 East Avenue, Suite 304
Austin, TX 78701
512-478-5161
www.environmentaldefense.org

Fairness and Accuracy in
  Reporting (FAIR)
130 West 25th Street, 8th Floor
New York, NY 10001
212-633-6700
www.fair.org

Farm Aid
334 Broadway, Suite 5
Cambridge, MA 02139
617-354-2922
www.farmaid.org

Financial Markets Center
P.O. Box 334
Philomont, VA 22131
540-338-7754
www.fmcenter.org

Global Exchange
2017 Mission Street, #303
San Francisco, CA 94110
415-255-7296
www.globalexchange.org

Global Trade Watch
215 Pennsylvania Avenue, SE
Washington, DC 20003
202-546-4996
www.citizen.org

Granny D
P.O. Box 1492
Dublin, NH 03444
www.grannyd.com

Association of State Green Parties
P.O. Box 18452 20th Street Station
Washington, DC 20036
202-232-0335
www.greenparties.org

Independent Media Institute
77 Federal Street
San Francisco, CA 94107
415-284-1420
www.alternet.org

Institute for Agriculture and
   Trade Policy
2105 First Avenue South
Minneapolis, MN 55404
612-870-0453
www.iatp.org

Institute of Policy Studies
1601 Connecticut, NW, Room 500
Washington, DC 20009
202-234-9382
www.ips-dc.org

The International Law Project
   for Human, Ecological and
   Environmental Defense (HEED)
8124 W. 3rd Street, Suite 201
Los Angeles, CA 90048
213-736-1000
www.heed.net

Jobs With Justice
501 Third Street, NW
Washington, DC 20001
202-434-1106
www.jwj.org

Labor Party
P.O. Box 53177
Washington, DC 20009
20-234-5190
www.labornet.org/lpa

Multinational Monitor
P.O. Box 19405
Washington, DC 20036
202-387-8034
www.essential.org/monitor

National Farmers Union
400 Virginia Avenue, SW,
   Suite 710
Washington, DC 20024
202-554-1600
www.nfu.org

National Labor Committee
275 7th Avenue, 16th floor
New York, NY 10001
212-242-3002
www.nlcnet.org

National Low Income Housing
   Coalition
1012 14th Street, NW, #1200
Washington, DC 20005
202-662-1530
www.nlihc.org

National Priorities Project
Sullivan Square, 3rd Floor
17 New South Street
Northhampton, MA 01060
413-584-9556
www.natprior.org

New England Burma Roundtable
   Trillium Asset Management
711 Atlantic Avenue
Boston, MA 02111
800-548-5684
www.trilliuminvest.com

New Party
88 Third Avenue, 4th Floor
Brooklyn, NY 11217
800-200-1294
www.newparty.org

The Preamble Center for Public
  Policy
1737 21st Street
Washington, DC 20009
202-265-3263
www.preamble.org

The Program On Corporations,
  Law & Democracy (POCLAD)
P.O. Box 806
Cambridge, MA 02140
508-398-1145
www.poclad.org

Public Campaign
1320 19th Street, NW, Suite M1
Washington, DC 20036
202-293-0222
www.publicampaign.org

Public Citizen
1600 20th Street, NW
Washington, DC 20009
202-588-1000
www.citizen.org

Reform Party
P.O. Box 9
Dallas, TX 75221
www.reformparty.org

Rocky Mountain Media Watch
P.O. Box 18858
Denver, CO 80218
303-832-7558
www.bigmedia.org

Shadow Bureau of Government
  Statistics
P.O. Box 348
Hawthorne, NJ 07507

Sindlinger Fax
405 Osborne Lane
Wallingford, PA 19086

Sustainable Energy & Economic
Development (SEED) Coalition
401 W. 29th Street
Austin, TX 78705
www.seedcoalition.org

Texans for Public Justice
609 W. 18th Street, Suite E
Austin, TX 78701
www.tpj.org

TomPaine.com
1636 Connecticut Avenue, NW,
  Suite 30
Washington, DC 20009
202-332-2881
www.tompaine.com

United for a Fair Economy
37 Temple Place, 5th Floor
Boston, MA 02111
617-423-2148
www.stw.org

United Students Against Sweatshops
1413 K Street, NW, 9th Floor
Washington, DC 20005
202-NO SWEAT
www.usanet.org

US Public Interest Research
Group (PIRG)
218 D Street, SE
Washington, DC 20003
202-546-9707
www.pirg.org

INDEX

Perennial

Books by Jim Hightower:

THERE'S NOTHING IN THE MIDDLE OF THE ROAD
BUT YELLOW STRIPES AND DEAD ARMADILLOS
A Work of Political Subversion
ISBN 0-06-092949-9

Hightower takes aim at those bedrock institutions that drive the economic and cultural life of the country. In this lucid, viciously funny, downright refreshing book, Hightower argues that government, the media and corporate conglomerates have put us smack-dab in the middle of the mess we're in today. Revised with a new introduction.

"If you don't read another book about what's wrong with this country for the rest of your life, read this one. I think it's the best and most important book about our public life I've read in years."—Molly Ivins

IF THE GODS HAD MEANT US TO VOTE,
THEY'D HAVE GIVEN US CANDIDATES
More Political Subversion from Jim Hightower (Revised Edition)
ISBN 0-06-093209-0

A piece of Hightower's mind on "Candidates 2000" and the whole stinking political mess. Fully revised and updated with election results and new material, this new book offers a plain-talking, name-naming, podium-pounding, point-them-in-the-right-direction, populist prescription for 2000.

"Forget all the political insider books about America's elections, here's the outsider book that tells you what's really going on in the 2000 election, why, and what we have to do to make politics work for us again."

—William Greider